HERE'S WHAT THEY SAID ABOUT THE FIRST EDITION OF THIS BOOK

*"The world of filmmaking can be fun and exciting, and also successful for those who take the correct approach. Wiese . . . writes a highly personal book on how to finance, produce, and distribute one's own films. No other book like this one has appeared on the market. Highly recommended."*
**Choice Magazine**

*"Detailed and up-to-date manual. . .Wiese draws on his own expertise to give practical and creative advice."*
**Video Magazine**

*"A practical handbook on financing, production, and distribution."*
**Millimeter Magazine**

*"Wiese reviews tried-and-true procedures and techniques in a valuable and detailed book. This knowledgeable volume encompasses every aspect of a project. . .is clear and forthright, offering creative suggestions and practical advice."*
**Back Stage**

*"In these days of expanding budgets and seemingly shrinking possibilities, this book is a welcome helping hand."*
**Film Arts Foundation Newsletter**

*"This book is handy. . .it encourages clear thinking: the making of reasonable predictions about economic realities."*
**Washington Area Film/Video League**

*"Wiese's guide offers some very useful information."*
**The Independent**

*"Practical advice on the fine arts of money-raising, partnership formation, budgeting, distribution, negotiations, television deals, self-distribution. Basic survival information that any working filmmaker hoping to make a first, much less a second, film needs to know."*
**Film Quarterly**

i

*"Provides informative and experienced advice on the financing, production, and distribution of documentaries and shorts."*
**American Cinematographer**

*". . . a complete package for filmmakers, both veteran and beginner. Should prove indispensable in an area of research where so little information is available."*
**Sightlines**

*"No matter how experienced a producer you are. . .must reading. This is a common sense, 'I've been there and I ought to know' book written with a touch of ironic humor. If you want to make your life easier in the financial area of film/videomaking —buy the book. Enjoyable reading even for those that really hate budgets but like profits."*
**Informational Film Producers Association**

*"A straightforward and clear overview on the business of making films or videos. Wiese covers the most important (and least taught) part of the job: creative deal-making. The book is full of practical tips on how to get a film or video project financed, produced, and distributed without sacrificing artistic integrity. A must for any aspiring independent producer."*
**Co-Evolution Quarterly**

*"I'm a Wall Street lawyer working with a major talent agency to create a package to bring to investors. . . Wiese's books provided me with incredible insight in the course of a single afternoon. Best money I've ever spent!"*
**Keith Styrcula, Attorney**

*". . . a standard classic that somehow manages to stay on the cutting edge. I can hardly wait to get my eyes on the new edition."*
**Edmond Chibeau, Video-Artist/Scholar**

*"The International Documentary Association refers our members to Michael Wiese Productions books at least once every day. These books have the information documentary filmmakers need to survive."*
**Besty McLane, President,**
**International Documentary Association**

# THE
# INDEPENDENT
# FILM
# &
# VIDEOMAKER'S
# GUIDE

## 2ND EDITION

MICHAEL WIESE

Published by Michael Wiese Productions, 11288 Ventura Blvd., Suite 621, Studio City, California 91604, (818) 379-8799, (818) 986-3408 fax, mw@mwp.com, http://www.mwp.com

Cover Design by Wade Lageose, Art Hotel, Los Angeles
Proofreading by Bernice Balfour
*Coyote's Honor* photographs by Geraldine Overton

Printed by McNaughton & Gunn
Manufactured in the United States of America

For classroom adoptions only, please contact Focal Press, 313 Washington Street, Newton, MA 02158, 1-800-366-2665

Disclaimer: The information presented in this book is for educational purposes only. The author is not providing business, financial, or legal advice. Readers should consult their lawyers and financial advisors on their business plans and during contract negotiations. Neither the author nor publisher of this material, is liable for how readers may choose to use this information.

Printed on recycled stock.

Library of Congress Cataloging–in–Publication Data

Wiese, Michael, 1947–
    The independent film & videomaker's guide / Michael Wiese. -- 2nd ed.
  by Michael Wiese. -- 2nd ed.
        p. cm.
    ISBN 0-941188-57-4
    1. Motion pictures--Production and direction--Vocational guidance.
I. Title.
PN1995.9.P7W5   1998
791.43'023'023--dc21                                98-18056
                                                        CIP

MICHAEL WIESE PRODUCTIONS
www.mwp.com

Since 1981, Michael Wiese Productions has been dedicated to providing novice and seasoned filmmakers with vital information on all aspects of filmmaking and videomaking. We have published more than 50 books, used in over 500 film schools worldwide.

Our authors are successful industry professionals — they believe that the more knowledge and experience they share with others, the more high-quality films will be made. That's why they spend countless hours writing about the hard stuff: budgeting, financing, directing, marketing, and distribution. Many of our authors, including myself, are often invited to conduct filmmaking seminars around the world.

We truly hope that our publications, seminars, and consulting services will empower you to create enduring films that will last for generations to come.

We're here to help. Let us hear from you.

Sincerely,

Michael Wiese
Publisher, Filmmaker

*For my wife Geraldine*

*and daughter Julia Bronwyn,*

*My two joyous beings who could only have come from heaven.*

*And for my dad, B. B. Wiese,*

*a man of great integrity and humor who recently returned to heaven.*

# TABLE OF CONTENTS

## PRODUCING

## INTRODUCTION TO DISTRIBUTION

## THE THEATRICAL BUSINESS & DISTRIBUTION

## THE VIDEO BUSINESS & VIDEO DISTRIBUTION

## TELEVISION

## THE LIMITED PARTNERSHIP

## OTHER CREATIVE FINANCING MODELS

## THE BUSINESS PLAN/PROSPECTUS

## PRESENTATIONS

# A No-Budget Movie–"Coyote's Honor": A Case Study

# ACKNOWLEDGMENTS

When I step back and view the wide and diverse information contained in this book I realize that, while I may have been the filter, many other people contributed ideas and principles throughout my career(s), helped shape my thinking, and refocused my commitment. The key contributors, out of hundreds, whom I would like to thank include:

• The thousands of filmmakers who, since 1981, have participated in my seminars and workshops, and through our exchange, interaction, and dialogue have helped me identify and focus on the issues and needs that are explored in this book.

• The over 200 film schools (and their deans and instructors) who are using our books to train the next generation of "communicators" for your willingness to share with us what works and what doesn't in film education.

• Filmmaker-friendly organizations such as The Independent Feature Project, The International Documentary Association, The International Television and Video Association, AIVF, Film Arts Foundation, The University Film and Video Association, The American Film Institute, Women in Film, Bay Area Video Coalition, and Eastman Kodak company, who've invited me speak to their groups in what is really a mutual learning experience.

• Ken Lee has paddled on the other side of the canoe called Michael Wiese Productions, through lowtide and torrents, and occassionally upstream. Besides lobbing various film and television projects in his lap, he also has the ongoing day-to-day responsibilities of managing this publishing company, which in recent years has expanded to international publishing as well. Without his constant attention to detail, his devotion to fashioning the finest product possible, and his

1

interaction with the outside world, you probably wouldn't be reading this book. (Ken also designed the "Self-Quiz" in the Appendix.)

• Marie Lee of Focal Press, who helped shape this book by sharing content outlines with film instructors and forwarding to me their comments and ideas.

• Chris Whorf and Wade Lageose of Art Hotel, who for many years have provided what I believe are the best covers in the world for our books. I appreciate their willingness to struggle with me through various concepts and revisions until the cover fully expresses the contents of the book.

• Michele Chong, who helped pull in research and materials for this book in addition to maintaining our book sales operations.

• Steven Kulczycki, former station manager of KCET, for his illuminating insights on the inner workings of PBS.

• Chris Vogler, who continues to inspire me with his insights into screenplay structure, human behavior, and folktales.

• Mark Travis and Judith Weston, two directing coaches who approach the dangerous art of directing from two very distinct perspectives, who have shared with me "the secrets" and encouraged me to develop my own style. I shall be forever grateful.

• Jeremy Tarcher, founder of Tarcher Publishing, in my mind one of the giants of consciousness in publishing, who has mentored me with my publishing company.

• Ralph and Joan Singleton, founders of Lone Eagle Publishing, fellow film book publishers and producers, whose friendship and support make me proud to be a contributor to the filmmaking community.

• My early film partners — Steven Arnold (*Messages, Messages*), Ernie Fosselius (*Hardware Wars*), John Knoop (*Dolphin, I Move, Silver Box*), Dorothy Fadiman (*Radiance*), Hardy Jones (*Dolphin*), Larry Reed, and many other independent filmmakers — whose collaborations set the foundation for everything else that was to follow, and gave me the body of knowledge from which I drew on in both the first and second editions of this book.

• My Vestron colleagues — Jon Peisinger, Austin Furst, Stephen Einhorn, Ray Bernstein, Richard Charnoff, Steve Monas, Ruth Vitale, C. J. Kettler, Larry Kassanoff, Greg Johnson, Kathy Gould, Rob Straight, Sharon Streger, Michael & Nancy Karaffa, Shelley Rabinowitz, Adam Platnick, Bill Quigley, and Steve Reuther — who virtually invented the business in the "go-go" years of home video.

• Richard Barrows, Tim Hartin, Steven Parker, Doug McCord, and the cast and crew of my digital video movie *Coyote's Honor*, a trial-by-fire exercise to see if we could really make a movie for no money. (We did.) Who, regardless of the odds, jumped in there with me as documented in a case study herein.

• Robert Faber for applying his FilmLook® technology on Coyote's Honor in my quest to make digital movies look like film.

• The legal beagles — Ed Labowitz, Greg Bernstein, Ray Gross, Jonathon Kirsch, and the late Harold Messing — who patiently taught me more than I ever wanted to know about entertainment law.

• Jeff Hardy of Big Horse Productions, whose amazing FilmProfit software program is an education in itself, for his creative insights and market research analysis for the Bali prospectus used as a sample in this book.

• Most of all, my remarkable wife Geraldine Overton, who embraces the importance that writing and teaching have for me, and has accommodated my writing of this book during a vacation to Cornwall, England, where we juggled the book writing schedule with exploring the moors, visiting bell-ringers, or splashing with our daughter Julia at the beach in St. Ives.

• And to Julia, my five-year-old jump-roper who one day walked into my office with a gift drawing which reads, "You make good books. You make the greatest books in the world. I love you." I hope this book lives up to her ideal.

# Purpose of This Book

Entertainment is America's "culture." It is how we spend much of our time and is our greatest export. The lifestyle reflected in American entertainment is what people aspire to in every corner of the planet. This culture is exemplified by the films and television of a few entertainment media giants like Time Warner, Disney, Geffen, and Westinghouse — a few voices speaking to larger and larger audiences, blurring the quest for authenticity.

The book is intended to empower and give strength to independent film– and videomakers so that their work may be more widely seen; and so that more voices may be heard from all the cultures of the world.

## How to Use This Book

This book had its genesis sixteen years ago when I prepared some handouts for my first filmmaking seminar that I presented when I lived in San Francisco. It occurred to me that these handouts may have a life as a book and so I rewrote and published them as a book. Since then over 40,000 books have been read by students in 200 film schools and by advanced professionals throughout the world. Many people who read that first edition when they were first starting out are making feature films, television shows, and CD-ROMs today.

The purpose of the book today, as it was then, is to assist you in getting your works produced and distributed as widely as possible. I don't want you to miss any opportunity or idea that may apply to your film or video idea.

Since my first book (this is my eighth), I've worked for ten years as an independent, another ten years inside the industry, and these last ten years again as an independent (except with the insight and experience of having worked in the big time). What I can offer you is the perspective of having experienced filmmaking from both sides. I can share insider's tips that will give you an advantage you might not otherwise have when dealing with suppliers, distributors, agents, actors, sponsors, and so on.

What I have to offer that is different from other producers and film book authors is that I am a generalist. I see the whole arc of the creative process which extends from program conception through marketing and distribution. Having this orientation I suggest you bring marketing elements into your program's design as soon as possible so that it will have as wide an audience as possible. But more on this important principle later.

I live in Los Angeles and travel frequently. As for Hollywood, I choose to say that I am "in it" but not "of it." It is the ultimate destination when you have something to sell, but independent films can be and are made almost anywhere. I am able to pursue only those projects that interest me and make a contribution. (While I may reference Hollywood filmmaking in this book, making films for the Hollywood system is not what this book is about.)

This professional objective has not come about overnight. But I have had it in my mind's eye since the beginning, so even though you will find your own path, the advice in this new edition offers up some ideas that you may find very useful as you do your own career planning.

But you have to be prepared. You have to be able to evaluate your opportunities and ideas: to see them from beginning to end to determine whether they will work and are worth pursuing. This book will help you do that. Most of this book is entirely new. My suggestions are the very same considerations that I too must embrace every time I start a new project.

## Who Should Use This Book?

This book will be useful to anyone interested in understanding and pursuing the art and business of filmmaking (or videomaking) or any of the other new media arts. You could be someone with an idea for a film, a writer, a producer, a director, a communications student, a multimedia developer, a web page designer, or someone interested in developing, producing, and distributing your own works.

I'll try to be as practical as possible, sharing insider information, principles, conceptual insights, and hard-earned ideas. Take what you need and leave the rest.

My job is to lay it out for you. Your job is to apply it to your own projects. If something you read inspires you with a whopper of an idea, stop reading and start writing in the margins or on a separate sheet of paper. I want you to get very turned on about your own ideas, about how to get it done. I want you to feel this book is truly your "guide" and friend that you can turn to when you have questions or get stuck. I've never felt there was enough sharing of the real, hard information in this business. Somehow people feel if they keep it to themselves they'll excel. I feel just the opposite. The more you give away, the more you get. So come and get it!

I want you to be dreamers. I want you to be entrepreneurial. I want you to break the rules. But I also want you to be practical and make choices where you can actually complete something. Sitting around drinking cappuccino bragging that your project is "in development" is not what this book is about. The real learning comes in seeing your own ideas brought into reality and shared with others.

## The First Exercise

Fill in the blanks:

*My project is: _____.*
*The career I wish to have is as a: _____.*
*Here's what I need to learn to accomplish my goals:_____.*
*Here's what I hope to get out of reading this book:_____.*

Just answering these few questions will turn on the creative faucet. It will focus you on getting your needs fulfilled so that you can begin your work.

What's your objective? Are you just generally interested in moviemaking and think you'd like to try? Do you have a specific notion for a movie or video you'd like to make? Are you already a producer but want to hone your financing or marketing skills? Are you trying to raise money? Come up with the next breakthrough independent film?

Whatever it is, now would be a good time to write down as specifically as possible what your objective is in reading this book. That way, you will have set your unconscious to scan and find the gold nuggets in your path. You'll find the answers somewhere between these pages or in your own creative mind. If you just read the book without "setting your objective," you may find it interesting, even fascinating, but not as useful as I'd like to make it for you.

Now I know that most of us (I count myself in here as well) are kind of lazy and would rather just keep reading than set the book down and have to do something. But from time to time in this book I will recommend things you can do that will assist you in your process. You don't have to do them but those that do will benefit the most. Besides, these little assignments are accumulative and by the time you are done you will have accomplished a great deal toward your goal.

I will supply many of the conceptual models that you will need; however, you'll have to do the networking, make the phone calls, and search the trade newspapers and magazines for updated information. I wish I could just pour the magic elixir into your brain but alas, it doesn't work that way. You're going to have to do some work, but not to worry, I'll take you through the process step-by-step.

I will talk about production techniques; however, this information is most readily available and not as difficult to find as some of the other material I'll cover (e.g., financing, distribution, marketing). The film schools do a pretty good job covering production as would any internship in a production company where you learn by doing. The areas that

I will primarily address are what the film schools skip over and the movie moguls hide. (Note: Many distributors dislike my books because I reveal many of their closely held secrets. But why not? I want there to be a level playing field when producers come into contact with distributors who are about to gobble up a work that has been years in the making.)

It is not easy to find information about how to develop marketable ideas, raise financing, create marketing plans, or qualify distributors. I hid from this knowledge during my first ten years as a filmmaker. Unbelieveable but true! And from my consulting practice I have seen with my own eyes that 95% of all producers ignore and/or are unaware of the value of marketing as they produce their programs. It's like they've got a patch over their "marketing eye." They'd rather be making something than figuring out whether that something is going to work in the marketplace. If you finish this book you will have a great complement to everything you've discovered up until now or will learn in the future. You will literally jump ahead of your colleagues who, in their rush to produce, have missed some valuable information. They may wonder why your projects find a distributor, find an audience, and why theirs may win film festivals but fail in the marketplace. (Tell 'em to buy the book!)

In these pages I'll share some magic formulas with you and then tell you why not to use them. Formulas don't work for every project. Instead I hope you'll learn to think creatively and on your feet; how to take conceptual principles and apply them to your own work. This creativity will not only be applicable on the screen but in the development of your ideas, in your deal making, and in marketing yourself and your project.

It's not about doing what someone else has done, but modeling from that and creating a new opportunity for yourself. Some of you will get this, most will miss it altogether.

A warning: although this book is laid out chapter by chapter and step-by-step, creating something from nothing (a film or video from an idea), doesn't follow a linear process. It may look like it. Books and teachers may explain it that way, but it's not an A, B, C kind of thing. There are other forces operating here. Like "intention." I have found that if you are very clear about what you want (high intention), then you will discover very creative solutions for how to get what you want. (Sometimes it's almost as if the solution finds you!)

Now normally the steps would be: get an idea, write the script, raise the money, produce the film. Recently I found a source for the money for a project before I'd written it. In another case, I finished the shoot and made a major sale before I found financing. Now if that isn't backwards. . .

So whereas I used to teach the A, B, C's of this process, I now allow it to happen as C, B, Z, A, Y, if that's what it takes. If you can relax enough and trust that you'll get what you need, then marvelous things happen. I'll give you many of the tools, but you'll need to be open to the process happening in any order! Think of it as a "painterly" approach to producing.

You are going to have to get comfortable with the thought that this is not a paint-by-number kind of process or business. Every idea you have is a new one. Every movie is a new product and requires its own test marketing. You won't find a cookie cutter here. It doesn't get any more entrepreneurial than this. That's why no one has a crystal ball in show business. Experience helps and that's what I hope to share with you here, but it's not the end-all. That's why you see new filmmakers with innovative no–budget films breaking through every year. The studios can't bottle the process or the product as hard as they try. This is where the little guy can excel.

## What's Missing for You?

I've learned that in this process, you not only have to get all the pieces right but you also have to think about the process as a whole. And then think what's missing and draw it to you. If you can identify what you need, you'll find it quickly. If you don't look, your project may have a big hole in it.

I've done everything from write, to shoot, to edit, to produce, to distribute. I've directed and produced many documentaries, short films, PBS programs, and home video but very few dramatic pieces. For me, experience with dramas was missing. I now have a dramatic property that I want to direct and I need to understand how actors work and how to communicate what I need so they can give it to me. This is a problem a lot of directors have. In fact many work very well with the camera but avoid directing the actors. This is the single biggest complaint from actors: directors cannot communicate what they want. So, regardless of how uncomfortable it was at first, I sought out directing workshops, mentors, fellow directors, and directing jobs over the last three years. My directing skills are light-years ahead because I focused attention on them rather than skirting around the problem. (I could have found experienced directors, I suppose, to direct my film, but that is not what I thought would be best for the film.)

## Another Assignment

The principle here (and another little assignment) is to write down what personal skills you need that you think are missing. It may or may not directly relate to filmmaking. You can write down "accounting" or "figure drawing" or "learning a foreign language." It counts.

I love it when I give a seminar and I say something and everyone gets inspired and writes it down. But I also want you to pay attention to things that I say that you violently object to or don't believe or that disturb you. If you have a strong negative charge on something, it usually means it's something for you to look at. Got the idea?

So I want you to be either very inspired and write down your ideas that are generated from my ideas. Or, I want you to really hate something and explore why you hate it and to find value for yourself. In both cases, there is a strong likelihood that you will find something you will need that is extremely valuable. All the other stuff in the book is like a smorgasbord. You can come back and get it if you find you need it later; you'll know where to find it.

## What's in It for You?

After reading this book you will have:

- new ways to think about what you do and what you want to do
- new ideas — program, marketing, business, money–raising — about every aspect of making film and video
- the ability to leverage new resources
- new elements to add to your package
- ideas about how to market yourself
- a real feeling that you know what you need to do
- a feeling of strength and confidence about your special gifts
- the beginnings of an action plan

When you finish with a chapter, I want you to feel a real sense of mastery in that area. If there is something you don't understand, reread that section, read some of the suggested books listed in the bibliography, or discuss the ideas with your colleagues.

Besides getting the information and putting it to use, I'd like you to think about doing something of value with it, something with integrity. I'll be hinting at this from time to time and may even give some examples of what that means to me.

If you are able to approach your work from the most sweeping scale and with little fear of failure, you just may accomplish something quite magnificent.

It is my desire that this book empower you to go beyond your own limits to fulfill your own goals and objectives. I hope that you select projects worthy of your life's work. And that as viewers we may marvel and delight in what you may bring us.

Michael Wiese
Cornwall, England

# INTRODUCTION TO YOUR INDEPENDENT FUTURE

## Low Cost High-Tech Gear

The miniaturization of technology has brought the cost of high quality production gear to bargain basement levels and within the reach of individuals. There is a proliferation of "project studios" where auteur producers can edit and postproduce their footage (shot on Hi-Band 8mm or Digital Video 6mm cameras) with all the special effects and graphics and sound mixing in home studios that only a few years ago had to be rented by the hour at extraordinary rates. You can originate in either film or video, depending on your intended market, and edit in both mediums as well. I just shot a no-budget feature with a tiny digital camera (more on this later).

## New Audiences

Independent films are finding audiences throughout the world. In 1996 winning most of the major Oscar® nominations were independent films. Home video distribution has opened up the distribution channels even further. Thanks to video stores, you can study the great films of all time, slow them down, and replay them to study editing and structure. In the "old days," it was very hard to even get film prints to study.

## Distribution Channels

The number of distribution channels has never been greater. Cable and pay cable systems are growing by leaps and bounds throughout the world. In recent years two new cable channels were launched: the Sundance Channel and the Independent Film Channel, both devoted to free-spirited independent films. New programming and media forms — CD-ROM, Digital Video (DVD), the Internet, and Interactive Television — are still in their infancy. Some say that DVD-ROM will be the distribution of choice in the early 2000s. Venture capitalists abound for new technology and software start-up companies. Last year saw a record number of technology related initial public offerings (IPOs). Television is expanding throughout the world at phenomenal rates.

Documentaries (renamed by broadcasters as "reality-based programming") have been adopted by major broadcasters worldwide as a popular, low-cost alternative to dramatic programming. Animation is experiencing a renaissance. Not only has the new technology given animators fast, new, high resolution tools, but the public's hunger and interest have caused more animated family features to be produced than ever before.

Tomorrow the art and business of entertainment will look entirely different and it's time to get prepared. When I started my career I looked through a Speed Graphic press camera with flash bulbs. A month ago I used a high resolution digital video camera that barely weighed a pound. My first film was edited by scraping the emulsion off film and gluing another piece onto it. Today I use nonlinear AVID or Abekas Stratasphere editing systems for on-line editing.

But that's nothing compared to what's coming.

We'll soon start to see digital video shown in theaters and over the Internet. No longer will prints be shipped around the country but there will be one or a few master prints. Theaters will offer hi-tech kinetic and visceral experiences; a combination of theme park rides and IMAX-style imagery. There will be moving seats, screens, and other sensory and virtual reality stimulation to assault the senses.

In the homes there will be video on demand movies delivered through the convergence of television, the Internet, and sales of DVD-ROMs that will reduce the number of video stores.

Producers working out of their own homes will use the Internet and web pages to transmit video, sound, and text in multimedia forms. Much like the audio revolution of the seventies enjoyed by musicians and composers with their low cost synthesizers, one–man band-style video auteurs in "project studios" will create, market, and distribute their own works. Middlemen distributors may be circumvented or reinvented altogether. CD–ROMS and DVD (digital video discs) will carry more information at greater resolution and replace video cassettes as a transportable medium. Manufacturing costs are already less than $1 per unit. Soon, it will be as cheap to buy a video/CD/DVD as it will to buy a movie ticket.

Vast new audiovisual networks and databases called "intra-nets" will be created within institutions and businesses. This private World Wide Web will need thousands of multimedia artists and programmers of all kinds. Those creating web pages today will create networks tomorrow. The promised 500 channels of communication today will seem like a pittance when you add up all the various ways people will get their entertainment, news, and educational information.

While the major cable, telephone, entertainment, and on-line companies scramble to control the distribution mediums, they will be unable to completely control content creation which rests in the minds of creative individuals. That's where independents will have a beachhead.

Now with all this activity there is not a single executive that can keep up. I don't care how many consultants they hire, how many trade magazines and high-priced special reports they stuff in their briefcases or how long they surf the Internet. Just ask them. The powers that be cannot keep up! This means there are lots of opportunities for independent entrepreneurs who have an idea that they can develop themselves. Every year there are new films that are made outside the studio system that catch the majors entirely by surprise. That's why studio executives and venture capitalists with open checkbooks troll Sundance Film Festivals, multimedia conventions, and the Internet.

## International Coproductions

As fate would have it, English is the international language. This makes English language producers the lucky ones. If you produce in English, the worldwide markets are more readily available to you. With the exception of France and India, American-made pictures dominate every country's screentime. In order to combat this cultural erosion and boost the local film industry, the national governments of many countries underwrite film production. This has led to a stagnation of marketing creativity. Why should a producer learn engaging storytelling or look for marketing hooks to include in his or her program when the government will fund the film anyway? So what is happening is that many of these films are either unwatchable or are only shown on local screens for a few days before disappearing altogether. They aren't distributed outside of their country because most films cannot compete.

In the U.S. producers have to scramble for good stories, casting, and production values, and their distributors must come up with innovative marketing campaigns to make it onto U.S. screens. Even if a film fails domestically, there's always the foreign markets for recoupment.

The U.S. market makes up only about 40% to 50% of the revenue stream for its filmed products. The rest of the world brings in another 50% to 60%. With half or more income from the U.S. market already in hand, U.S. producers have great leverage for finding international coproduction partners. The Europeans have been doing coproductions for years and are getting very good at it. Half of the approximately 150 films made in France last year were coproductions with other European or U.S. companies.

I am not particularily pleased by the fact that Hollywood-style films dominate the world market and spread unquestioned Western-style values. Our cultural imperialism spread through U.S. films undermines local values and customs. One–way cultural exchange is not an exchange. Hollywood's coffers are filled with foreign cash, film being one of our largest exports. While taking full advantage of nearly 90% of worldwide screens, we've protected our own screens from most foreign fare from which we could, if we wanted to, learn a great deal. But it's not about learning, it's about money.

U.S. movies make the rest of the world want to emulate our lifestyles. Do we really want to see blue-jeaned clad teenagers in modern malls through Eastern Europe and Southeast Asia? The bigger-than-life images from the Hollywood image machine convey enormous cultural and psychological power. How can the icons and cultural values of traditional cultures survive when the West's magic seems so much greater? Perhaps we need to be more responsible with the stories we choose to tell and the way we tell them. There may be a terrific cultural advantage to creating coproductions as a means of enriching our own culture and assisting other countries to develop competitive cinema.

Today you can make a film or video anywhere in the U.S. (with minimal expenses and equipment) which can be seen in dozens of countries around the world by millions of people. This is not fantasy. This is a real possibility that exists for you. Take your best shot.

Are you excited? Terrified? Challenged? You should be. You might start thinking: Where do I fit in? What should I be doing? What can I produce? These are all good questions.

What kind of future do you want it to be? Imagine it. Do it. You have the power to both choose and create. For many of you, this is the beginning of your career; for others, you may be going through yet another "career change." (I go through one every three to five years!)

Now is the time to gain all the experience you can and put your knowledge to work in new ways and in new forms. When you study film theory, you'll quickly learn that there are many approaches to the cinematic form. Cinema is quite a new art form and American filmmakers tend to dwell on formula story structures. Study the traditional forms to gain a firm footing in the emerging new forms. As Marshall McLuhan informed us, the old forms tend to be emulated in the new.

It's time to start thinking and planning your own strategy for the future.

# IMAGINE THIS

## The Three Secrets to Filmmaking

I'll cut to the chase. Here's the whole deal. I'll explain the three secrets to filmmaking right now. Here they are:

1. See the film in your head before anyone else.

2. See the entire success of the producing enterprise in your head.

3. Build agreement for your vision of #1 and #2.

That's it. Got it?

If you can get a glimpse of your film and then start seeing it clearer and clearer, writing it down, drawing it, and telling the story of it, you are on your way.

At the same time, the producer in you has to start seeing how this is physically going to get done. Get it made. In the same way you can see the story in your mind's eye, you can see people making the film as well.

This is not an idle waste of time. This is prep. This is getting powerful images in your head around which you are going to communicate to other people who will in turn get the story and "how to do it" in their heads as well. It's this last step that brings it into reality. You need to have a vision, communicate it well to other people, and get everyone to say, "Yeah, great, let's do it!"

That's it. That's all there is. Now the rest of this chapter will help you work on #1 and the rest of the book will deal with #2 and #3. See it and get it done.

## A Glimpse of Your Own Future

Would it be helpful if you could see your future? Sure would. Think you can? No way!

That was my answer too until I tried a little meditation exercise twenty years ago. It was quite simple. I found a quiet room, turned off the phones, made sure no one was coming over, and sat in a chair and began to imagine my ideal work/play/create environment.

In my mind's eye I saw a large Japanese style tatami floored room surrounded with sliding paper doors. In front of me were a bank of video monitors that were pulling in images and sounds from all over the world, from the past, from the present, and from the future. I was synthesizing images and sounds through a miniaturized mixing board and broadcasting them out to colleagues and theaters around the world. Occasionally I'd pour myself some green tea.

I directed myself in this visualization exercise in 1976. Today, with my computer and the World Wide Web, my office looks very similar to what I had imagined twenty years ago (minus the Japanese shoji screens and green tea)!

If you can "see it" or pre-visualize it first and get an idea of where you may be heading or would like to be heading, then you can do something about making it so.

I told my film producing partner, Steven Arnold, in the late sixties, "If you can think it up, I can do it." And I meant it. Somehow, no matter what we dreamed up, we always found a technical way to do it for the camera whether it was to make someone fly or transform. If we can see it in our mind's eye, we can bring it into form.

I do this with all of my projects. Sometimes it starts with just a single image, a few words, a character, a piece of music. You can start anywhere and build.

Why not do this with your film projects? Your career? What would you like to have in the future? What sort of people would you like to be working with? What would you like to be making?

What's to lose? Worst case, you see nothing. Best case, you get a peek into the future.

**See It First: A Pre-visualization Exercise**

This is the first step in planning your film or your career so treat the process with respect. You have to draw out the Muse. Set up a quiet space. No phones. No visitors. No distractions. Close your eyes and spend thirty to sixty minutes on this exercise.

If I could be doing something right now, what would I be doing? Producing a film? Directing a film? What film? Where?

Ask yourself questions like these and dwell on them for a while. Ask them to yourself over and over. (If you allow it, you will get a wide range of answers to the same questions. That's fine.) Imagine a specific instance or example. See yourself doing what you would most like to do. See yourself doing it better than anyone else. See yourself thoroughly enjoy what you are doing. See yourself being paid very well for what you enjoy doing! (Fun, isn't it?)

Make it very real. What do the people helping you look and sound like? Where is this taking place? What does the room or environment look like? Smell like? Feel like? Is it hot or cold? What objects are in the room? What do they look like? When is what you are seeing taking place? Next year? In five years? In ten years?

Just allow yourself to enjoy what you see. When you feel you've visited there long enough come out of your meditation and write down what you've seen and experienced. Write down how you feel about it. Make as complete a record of your experience as possible. You'll use these images later as you gather the images for your project. This is the rocket fuel that turns dreamers into doers. This is where the magic begins. What you gather here you will share with others who will support you and help you make your film or video.

19

## Imagine Success

Here's an exercise that we do in my filmmaking seminars. I ask the participants to tell us what would be the biggest payoff for them and their film. What would it look like? What is one specific moment that you want to have happen as a result of making a great film or video? Here are some examples of what they've said:

> *I overhear people discussing my film in a restaurant.*
> *The audience laughs at the funny scenes.*
> *I get a stack of contracts from the major distributors all wanting my film.*
> *Children around the world sing the theme song to my animated film.*
> *There are lines around the block, I can't even get in to my own movie.*
> *The film starts a debate in the editorial column of* The London Times.
> *My photo appears on the cover of* Premiere *magazine.*
> *I open a letter with a check for $1 million.*
> *My father tells me he's proud of me.*

What's amazing here are the things which drive people to make their films. It's all over the board. There are the expected things like fame and fortune, good reviews, and the best seats in restaurants. But there are other things that people have said that go deeper like having the respect of their family, teaching children, or raising money for a cause.

I believe it's important for you to determine at the start what is important to you in the project. Dig down and see what you really want to get out of it. If it's money, fine. If it's recognition, fine. Whatever it is, get clear about it. Because this will be the measure (in your eyes only) whether you are successful. It's important that you get the payoff you are looking for. The more depth and meaning you can find in your project, the more inner resources you are going to have to get you through the whole process.

(Note: I have found that "get-rich-quick" movie schemes do not work. Why? Because the motivation to "get rich" is not deep enough and doesn't provide enough firepower to get someone through all the months or years of production. They run out of steam. Seeing a class full of kindergarten kids laugh has for some people more "oomph" than the desire to get rich.)

Write down what you want to get out of the project. Write as many ideas as you want. Then prioritize them. For some of you this will be very easy. For others, you may have only the foggiest notion. Don't skip over this exercise. These are the building blocks that will take you over the finish line later. That's what this book is about. Making your vision real.

If you can see it, you can do it.

# Drawing Back The Bow

## Know Where You Are Going

If you want to hit the target you must first draw back the bow. If you want to produce a film, start a successful film or video production business, or change careers you must first draw back the bow. Here is a single exercise that you can do to increase the impact of what you want to accomplish.

(Throughout the book there will be other tips and principles that will greatly enhance your ability to get it done. They will help get you focus and plan. By now some of are probably asking, "But Michael, when are we going to learn how to get the money? Make the film?" I say, "Don't worry, we'll get there. Be patient. First things first. Now you've got to draw back the bow.")

The first thing is to know where you are going. Every film released is its own test case. It is being marketed for the first time. And it's an all new marketing campaign and approach. (Except perhaps for sequels.) In the same way, every individual is different with different skills, needs, and definitions of success. Therefore, you will need to create a one-of-a-kind road map for yourself. It's something I can't give you. You are a specially skilled visionary who is going to do it yourself. Do what? Write a mission statement.

## Write a Mission Statement

A mission statement is both broad and specific, and has the power to frame your activities for your entire life. It is a concise definition of who you are or what your company is about that you are willing to share with the world. Someone reading it can very quickly understand your goals, your aspirations, your intentions, and your position which is unique from everyone else's. Corporations have them in their annual reports. A mission statement doesn't have to be long: it can be a sentence or a paragraph. It says what you stand for.

Ours is:

*Michael Wiese Productions is a successful communications company which creates, produces, and distributes communication pieces that inspire, inform, and empower.*

Since we produce a lot of different things I prefer to call them "communication pieces" rather than films or videos which is too limiting. I could say we do communications about the environment, or health, or technology but I haven't specified a genre. You can if you want.

Whatever we do I want it to have a positive and beneficial effect on those who see it or read it or hear it, so I say that our work "empowers" people. I could also say that I want our company to be profitable and make lots of cash, but instead I've said we are successful so that all my other definitions of success are included as well. Nothing wrong with being successful. You want to make success part of your mission, don't you?

Every six months or year I might tweak our mission statement to bring it up to date to my current thinking.

Ideally you write the mission statement with your closest colleagues and partners. Everyone in the office can contribute to it, making it say precisely what you intend. You want everyone to fully understand the mission, embrace it, and be part of it as you move forward.

The mission statement does not include "deliverables" such as making a ton of money or getting to the top. Rather it is a rationale for professional life and your personal lifestyle. Stress what you want to be, not what you want.

What happens when you create your mission statement is that, first, you immediately have an identity. You are something special. You see something that others don't. You are something that others aren't. People see that you have something special to offer. Either they line up with your mission statement or they don't. Your mission statement is like a filter that you can use to review projects or people with whom you may like to work.

My office gets dozens of calls a week from producers or writers with projects. They usually want us to participate in some form or another: executive-produce, coproduce, direct, market, consult. The first thing that the person who answers the phone does is to see whether this falls within our mission statement or not. Most often it doesn't, so the inquirers are sent on their merry way. They may say, "But it's a great idea and will make you a lot of money." We say, "Terrific but it doesn't fit our mission statement." Then they say, "Well, then how about just consulting on it, helping it along." And we reiterate, "It doesn't fit our mission statement, we're sorry." It's a great filter.

We are not trying to cop an attitude; we simply want to be very clear with people what we are about. When someone brings in a project knowing our mission statement, they have a much greater chance of our working together. In the same way, if you are looking for a distributor, you'd best understand their mission statement and what kind of products they distribute or you are wasting everyone's time. It's a matter of finding the right match. Putting your mission statement out there is a great way to start.

Having a clear mission statement attracts exactly what you want. When you put out very clearly who you are and what you want to do, not only do you find support for that (not from everyone) but you also attract people and projects to you that do fit your mission statement.

I spent years operating without a mission statement. Being entrepreneurial, I was like an untethered boat and would go off in any direction and get involved in all kinds of projects. There was no rhyme or reason or strategy to build something. That's why I offer up to you this notion of creating a mission statement for yourself early on as I know that it will be extremely helpful; your own guiding light. If you get confused or something comes along that offers get-rich-quick potential (it never is!) then you can apply your mission statement and see whether it fits, secure in knowing that you've spent serious time thinking about what you want to do with your time and your skills.

There are two things you should do. First, visualize what you want to be, do, or have. And secondly, articulate that in a mission statement so that it will be clear to yourself and other people.

Try writing a mission statement right now. It doesn't have to be perfect. It will get you thinking and committing something to paper. You can revise it as you go. After all, it is a work in progress and is meant to serve you.

# DEVELOPMENT: CATCHING BIG IDEAS

## The Development Stage

You have a vague idea. Maybe it's just a single image. Or maybe you have a whole dramatic story outlined in your head. Maybe you don't have an inkling of what to do and are looking for new ideas. This is development: bringing your ideas to paper so that they may be shared with others.

What's great about this initial stage of filmmaking is that you haven't spent anything yet! You are still in the metaphysical stage. You have an idea; it doesn't weigh anything. It has no physical properties. You can fix it and it won't cost you anything. You aren't under any pressure to get something done on time or budget. You can rework your idea until it's just right.

The studios would call this the "development" stage. Producers strut around and say they have projects "in development." It means they are working on an idea or a script or it might mean that a studio has put up some money to have a writer develop an idea that the producer has pitched. This isn't as easy as it sounds. If a studio puts up money to have you write a script, they control your idea and the script from that moment on. They may produce it but probably won't. Most likely it will go onto a shelf with the thousands of other scripts they've developed over the years.

I advise producers to develop an idea and take it through the script stage by themselves without taking development money. That way a studio or investor can buy it if they like it and it never ends up on a shelf because you own it. Nevertheless, undercapitalized producers always ask me about "development money" or "seed money."

26

## Development Money

Yes, there is such a thing. You can go to an investor (or studio) and ask them to invest in you hiring a writer to develop your idea into a script. This is the most risky investment of all because not only does the investor have no assurance that a film will ever be made, he has no assurance that a good script will ever be written.

From the producer's point of view, development money is the most expensive money there is because an investor must be compensated for his or her considerable risk. The investor may want a very high multiple return on his cash investment such as two or three times his money back and profit participation! The producer has already given away a substantial portion of the upside in his or her film (if any) and the film is not even in production.

The best thing to do is to bite the bullet and develop the script yourself. Maybe you have to pay a writer a little something. Or maybe not. There are plenty of unproduced writers who would write a script on "spec" and be thrilled in working with a producer, hoping their film will get made. Get inside a writer's head. What do they want? They want to be produced! That's what you have to offer. They want a screen credit (that's easy), a little cash, and maybe (or maybe not) a percentage of profits. It's entirely negotiable.

The only way for producers to control a project is to control the underlying material: the script. So either write a script or have someone write one for you. The script is the only thing that cannot be taken away from you. Ideas can. Scripts, stories, and books that you do not own (or have not optioned) you cannot do anything with. Get a script that you control.

## Finding a Great Script

This is the essence of the game and is what every producer and studio in Hollywood are trying to do. The studios spend millions of dollars a year developing ideas and reading scripts so it's unlikely that you are going to see a great script before they do. However, there are tons and tons of scripts out there. Over 70,000 scripts are written each year! Ninety percent or more are written by people who don't know what they are doing so there's a lot of dreck to flip through. If you don't write one yourself, you have to be willing to spend quite a long time looking for scripts. How do you do that?

You contact agents who have a roster of writers. Maybe you start with the smaller agencies. If you can convince them you are a bonafide producer they will send you scripts, most of which the studios have already seen and passed on.

Samuel French Bookstore (213-876-0570 in Los Angeles or 212-206-8990 in New York) sells directories that are filled with writer's agents. Get one of these books and call the agents. Describe the genre or story form you are looking for. Sound professional or you won't get past the receptionist.

Don't waste your time with an ad in *Variety* or *The Hollywood Reporter.* If you do, you'll get swamped with so many bad scripts you won't know what to do.

You can also befriend story editors or script readers who may have read something that they liked but their employer passed on.

Search the Internet. Among the newsgroups you will find several writer forums where you can post your interest in reading scripts of a specific nature. Perhaps you might ask for a one page synopsis first. Use the search engines and search under "film scripts." You'll find many sites that pitch scripts. How good they are is for you to find out.

Scripts are plentiful and they are out there. But don't expect to find a good one right away. Some one- and two-man script development companies that I know only expect to find a handful of scripts worthy of development (e.g., rewriting) a year, and they work full-time at it.

When Vestron (where I worked for four years) announced it was going into the film production business, we received 10,000 scripts in just the first year. When I left Vestron, I said to myself, "I'll find something good in here that everyone else missed." I went through the "coverage" on the scripts submitted. Coverage is a one– or two–page synopsis of a script with brief criticism and analysis. Executives can read the coverage very quickly. If a script gets good coverage from a variety of readers, then maybe the executive will read the script and maybe it will make its way into a discussion about development.

I started with a three-ring binder of coverage titled "A" which was the size of the Manhattan telephone directory. Three days later when I was halfway through "C" I realized that it was a hopeless endeavor. I was not going to find a great script in this lot. These coverage pages described some of the worst story ideas I have ever heard in my life. It is far better to come up with your own idea, something you care about, and develop a screenplay.

## Developing Great Ideas

There are lots of ways to come up on a good idea. They are all around you everyday. An incident or character may suggest a story idea. A life story in a magazine or newspaper may be your inspiration. Perhaps a historical event.

I go to the Book Expo (formerly ABA) convention each June. (Europeans in mid-October go to the massive Frankfurt Book Fair which is ten times larger than Book Expo.) I spend three days walking through more than a thousand booths of large and small publishers. Here you can find new books which you can option and develop into screenplays. The show is attended by many studios and independents looking for that one great book. But with 50,000 new books published each year, there is plenty to look at. You can also meet editors and find out what books they have on their drawing boards.

The Book Expo is also a great source for special interest home video material. I found the books *Diet for a New America* and *The Courage to*

29

*Heal,* among others, from which I developed two PBS specials. I saw *Men Are From Venus and Women Are From Mars* long before it was published. I saw *Chicken Soup for the Soul.* I saw Deepak Chopra's books. All became hits a year or two later.

Plays are also a good source for material especially because they have few locations, which is good for low-budget independent films. Samuel French in Los Angeles and Drama Books in New York have numerous plays both old and new.

Look at historical events which are already well known from which to draw. Place your character in the context of that event.

There are well-known novels and authors that you read in high school that may be relevant to today's audience if redressed. Look at the resurgence of Jane Austen's stories. Is there anything she's written that hasn't been made into a movie?

Your own library is a great source. These old friends stacked along your walls were once an inspiration to you. Maybe they still are. What was it about them that inspired you?

What about biographies of great people? A prepromoted aspect is already built-in, which will help you later on.


**Trends**

Stand and look at the big picture first. Look at cultural trends and see where things are going. Attending Book Expo gives me an idea for future trends. I saw the emergence of book publishing trends for New Age, environmental, recovery, multicultural movement, and the Internet long before these trends emerged in the mass market. Since it takes a year or two to get your idea into production, if you pick your idea soon enough, then your program can hit about the same time the culture is ready for it. If you wait too long, by the time you get into production it may be too late.

I have found Faith Popcorn's first book, *The Popcorn Report*, to be excellent reading. She identifies various cultural trends. Fads, she says, are short-lived, but trends last for ten years or more. There are professional trend watchers with newsletters that keep you abreast of cultural and demographic changes that could very well affect the information that people want and the stories affecting their lives. Check out the Internet. Read Ken Dychtwald's book, *Age Wave*.

Do not study the current "hot" film genre fad unless you want to learn what to stay away from. By the time you figure out what the fad is, it's over. One year it's erotic thrillers, the next "independent art movies." By the time you get your movie finished, the market will be flooded with similar, unsaleable material. (For a real shocker on "me-too" producers, attend The American Film Market in Los Angeles where films are bought and sold internationally by the barrelful. Many copy last year's hit movies.)

## Original Ideas

So you want to be original? Great. What about original ideas? Develop your own stories or series ideas. Avoid buying or optioning other people's properties: there are no net profits you have to share! If you have the skills to create your own material you are much more in the driver's seat.

Many first-time novelists use their own life stories for material. While there may be a bias in the filmic and performance arts against using your own life as script fodder, it is a source of material that is rich and meaningful. Don't rule it out. If there are themes, conflicts, and struggles in your own story that are universal and will draw empathic viewers, why not?

Here are some idea-generating tools, both linear and intuitive, that have worked for me. Be open, try them out, and use what works for you. If they aren't helpful to you, don't use them. Unless you give them a try you won't know how powerful they can be.

## Mind Maps and Idea Fishing

You don't need much, just a kernel of an idea or a word, and you can start using associative techniques described in the books *The Idea Fisher* by Marsh Fisher or *The Mind Map* by Tony Buzan with Barry Buzan. The catalysts are words which spread by association through word links.

## Try This Exercise

Take any word and find as many associations that you can from the word. List the words. Don't critique the words. Just write them as fast as you can in a long list. After five minutes go back and circle the words that appeal most to you.

Then do word associations using the circled words. After you've done this start to identify some ideas or threads of ideas that appeal to you. You may start getting character or story or location ideas. These are the basic ingredients for your story idea that you have pulled out of your brain through word association.

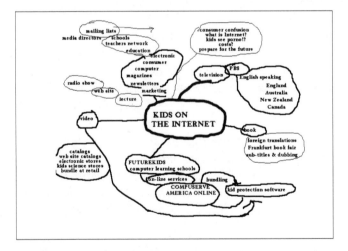

The mind mapping book says that the mind does not work in a linear fashion and therefore suggests you write down the words and link them in patterns of words and circles and connections until you start to discover relationships that you like.

This is an example of mind mapping that I did around a project to help determine what the distribution channels would be. (You can use this technique for just about any creative design from copywriting to marketing, storytelling to character development.) Try it.

*The Idea Fisher* is a bit different. Here, you work with words as "bait" to fish for even better words and ideas. You start with the words of whatever idea you already have and using each word for bait, you fish for new words and ideas.

*The Idea Fisher* suggests you classify your ideas into three different groups or categories of ideas (e.g., "ocean, seas, tidepools"). An ocean is bigger than a sea which is bigger than a tidepool. Sort your words according to these categories; from the general to the very specific.

Maybe all you have for your story is a physically impaired old man beats others to gold in the mountains.

I did this list in about five minutes. You can continue to add to this list going from right to left, or left to right. Go from the general to the very specific. As you brainstorm you will come up with more and more specific ideas that you will like. You get more specific going to columns in the right, and more general going to the left. I could continue to associate and get even more specific; adding other locations and characters and conflicts, and a story would start to emerge. You pick your favorite elements and brainstorm some more. Got it?

Using our sentence you might have something like this:

| OCEANS | SEAS | TIDEPOOLS |
|---|---|---|
| | *physically impaired* | |
| | | *blind* |
| | | *deaf* |
| | | *dumb* |
| | | *amputee* |
| *wrinkled* | | |
| | *experienced* | |
| | *learned* | |
| | *100 years old* | *Grandpa Moses* |
| | *immortal* | *2,000 year old man* |
| *man* | | |
| | *sage* | |
| | *guru* | |
| | *drunkard* | |
| | *scholar* | |
| | *athlete* | |
| *gold* | | |
| | *elixir* | |
| | *knowledge* | |
| | *fountain of youth* | |
| *mountain* | | |
| | | *Mt. Everest* |
| | | *Kilimanjaro* |
| | | *Smoky Mountains* |
| | | *Rocky Mountains* |

This technique is very useful for opening up your mental powers. You'll be surprised what is stored there and how fast you can come up with ideas. It's also a great technique to use with your creative partners or a group of people to brainstorm. Get a large piece of paper and tack it to the wall or use a blackboard so everyone can see the contributions as they are being made. Try it!

Both mind mapping and idea fishing work well for developing story ideas, characters, dialogue, descriptions, movie titles, and copy lines.

## The Title Machine

Roger Corman, possibly the most successful exploitation B-movie producer of all time, it is told, would come up with marketable titles first, test them, and then, using the most successful titles, write scripts and produce them. He has a nearly perfect profitability track record so he must be doing something right. The story goes that Roger Corman agreed to produce Ron Howard's first film, *Grand Theft Auto*, once they found a marketable title.

Charlie Band, a producer of horror and fantasy films, uses a similar technique. He would come into Vestron to pitch ideas, not with a stack of scripts but with a stack of theatrical posters for the films he wanted to produce. They were mostly scantily-clad-Amazonian-woman-with swords-fighting-dragons kind of stuff that illustrator Boris Vallejo and others had illustrated. The Vestron movie executives would flip through the posters. "Yeah, we'll take that one, and this one, hey, that one's pretty good." Then they'd send Charlie off to come back with scripts based on the titles and artwork that they liked. I tried another version of this technique. I put every word from the 100 top-grossing movie titles of all time into a computer. I asked the computer to deliver every two-word combination. The computer spit out a phone book size book with two-word combinations. I read the book and passed it around to my staff and asked them to circle every two-word title they thought was good.

We found that we could put the word "deadly" in front of just about any word and get a good, exploitation type title: *Deadly Friends, Deadly Curse, Deadly Nightmare, Deadly Garden, Deadly Blanket.*

I thought *Deadly Breath* could be a kung-fu parody! A few years later I was speaking at the Cologne Film Festival and I told the audience this story. A German investment banker came up to me at the reception and told me he had invested in two films which both had the word "deadly" in them. Excited I said, "How'd they do?!!" He said, "Both flopped."

## Tapping Into the Unconscious

Another technique that is very useful when you are really stuck on something is to give your unconscious an assignment. Not just any assignment — a tough assignment! The more important the better.

Before I go to sleep, when I am relaxed, I give my unconscious the problem and then I forget about it, knowing that my unconscious (which has the ability to tap into a great reservoir of knowledge) will deliver an answer. When I ask the question, I also ask that I receive the answer at a specific time, such as when I open my car door in the morning.

Usually what would happen is that I would forget about the whole thing until I opened my car door. And then, whammo, I got an image, or a set of words, or a feeling that would have within it the information I needed. Try it!

Once at Vestron Video, when I was trying to bring National Geographic into the home video business and was competing with CBS Video who were also bidding on the project, I had this terrible feeling that they were going to get the deal. I racked my brain: What haven't I done that would close the deal?

Both deals were very similar in terms of money so it would have to be something else that would close the deal. CBS had, I believed, a better brand name than our much smaller company.

So I asked my unconscious: What could I do that would close the National Geographic deal? then I went to sleep.

The answer I got was simple and cost absolutely nothing! I later found out, it was the one thing that allowed Vestron (little David) to beat out CBS (Goliath) for the rights to distribute National Geographic's library of television specials in home video. A deal that turned out to be worth over $40 million.

The answer I got was, "Take Vestron's president to a meeting with the National Geographic folks." Simple as that. It worked. CBS also had not brought forth their president. National Geographic needed to see and hear Vestron's head guy say, "This is a priority for our company" and mean it. It was not about money, it was about respect for their programs. It was about integrity.

## Creative Tools Are a Must

If you are a writer or a producer or director, then your livelihood depends on developing ahead-of-trend ideas, innovative story lines, and marketable projects. You will need to collect your own arsenal of brainstorming and mental pump–priming tools. These are but a few of the ideas out there. In the biographies of painters and sculptors you'll find many, many more techniques. Develop your own techniques, chuck the rest.

These are just a few of some of the techniques I've used to jog the brain into new ways of thinking. There are many, many more. I encourage you to discover your creative tools that support your creative process.

# Producing

## The Producer

A producer is involved in a film or video from the conceptual stages of the project, beginning with the preproduction, research, and writing, through the casting, shooting, editing, and postproduction. But that's not all. The job continues with negotiating the distribution contracts and arranging for the promotion and exhibition of the piece.

The producer is the first one on a project and the last one off. I am still responsible for managing the ongoing business of films that have been in distribution for over twenty years! I still collect royalties and license fees from distributors and disburse them to the investors and my creative partners! Some films will require attention as long as they are earning income.

When a project is just getting off the ground, the producer represents the film to potential investors during the fund-raising. When the film is in production, the producer keeps the ideas alive with his/her coworkers. The conceptual idea for the film may have been created by someone else (like a writer or director), but it is the producer that stays with the job the longest.

The public thinks of a producer as the one with the big cigar and a roll of money. That's not so, at least among independents. He/she is the one responsible for raising money and paying the crew. The producer keeps the production on schedule. Much of the job is an administrative one.

It is not a job for everyone because it requires a stick-to-it-ness. Many filmmakers find they are much happier doing other jobs like writing, camerawork, or editing. A producer's job has a lot to do with the business of filmmaking. If you do not have the personality to negotiate the business (pitching, financing, promotion, publicity, and advertising) involved with producing films, then find someone who does. These aspects are crucial to the success of any film.

## Relationships

Good working relationships with people are more important than any idea. This may sound a bit extreme but it's true. In filmmaking, it is people cooperating with each other that make ideas real. Many people have wonderful ideas for films but can't work with others. Their ideas will probably not be realized in a film, which is very much a cooperative effort.

Many of the people you meet will continue throughout the years to make films. Their skills, talents, and contacts will grow as will yours. Once you have built working relationships with these people you will want to continue to work together. The best way to begin is with agreements.

## Agreements

An agreement is a tool for establishing and maintaining good communication — a clear understanding of what one's responsibilities are and what the exchange is. Agreements (or contracts) represent the place where this is acknowledged and written down.

Very often two or more people will begin a film or tape a project with very different ideas of who will do what and who will get what. They'll work for many months, having very different expectations about responsibilities, money, screen credits, and profit sharing. These aspects of the working relationship need to be clearly and firmly established from the outset.

For one thing, it clears the minds of everyone. You no longer have to struggle to get what you want because you have all already agreed on salaries, credits, profit sharing, and responsibilities. Your energy can go toward working as a team and not manipulating or fighting with one another over who gets what.

Do not be afraid to put your cards on the table and say what you want. Encourage your partners to do the same. Out of these discussions you can determine what is the most workable agreement for everyone.

An agreement is something you all create and agree to. It is not something that is created by someone and forced upon someone else. All of the participants may not get what they want. Compromises may need to be made, but at least everyone will have created the agreement and will support it. There is nothing worse than people sabotaging the film because they aren't getting what they want. Written agreements align everyone and allow the film to get made.

Create agreements very early on. If it turns out that someone does more work than someone else, then revise your agreements. Have a basis on which to build. An agreement is something you can refer back to 12 months later when all of you have forgotten what you agreed to.

Similar agreements can be created for the crew and other participants in the film. They can state what their responsibilities are and what the exchange is (money, percentages, and credits). The period of employment is established. Travel and other reimbursements can be clearly defined.

Many people in film and video projects have disagreements because there wasn't a clear understanding in the beginning. Everyone had a different idea about who would get what. It is extremely destructive to the morale of the cast and crew and the filmmaking community as a whole. Written agreements can alleviate much of the misunderstandings and subsequent bad feelings that arise when artistic people join in creative and business ventures.

**Rights & Clearances**

Written agreements (which are legal contracts) extend into the area of "rights." You will have agreements with your creative partners (writers, directors, associate producers) and with anyone who contributes anything to your film.

A film is a bundle of rights. Everything and everyone that appears in, or participates in, the making of the film needs a contract or agreement. Sometimes this is with unions and sometimes not; sometimes a mixture of union and nonunion. You must obtain all the rights in the film, including all the various media rights (theatrical, broadcast, home video, multimedia, etc.) in order to "sell" (actually license) the film to distributors, broadcasters, etc. If you inadvertently leave out the rights for one participating actor or key creative talent, it is likely the film will get held up from distribution as a distributor will require that you show proof that you have cleared all rights in a film.

Warning: Distributors and broadcasters do not mess around. If you have not secured *all* the necessary rights in your film, they will not license or distribute it. All your hard work will end up on a shelf. Do it right. Secure all rights up front.

Get signed agreements with everyone involved with your production, particularly if they are friends or family. Once you've all signed the agreement you can put it in a drawer and get to work. Without agreements relationships can become difficult, especially with those people who are close to you. In my consulting business I see it frequently. If you don't get a formal contract, at least have all parties sign an agreement letter. If you are really serious about your filmmaking, you will be absolutely sure that your agreements are buttoned-down in every conceivable area. It's the only way to go.

**The Twenty-one Basic Agreements**

Here is a brief summary of the primary agreements that you will need for your film which lawyers will prepare. Any good entertainment attorney will have form contracts for these agreements on their word processor and will be revising them for your particular project. They should not have to write them from scratch but only amend and negotiate existing agreements with the various parties involved.

41

## 1. Underlying Rights

Often there is a preexisting work, a play or book, on which a film is based. The rights must be obtained from the original owner. If the author is no longer living, you may need to deal with heirs or an estate. Or, you may need to acquire the "life story" rights. If so, you obtain an option which includes the financial terms on which the property will be brought, if and when the film goes into production. An option may or may not cost you something depending on your negotiation skills.

## 2. Writer's Agreement

This agreement may be with a Writer's Guild member or not. In either case, the agreement will specify how many drafts you require, the payment for each, credits, and the transfer of the copyright. If you have hired a Writer's Guild member, then your production company will need to be a signatory to the WGA (Writer's Guild of America) agreements which specify minimum rates, credits, working conditions, etc.

## 3. Development Agreement

You may get "seed money" from a private investor, a studio, broadcaster, distributor, or film company. You will want a clear agreement that protects their investment and specifies how they will be repaid. Will the repayment be in cash, a multiple of their cash, equity, or all of the above? You certainly want to consult a lawyer so that you don't inadvertently tie up valuable rights in your development deal. This being the riskiest of film investments, the investor may want a very tough deal. The contract should cover exactly what is to be created (a treatment, a final draft script, a polished script) and by whom, and whether or not the producer, who oversees the process, will also be paid. If the deal is with a studio, then you should negotiate "turnaround rights" which will enable you to get your property back (usually for the recoupment of their outlay and then some) if the studio fails to get your script into production within a specified period of time.

### 4. Production Company Agreement

This is an agreement with the production company which will be responsible for actually producing the film. Your production company may have an agreement with a limited partnership (if that is how the film is financed). The contract will specify who will actually produce, credits, a payment schedule matched against delivery (script, principal photography, rough cut, fine cut, master delivery, etc.). As producer you don't just get a tub of money to spend on the first day. It is doled out to you as you meet your schedule with the final payment withheld until delivery of <u>all</u> the required materials, which is more than just the master negative of the film.

### 5. Cast Contracts

Cast agreements need to be signed by everyone appearing in your film from stars to walk-on extras. The agreements cover their performance, how many days they will work plus contingencies, their fees per diems, residuals, and credits. The producer is authorized to publicize the film using their likeness, photograph, and biographical information. Producers should always "buyout" the entire body of rights (film, broadcast, home video, multimedia, etc.) so that a film is not tied up when, say, the television rights for one actor were not obtained. In the U.S., the production company will become a "signatory" to the Screen Actors Guild (SAG) and promise to abide by its rules and rates. Without being a signatory to SAG you cannot hire guild actors. The guild will reduce actors' fees on low budget productions.

### 6. Producer's Agreement

The production company (even if the producer is also the general partner of a limited partnership) will need to have an agreement with the producer producing the film. This agreement will state that a professional quality motion picture is expected to be delivered at such and such a date, of a predetermined length, for a certain budget. If the producer goes over the budget, the contract may specify that any "overages" are deducted from the producer's salary. There is a payout schedule as to when the producer shall be paid and a certain amount often withheld until delivery. Since the financial onus for coming in on budget and on schedule is on the producer, the agreements may make the producer personally fiscally responsible for the film's costs. The contract will specify the producer's fees and equity, profit participation or royalty position in the project, and credits. (In my producing contracts as producer, I sometimes guarantee to the financing entity that I will deliver a film or video for a specific "guaranteed" budget. If I go over budget then I am responsible for all overages. If I come in under, then I am allowed to split (50/50) the savings with the production company. This is an incentive for me to stay under budget (which the investors like) and also compensates me for taking the financial risk on the picture. Depending on the size of the project and your financial standing, your investors may or may not accept this clause and may, instead, insist on a completion bond company (see below) to protect the film from going over budget.

### 7. Director's Agreement

This agreement is written between the production company and the director and covers the responsibilities of the director, specifies a delivery date, the director's fees, profit participation, and credits. The director's salary might be a percentage of the budget, or a fixed buyout (covering all media rights). The production company will need to be a signatory to the Director's Guild of America (DGA) in order to use guild members and must abide by DGA rules and regulations.

### 8. Facilities Agreement

You will need contracts with everyone that supplies you with equipment. These agreements will specify negotiated costs and equipment insurance requirements. Sometimes a rental house or facility will have insurance, sometimes you will be required to provide it or supplement it. The agreements may cover such things as camera rental, film purchase, lighting and grip gear, catering, lab, postproduction houses, specific effects suppliers, etc. It's important to be very clear what is expected of the facility in the agreement so that there are no misunderstandings. (Sometimes you can bring in a facility as an investor in the project which will require yet another agreement where in-kind contributions are treated like capital contributions in the project. Depending on how you structure it, they may or may not be a limited partner.)

## 9. Crew Agreements

You need to have agreements with absolutely everyone that is working on your film. The agreements will cover what services your crew are performing, what rights they are conveying to the production company, their fees and credits. The agreements may or may not involve signing with a guild such as IATSE.

## 10. Stock Footage/Music Agreements

If you are producing a documentary compilation that involves clips from other films or television programs, you will need to clear a variety of rights. For "The Beach Boys," a documentary feature film which I executive-produced, we needed to clear nine separate rights on one two-minute segment that appeared on a Bob Hope special. Nine separate payments needed to be made to:

> 1) the owner of the footage itself
> 2) the Jack Benny estate for his appearance
> 3) Bob Hope for his appearance
> 4) WGA for the writer of the TV show
> 5) DGA for the director of the TV show
> 6) AFTRA for the go-go dancers in the background
> 7) AFM for the musicians in the background
> 8) music publisher for the compositions
> 9) record company for the master recording rights,
> 10) the Beach Boys themselves (already covered in an overall agreement with the band)

## 11. Music Rights

The simplest music agreement is for music that has already been recorded. You acquire the rights (in all media) to use a specific piece of music. More complex music agreements cover the composing and recording of an original score for your film which include the composer's fees, copyright issues, publishing issues, and more.

Besides an agreement with the composer, you will need an agreement with the composer's publishing company (which owns the rights to the score). The master recording rights and the synchronization rights allow you to use a specific piece of music and to sync that music with your images. These rights are generally held by the record companies. If you are dealing with a popular song, then you will definitely deal with the record company's business affairs office. You will also need to get the "mechanical" rights which allow you to manufacture the music in the form of a film or home video or CD.

For low-budget films, the fees for the sync rights and master recording license may be around $12,000 per song.

If you are dealing with a film composer (who does everything himself on a synthesizer), then you may only need one agreement with just the composer who can grant you all the rights you need.

There are music "paralegals," of great value when acquiring music rights for your film, that are cheaper than lawyers and can negotiate the various rights for you and keep detailed records. The advantage to using them is that they have extensive contacts among music publishing houses and know fair prices and costs. (Our rights book for the Beach Boys film was the size of the Manhattan phone directory and took over a year to complete!)

*12. Production Finance Agreement*

This area actually covers a wide range of different kinds of financing agreements. It is entirely dependent on the financial vehicle you choose to use for funding your film. It could be an agreement with investors in the ever-popular limited partnership agreement, or a limited liability corporation, or a joint venture. The financing may be a loan from an individual, a corporation, or a bank. Financing may come from selling equity in the film, as a loan, from presales, or a combination of all these things. An experienced entertainment attorney can recommend the best strategy to employ based on your specific needs, abilities, and resources.

## 13. Presales Agreements

Films are licensed all around the world. One strategy for financing films is to "presell" the rights to your film in different territories (e.g., Japan, Germany, France) and to use these agreements to secure a loan from a bank. A foreign sales agent will sell these rights for you at various film markets such as American Film Market, Cannes, or MIP. You will need a contract between the owner of the film (possibly the limited partnership) and the foreign sales agent who represents the film. You will also need individual agreements between the purchasing countries (which the foreign sales agent will obtain).

## 14. Security Agreement

If a bank loans you money on your presales agreements, it will hold these agreements as collateral but may also require another agreement that prohibits the filmmaker from selling territories without the bank's consent until the bank gets paid back. The bank wants to protect their loan and also uses the copyright, and all other underlying rights in the film, as its collateral.

## 15. Completion Bond Agreement

A completion bond or completion guarantee is a form of insurance policy which assures a film's investor(s) that the film will be finished even if it goes over budget. The completion bond company oversees and monitors production. If the film begins to run over schedule or budget the completion bond company may step in, fire the current director, and complete the film using its own director or producer. The completion bond company may also require the producer to reduce his or her fees and credits if it must take over the film. The fees for the completion bond company are approximately 3% to 6% of the production budget. If the film is completed on time and schedule, then 2% or 3% of the bond is rebated.

## 16. Producer's Insurance Package

You will need an agreement with an insurance company (which they will provide for negative insurance, equipment insurance, key man insurance, cast insurance, liability, theft, workman's comp and disability, as well as errors and omissions insurance). If it is insurable, there is a policy for it.

## 17. Collection Agreements

In some cases, key talent (and others) may require that funds be set aside in an escrow account from the film's proceeds to assure that they get paid their profit participation.

## 18. Escrow Agreement

There may be an agreement between the production company or limited partnership and their bank for an escrow account while fund-raising. If the minimum amount needed for the film is not raised by a certain time, the money already collected in the escrow account is returned to the investors with interest.

## 19. Foreign Distribution Agreements

You (or your sales agent) will need to negotiate distribution agreements with any territories not already presold. This may or may not be handled by your presale agent.

## 20. Television and Pay Television Licenses

When a film is sold to television, it is licensed for so many plays during a specific "window" or period of time. A contract defines the time period when the film may be broadcast.

## 21. Theatrical (and Home Video) Distribution Agreement

In the early days of video, a producer could make one deal with a theatrical distributor and another deal with a home video distributor. This was called "splintering the rights." Today, because of the high costs of releasing a theatrical film (film prints and advertising, "P&A"), theatrical distributors will want to protect their downside by also controlling the home video rights, even if they do not have their own home video company. This bundle of rights is generally sold on a territory by territory basis (sometimes along with television) by the distributor or the distributor's sales agents. A sale of all rights is called an "all rights" deal (e.g., "all rights domestic" or "all rights foreign" or "all rights worldwide."

Have an entertainment lawyer familiar with these various agreements to prepare them for you. For self education you might study attorney Mark Litwak's great book, *Contracts for Film & Television*, which has examples of many of the agreements mentioned here.

### More About Music

Music rights can be difficult and troublesome to secure. Music that has already been recorded on records involves getting signed releases not only from the recording artist, but from the composer, record company, and publishing company. Furthermore, the musicians' union requires that you pay "re-usary fees." (In the case of a prerecorded orchestral piece, those fees alone could amount to $3,000 to $10,000.)

Do not take music from a Beatles album, edit your film to it, and expect to get the rights later, as so many have done. Even if it's "okay with Paul," is for a good cause, and is nonprofit, you probably won't get permission. Large record companies simply won't bother with you unless there's a large fee involved.

Deal instead directly with small, independent record or publishing companies that are owned by the recording artists themselves. You can make an arrangement for the rights with one person (usually the musician/composer) and be done with it. Good classical music may also be found by contacting small European record companies. If you try negotiating with the larger European companies (EMI, BMG, Deutch Grammaphone, Polydor), you will encounter the same difficulties.

A very simple and effective way to handle music rights is to hire a composing student from the music department of a local university to do the score. Not only will he/she be delighted to get the experience, but given the opportunity will probably deliver a great sounding track. You can then either record union or nonunion musicians. If your budget can afford it, hire a professional composer. You can find their listings in local production directories or track them down from other movies that you've seen and liked. (Lone Eagle publishes the *Film Composers Guide — 5th Edition* which you may find useful for locating accomplished film composers.)

You can also go to a music library and pay "needle-down" license fees for music. The rates vary depending on how many selections you choose, the total length of your film, and the market (educational, television, theatrical). The fees are called "needle-down" because you are charged every time the needle is put down on the record and you use that music (even though nowadays music libraries are on CD's!). These fees are reasonable ($50 to $200) and while, in my opinion, much of the music is absolutely awful, if you listen to enough of it, you will find some good selections. There are also sound effects libraries you can license or purchase outright.

You can find these music libraries advertised in trade papers such as *Variety*, *The Hollywood Reporter*, *Videography*, *Movie Maker*, etc., or in your local yellow pages. The sound department of your local film laboratory, recording studio, or postproduction facility may also have music libraries, although the largest are to be found in the major cities.

There are also composers who cut CD's and sell "all rights" to producers for anything they want to do with it. You can find them listed in the back of production magazines such as *Millimeter* or *Videography*.

For $75 to $100 you can get an hour of music with several dozen cues. Some of it is very good although most likely will be heard on industrials far and wide. You can negotiate with the composers to do special music for you if you like their style.

## Other Rights

The rights to use art work, paintings, still photographs, or other copyrighted material may be obtained by paying a flat fee ($15 to $300) to the owner of the material. The same is true with stock footage which is purchased on a per foot basis. Stock footage is more and more expensive (e.g., $35 per minute). The price is usually dependent upon your use: educational, documentary, feature film, television, music video, etc. The U.S. National Archive film material, such as NASA footage, may be obtained for free since it is publicly owned. You will, however, pay search fees, laboratory duping costs, and shipping.

## Copyrights

Copyrighting your film is not as mysterious or difficult as you may be led to believe. The steps are relatively simple:–Here's how to get your film or video copyrighted. *Note: This process takes up to six months so it pays to be prepared by ordering the appropriate forms very early in your production process.*

Step 1:
• Call the Copyright Forms Hotline at (202) 707-9100.
• Order Copyright Package #110.
*Note: This application form applies to any audio visual work.*

Step 2:
• Once you receive your application, fill out the
Package #110.
• In the end titles at the end of your film/video project, list the copyright notice as follows:  © (Indicate the year of first public distribution of work)  Name of Copyright Owner.  Here's an example:
© *1999 Joe Smith Productions*

- Enclose one non-returnable copy of your film or videotape.
- Enclose a Filing Fee of $20.00.
- Send your entire package via Certified Mail to ensure delivery to:

U.S. Copyright Office
Library of Congress
Washington, DC 20559

Step 3:
- In approximately six months, you will receive a certificate of registration which will include a reproduction of the application form and a registration number for your project.

That's all there is to it. You will soon no doubt begin to feel pangs of immortality!

Note: One part of the form that can cause some confusion is where they ask about Compilation or Derivative Work. In this section you list any material owned by someone else that you got permission to use in your film or tape. This includes stock film footage, paintings, sound effects, music, and so forth.

In the second section of this form you are to "give a brief, general statement of the material that has been added to this work and in which copyright is claimed."

This is very confusing. What they want you to do is list all the "elements" in the film that you wish to copyright. You can write, "photography, editing, continuity, script, new music, sound effects, and all other cinematographic materials excluding preexisting material listed above." That means that you have copyrighted every element in the film, including the edited sequences, as well as the film as a whole.

If you have any questions call the Copyright Office. The people are very friendly and quite willing to help you. They are sticklers, however, when it comes to filling out the forms exactly right. If you don't, the forms will be returned to you.

If you have more questions call the helpful folks at the Copyright Office Information line at (202) 707-3000 or visit www.loc.gov\copyright.

## Producing As You Go

Many filmmakers are unable to raise their entire budget from the get-go. Most first–time filmmakers get a little money, shoot a little, get some more money, shoot some more, get money for editing, mixing, and so on. It's a very hard thing to do and for many takes years.

This is not the best way to do things, but often filmmakers feel they have no choice. They have nothing to show nor the experience to raise large sums of money. I hope some of the ideas later in this book will make this less daunting.

The lucky ones may raise the first $50,000 of a $100,000 project. That's just enough money to get into serious trouble. The money is spent and they are unable to raise more. I've met many filmmakers who have been in this predicament for years! Something they once loved and thought would be so enjoyable to produce is something they now resent. It is a considerable risk for your investors if you start before all the money is raised.

How you proceed should be clearly stated in your Limited Partnership Agreement. You can write it up anyway you like. Some agreements let you start when you've raised a minimum amount of money (enough to get a project done) while others require the entire amount to be in escrow before it is released. If the budget is not raised before a specified date, then all the monies, including interest, are returned. Other partnerships allow some or all of the collected money to be spent before all the money is raised.

The advantage to beginning before you have all the money is that you will have something to show to potential investors and you will continue to move toward your goal. I've produced several projects that started to spend money before we had raised any money. (Nowaways it's called credit card filmmaking.) As it turned out, the "pilot" film we made "on spec" helped us raise the necessary money but our first shoots could have been a disaster.

The disadvantage of raising only a part of the total budget money is the pressure you will feel holding two jobs — one as a filmmaker, the other as a fund-raiser. If, as you are proceeding, the film looks good, then money will be easier to raise. If your footage looks bad, then money will be difficult to find. (Sometimes it's better to put a dream into someone's head and not show them any footage.) Unfortunately, even the best films look awful in the early stages. I hate to screen my works-in-progress for anyone, especially investors. Without color correction, effects, titles, and a sound mix it's hard for anyone to "imagine" what's not there. Besides, a minute after you've made your disclaimer about what is not there and the lights go out, everyone will believe he or she is watching a real film. Even though you tell them beforehand, most people will think they are watching your finished film. The result — your investors don't think you make very good films!

## Budgets

One of the key jobs of the producer is to prepare the budget. When the script is finished, it is broken down by scenes. The producer (or assistant director) figures out how many days it will take to shoot the film. This begins to give you the key information for your budget because until you know exactly how many days you will be shooting, how many days you will need your lead and secondary actors, your shooting ration, etc., you can't budget.

The budget is one of the most important pages in your presentation. It must realistically anticipate every cost in your production. An error can cause severe repercussions. Writing a budget means researching costs and becoming creative when you break down your shooting script. You must find the most economical ways of doing things. If you are honest and very conscientious about preparing your budget, your certainty and confidence will be reflected in both your written and live presentations. If you have fudged here and there, underestimated, padded, or are in the dark about costs, you will run into trouble. Eventually bad numbers catch up with you. If not now, then later. Some of the most difficult questions you will receive in your presentations to investors will be about the budget. These questions may come from investors who have little or no experience with how films are made or experienced business people who don't understand how films can cost so much.

I am always being asked, "How much does it cost to do animation? Or documentaries, how much a minute? Give me a ballpark?" I usually say, "How much for a house? A Frank Lloyd Wright? A geodesic dome? A bamboo hut?" Using "rules of thumb" no matter who told you is dangerous. I know generally what it costs to make certain kinds of films or videos. These budgets are based on very similar programs that I've produced in the recent past. But it's very irresponsible to pull numbers out of a hat because you are lazy. (Filmmakers tell me, *"I'll just tell them a number and if they invest, then I'll do a budget."* It's folks like this that give filmmakers a bad name because usually they have to go back and ask for more money and no one's happy. Do it right the first time.

It is not within the scope of this book to cover budgets in great detail. If you want actual examples of different kinds of projects from documentaries, feature films, music videos, live concerts and more, in both film and video formats, please consult the 500 page book that Deke Simon and I wrote called *Film & Video Budgets*. There you will find budget formats that will help you budget your project plus an extensive description of items that you may wish to include in your budget.

Budgeting is one of the most important steps you will need to do to make your film. It's exciting. It's a veritable shopping list of everything that you will need to realize your dream. Don't avoid doing it. Get in there in the process. It's a terrific learning experience on which you will build for years to come.

## Negotiations

Since we're on the topic of budgets, we should briefly discuss negotiating. This is where the rubber hits the ground. If you are good at negotiating, you'll be good at producing films.

"It's all negotiable." Remembering that will make a great difference on your bottom line. An exciting thing about moviemaking is that there are few rules. It is an entrepreneur's business. You can make movies with a small budget or with a big budget. It all depends on the skill of the entrepreneur (producer). I recently made a "no-budget" film which was the supreme test of my negotiating and persuasive skills.

Approach negotiation with an attitude that people already want to work with you. The people you want to borrow or rent equipment from already want to loan or rent it to you. The owner of the restaurant you want to use for a location would love it. This will put you in the right frame of mind when approaching people. In reality, they may not want to have anything to do with you. It doesn't matter. You'll find people who will. It's a game. It's a treasure hunt. Have fun with it.

Maybe you have $2,000 to rent a great house for one day. But, you probably don't. Sharpen and develop your skills as a negotiator. You know how much you have to spend. As my grammy used to say, "Don't spend it in one place." Good advice. The more you can save in each area the more you have to spend elsewhere. And believe me, that "elsewhere" is just around the comer.

Some people will want to work for what you can afford. Others won't. Don't let that stop you. Go on to the next name on your list. If, in speaking about your film, you imply that no one is getting paid (and that's true), you might get a star and crew for free. Don't pay one person and not the others. The news will travel faster than you can say "action." It'll create bad feelings all around. Even though it's your business, a crew will question how you can pay one person and not others. Be consistent. Either pay no one or pay everyone something, even if it's very little. If the cast and crew perceive inequities you'll pay dearly (in screwups and on-set delays). Tell the truth. If you can't pay people, tell them that. Don't lead people on. In our business, honesty is a rare commodity and when it shows itself, it is greatly appreciated.

For talent, services, and materials always offer less than what you could pay if pressed. You have to start saving your money. You may be surprised when people accept your first offer. Some won't and in some cases you may be forced to pay more than you planned.

## The Five Rules of Budgeting

There are five basic rules to keep costs down.

*1. Question every price.* I don't care what the price tag says. There's always room for reductions. Always ask if the price could be lower. What if you rented it for more days? Over a weekend? What if you video-edited at night? On weekends? Be creative. Offer the supplier some other value that they may not ordinarily receive. Is there any promotional value in what you are doing that they could share? Don't accept the first quote. Somewhere, someone will do it cheaper and perhaps better.

I once needed a special effect for a commercial. The first quote was $4,500. The fellow said, "Bub, there's only one way to do this effect." I wasn't convinced. My second quote was $2,000. My third quote was $600. As I went from quote to quote, I learned problem-solving techniques. I figured out how to do the effect for $300; 6% of the original estimate!

Remember, price is flexible. It's not unusual to receive anywhere from 5% to 50% off. Be courageous.

*2. Shop around.* Take the time to ask lots of questions, make phone calls, interview technicians, visit studios. Get out your production directories. Explore. Ask people for recommendations. Make lists of contacts. Check out every lead until you're an expert on people, places, and prices. Then spend your money.

*3. Collect information.* If you question every price and shop around, then automatically you are collecting information. Often it's the information about a technical process or approach that you are paying for. Most information is free. But you have to be motivated to do some research. The more you learn, the more options you'll have. Filmmaking is problem solving. Lots of problem solving. The more time you spend in preproduction collecting information, the more you'll save (and the more you'll be worth as a producer, director, or production manager).

*4. Give yourself time.* Too often producers and production managers don't have (or take) the necessary time to research every aspect of their production. They get forced into corners. They end up paying high prices to get the job done. This happens all the time on commercials. The client needs it done right away. It's rush, rush, rush. Rush charges double or triple costs. The suppliers love it. It's the same amount of work for them. They just may have to work at night or on weekends. They know that when clients are in a hurry they'll spend more money. Don't let this happen to you. If you're a production manager you know that it's cheaper to hire a unit manager, production assistants, location scouts, or field producers for a few extra days (or weeks) of preproduction, than get caught short later.

Careful planning will make for a smoother, more cost efficient production. Some production companies operate with a "crisis mentality." They rush around unnecessarily. Decisions wait until the last minute. There's no time for prep. Everyone works late, works weekends, skips meals. I guess emergencies make people feel like they are doing something important. Makes them feel like martyrs. (The job isn't any better because they stayed up all night to do it. It says to me they didn't plan their time well.) I don't think they're heroes. I think they're stupid. They've misused time and energy. Furthermore, the cast and crew quickly perceive this lack of professionalism. It damages morale.

*5. Plan, plan, plan.* This really incorporates all the other rules. Spend as much time as you can in preproduction. Here it costs little. When you are in production every day is tremendously expensive. Do as much of your creative thinking, rewriting, planning, scheduling and rehearsing in preproduction when the big clock isn't running. You'll hear this over and over again from production managers and producers everywhere. No one has enough time to plan. Get the message. Plan. For every hour you spend on problem solving and anticipating your needs, you will save thousands of dollars in production. Successful low-budget filmmaking only works with great preproduction planning.

## Money-saving Tips

Every single decision you make on a film costs money. Therefore, if you examine every step, you'll eliminate waste and create savings. Here are a few thoughts on how to keep expenses down.

*1. Prepare a detailed script.* The cost of writing a detailed script is minimal compared to what it costs "being creative" on a set with a dozen people standing around. Storyboard every nuance in advance — the action, dialogue, technical requirements, camera angles, color schemes, costuming, blocking, lighting, sound, etc. The more planning before the cameras roll, the more you'll save. Most productions could use more planning.

*2. Rehearse Your Actors.* I can't say enough about rehearsing your actors weeks or months in advance. Build trust with your actors. Share the experience of discovering who the characters are and deepening the scene. When it's time to go on the set it may only take a word or two to get your actors ready for the camera. The savings are enormous, plus you'll look like a directorial genius working magic. You're not, you're just prepared.

*3. Communicate with your department heads* (director of photography, production manager, lighting director, costume designer, set designer, soundman, etc.). There should be many preproduction meetings where every script detail is discussed. The department heads can take notes, do their own research, come up with questions for future meetings.

Once you are in production there should be a meeting at the top of the day to go over what you expect to cover, and a short ten-minute meeting at the end of the day to go over what's coming up. (That way everyone can be moving forward and thinking about what's to come. They can sleep on it.) When people know what is expected of them, they perform their best. If they sense (or see) that the director doesn't know what he or she is doing, then they lose respect and enthusiasm for the project. Eveyone wants to work on a first-class film. Make it first-class by communicating with your staff.

4. *Don't spend money on unnecessary things.* This may seem obvious but many first time filmmakers with little or no money spend it on the wrong things. Maybe you can't afford to pay a cameraman. Maybe you need the money for film and processing. Then you must get a cameraman for free. Be smart. Your money is well spent if it appears on the screen.

Nothing wrong with setting up a "no budget" movie. People understand that. Either they want to work with you or they don't. If you are enthusiastic enough, you'll get your movie made.

5. *Use "buyouts" when working on low-budget project.* You need to contain costs, but this is hard to do when you don't know how long it will take to shoot each day. So you hire your cast and crew on a "buyout" basis. This means that you pay a flat daily rate regardless of how many hours are worked. Or you pay a flat weekly rate. Then you know exactly how much the cast and crew will cost at the project's outset, and you will avoid overtime charges which can quickly send you over budget.

Negotiate lower rates for cast and crew by offering them long-term employment. For example, if a cameraman's rate is $500 per day and you need a cameraman for a week, then an offer of $2,000 may be acceptable. You've saved $1,500 right there. And, rather than rent the camera equipment from a rental house, hire your cameraman's gear for less than what you'd pay at an equipment house.

6. *Options.* The normal practice is to "option" rather than "buy" literary properties. If you can't get the project off the ground then losses are minimized. Perhaps you can get a free option. Give it a try.

Put a crew "on hold." Only "confirm" when you are absolutely certain the shoot will take place. If you don't put them on hold, you could be liable for full salaries if the shoot doesn't take place for whatever reason.

When you are selecting stock music for your film or tape, only pay the search and transfer fees. Never pay the license fees until you have a fine cut of your film or until you are absolutely certain that you will use the music. Some filmmakers only purchase the "festival rights" on their music. This way they can show the film in festivals, and if a distributor wants it, and requests music changes, they won't have spent money on music they'll never use.

7. *Consultants.* Consultants can save you tremendous amounts of money. You can hire all kinds of experts for every phase of your project, keeping them only as long as you need them. An assistant director can break down your script. A production manager can prepare a budget. Their ideas alone may save you thousands. A script consultant can review your script for structural or pacing problems. A dialogue or comedy writer may improve certain scenes. A stunt coordinator or combat choreographer can help you stage some of the action scenes. A producer's rep can help with distribution, marketing, or publicity. There are consultants for everything. You pay for their knowledge only when you need it. They are not on staff. A consultant can guide you away from costly mistakes.

The greatest weakness of young filmmakers is that they are unwilling to admit they don't know something. Big problem. We all have to learn something sometime. So my advice to you: Get over it! Ask questions. Seek mentors. Find older friends with experience to help. There are lots of people out there willing to help if asked. Too much attitude is destructive to the learning process. Forget copping an attitude. Your job is to get the information and figure out how to make your film. You may only get one chance as a filmmaker. Don't be in a position two years from now where you look back and say to yourself, "If only I would not have been such a jerk and took the time to find out."

*8. Narrators and actors.* When you hire a narrator or actors negotiate a flat fee, that includes "pickups." You will probably have lines you'll want to redo as narration or loop. This won't become apparent until you start editing. A line may be too long or too short. Maybe it was recorded poorly or an airplane flew over at the wrong time drowning out the line. You'll want to go back in the studio and rerecord certain sections. This can be costly unless you negotiate for these audio pick-ups in advance.

*9. Equipment.* Rent equipment over the weekend. A weekend rate is the same as a one-day rate. You get two days of shooting for the price of one. (Be careful, however, not to pay crew overtime for the weekend.) Strike deals with postproduction editing houses to edit at night or on weekends. Use equipment during off-hours and you can receive price breaks.

*10. Props and Costumes.* Can you get props or costumes in exchange for an on-screen promotional credit? Maybe. Try it. Also, you don't always need full costumes. I've filmed costumes which didn't have backs or bottoms. Silver paint turns cardboard into metal. Cheap costume jewelry can photograph better than the real McCoy. Try local thrift shops for period costumes and props. On my student film I used a $50 roll of white butcher paper to build seven sets! We changed the look merely by relighting it. A little movie magic goes a long way. The film was invited to Cannes! Its total budget was $800!

*11. Editing.* Will transferring your film to videotape for editing provide any savings? Will you edit on film or on video on a nonlinear editing system like the AVID, Media 100, or Stratasphere? Video editing is fast and you can save various versions of your edit should you want to go back to something that worked better earlier, but it is more expensive than film editing. Run the numbers both ways. How are you most comfortable working?

*12. Film.* If you can't afford film you might beg or buy "short ends" from other productions: it's film they bought but didn't expose. Or you can buy it from Studio Film & Tape Exchange in Hollywood. Kodak gives discounts if you pay cash. Remember everything is negotiable.

*12. Feed your crew well.* Have coffee and danish and fruit in the morning. Have snacks throughout the day that they can just grab. If you are on location in the summer have big tubs of cold drinks (or hot drinks if you are in the snow) available at all times. Lunch can be catered in so you don't have to disperse, drive somewhere, and then worry about everyone getting back on time. Dinners can be pizzas if you're really on a tight budget. People get very hungry. A well-fed crew is a happy crew and they will work 2000% better if you look after their dietary needs. (Keep sugar and candy bars, which give a momentary rush with a crash at the end, away from the set. Healthy nutritious food is where it's at.)

*13. Keep everyone healthy.* Pushing your crew, cast, and editors to their physical limits may seem to save time, but you may burn them out. Nothing is more destructive to your crew's motivation than being exploited at every turn. Skipping meals and sleep is damaging to their health and reflects poor planning. Plus there are diminishing returns when people are tired. They may only be working at 10% efficiency when you are paying them time and a half. It doesn't make sense. When a principal cast or crew member is sick, you're out of business. Keep your staff in good health; it will pay off.

14. *Reuse sets.* An old Roger Corman trick is to reuse and redress standing sets. They are cheaper to rent from someone else and tear down (saving them money). You get a whole set for peanuts. Call other production companies and find movies or commercials that are wrapping and make deals to use their sets.

15. *Get free locations.* People love to watch movies being made. At least they think they do and may loan you their house or property to shoot on so they can be around the filmmaking process.

16. *Get a lab to defer half their fee.* Some labs are great supporters of independent films. They want your business now and in the future. If they do you a favor, maybe your release prints will be struck there which is where their real profit is. Perhaps they will defer part of their fee. This could be a huge savings.

17. *Long rehearsal period.* While impractical when working with high–priced stars, do try to schedule a long rehearsal period. Longer than the shoot itself if necessary. This is one of the secrets of low-budget filmmaking that will get you more prepared than just about anything else you can do.

18. *Script in your resources.* Write or have a script written that uses all the producer's assets (cars, motorcycles, houses, locations, etc.) or anything else that the producer and staff can get their hands on. Write it in the script. If you own a motorcycle, write it in the script. Survey what you know you can get and use it.

19. *Edit at night.* Make late night and weekend deals with postproduction facilities for flat-beds or nonlinear editing systems. The gear is usually down at night so anything the facility makes on it is a bonus.

20. *Confidence game.* It is a confidence game. It is an overconfident writer and/or director and/or producer who enrolls everyone else in getting the film made.

These are just a handful of suggestions for keeping expenses down and getting your movie made. As you develop your script and budget you will discover many more on your own. Or check out *Film & Video Budgets* for more ideas.

## Pitfalls of Independent Filmmakers

Where do most filmmakers get into trouble? Read on.

1. *Filmmakers do not get clearances from everyone involved.* You absolutely must clear the rights to everything and everyone that appears in your movie. Without releases you will not get "errors and omissions" insurance. Without "errors and omissions" insurance, a distributor will not release your film.

2. *Music is often overlooked until the last minute.* Costs are underestimated. Let's say you've got a film with a lot of music — 22 songs. The fees to the music publisher per song will range between $4,000 and $15,000 depending on the notoriety of the song and your negotiating

skills. You must also obtain master sync rights from the record company. This will range between $2,000 and $15,000 especially if you clear a lot of songs from one record company, more if you use a number of record companies. Figure an average is about $12,000 for both sync and master license. Your 22 songs for your feature will cost about $264,000. Time to rethink your music needs? You might also find a first-time composer with synthesizer who can do your whole score for a modest fee for his big break.

3. *The blowup.* If you shoot in 16mm you can strike an answer print and be shown in festivals. If you want to do a blowup from 16mm to 35mm, you will spend around $40,000 to $50,000.

Even if you shoot on video, a transfer to 35mm film will cost about $395 per minute ($35,550 for a 90-minute feature; 16mm is less). If you are in 16mm you will eventually have to go to 35mm for most theaters.

4. *Produce as you go.* The most tenacious independents will shoot a scene or two and use that to help with their financing. It is a world of taped together, start and stop financing where the film eventually gets made or the filmmaker burns out and crashes.

## Summary

Producing is anticipating what will be needed before it is needed. It is anticipating what will go wrong before it does, so it won't. It is all about trying to wrestle order from chaos, keep a calm cool exterior, so that cast and crew and your director will feel everything is being taken care of. The contracts that we've discussed here are one way to start thinking about covering every contingency as they describe who is doing what for what compensation.

Producing is also about endless negotiations for everything that appears in the film. The producer may stay on top of every detail.

Every producer will have his or her own strengths to bring to a production. Weaknesses can be covered by clever hires. What I've tried to outline above is to get you thinking in this direction. It's endless, but through time and experience you will get what others perceive as a firm grasp on reality and you will set their minds at ease.

# INTRODUCTION TO DISTRIBUTION

## The Distribution 'Pie'

Surprisingly enough, many filmmakers overlook distribution. They feel it's an alien business, at odds with content and the creative process. They think of distribution as the enemy, mainly because it's so foreign and unknown to them. So they jump into production with little concern about what will happen when they finish their film. This has got to change, because when the filmmaker emerges from the editing room, he or she may soon discover that they have created a film that cannot find a distributor, and hence, there will be no audience for their celluloid vision. Distribution must become a priority for filmmakers. It's part of the responsibility that comes with calling yourself a "filmmaker."

A way to make the economics of filmmaking work is to start thinking bigger. Start being responsible for the whole process. As we discussed

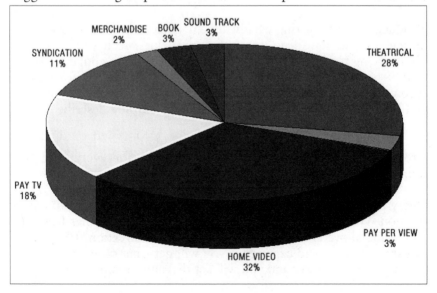

before, think of yourself as a "filmmaker" and you can only make films. Think of yourself only as a "videographer"; then you can only make videos or television. Think of yourself as a "communicator" and you can produce "communication pieces" for many different media markets, thereby increasing your revenues streets. The Distribution "Pie" gives you just some of the many income-producing possibilities for your films and videotapes.

This is a hypothetical chart. While there is a relationship between theatrical exhibition and home video sales, no inference should be made by these percentages. There are lots of different markets (and more besides these) for "communication" products, and you should think about how your concept can be successful in many of them to maximize profits. Once you've identified the kind of product you are making, your search for a distributor begins.

## Finding Distributors

A key to success in filmmaking is distribution. Without distribution, no one will ever see your film or video. With a favorable agreement with a reliable and reputable distribution company who also excels at marketing, your film or video can be seen around the world. Your job is to create a marketable product that can be successfully distributed.

A first step (before, during, or after production) is to find a distributor. Take your time finding the right distributor. There are hundreds of distributors for theatrical films, home video, educational, and television programs. (A relatively current list of distributors can be found in the appendix to get you started.)

Let's sort out the different kinds of distributors for media products.

### Theatrical Distributors

They distribute every genre of feature film from action adventure and horror to drama and art. These could be big budget studio films, low budget exploitation films, independent features, or foreign fare. They distribute film prints to movie theaters and receive anywhere from 35% to 60% of the box office gross which is shared with the producer.

## Home Video Supplier/Manufacturers

They distribute videos through wholesalers and also through direct sales to video retail stores and chains. The videos can be for sale or rent. The studios have their own home video divisions. A feature film will carry a retail price of $100. A sell–through consumer video sells for $4.95 to $19.95. Producers receive a royalty based on the whole-sale price ranging from 5% to 30% depending on whether it is a low–priced sell through tape or a high priced rental tape. There are hundreds of video distributors carrying everything from movies and exercise to sports, music videos, documentaries, travel, etc. The home-video market is dominated by very commercial products.

## Nontheatrical Distributors

This is a fading marketplace thanks to the burgeoning low-priced home video market. These distributors sell videos to schools, institu-tions, prisons, corporations, hospitals, businesses, summer camps, oil rigs, etc. Their product could be feature films, documentaries, or edu-cational short films. Prices had been high in the days when 16mm film prints were rented and sold. Now the pricing has fallen within the range of the home video market. (The videos are sold directly by the distributors and do not go through wholesalers like the video con-sumer market.)

If you are making a film for the educational market it is important to know how your film will be used in the classroom. Generally speak-ing, teachers and film users buy films with lots of information in the narration. They do not like abstract art or experimental films because they neither understand them nor know how to use them for teaching purposes. It is a very traditional marketplace and not open to much experimentation. Classroom time is extremely limited so they will more likely use a short film or video (under 18 minutes) that comes with a study guide and is closely tied to their curriculum.

*Educational*

Nontheatrical, educational distributors sell to a variety of related markets including elementary and secondary schools, colleges and universities, libraries, museums, the military, and other educational institutions.

The home video revolution in the mid-eighties and nineties hit the nontheatrical, educational business extremely hard, wiping out many distributors. Media lost its "perceived value" among educators at about the same time as the educators lost their government underwriting. Low home video prices cause educators to ask, "Why do prices for classroom media have to be so high?" They don't understand the economic forces at play: a Disney video may sell millions of copies allowing for low prices. An educational title may sell a few hundred.

Prior to videos, distributors sold 16mm film prints for $800. Nowadays, perceived value has changed, particularly when home videos can be bought for less than $19.95 and institutions rarely pay more than $99.00 for educational titles (that include a "performance license" allowing them to show it in group situations. With the new emerging delivery systems such as the Internet and DVD, there is anticipation that even greater changes will come which may erode the video distribution. If the educational distributor isn't able to increase sales volume to targeted niche educational markets, he may become extinct.

The largest educational distributors have full time staffs and thousands of titles in their catalogs. Prices range from $29.95 to $99.00. A title needs to sell 2,500-3,000 units to be considered profitable.

Smaller distributors may have a couple of hundred titles in their catalogs and sell at prices between $100 and $250; here 200-300 sales are profitable and 600-800 are considered "a hit."

Very small boutique distributors, such as New Day Films, limit their catalog to a hundred or less and sell them for high prices ($200-$350) but over time reduce them to $59 or less. If they can sell 300 copies of a single title, it is considered "very good."

Royalties to the producer are 20% to 30% of the selling price. Most of the films in a distributor's catalog will perform poorly with only a handful bringing the lion's share of the revenue and helping to cover the distributor's marketing costs.

Pricing structure is all over the map as distributors try not to lose customers. The starting price for a title might be $250 (sales to universities) but would be reduced to $125 during special promotions, or $89 to libraries and $75 to public schools. These different price structures confuse the marketplace, but for survival sake, the distributor tries to make as much from each market as possible. Even then, if title sells 300 copies at an average price of $125, that is $37,500 in gross revenues. At a 25% royalty the producer makes $9,375 and the distributor retains $28,125 for duplication, marketing, and overhead. Some titles may only sell 100 copies which reduces the producer's income to around $3,100. Hardly a living, let alone payback to the investors.

Titles that are produced specifically for the educational market have a much greater chance of success. They will be designed to match curricula, they will be no longer than 18 minutes, and there will be no inappropriate content for the audience. Of course, there may be no other market for such a program if it is designed solely for the educational market. Since most independent films and videos tend to be very subjective, they are seen as not appropriate for classroom use.

If you have a documentary that has educational and entertainment value, you should consider releasing first to the educational market (where you can get a higher dollar per unit) and later going to the home video market. In essence you have to create two distinct "windows" for your film, otherwise the home video prices will cannibalize your sales. Your educational distributor may insist on an exclusive window before they will even take on your film as they do not want to go to the expense of marketing your title only to have a teacher buy it through a catalog for $19.95.

You may create a documentary or informational film that could have a large market if the film targets a very specific cultural experience, or a health issue (e.g., AIDS). The film or video can be even more successful if it has a broadcast on either HBO or PBS, which acts as its "theatrical" window bringing widespread exposure to your film.

The educational markets were, for several decades, the primary ancillary market for independent documentaries and shorts. Without them, there is little chance that independent titles can compete with Hollywood fare, which utilize fast-food chains in massive cross promotions yielding tens of millions of consumer impressions.

### Corporate Training

Sometimes *nontheatrical* can also refer to the niche market that sells training tapes to the Fortune 1000 companies (and others). Prices range from $89 up to $1,000 or more for videos, workbooks, and other training materials. Producers receive a 25% to 30% royalty of the selling price.

### Television

Most independent films (except for the rare documentary) will not be shown on network television. The most lucrative markets for independent features and hard–hitting documentaries are the pay cable systems such as HBO and Showtime or smaller markets such as Bravo or A&E, the Independent Channel, and the Sundance Channel. PBS shows a few independent films and documentaries; however, the license fees (if any) are a pittance.

### Foreign Distribution

All classes of distributors have their counterparts in foreign countries. Feature films travel best. Some feature films may never be released theatrically in the U.S. but will be exhibited in foreign territories. The more suitable your film is for domestic and international distribution the greater revenues are possible. Very few corporate training and educational tapes usually are sold internationally. Documentaries, and especially wildlife films or videos, can be sold worldwide.

## How to Find Distributors

There is a list of some distributors in the back of this book. Do not waste your time and resources sending your film (or proposal) to everyone. You want to find distributors who carry similar genre films or videos as the one you have made (or are making).

You could call them and request a catalog or ask what genre films or videos they carry. A faster way to cull the list is to attend the major markets and festivals or purchase a copy of the *Variety* issue for the specific event in which you are interested.

For Feature Films

The best way to get an overview of who distributes what is to attend any of the major film markets and television markets. These are <u>markets</u> where films are bought and sold by distributors to international buyers. (Markets are not to be confused with film festivals, where films are also shown.)

| | |
|---|---|
| NATPE *(National Association of Television Program Executives)* | *Early January* |
| AFM *(American Film Market)  Los Angeles* | *Late Feb/March* |
| MIP TV | *Mid-April* |
| CANNES | *Early/Mid-May* |
| IFFM *(Independent Feature Film Market)  New York* | *Late September* |
| MIFED  *(International Film, Television & Documentary Market)* | *Mid-October* |
| MIPCOM *(Cannes)* | *October* |

A one-day pass to the AFM in Los Angeles costs about $100 or so. A suite (where you can display your film's poster, trailer, etc., costs about $10,000.)

While this may not be practical for most, you could call *Variety* at 1-800-323-4345 to order back issues of the special issues that cover these film festivals and film markets. The issues have an extensive listing of the distributors or sales companies, address, phone numbers, and executives names. They also list the product for sale from each distributor. In addition these special issues are crammed with advertisements so you can quickly access who markets what kind of films and how they do it.

For Video (Movies and Special Interest)

Same approach as finding film distributors. Attend the VSDA (Video Software Dealer's Association) show which is held in July each year, usually in Las Vegas, or request their show catalog. For a few hundred dollars they also sell their 3,500 members mailing list, which lists all the current video players from distributors, wholesalers, retailers, and manufacturers. (Their number in Sherman Oaks, California, is 818-385-1500.)

For Television

Attend NATPE (National Association of Television Program Executives) in early January or call *Variety* magazine (1-800-323-4345) for their NATPE issue.

A Strategy

Once you've obtained an overview of the playing field and the players most suitable for your product, prepare a "hit list" and prioritize the distributors who will most likely be interested in your film or video. This should not be pie-in-the-sky time. If you've done a no-budget movie, Paramount is not going to be interested so don't kid yourself by putting them on the list. There are several ways you can get your proposal/work-in-progress/finished film to distributors:

> 1. Get shown in prestigious hip festivals like Sundance, Toronto, Telluride, etc.
> 2. Take a booth or executive suite during the film/TV market.

2. Have a friend who knows an executive hand-deliver your work.
3. Have an agent or entertainment attorney solicit your work.
4. Set up screenings and invite distributors.
5. Call the distributor, make contact on phone, follow up with a tape/screening.

Ideally, your pitch to a distributor should be extremely well thought–out. Spend time to think about how to raise the "perceived value" of your work. Casting is vitally important. Pitching and presentations will be discussed in other chapters in this book.

**Pitching Your Idea to Distributors**

As you prepare your prospectus (a written presentation for film financing) you may discuss your film or video with potential distributors. Even in the development stages, some distributors may be interested. If this is the case, have them write letters expressing their interest in seeing your film upon completion. While noncommittal, you may add these letters to your prospectus to show your investors there are potential outlets for the film or tape you propose to make.

Once you've made some films or tapes that are in distribution and have established relationships with distributors this process will be easier. You'll know where to go if you've made films that are successful in a specific market. You can call up your distributor friends and perhaps negotiate a deal with an advance or negative pickup that can pay for production. This isn't always the case, but if a distributor knows that your films have earned money in the past, he or she may be willing to finance your new projects.

If you don't know distributors, you can ask the end users of films (librarians, educators, theater exhibitors, video retailers, and television program buyers) to suggest reputable distributors.

Pay attention to the market needs, not your own. If you don't, you will end up with a film that does not find distribution.

## Distribution Contracts

In the early years of my career most of my films were rejected by distributors because I made them for myself and did not understand the market. Finally, I got an offer. Boy, was I happy! I was so thrilled that someone actually wanted to distribute one of my films that I paid very little attention to the contract I signed. It was a very expensive mistake.

The pages you are about to read are extremely important. If you are able to make use of this information, you may save thousands of dollars.

## Negotiations

Once a distributor has screened your film either in his or her office, at a screening room or at a film festival, he or she will let you know if they want to distribute your film. Do not take the first deal that comes along although you will be pressured to do so. Shop around. Remember, the deal you sign will be in effect for many years to come. Make sure you are making the best deal you can with the best distributor for your film.

Get as many offers as you can from reputable distributors. This will speak very highly of your film and will allow you to leverage a better deal. It also demonstrates that several distributors think your film will make money for them.

When you talk to different distributors, get them to tell you what they will do to market your film. See what kind of real commitment is there. What's the strategy? Will it open in exclusive theaters in selected cities and gradually roll out, or will it be a large release immediately? Why? Get a sense of their abilities to promote and sell your specific film. Listen to the stories about what they've done for other films, but ask what they are going to do for your film. Take notes or tape your discussions because it is easy to forget all the points of the negotiations, especially when you are considering several different deals at the same time. Get all commitments documented in your deal memo.

Take a large sheet of paper and make a series of grids with distributors listed in a row across the top and contract terms (advance, percentage, promotion, budget, markets, etc. ) in the left-hand column. The page will fill up as you talk with the various distributors and allow you to keep track of the points of discussion. This way you can compare various offers (should you be so lucky).

You may find it very difficult to get them to answer this next question (because it is a direct giveaway of how well they think the film will sell), but somewhere in their minds they have an answer. "How much do you think this film will gross in its release? What is the range? What is its potential? Based on what" Ask this, not so you can hold them to it in a contract, but so you can get a sense in specific terms of how well they think it will do. If they are reluctant to answer, say, "Make something up." The truth is, no one really knows how well the film will do until it has been released.

## Talk With Other Producers

No one will be more willing to talk to you about his or her experiences with a distributor than another producer. Before making any deal with a distributor, particularly one you've just met, contact other producers whose films are represented by the prospective distributor. (You find out what other films they distribute by studying the trades, getting their catalogs, and looking at the posters on their office walls. There are also on-line databases where you can find the credits for films. (Visit http://www.mwp.com for these sites.)

Since you are probably the only one who has ever asked, and because they usually have a lot to say, it can be a very rewarding exchange. If producers are happy with the distributor, they will say so and why. If they are displeased, they will be the first to tell you. Don't be shy about making these exploratory calls. What you will learn will be extremely valuable and put you in a better position to make your own decision.

Ask producers these questions:

> Are you happy with the job the distributor has been doing?
>
> Did they keep to their marketing plans?
>
> Do they listen to your comments and concerns?
>
> Did they keep to their promised release schedule?
>
> Could they have done better?
>
> Did they pay on time?
>
> How was your deal structured?
>
> What did they give on easily? What were stickler points and main concerns?
> Who was your attorney that did the deal?
>
> Did they pay for any finishing costs; remix, blowup, transfer, negatives, E&O insurance?

Give the producer lots of room to offer other valuable information. From these discussions you will get a very clear idea of how the distributor operates. (By the way, not everything you hear will be horror stories. You'll also hear many good things about distributors.) Sometimes you'll learn awful things and wonder how you got in the film business in the first place. Sometimes you may feel that you are forced to make a choice between the lesser of two evils. But it's better to find out early about a distributor's bad habits, rather than later when you've signed away your film.

Write down everything you learn in your discussions on that large sheet of paper. Then study the information you've gathered. Ultimately, it may break down to which distributor you think you can trust. Pick the one who you think will do the best job for you. It may not necessarily be the friendly one or the one you like the most.

Sometimes it may be wiser to take the highest advance you can get, since common wisdom says you'll get no more. Other times, if you believe in the strength and integrity of the company, you may take a smaller advance and a larger percentage of profits.

Only sign a distribution contract when you have received answers to all your questions and when you (and your lawyer) feel that you have explored all the options. Don't be in a hurry because negligence at this stage may result in your losing everything you have worked so hard to gain. Remember, if you have investors, you are representing them as well in any deal you make. They believe that you will not only make the best film you possibly can but the best distribution as well. Your signature can make the difference between a loss and a profit for them.

Once the papers are signed, what was once an adversary relationship becomes a partnership (in the nonlegal sense of the word), and it is no longer to your advantage to challenge your distributor. It is time to support him or her because now you are in this thing together.

**Summary**

Now you've learned about the different kinds of distributors for different markets. You have a sense of the pricing structures (without which you could not prepare an investor's prospectus or income projections). You've learned how to identify, find, and check out distributors.

# THE THEATRICAL BUSINESS & DISTRIBUTION

## Studio Theatrical Overview

The studios released 240 movies to the theaters and ancillary markets in the U.S. in 1996, up from 234 in 1995. The total number of releases among the studios and independents in the U.S. in 1996 was 471 compared with 419 in 1995.

According to Adams Media Research, the share of the studio's domestic revenue, which was $11.7 billion in 1996, breaks down as follows:

| | |
|---|---|
| Theatrical release | 23.0% |
| Video | 54.9% |
| Pay TV | 12.5% |
| Television | 7.4% |
| Pay-Per-View | 2.2% |

These percentages vary a great deal between films. Those films that are theatrical hits perform much better in home video.

With more than half the income resulting from video sales and rentals it's no wonder the studios have made such a strong commitment to dominating the home video marketplace. Studios have learned that, with the right film, they can make more money by releasing the video at low prices rather than higher prices. The strategy, of course, is to sequence the release of a film (into video, pay-per-view, pay cable, television) starting with the most profitable markets first. A film distributor's revenues are greater from the theaters in the first few weeks of exhibition. At the same time, the longer a film's run, the greater success it will have in the ancillary markets.

*Variety* shows a dramatic increase in the cost of film production and marketing:

|  | 1995 | 1996 |
| --- | --- | --- |
| Average Budget (millions) | 36.4 | 39.8 |
| Average Marketing (millions) | 17.7 | 19.8 |
| Total Budget/Marketing | $ 54.1 | $ 59.6 |
| Total Box Office Admissions (billions) | 1.26 | 1.33 |
| Total Box Office Grosses (billions) | $ 5.5 | $ 5.9 |

## Independent Features

But that's the world of the big guys. What about the independents? What's going on?  There are more independent features than ever being made. Sundance '98 reports that more than 1,200 films were submitted for around 150 slots.

An informal polling of Sundance filmmakers reveals that the median filmmaker's age is about 25. Maybe half of the filmmakers went to film school, the rest learned their craft in the street and on the job. Budgets for about a third were under $50,000. Most were made for under $250,000. Half of these one thousand films will make no revenue whatsoever.  Not only that, many of the filmmakers will carry a debt for many years. Why are more and more people willing to put themselves through development and production hell to make something that, chances are, will never see the light of a theater screen?  It's that great independent filmmaker spirit that, against all odds, its creator is going to make the great American independent movie.

## Independent Theatrical Distribution Issues

The good news is that lots of independents are making movies. (I estimate nearly 4,000 feature films a year.)  The bad news is that in any given year, the independent distributors' share of the U.S. box office is between 3% and 5%. There are only about 600 screens for independent films. Nevertheless, independent distributors continue to look for a way to counter-program against the majors by releasing independent films at unconventional times such as during the summers, which is usually flooded with action films. Sometimes the economics really works as evidenced by the cost–to–return ratios of these films (most of them independently produced).

## Cost-to-Return Ratios

| Film | Gross | Budget | Cost/Budget Ratio |
|------|-------|--------|-------------------|
| 1. Trainspotting | 72.1 | 3.5 | 20.6 |
| 2. Il Postino | 80.5 | 4.5 | 17.9 |
| 3. Seven | 310.0 | 26.0 | 11.9 |
| 4. Independence Day | 788.0 | 70.0 | 11.3 |
| 5. Leaving Las Vegas | 49.8 | 4.6 | 10.8 |
| 6. Toy Story | 359.0 | 35.0 | 10.2 |
| 7. Rumble in Bronx | 75.8 | 7.5 | 10.1 |
| 8. Babe | 246.0 | 25.0 | 9.8 |
| 9. Secrets & Lies | 39.6 | 4.5 | 8.8 |
| 10. Dangerous Minds | 180.0 | 23.0 | 7.8 |

The secret to profitability is making a film for a low budget and still having upside in your particular genre. In the preceding chart you can see that all but one of the budgets were "low budget" by Hollywood standards and were thereby able to have a very large ratio between cost of the film and gross revenues. That's what you want to do without sacrificing production quality. Three of the movies made this list because a relatively low-cost ensemble cast was employed and special effects were the stars (*Independence Day*) or the star was a pig (*Babe)* or the film had no human actors at all (*Toy Story*). *Leaving Las Vegas* did have stars who worked for scale and thus the budget was reduced. Food for thought?

## Seven Steps for Selling Successful Indie Films

Those independent filmmakers whose films have shown widely agree on the things you need to do for a successful film. They are:

1. Write, find, or option a great script that attracts great actors.

81

2. Make sure you are passionate about making this film.

3. Be persevering, tenacious, enthusiastic.

4. Get a good casting director.

5. Spend money on promotion.

6. Find someone who can help you get attention at Sundance such as a producer's rep (who may command 7.5% of any advance you get).

7. Have distributors see the film in a good setting with an enthusiastic crowd. (Load the seats with your friends if you have to.) Don't sell them, rather let them "discover" you.


## Marketing Your Film

It's the producer's job to do everything possible to gain attention from distributors for their films. You can do this in a variety of ways. Get their attention with a good film so they can see its market potential.

Set aside about $25,000 to market your film. Send postcards or one–sheets to every distributor. Get them excited about your film. The more information and visibility you have in front of distributors, the more interest they may have and hence the higher offer you may receive. However, there is a fine line between overpromoting your film and having it "discovered." Buyers like to discover films. They like to feel they are the ones responsible for bringing them to their companies and to the world. There is obviously a contradiction here. The objective is to find a way to let them know about your film so that they can discover it.


## The Deal

So suppose you've shown your film to a distributor during a private screening or at a prestigious festival (better!) and they want to tie you up quickly with a "deal memo," which is a binding contract that high-lights the key points of the deal. (Ever seen a spider wrap up a fly that's flown into its web?!) You too want a binding deal, but you want to be sure you're not going to get done in by the "boilerplate." (The fifty–page contract with definitions that comes later.)

You will need expert help. Take a producer's rep or a lawyer with you to negotiate the deal memo. You eventually will want to go to a full contract or the deal memo will be interpreted in favor of the distribu-tor. A one- or two-page deal memo cannot cover all the contingencies.

Some deal memos will have a last line in them that says something like "This agreement will serve as a binding agreement in the event a full, formal agreement is not made." Then bingo, the distributor has no reason to go to a full agreement and can interpret the deal memo in their best interests. We'll look at the deal memo in a moment but back to the offer.

The distributor makes a "preemptive strike" with an advance offer. What they want is for you to stop considering any other offers: stop talking to anyone else and decide whether or not to take their offer. They want a period of exclusive negotiation. While it's great to have interest, it is to the advantage of the buyer to "take it out of the mar-ketplace" because it takes your film out of competitive bidding. No distributor wants a bidding war to ensue where they will have to pay even more money for a film they've "discovered."

Of course you want to license your film, but you are feeling pressured and leveraged. What do you do? You ask them to raise their offer if they expect you to take it out of the market. Maybe you'll get more. Or, you ask for time: "I'll decide in three days." They may figure that's not too long. The offer hopefully stays on the table. And you work like crazy to shop it to other distributors over the next three days. Their offer has actually helped you because now the leverage is in your court. You've got a bonafide offer and you can see whether you can get a better deal elsewhere. The pressure is on the newly pitched distributors to match or exceed your offer. (There is nothing that makes a distributor want your film more than an offer on the table from a competing distributor. Everyone's judgment goes out the window and it's ego time. You don't care. You get a higher advance while everyone else gets a little crazy.)

But this is a high stakes game. Distributors can be very fickle and even when you've got a lot of bidding going on, they can all go away! Sometimes a distributor sees a film at a festival; there's a lot of buzz and then "festival helium" sets in making everyone temporarily lose their senses and make unrealistic bids. When the marketing guys back home hear from the acquisition people what they've bought they go ballistic and the distributor's offers start evaporating if deals aren't closed. So you've got to be very careful and level-headed about all this, which is extremely hard considering that you've been living with your film for months or years and have placed a high value on it.

While I was at Vestron Video, a common approach among the buyers would be to pressure the seller into making a quick decision: "You have 24 hours to accept our offer or it goes away for good." Pretty strong medicine. Most of the time this was a bluff which wouldn't be called and the seller would sell. The window was very short because the Vestron buyers did not want their offer to start a bidding war. As a buyer, I was always more interested in a project if I knew a competitor had already made an offer. (Acquisitions people are very competitive which is good for you. If you can, fan the flames.)

A producer can rebuttal with a bluff: "Your offer of $200,000 is very nice but another distributor has offered me $400,000. Come up to $500,000 and its yours." Bluffs usually don't work because all the buyers know each another. It only takes one call to check on the validity of your statement.

The best strategy, if you know you have something hot, is to keep cool, accept as many offers as you can, and tell them *you'll give them a decision soon*. Be courteous, be gracious, make them feel like they are the only distributor in the world. This way you can compare the various deals, go back to the distributors with questions, or ask for the deals to be improved. You write your own ticket.

If, on the other hand, you have a film that's not very good and not very desirable, you should take whatever offer you get before the distributor comes to his or her senses. Here's where clear-headed honesty about what you've made comes into the picture. I've seen producers with offers hold out, not realizing how lucky the initial offer really was, and eventually ending up with no deal. A producer's rep can help enormously. Filmmakers cannot be objective. They see only "their baby." A producer's rep sees "product" and knows how to raise its value to the buyer.

What can you expect these days from a deal? Not long ago the terms (length of the contract ) was 7 or 10 or 12 years. Now distributors will try for "perpetuity." Also it's hard to splinter or segment the theatrical and home video rights and make separate deals; probably impossible. You may be able to hold onto television (but they'll ask for this as well), and you'll be able to exclude sequel/remake rights, books, merchandise, or interactive rights.

The distributor will pay, hopefully, a significant, nonrefundable advance which is recouped from future profits. Distributors normally receive a 25% to 35% distribution fee from collected theatrical revenues plus a 25% to 35% fee for sublicensing television, home video, and foreign rights. Try to negotiate even better terms.

The distributor also pays P&A (prints and advertising) and other promotional costs. You want your distributor to show that they are going to spend money on your film to suppport it. Once the film has recouped the P&A promotional costs, then a producer hopefully can look to "overages."

## Sample Deal Memo #1

The deal memo is a few pages of main deal points, negotiated by your lawyer, agent, or producer's rep with the distributor. Here's what a deal memo for an independent feature might look like:

TITLE:   "YOUR FIRST FILM"

Term:   15 years, all rights worldwide

Advance:   $400,000 payable as follows:

> $100,000 on delivery less
>> -$20,000 to lab for initial film prints
>> -$10,000 for E&O insurance
>> -$30,000 for Cannes festival expenses (prints, travel, lodging, promotion)
>
> $100,000 on the first day of theatrical release
>
> $100,000 90 days after the first day of theatrical release or April 1st whichever comes first
>
> $100,000   180 days after theatrical release

Advance is recouped as follows:

U.S./North America Advance

$200,000
30% distribution fee, costs off top
30/70 pay cable
35/65 television syndication
15/85 network sales
video, 100% of 20% royalty on
wholesale gross receipts

Worldwide Advance

$200,000
17.5% sales fee to recoupment, then a 20% sales fee with costs off the top

Maximum of 50% cross-collateralization between the U.S. and world.

Producer has right of consultation on marketing, sales sheets, trailer, ad and poster design, and all printed sales materials.

No cuts can be made in the film without producer's approval. Distributor shall advance the cost of any changes as a distribution cost.

## Notes on Sample Deal Memo #1

When you hear a licensing fee bantered around the Sundance Film Festival you really don't know what they are talking about. Someone says, "Yeah, that film got a $400,000 advance." So? Is that U.S. only? Worldwide all rights? Does that include the prints and advertising expenditures? What exactly is it? Producers will, of course, tout the largest number possible without explaining what it actually is. Maybe it's just the print and ad money, with no advance! A producer doesn't want to feel like a fool giving his film away for no cash but maybe that was the only deal he could get. So you have to take these numbers you hear and read with a grain of salt.

Distribution costs should be only the direct, out-of-pocket expenses for the movie that is being promoted. However distributors will some-times charge other movies to a film's account. This can be found and eliminated through auditing. A minor audit can cost as much as $10,000. Then, as all things in the movie business, a settlement is negotiated.

On a $250,000 first feature the director's deferment for the director might be $30,000, higher or lower.

Notice that the deal memo says "costs off the top," but in fact the dis-tributor will take their distribution fee first (because it will be larger) and then the costs (hopefully only direct hard costs) will be deducted.

The distributor does the most work theatrically and gets paid a 30% fee. Pay TV and syndication fees are fairly standard. Network sales of an independent feature is highly unlikely and put in just to widen the eyes of the producer. It's not very realistic so don't get your expecta-tions up.

The video deal is written as "100% of 20% of the wholesale gross receipts." Without this clause the distributor would take a distribu-tion fee when in fact many have their own home video divisions and they are just sending it across the hall. I call it "double dipping". The studios are notorious for this insidious practice.

On the foreign side, the distributor is actually rewarded by a higher sales fee when the advance is recouped. A good notion which motivates them. If they recoup, then you've recouped and will start seeing overages (which is a position you want to be in). Usually, <u>distributors do not want to recoup their advance</u>. I know this sounds crazy but it's true. If they don't recoup their financial liability (the advance), they don't owe the producer any more money. That's what they want. So, they will try, through creative accounting, to keep piling on expenses and interest and overhead charges in order that the advance is <u>never</u> recouped. Got it? That's why most studio movies never go into profit no matter how much money they make at the box office. A good long-form contract can get rid of many of the very issues that can keep every penny in the distributor's coffers.

Notice that there is a clause that says only "50% cross-collateralization between the domestic and foreign revenues." You do not want the territories to be "crossed." Say the film is highly successful in foreign sales and is about ready to throw off overages (beyond the advance) to you the producer. But if the distributor has "cross-collateralized" the advances, then he can apply the overages from foreign sales to the domestic (U.S.) side where the film still has not recouped. Then the distributor can recoup domestic losses by keeping the foreign overages.

I did five television specials for PBS that later went onto home video. The deal was cross-collateralized. Financially, of these five shows, one was a home run, one was a double, and there was a single and two strikeouts. If they were not cross-collateralized I would have received additional income from the two successful shows which recouped their costs, but because they were "crossed," I did not.

Note that the producer gets "consultation" on the marketing materials. All very well and good, but consulting does not mean approval. It means the distributor can send the sales material and the producer can say whatever he or she wants about it, but the final call is with the distributor. Giving a producer "consulting rights" looks good but is not of any real value for the filmmaker.

Here's a more detailed deal memo with better terms and more definitions. You can only get these clauses in a deal memo if the film is highly desired by the distributor.

(Deals can be very creative, and can be structured in many ways.)

## Sample Deal Memo #2

TITLE: "A VERY HOT FIRST FEATURE"

Advance $500,000

33% on signing deal memo
33% on delivery
33% on theatrical release

P&A    $1 million in North America within the first 4 months of release

Bonus: $100,000 upon reaching $4 million North American box office gross plus $100K upon reaching $5 million North American box office gross. Bonuses are payable within 10 days of gross target.

Fees — Domestic
30% theatrical
25% pay cable
30% pay-per-view
20% network television
35% syndication and other television
50% nontheatrical
25% home video royalty on wholesale price

Fees — Foreign
25% total to be divided between North American distributor and foreign sales company.

Distribution Costs
1. Direct costs only.
2. No interest charged on advance.
3. No expenses charged to film that predates signing.
4. Distributor to pay for
        —lab costs, sound remix, title reshoot, blowup,
         internegative, interpositve
        —music clearances, not to exceed $75,000
        —clip clearances, not to exceed $100,000
        —MPAA rating
        —E&O insurance

Accounting, monthly for the first 6 months, quarterly there-after. Producer royalty reports to be sent and payment if any within 154 days.

Delivery:  (only two items)

1. Chain of titles.
2. Access to negative and picture and sound elements.

Rights Excluded.

> Publishing
> Television series
> Remakes & sequels
> Merchandising

Artistic/Creative Control
1. Title will not be changed.
2. Film will not be reedited.
3. Producer can supervise video transfer, subtitling, inspection of release prints, and take possession of any that are not of release quality.

Marketing:
1. Minimum $1 million P&A commitment.
2. Producer full approval of all marketing decisions and materials such as trailer, one-sheet, newspaper ads, merchandise and theater selection.

The "key man" shall remain in place at the distribution company and be available to supervise all aspects of the release of the film on a regular basis.

Specific release strategy.

Release territories by:
1. NYC and LA          February
2. Top 20 markets      March
3. Top 50 markets      April

Distributor will release no other films during the period of initial release.

Merchandise divided 50/50.

Previous film festival commitments will be honored.

Home video release not earlier than 9 months from last release date.

```
Producer shall receive one 35mm and one 16mm print for ben-
efits, his own showings, etc.

Producer will promote the film for 6 months. Distributor pays
per diem, hotel, coach travel whenever producer requests
travel to any festival or market (except outside the U.S.
which shall be business class travel).
```

## Notes on Sample Deal Memo #2

In this deal memo there is a larger advance. You get the money soon-
er; it is not held back until the film is in release. Unlike deal memo #1,
there is a commitment for P&A (prints and advertising) and a time
period where it must be spent.

Bonuses are built in so that there is additional money forthcoming
without accounting delays. While not specified here, they are no
doubt treated like advances and still must be recouped by the distributor from the producer's share of profits.

The fees are the same as in deal memo #1. Perhaps, if the film is very
desirable, you could knock 5% off some of the fees.

Foreign is specified differently so that only a maximum of 25% may
be deducted. With the first deal memo the fee is less but there is no
telling how much of a fee the foreign distributor takes. The distributor does not have an in-house foreign sales team.

Here, distribution costs are clarified to be only direct costs; no interest is charged on the advance or overhead or P&A. No expenses can
be charged to the film that predates this agreement.

In this situation the producer has finished a 16mm film and the
distributor agrees to pay for the remix, the blowup and negatives,
plus music clearances up to $100,000. The distributor also pays for
the rating and the E&O insurance, all of which will be deducted as
distribution costs.

The accounting period is monthly when the film is in release, then quarterly. Statements are to come quickly. A common complaint among producers is that they are frequently paid by distributors much later than the contract specifies. The popular income projection software program called *FilmProfit* builds these delays into their projections as if it were an industry standard!

Distributors will not pay an advance until all the deliverables are made. This could include a two-page list of items including the negatives, workprints, still photographs, synopsis, final shooting script, bios, etc. In this deal memo, only the chain of title and access to the negative are considered a deliverable.

While contracts "include" various rights, they should also specify what is "excluded." Here the publisher hangs onto the publishing, television series rights, remakes and sequels, and merchandising.

The distributor has further agreed not to change the title, not to edit the film, and that the producer can monitor the video transfer and printing of release prints.

A commitment of $1.5 million for P&A is made and the producer can "approve" all marketing materials. This means something.

In addition, the filmmaker made the deal because the head of marketing carried on about all the great things he would do for the film. When he ranted and raved about it, the filmmaker wrote it all down and the filmmaker's lawyer included it as part of the agreement. The film will open in February in New York and L.A., build word–of–mouth and reviews, then go to the top 20 markets in March, continue to build and then roll out in April. Now it's contractual. The "key man" has to stay at the company during the film's release and actually supervise it.

Assuming the distribution company is small (and not a major), the filmmaker doesn't want the distributor's limited staff and resources spent on another competing film at the same time so the distributor has agreed not to release another film during the initial release.

The filmmaker had preexisting agreements with various international film festivals. The distributor allows that these showings be honored and all other festivals will be determined by mutual consent.

The filmmaker believes that the film will do well if the word of mouth builds and the theatrical campaign slowly rolls out, and therefore does not want the film rushed into the home video market. The distributor agrees to wait 6 months from the last play date.

The filmmaker also receives his own 16mm and 35mm film print for his own showings, benefits, etc.

The distributor agrees to pay the expenses of the filmmaker when he travels in order to promote the film.

Deal memo #2 is much more detailed than deal memo #1 and should give the filmmaker additional comfort. But it still isn't a long form contract which is what is really required. Perhaps the filmmaker's lawyer can build in a clause that if the parties do not come to an agreement on the long form contract in less than 30 days in good faith negotiations then deal memo will be null and void.

Any contract is negotiable. It is a function of how much the distributor wants the film as to how much they will bend on their so-called standard agreement. No matter what a distributor tells you, every contract in his file is different. The "standard contract" is what they can immediately agree to (because it's all in their favor).

## A Note About Distributors

Am I giving you the impression that distributors are out to take advantage of you? Not necessarily. However, it is a tough business and the more information you have about dealing with distributors the better. The test of a good distributor is if you are able to work together in successfully distributing and promoting your film. You want a relationship that is beneficial to everyone.

You may hear horror stories about how a distributor made some huge mistake, but before scratching that distributor off your list I suggest you probe deeper. Distributors, like anyone else, make mistakes. Good distributors are those that take care of their mistakes quickly and responsibly. (That could be said about good filmmakers as well!) Good luck in finding and signing with the best distributor for your work.

## The Distribution Contract Basics

Before describing distribution contracts, I want to make it very clear that you never "sell" your film to a distributor. You don't sell your film to anyone. You "license" it. You always keep ownership of your film and allow others, by means of a licensing agreement, to do things with the film, such as show it on television, distribute it, or exhibit the film in a theater. Selling your film, that is, your ownership in your work, should never be done. (Although some will argue that a contract in "perpetuity" or for the length of the copyright, is as good as selling your film outright. You may own the copyright; however, with an extremely long license period the distributor has pretty much tied up the property.)

There is no "standard contract," although that's exactly what a distributor will offer you and lead you to believe. For the distributor, a standard contract is the deal they would like to make. For you, it is only a place to begin your negotiations. Remember: Everything is negotiable. <u>If a distributor wants your film, concessions will be made that deviate significantly from the initial standard contract</u>. If they are not terribly interested in your film, their standard contract may be the best offer you'll get. (In which case, you should ask yourself whether you are completely happy with the advance you receive as the only monies you'll ever see, because most distribution contracts will have so much "magic" in them that the producer will never see any net profits.)

Most of the standard elements in most long form theatrical film distribution contracts will be expressed the deal memo,which may precede a negotiated long form contract.

94

Here are the major issues to be negotiated in the deal memo and distribution contract.

1. Term. The length of the agreement in years. Distributors will want as long a term as possible. You will try to limit the length of time. Never sign the rights away for perpetuity if you or your investors have paid for the film.

2. Territories. This could be U.S. only or worldwide or specific territories. Sometimes you may only be licensing rights for one country (e.g., Japan), sometimes it's a continent (e.g., South America).

3. Rights included. Theatrical? Home video? Television? Multimedia? Sequel rights? Be as specific as possible. Distributors will undoubtedly ask for as many rights as possible. They may ask for the videodisk format rights even though they do not distribute videodisks. What they will do is sublicense these rights to another distributor who distributes videodisks. Only grant those rights to those distributors who are powerful and successful in distributing in that specific format.

A red flag should go up whenever you find that a distributor asks for rights in *any and all media now existing or which may exist in the future.* That means if any new format (like DVD or whatever) comes along and can be marketed and distributed, then the distributor will have those rights as well. If you had signed a contract with a distributor that contains this kind of language, then you may lose a great deal in the future. How can you value the rights to a medium that doesn't yet exist? Delete this line and, if and when another format comes along, find an appropriate distributor then. You will, in the long run, earn more money by being very selective in regard to what rights you grant to a distributor.

4. Rights excluded. Publishing, sequel, Internet, merchandising? Whatever rights you keep should be clearly specified as "exclusions." Some agreements are written in a vague manner where you could accidentally give away some rights without knowing it. To safeguard yourself from this, be very specific in stating what rights are "included" and what rights are "excluded."

5. The share of profits. Usually the distributor gets a distribution fee (of gross revenues), then expenses are deducted, and the producer sees his or her share.

How profits are defined is one of the most complex and most fiercely debated areas of contract negotiation. It's all in those little words and how they are interpreted by lawyers and accountants as to if and when you will ever see any profits. If at all possible, have your profits defined as a percentage of gross revenues. That means you participate from the first dollar received by the distributor before any deductions are taken out. Gross participation is usually reserved for top stars. This eliminates creative accounting because to determine your share all you have to do is calculate a percentage of all the revenues that the distributor receives. (Distributors will fight against a gross deal in order to keep the magic language in their contract, which will allow them to flow more money to themselves. For example, you may get a large home video advance in paragraph 12a but by the time you are thirty pages into the contract, paragraph 32.2.b and later paragraph 66.2.c will little by little take away percentage points, thus diluting the royalty you thought you received. These nasty little land mines can significantly diminish your returns. Only an eagle-eyed entertainment lawyer who has dealt with distribution contracts before and is savvy about contract structure will be able to spot and eradicate this deceitful standard business practice.)

6. Delivery Requirements. What elements does the distributor need that constitute delivery? Negative? Press kits? Music? Publishing? M&E tracks? E&O insurance? The longer the list, the more expensive it is to pull together. For features, the deliverables could cost between $25,000 and $100,000.

7. Who pays for such things as E&O insurance, blowups, etc.? Maybe the distributor will pay for some of the delivery elements required?

8. A marketing commitment expressed as P&A dollars, a release date, and schedule.

(Many will be reluctant to define exactly what they will do.) Try to get a specific dollar amount in the contract and a release date; otherwise your film could be indeterminably held up.

9. Advance payment schedule. When? A percentage upon signing, upon delivery, upon release, and upon a number of days after release? An "advance" is a portion of your profits or royalty, given to you in advance before your film has actually earned it. Distributors are less interested in giving you an advance than you are in receiving one. In some cases an advance will be used to entice a filmmaker to sign a deal. The advantage in receiving an advance is that you can actually receive some cash in hand to repay your investors. It could very well be the only money you'll ever see because of "creative accounting" by the distributor.

10. Bonuses or bumps. How about including clauses for additional cash advances based on box office grosses?

11. Specification of allowable deductions (e.g., distribution costs) by the distributor. If deductions aren't specified, the distributor could charge all kinds of expenses against your film, slowing down or keeping the film from recouping altogether. This, unfortunately, is a standard practice employed by many distributors.

12. Accounting schedule. When are the producer's income statements and payments due? They should come monthly during the release, and later can revert to quarterly.

13. Audit rights. When and how often can the producer audit the distributor's books and records? Some distributors will try to cap the time the producer can audit. In other words, if the producer doesn't question (audit) a report before a year is up, it is deemed acceptable. This means the distributor could have accounted improperly but if the producer doesn't audit, the distributor is entitled to keep the monies in dispute.

14. Various warranties and indemnifications.

15. Copyright? Change of title?

16. Rating goal. R? PG?

17. Creative Control. The contract should state that the distributor cannot edit your film without written permission. They can, however, insert their logo at the head or tail of the film. This lets audiences know who distributes the film, which is very important. Some logos are quite nice and add a real snazzy look to your film. Never mind that it will give the impression that the distributor produced the film. They may want the right to edit, if the film has to be cut for broadcast on television.

18. Filmmaker has "consultation" or "approval" rights over marketing elements. Consultation means he can speak but the distributor doesn't have to listen. Approval means the distributor cannot proceed without written approval.

19. Festival commitments. The distributor agrees to enter into a number of festivals and pay travel expenses for the filmmaker.

20. Publicity commitments.

21. Credits. It should be specified how all the credits will read in the distributor's ad and marketing campaign. You have agreements regarding credits with your actors and principals which terms you must pass on. The distributor has to honor your agreements with others in regard to credits and will only do so if this is made contractual in your distribution agreement.

By now, we have substantially altered what was once the distributor's standard contract.


## My Amendments

Whatever they may be, always try to get all your own amendments and concerns into the contract. When you negotiate, each side must give up something. Amendments will give you a more favorable contract. It also allows you to have something to give up when necessary. If you don't give up something that is relatively insignificant to you, you will have to give up something important.

You can be sure that the distributor has already loaded the contract with dozens of things that they are instantly ready to give up in order to let the opposing lawyer feel that he is making progress for his client and to slow him down on the big issues. What is actually happenning is that these *give-me's* are a smoke screen to divert attention away from other things that the distributor is trying to hold onto. So come up with some *give ya's* of your own.

Here are some things you can ask for:

1. The rights to purchase prints (or videos) at cost. You may want a film print for festivals or videos to give out when promoting your film.

2. A supply of theatrical posters, flyers, etc., for your scrapbook.

3. Ask that the distributor pay all entry fees and shipping to film festivals. Reserve the right to request festivals. The more festivals, the greater visibility. Ask that they enter their cassettes and prints. Any cash awards or trophies go directly to the filmmaker or videomaker.

4. The distributor will ask that you indemnify them from any lawsuits you may have. You should always flip-flop the warranties and indemnification paragraph so that it applies equally to both of you.

5. Have a clause where any disputes are handled by an arbitration council. This is much cheaper than going to court which you cannot afford. A distributor knows this so might take liberties knowing that your lack of net worth protects them from lawsuits. Arbitration is cheaper, however, and equally binding. This gives you some edge to keep them honest.

6. If the company is sold, all rights to distribute should revert back to you. I ask for this because some deals I make are based on who is run-

ning the company. If another company buys the distributor out, a new sales policy may place my film on the shelf for the remaining years of the contract. Only with some distributors (the smaller ones) will you be able to get anything like this.

7. A sliding scale for royalties on home videos. As the video grosses increase so should the royalty, the assumption being made that the distributor has recouped marketing costs and the filmmaker should share more equally in profits.

The above is meant to give you only the most superficial understanding of distribution contracts and what to watch out for. It is not within the scope of this book to explore this subject in great depth so you'd be well advised to consult with an entertainment attorney familiar with motion picture, television, and home video contracts specific to the company with whom you are negotiating.

## Summary

In this chapter, you've gained a sense of the overall marketplace, the number of studio films and independent films released, and what constitutes a successful film. You've learned how deals are negotiated, using both deal memos and long form contracts. The more you understand the inner workings of a distribution agreement, the more power you have to ask intelligent questions and make your lawyer fight for the things you, your investors, and your film deserve.

# VIDEO BUSINESS & VIDEO DISTRIBUTION

## Home Video Market — An Overview

Today about 86 million U. S. households have VCRs. It is clearly a household appliance.

According to a "white paper" prepared by VSDA (Video Software Dealers Association; 818-385-1500; http://www.vsda.org), Americans spent nearly $8.7 billion renting videos in 1996. Every month, nearly half of all U.S. consumers (100 million people) rented a video at least once. On the sales side, nearly $7.5 billion was spent on prerecorded videos. The total video revenue exceeded $16 billion in 1996. Besides video, only gambling and cable television were greater than the video expenditures.

The studios rely on home video sales and rentals for about 55% of their domestic revenue. The rental market continues to be strong with small, entrepreneurial operators still holding a significant lead over chains such as Blockbuster (3,700 stores), Hollywood Entertainment (540 stores), Movie Gallery (965 stores), Video Update (200 stores), West Coast Entertainment (120 stores), Moovies (120 stores), and Family Video (87 stores). The chains claim about half of all the rental transactions.

Emerging threats to the home video market appear to be DBS (Direct Broadcast Satellite) with their inexpensive small dishes, and the Internet. In a survey by *Video Business* magazine, only logging onto the Internet has risen in the 14 leisure actitivies which they track.

Who are these people that rent and buy videos? The core users are households with children under 17. The deciding factor for what to rent is usually the child. Households with children are more than twice as likely to rent videos more than once a week, compared to childless households. The same is true for purchases. (A trend which has not gone unnoticed by the folks at Disney!) The older audiences are the least frequent renters.

Video renting and viewing is a group event. Nearly 40% of all renters said they watched videos with other adults and children. Women, more frequently than men, are the primary renters of movies watched by families.

Consumers, between 18% and 35% of them, purchase a video at least once a month. Although renting tapes is still a very popular activity, purchasing tapes has risen dramatically. The total consumer spending on video purchases will soon surpass video renting. The average U. S. household owned 41 videos in 1996. The heaviest buyers own 81 videos. The VSDA survey also discovered that people who rent videos also buy videos.

Three years ago there were fewer than a dozen movies that went to "sell-through" at low retail prices. In 1996 there were about three dozen priced to sell movie titles.

In the "go-go" days (1983-1987) of the video distribution and marketing business growth was phenomenal and retail video stores were mushrooming on every block. In those days the business was primarily rental. Today, the public has embraced the idea of owning videos, much like books. Prices are low enough so that consumers can own them, and view them again, or not. For years, the magic word among video programmers in regard to saleability was "repeatability." Unless a video was repeatable, like music or exercise, consumers wouldn't buy it. This axiom is no longer true. How many books do you own that you've read once or less than once? The analogy made in the good old days about "videos being collectible like books" has finally come true.

## Video Retail Environment

There are 25,000 to 35,000 video specialty stores in the U.S. and another 5,000 to 6,000 in Canada that rent videos. Other retail video rental outlets, such as supermarkets, convenience stores, drugstores, and others add another 10,000 to 12,000 rental outlets.

Most stores, between 75,000 and 100,000, sell videos, especially during the Christmas season, and include department stores, wholesale clubs, bookstores, music stores, electronics stores, supermarkets, and drugstores.

## The Major Players

Home video genres includes feature films, children's, exercise, sports, and many other genres. According to VideoScan, in late 1997 theatrical films made up 78% of video sales through mass merchandisers and retailers (not including discount outlets). Children's at 13%, television (3%), exercise (3%), sports (1%), and miscellaneous (1%) made up the balance.

During 1997 the market share leaders in all categories were:

| | |
|---|---|
| Disney | 20.95% |
| Universal Home Video | 19.25% |
| Warner Home Video* | 16.10% |
| Fox | 11.19% |
| Paramount Home Video | 7.61% |
| Columbia | 5.13% |

*includes MGM, HBO, Turner, New Line, and Warner Vision*

The bulk of the business is features, and six studios dominate the market. However, there are occasional windows for smaller independents with specialized products as demonstrated by the showing of smaller distributors in the exercise category.

## Niche Performers in Exercise

Here is Videoscan's year to date (October 5, 1997) share of the exercise video sales and the current top-selling exercise videos:

| | | |
|---|---|---|
| Warner Home Video | 22.84% | *Kathy Smith Functionally Fit* |
| PPO Entertainment | 22.30% | *Denise Ausin* |
| BMG Video | 12.82% | *The Firm: Low Impact Aerobics* |
| Anchor Bay | 10.44% | *Tai Chi for Health* |
| Polygram Home Video | 7.78% | *Dance Step Reebok* |
| Goodtime Home Video | 4.49% | *Richard Simmons: Sweatin' to the Oldies* |
| Sony/Sony Wonder | 3.45% | *The Grind Workout* |
| Healing Arts | 2.81% | *Yoga: Practice for Beginners* |
| Live Home Ent. | 2.80% | *Paula Abdul's Get Up and Dance* |
| United American Video | 1.90% | *Kathy Ireland: Total Fitness Workout* |

In this specialized category there are five or more smaller, independent distributors represented. Notice also that five of the top titles feature "A" level, well-known celebrities and models. The other tapes are "high concept" or have a well-known brand attached. Also notice that there is a trend away from traditional bounce–around exercise into quieter meditative stretching exercise regimens such as tai chi and yoga. As baby boomers age they want softer exercise programs.

The studios control the video movie market. The good news is that with specialized programs (independent features or special interest videos) there is room. The studios do not bother with the lower, economic end of the ladder and in a $16 billion or more industry, there are plenty of crumbs.

Another reason the studios do not market special interest videos is that the price points are low. To run the studio distribution machine they need to generate a lot more sales to cover marketing and overhead so they will always go where the dollars are. Pure economics.

What's common to both the studio and independents is that everyone is looking for branded, high-concept titles with stars. You need a pre-promoted element in your video. Occasionally a title like *Tai Chi for*

*Health* will break through where tai chi is the star, but that's the exception.

## Economics

The wholesale price for rental videos (e.g., movies) is $70. Between 1,000 and 2,000 new titles are released to the market each year, which means hundreds of new titles appear each month. The stores have limited "open to buy" dollars so may only select a few from these hundreds of offerings. A store might reinvest 25% of its revenue into new purchases. The most consumer demand is within the first 3 weeks of a video's release and then tapers off quickly. A store must make its money back on the number of "turns" of a video.

Video stores want as long a "window" as possible before the film makes its way onto cable. The home video rental window lasts between 30 and 75 days depending on the title. A film's journey now goes from theaters, to video, to pay-per-view, to pay cable, to broadcast and cable television. (Sometimes after the pay-per-view window, a video movie will be rereleased at a sell-through price.)

In recent years, some Hollywood studios have decided that they can make more money by pricing their videos at wholesale prices of $12 to $15 rather than the $70 rental price, which allows for retail prices of $19.95 or less. The good news is at the lower prices, the video rental store can recoup their investment after about 7 rentals as opposed to 30 rentals at the higher price. The bad news is that this sale-through pricing brings the video store into competition with the mass merchants such as Wal-Mart, Target, K-Mart, and others who are able to purchase videos in greater volume and sell at lower prices to consumers.

The mass merchants are where over 50% of all videos are sold. According to VSM/Chilton Research here is where consumers bought their videos during the fourth quarter in 1996:

| | |
|---|---|
| Wal-Mart | 25.9% |
| Blockbuster | 8.6% |
| K-Mart | 7.8% |
| Target | 7.6% |
| Sam's Wholesale Warehouse | 4.3% |
| Price/Costco | 3.2% |
| Best Buy | 2.7% |
| Columbia House | 2.5% |
| Other Direct Response | 2.5% |
| Suncoast | 2.0% |

Theatrical films account for 85% of all rentals and 82% of all video purchases.

## Release Schedule

The entertaiment industry is made up of different release windows and naturally the length of these windows is a case of dispute among the different participants. The theater owners want as long a window as possible (they do not want people waiting for home video), while the video retailers want the release to be near the theatrical release so that video renters remember the film's theatrical marketing campaign. The argument persists throughout the release sequence for any film.

According to NATO (National Association of Theater Owners), the length of theatrical windows is getting shorter with the average being 5 1/2 months in 1996. (More films need time on the screens, hence less time for a film to be in release.) Once the film goes to video there is a 30 to 45 days window before it can go to pay–per–view. Years ago this was not much of an issue because pay-per-view was a smaller business. Now, the pay–per–view window with access to 28.3 million homes adversely affects the video rental business. In 1996 pay–per–view generated $413 million. In addition, the release to DBS (direct broadcast satellite) and the burgeoning piracy of pay-per-view signals (perhaps as high as 4 million homes) further erode the video rental business.

Because of the increasing costs of producing and marketing feature length films, the studios want to move a film through the distribution pipeline as fast as possible. The longer a film is in a theatrical run, the shorter the studio's share of the box office so they move it quickly to home video and pay-per-view.

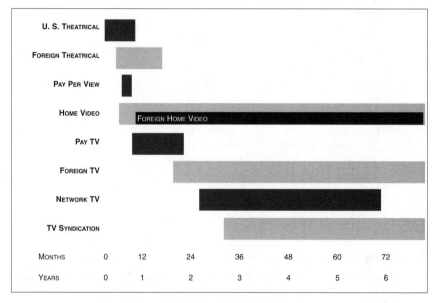

*Release Schedule - Market Sequencing*

In the early days of video, video distributors assumed that people only wanted to see a video once or twice and would therefore only rent it. Nowadays studios study each film to decide at what price to release the video. The usual wholesale price for rental product is between $60 and $70. Retailers pay $65 to $75. Major box-office movies sell 500,000 to 600,000 copies into the rental market, but most films sell well below the 100,000 unit mark. Without a theatrical release, most independent films sell less than 5,000 units.

The new strategy, championed by Disney and others, is to sell their smash hits at sell-through prices. So instead of selling 500,000 units at a high price they may sell 15 million units at a low price. The slimmer margin they receive is made up by vast volume.

## Top 50 Sell-through Titles by Genre

| Genre | Number of Titles | Percent |
|---|---|---|
| Action | 4 | 8% |
| Adventure | 4 | 8% |
| Animated | 17 | 34% |
| Comedy | 11 | 22% |
| Drama | 2 | 4% |
| Erotic Thriller | 0 | - |
| Family | 12 | 24% |
| Foreign | 0 | - |
| Horror | 0 | - |
| Romance | 0 | - |
| Romantic Comedy | 0 | - |
| Sci-Fi | 0 | - |
| Thriller | 0 | - |
| Western | 0 | - |

Source: *Video Store Magazine*

Children's titles continue to dominate the sell-through market. Animated and family release account for 58% of all titles on the list. Comedy also sells well with 22%. The genres that consumers want to own have broadened in recent years including adult-themed films such as *Forrest Gump* and *The Fugitive*.

## Release of Sell-through Titles by Quarter

| | |
|---|---|
| 4th Quarter | 38% |
| 3rd Quarter | 22% |
| 2nd Quarter | 22% |
| 1st Quarter | 18% |

Source: *Video Store Magazine*

## Top 10 Video Releases, 1995

|  | List Price | Sales (000) | Box Office |
|---|---|---|---|
| The Lion King | $ 26.95 | 27,500 | $312.1 |
| Forrest Gump | 22.95 | 14,800 | 321.1 |
| The Santa Clause (tie) | 19.98 | 11,500 | 144.8 |
| Cinderella (tie) | 26.99 | 11,500 | N/A |
| Batman Forever | 19.96 | 10,500 | 168.8 |
| Apollo 13 | 22.98 | 9,600 | 179.5 |
| Casper | 22.02 | 7,500 | 168.8 |
| Miracle on 34th Street | 14.98 | 7,000 | 90.5 |
| Mighty Morphin Power Rangers Movie (tie) | 22.98 | 6,100 | 17.2 |
| The Mask (tie) | 19.98 | 6,100 | 119.0 |

Source: *Video Store Magazine*

Clearly the bulk of sales occurs during the Christmas holidays and is flat during the rest of the year.

## New Technologies

### DBS

Direct Broadcast Satellite (DBS) came of age in 1995 when low-priced small pizza–sized dishes allowed consumers to receive video signals from satellites. DBS systems offer viewers about 150 channels including pay-per-view programming. One million systems were sold in 1995 and 3.5 million in 1996. When viewers buy a DBS system they stop going to the video store by about 70%. In addition, they not only stop watching videos, they also do not order pay-per-view movies with frequency; rather they simply watch all this expanded free programming. Some experts think the DBS market will tap out at about 15 million homes in the next five years; others are more optimistic.

## DVD

DVD (Digital Video Disk) is the latest new format. The technical formats have not as yet shaken down. The quality of DVD surpasses that of VHS video; it has surround–sound and interactive capabilities as well. Because of the large storage capacity (seven times that of a CD), additional material such as trailers, different endings, director's comments, and multiple language tracks may be included. The quality of the DVD is so high that piracy becomes an issue. Some feel that encoding will help prevent piracy.

Now that the consumers are accustomed to buying videos, this ownership phenomenon is likely to transfer to DVD as well which is expected to be the "next format" and firmly established within 5 to 10 years. At present, the promotion of DVD is targeted to the techno-market and "early adapters," which are males between the ages of 18 and 45. In the first year of release experts say DVD sales will generate about $70 million and are expected to reach about $10 billion in the next 7 years.

A Paul Kagan Associates report shows that by the year 2004, the DVD marketplace will equal the video retail business and surpass it by 2005. As DVD increases, and the overall revenues from all media (theatrical exhibition, retail video, DVD, and pay-per-view), the theatrical business will stay relatively flat. The expansion in the overall market will come from pay-per-view and DVD, while video retail will diminish.

### The Home Video Food Chain

Video programs, whether movies or special interest programs, go through an elaborate distribution process before reaching the consumer. Producers take their ideas and make movies or special interest programs. These are hopefully sold and distributed by "suppliers" or "manufacturers" like Disney Home Video or Mystic Fire Video. They in turn work with a number of "wholesalers" or "distributors" such as Baker and Taylor or Ingram. These 'wholesalers' sales reps take the programs to the video chains rental outlets like Blockbuster or Tower or Video Droid and try to sell rental copies. They also sell to the mass merchants like Walmart, K-Mart, and Target. Various promotions are worked out, sometimes originating with the supplier (or the wholesaler), with the purchasing retailer to bring consumer awareness to the videos for sale or rental. The merchandising of the videos are done through expensive posters, stand-ups, shelf-talkers, banners, or point-of-purchase displays. After all of this, perhaps the consumer either buys or rents the video.

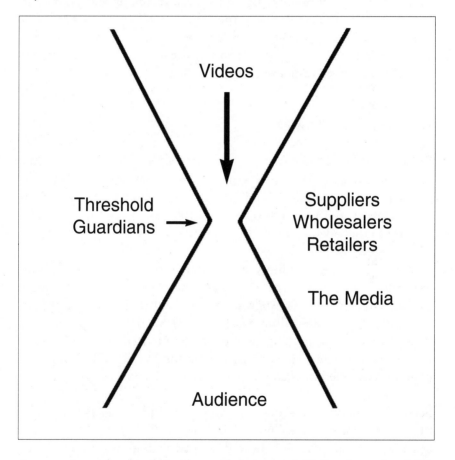

As you can see by the chart above, the process is like an hourglass with a lot of products at the top and a lot of consumers at the bottom. The supplier, wholesaler, and retailer are the gatekeepers. Get past them, and you get to the marketplace. What interests the gatekeepers are highly promotable titles which they know they can sell in sufficient quantities down along the video food chain.

Fortunately, there is also another way to get to consumers without going through this complex distribution process which is called "going direct." In this case, the video producer takes out ads in newspapers and magazines, buys air time on television, or sends out mailings directly to the consumer in the hopes of selling his or her video. Bypassing all the middlemen is an expensive process which can work for programs that are highly targeted and where the producer knows he will have a high response rate to his offer.

## Direct-to-Video Movies

Some feature films go directly to the video stores without ever having a theatrical release. With marketing costs for the average Hollywood movie hovering around $20 million, it is easy to see why some films never make it onto the big screen. In 1995 about 300 movies went directly to the video market.

There are three types of films that find their way here — horror, erotic thriller, and martial arts. They have their own stars like Shannon Tweed, Don Wilson, or Andrew Stevens and their own followings. The budgets for these films rarely exceed $250,000. A producer is happy to recoup his investment and several hundred thousand dollars. However, these films are having more and more difficulty competing in an overcrowded market.

Second, there are the sequels to Hollywood films. These are often titles that are well known among the public. *Aladdin* set the pace theatrically and then Disney followed with two straight-to-video releases: *The Return of Jafar* and *Aladdin and the King of Thieves*. *Jafar* sold close to 11 million videos earning Disney about $100 million. Both films went directly to the sell-through market at low prices. The budgets of direct to video films are considerably less than the originals and do not have the higher technical standards of the first, nor huge theatrical marketing costs. Disney created the "home premiere" business and offers at least one big title a month that "premieres" on video.

Lastly, there are Hollywood films deemed too weak (and expensive) to market theatrically. Mid-stream the decision is made to go straight to video which is what happened with Whoopi Goldberg's *Theodore Rex*. The studio is trying to recoup its investment without spending more in marketing.

The cost of producing and marketing highly promotable features and the scarcity of screen time mean that fewer and fewer films actually get to the screen. Home video is another matter. Many films that are never released theatrically can recoup some of their investment and even make a profit in the worldwide home video markets. Until recently made-for-video features generally had little or no prepromotion: no advertising, no publicity, no reviews, no television appearances by the film's stars, and no theatrical exhibition.

The direct-to-video budgets range from a high of $1 million, but are usually in the $200-$500,000 range. This buys about 20 days of shooting in limited locations, maybe a cameo by some "B" or "C" star. These films are marketed by fitting into highly recognizable genres with exploitable elements (e.g., sex and violence).

If you want to produce a profitable made-for-video movie, then select an exploitable genre and come up with a punchy title that suits the genre. Stick within the conventions of the genre. Genre audiences do not like their offerings mixed. Since they want to obtain as large an international audience as possible, they keep dialogue to a minimum. The pictorial elements are reduced to basic action and flesh.

Producers often shoot in 16mm and transfer to video or they shoot in video. They edit on AVIDs or other nonlinear editing systems. They prepare NTSC, PAL, and SECAM masters with split tracks (so that dubbing can be easily performed for foreign versions). Their films are represented by sellers at world film markets including Cannes, Mifed, Mipcom, AFM, and Monte Carlo where sellers license the video and television rights to the international markets.

Most films are barely indistinguishable from numerous films already in circulation except by title. Some producers of these exploitational videos *don't plan to do this forever* while others have made a business of it.

Here's only a very partial list of the direct-to-video titles that were in the international market at The American Film Market in Los Angeles.

*Final Justice, Appointment for a Killing, French Silk, Caged Seduction, The Voyeur, Exotica in a Moment of Passion, Heavy Petting, Acapulco Heat, Swimsuit, The Fraternity, Moll Flanders, Resistance, Inevitable Grace, Abducted 2, Cover Story, Cage II, Through Dead Eyes, Seduction of Innocence, Desert Steel, Street Warriors, When a Spider Bites, Squanderers, LA Wars, Hunt for the Blue Diamond, Paid to Kill, Meltdown, Another 9 1/2 Weeks, Red Scorpion 2, Sexual Malice, Sexual Outlaws, The Great Bikini Adventure, Stranger by Night, Body of Influence, Sins of the Night, Secret Games II, Body Melt, A Killing Obsession, Resort to Kill, Erotic Time Machine, Harem Heat, Lady Chatterly in Tokyo, Death and the Maiden, Cutthroat Island, No Angel, Young Lady Chatterly, Angel of H. E. A. T, Skinner, Tender Is the Hunter, One Man Army, Caged Heat 3, Killer, Masters of Horror, Fatal Past, The Silencer, Housewife from Hell, Whispering, The Seductress,, Making the Rules, Murders & Acquisitions, Rift, Beyond Fear.*

Get the idea? Basically, you are not a player unless your film's poster has a breast or a gun on it, preferably both.

### Independent Film on Home Video

There are a few video stores throughout the country (such as Video Droid in the San Francisco Bay Area or Video West in Studio City) that take chances and go out of their way to stock independent films. Most video stores follow a safer route. In fact, about half a video store's income is from renting the major studios' hit films. Even with the momentary (and cyclical) resurgence of press and Oscar awards to independent films in 1996, there has always been a limit to how many independent film videos that could be sold into the video rental stores.

Video analyst Tom Adams says the typical independent film which is financed, produced, and distributed outside of the studio system and earns less than $5 million will usually sell less than 30,000 units to the video stores. Three years ago, an independent film could expect to sell 60,000 units. As sales are falling, the ability to obtain financing for independent films also diminishes. Why is this happening? Because video stores spend more of their money on the tried-and-true Hollywood hits. They'd rather buy one more blockbuster than one more independent film. What's interesting, and a trend that video retailers apparently have not picked up on, is that the independent films (including foreign films) remain on the shelf and are rented long after the blockbusters are in the "under $6 bins."

## Home Video Royalties

There is much confusion among producers about how royalties are calculated. A royalty is usually based on the wholesale price of the video which is collected by the manufacturer/supplier when sold to a wholesaler. The wholesale price may range between 42% and 50% of the retail price depending on whether the wholesaler is selling a few units to a specialty store or many units to a mass market merchant. For example, a movie:

| | | |
|---|---|---|
| Retail Price | | $99.00 |
| Wholesale | | 41.58 |
| Royalty 25% | $ 10.39 | |
| Royalty 30% | 12.48 | |

For example, a sell-through title:

| | |
|---|---|
| Retail Price | $9.95 |
| Wholesale | 4.98 |
| Royalty 5% | .25 |

Let's suppose you license the video rights only in your program to a home video supplier/distributor like Paramount, CBS, Mystic Fire, or Healing Arts. A deal memo might look like this:

## Video Deal Memo

```
Rights:  Home video, laserdisk, (DVD?)
Territory:  Worldwide
Terms:  7 years

Advance: $50,000
Payable:
     50% on signing deal memo
     50% on delivery

Producer's Royalty
     20% royalty of gross wholesale receipts (for a
     film) (at $70 wholesale price)

Note: special interest video titles royalties esca-
late based on retail price.

     20% royalty of  wholesale receipts ($19.95 and
     above)
     15% royalty of wholesale receipts  ($14.95 and
     above)
     10% royalty of gross wholesale receipts
     ($12.95 and above)
     5% royalty of gross wholesale receipts   ($9.95
     and above)

     The royalties above are based on the wholesale
     price.

Distributor pays for
1. Marketing commitment of $200,000.
2. All packaging
Delivery Requirement
   1. Beta SP master/Digital master
   2. E&O insurance
```

3. All rights and releases
4. Color slides/promo stills
5. M&E (music and effects tracks)

Accounting quarterly with producer's royalty reports to be sent with payment, if any, within 60 days.

Artistic/Creative Control
1. Title will not be changed.
2. Film or video will not be reedited.
3. Producer can supervise video transfer, subtitling, inspection of release prints, and take possession of any that are not of release quality.

Marketing
1. Minimum $200,000 commitment.
2. Producer shall have full approval of all marketing decisions and materials such as trailer, one-sheet, newspaper ads, merchandise, and theater selection.

## A Deal With the Studios

If you independently financed your film and only sold the home video rights to a studio, you would receive a 20% to 30% royalty. If the studio finances your film (and sometimes even if they don't), they will give their home video division the rights to distribute the video. In turn their home video division will give a 20% to 30% royalty from which the studio distributor will also deduct a 30% distribution fee for "making the home video deal" even though it is with their own company. This is what we referred to before as "double-dipping."

Here's what the numbers look like for comparison's sake:

*Studio Deal*

$99.00 retail price
   62.00 wholesale gross revenues to the studio

deduct expenses

    2.00   duplication of tape, label & slip sleeve
    9.00   marketing (15%)
    6.00   overhead (10%)
  12.40   (a 20% home video royalty based on wholesale)
  <u>3.72</u>   less 30% distribution fee to studio
$ 8.68   to producer

-29.40   total expenses

$36.32   contribution to studio's profit

If 50,000 units are sold the producer receives total royalties of $434,000, assuming no additional "magic" is in the contract which allows other deductions.

*Home Video Distributor Deal (Self-financed Movie)*

  $99.00 retail price
   62.00 wholesale gross revenues to the studio

deduct these expenses

    2.00   duplication of tape, label & slip sleeve
    9.00   marketing (15%)
    6.00   overhead (10%)
  12.40 (a 20% royalty) no distribution fee

-29.40 total expenses

$25.68 contribution to distributor's profit

If 50,000 units are sold the producer receives total royalties of $620,000, assuming no additional magic is in the contract which allows other deductions. The producer receives $186,000 more. The home video deal with a studio distributor means the producer paid the studio a distribution fee of $186,000 for walking the project across the hall!

## How Home Video Advances Work

Producers are mystified how distributors determine advances. It's really quite simple. It is called the "how many?" exercise. How many videos do we think we can sell?

A home video advance is predicated on how many units the distributor thinks they will sell. Rarely will distributors ever pay more than they know the distributor makes back as an advance. If an independently produced action/adventure with some cast name value might sell 50,000 units, then the advance may be up to $620,000 (based on a 20% royalty of $12.40 per unit sold). You can assume distributors will always offer a lower advance, however, and only get to the higher number if pushed.

50,000 units x a royalty of $12.40 = $620,000 advance

In a studio's calculations, they will allot the royalty (less their fee) and come up with a different allocation.

50,000 units x a royalty of $8.68 = $434,000 advance

A studio will take a distribution fee of 30% from home video even though they are essentially selling it to themselves. On independent films which they have not financed one could argue that they are not entitled to a "distribution fee."

When a distributor makes an offer for "all rights" (e.g., theatrical, home video, television), you will get one number. You will not know how they did their projections to come up with the advance they are offering. So you should try to do some calculations on your own, or get them to break apart their advance by asking questions like *How much do you think the film will gross theatrically? How many video units do you think you can sell? What is the value in television or pay cable?* These are questions to ask of your distributor before a deal is made. The questions should be sprinkled through your various conversations. If you can get some clear indication of any of these numbers, you can start to work your way backward to see how they came up with their advance. This will help you and your attorney later try to figure out the real upper number in their mind, as they will always lowball it.

## Premiums

Another market, which can be quite lucrative, but hard to crack is the premium market. This is where a purchase of a large quantity of videos is made by a corporation. Perhaps they wish to give away your video with their packaged merchandise. Maybe it is an exercise video that is given away with some high priced exercise shoes. Or a pet training tape that is sold for $4 when you buy a 50 pound bag of dog food. Or a how–to–save–for–retirement video when you buy a $10,000 CD at a bank. There are a myriad of possibilities. The purchaser of the videos hopes that by adding value (a video) to his offer the consumer will be induced to buy.

The math is quite simple. You sell your videos in high quantities for $.50 to $2 above your dupe costs. The hope is that you sell enough videos with your initial order that you make a large profit from one sale. We sold our video, *Kids on the Internet*, to Compuserve who packaged it with some software they were selling. If you sell hundreds of thousands of videos, then you can offer them at a very low per unit price. If you are only selling hundreds or a few thousand, then you probably won't offer deep discounts.

While you can probably think of numerous possible purchasers of your video, that's not the hard part. The difficulty is knowing who is "open to buy." And there is really no way of knowing. I've been in the right place at the right time for almost all the premium deals I've done. They are extremely difficult to find and a great joy when they happen. It's an ancillary market and does not in any way negatively affect your other avenues of sale.

## Forced Distribution

Forced distribution is not too different from a premium sale. In this case you find a corporation or sponsor whose interests are to deliver your tape (and their message) to a specific audience. They pay you to duplicate and send out the videos. Our hard–hitting environmental video, *Diet for a New America*, appealed to an educational foundation who wished to inform school kids about the impact of their diet on the environment. They sent out a letter to thousands of schools with the offer that they would be sent this program if they showed it on Earth Day and if all the kids wrote a letter to them telling them about what they learned from the program. Ten thousand schools responded, and so this resulted in a sale of 10,000 units to the specific schools who said they'd have their kids write letters.

A promotional video might best be distributed to a targeted list of interested buyers/viewers. Sometimes it's better to find the sponsor or corporation that will put your video into forced distribution than to try to sell your video one unit at a time.

## Summary

Can we interpret any of these developments as to what it means to the video producer?

The good news is that people finally accept videos as a sell-through product. They want to own them and collect them. There is a sense of pride. They value videos. However, for the most part, movies and kids' programs are the top-selling genres, not special interest videos (which are best sold through direct response and direct advertising, not retail distribution). The sale of videos is now outstripping rentals in total income. Someday, the video market may develop where you will see a title breadth and depth similar to the superstore bookstores that stock both best-sellers and independent presses. (In the superstore bookstores, best-sellers only account for 3% of gross sales.) There is room for everything, not just the blockbusters, but this day has not yet come. When it comes time to sell your video, hope for a fourth quarter window, but look out — the marketplace is flooded with products.

For the present, if you want to produce videos for mass audiences you should stick to family features, animations, or comedy. But look out, Disney owns the playground!

The bad news. If you want to see your products in the video and mass merchant stores, they have to have a very highly promoted name or title. No store will stock your title unless it has high volume potential. In reviewing the special interest titles released this year, there are very few branded titles. Exercise has become saturated, and sports tapes are rare as well. Here and there are comedy tapes. The direct-to-video titles are in the exploitation genres (horror, erotic thriller, martial arts) with budgets in the $250,000 range. An average seller is about 5,000 units which domestically will allow a producer to recoup 30% or more of his budget, the balance coming from foreign television and home video sales.

# Television

## Pay Cable

Pay cable television, both in the U. S. and abroad, are burgeoning markets for films and programs of all kinds. There are so many new, niche channels that will have to fill airtime, resulting in many sales opportunities. Of course, as audiences get more and more fragmented, so do license fees; therefore, you may not receive as much from broadcasters as in the past, since they are reaching fewer people.

HBO and Showtime have realized the marketing value to their paid subscribers of the "premiere" movie. They are willing to pay for independent films that premiere on their networks. Prices were around $1 million but have fallen to $600,000 recently. In some cases, the pay cable premiere and publicity gave the film more visibility than even some theatrical films receive. Since not everyone gets pay cable, it is sometimes possible to release the film theatrically <u>after</u> the pay cable window which is contrary to the usual release pattern. (A cable premiere, on the other hand, is said to negatively affect foreign presales because they would rather see a theatrical release in the U.S.)

Deals are fairly straightforward. Both the license period (one year, 18 months, etc.) and the number of plays (which could be 12 or unlimited) are defined. A large cable system like HBO will want an exclusive license where you cannot license to a competitor until the HBO license period expires. Sometimes renewal options are written into the agreement so that if the show is successful, the licensor may relicense it at a predetermined price.

## Cable Television in the U. S.

As of 1997, A. C. Nielsen Company claims there are about 65 million basic cable subscribers representing about 68% percent of households. In 1995 about 48 million pay subscribers represented about 78% of all basic cable users. In 1995, the average monthly basic rate was $23.00 and the pay rate (per system) was $8.50 per month.

The Multi-system Operators, depending on the size of their system, are able to package and offer to the consumer basic and pay television program services. You do not go directly to these operators with your programming. These are the systems that decide what pay and basic television programming services they will carry.

## Top 50 Multi-system Operators (MSO)

| MSO Rank Subscribers | MSO | |
|---|---|---|
| 1 | Tele–Communications, Inc. (TCI) | 16,009,000 |
| 2 | Time Warner Cable | 12,100,000 |
| 3 | MediaOne, Inc. | 4,754,000 |
| 4 | Comcast Corporation | 3,447,000 |
| 5 | Cox Communications, Inc. | 3,235,000 |
| 6 | Cablevision Systems Corporation | 2,435,000 |
| 7 | Adelphia Cable Communications | 1,824,000 |
| 8 | Jones Intercable | 1,437,000 |
| 9 | Marcus Cable | 1,275,000 |
| 10 | Century Communications Corp. | 1,249,000 |
| 11 | Lenfest Group | 1,105,000 |
| 12 | Falcon Cable TV | 1,077,000 |
| 13 | Charter Communications | 930,000 |
| 14 | InterMedia Partners | 928,000 |
| 15 | Prime Cable | 821,000 |
| 16 | Scripps Howard Cable | 809,000 |
| 17 | TCA Cable TV, Inc. | 627,000 |
| 18 | Cable ONE | 588,000 |
| 19 | Fanch Communications, Inc. | 498,000 |
| 20 | Multimedia Cablevision, Inc. | 460,000 |
| 21 | Triax Telecommunications Company, L.L.C. | 398,000 |
| 22 | C–TEC Cable Systems | 382,000 |
| 23 | Rifkin & Associates, Inc. | 314,000 |
| 24 | Service Electric Cable TV, Inc. | 292,000 |
| 25 | SBC Media Ventures, L.P. | 255,000 |
| 26 | Harron Communications Corp. | 253,000 |

| | | |
|---|---|---|
| 27 | Tele–Media Corporation | 247,000 |
| 28 | Greater Media, Inc. | 246,000 |
| 29 | US Cable Corp. | 239,000 |
| 30 | Media General Cable | 225,000 |
| 31 | FrontierVision Partners, L.P. | 215,000 |
| 32 | Bresnan Communications Co. | 215,000 |
| 33 | Garden State Cable TV | 205,000 |
| 34 | Northland Communications Corp. | 201,000 |
| 35 | Armstrong Utilities, Inc. | 196,000 |
| 36 | Galaxy Cablevision | 177,000 |
| 37 | Classic Cable | 173,000 |
| 38 | Insight Communications | 167,000 |
| 39 | American Cable Entertainment | 164,000 |
| 40 | Pencor Services, Inc. | 159,000 |
| 41 | Blade Communications, Inc. | 153,000 |
| 42 | Susquehanna Cable Company | 148,000 |
| 43 | Prestige Cable | 140,000 |
| 44 | Booth Communications | 138,000 |
| 45 | Midcontinent Cable Co. | 133,000 |
| 46 | Buford Television | 133,000 |
| 47 | Coaxial Communications | 125,000 |
| 48 | Sonic Communications | 117,000 |
| 49 | Wehco Video | 116,000 |
| 50 | Helicon Corporation | 115,000 |

## Cable Network Program Services

These programming services listed below all license programs for rebroadcast. Some produce their own programming. In order to license your short film, documentary, or independent feature you must contact the vice president or director of program acquisitions. They will tell you how to submit your film for review. After review they will either return your film (they screen on videocassette) or they may make you an offer. An offer will be based on how many times they wish to air it over what period of time. They may want "unlimited plays" over a six–month window. Or a specific number of plays. This is all negotiable.

You could also ask the acquisitions person or programmer if there are agents with whom they frequently buy programs. Get the phone number and call that agent. They may have a better sense than you of the fair market price for your programs. While it will cost a fee (10%-25% of the license fee), a sales agent might be able to obtain a much higher price for you as well as be familiar with the intricacies and eccentricities of the cable network's licensing agreement.

Before submitting a program you should study a network's program schedule to make sure that they are an appropriate broadcaster for your work. Do not assume your show is for everyone. It's not. Cable television targets their audience by demo- and psychographics, and special interests. If you do not fit into their already determined program category, do not submit your film to them. You are wasting everyone's time. The more targeted you can be, the better your results. You may find several buyers. Many will want exclusivity for which they should pay more. This means that your work can only be shown on one service during a certain period (six months, one year?) at a time.

You may obtain the addresses and phone numbers of some of these services online.

A&E Television Network (A&E)
Action Pay Per View
Adam & Eve
Adultvision
All News Channel
AMC (American Movie Classics)
America's Health Network
ANA Television
Animal Planet
Asian American Satellite TV
BET (Black Entertainment Television)
BET on Jazz: The Cable Jazz Channel™
Bloomberg Information Television
Bravo Cable Network
C-SPAN (Cable Satellite Public Affairs Network)
C-SPAN2
c/net: the computer network
Cable Video Store
Canal de Noticias
Canal Sur

Cartoon Network
Channel America Television Network
Children's Cable Network
Cine Latino
Cinemax
Classic Arts Showcase
Classic Sports Network
CMT: Country Music Television
CNBC
CNN (Cable News Network)
CNN/SI
CNNfn – the financial network
CNNI (CNN International)
Comedy Central
Consumer Resource Network (CRN)
Continuous Hits 1, 2, 3, 4
Courtroom Television Network (Court TV)
Deep Dish TV
Discovery Channel
Discovery Civilization
Discovery Kids
Discovery Science
Discovery Travel & Living
E! Entertainment Television
ENCORE Thematic Multiplex SM
ENCORE®
ESPN
ESPN2
ESPNEWS
Ethnic–American Broadcasting Co. L.P.
EWTN: Global Catholic Network
FiT TV
Flix
Fox News Channel
Fox Sports Américas
FoxNet
FREE SPEECH TV (FStv)
fX (Fox Basic Cable)
fXM: Movies from Fox
Galavisión
Game Show Network
Gay Entertainment Television
GEMS International Television
Global Shopping Network

Great American Country (GAC)
HBO (Home Box Office)
Headline News
Home & Garden Television
Home Shopping Network (HSN)
Home Shopping Spree (Spree!)
Hot Choice
HTV
International Channel
INTRO TELEVISION
Jewish Television Network
Jones Computer Network (JCN)
KALEIDOSCOPE
Knowledge TV
Ladbroke Racing Channel/ Meadows Racing Network
Las Vegas Television Network
Lifetime Television (LIFE)
M2: Music Television
MOR Music TV
MSNBC
MTV Networks Latin America
MTV: Music Television
MuchMusic USA
My Pet TV
NASA Television
National & International Singles Television Network
NET – Political NewsTalk Network
Network One
NewSport
NewsTalk Television
Newsworld International
Nick at Nite's TV Land
Nickelodeon/Nick at Nite
Nostalgia Television
Odyssey
Outdoor Life Network
OVATION - The Arts Network
Planet Central Television
Playboy TV
Plex - encore 1
Prime Network
Product Information Network (PIN)
Q2
QVC

Request Television
Sci–Fi Channel
SCOLA
Shop at Home
Showtime
SingleVision
Speedvision Network
Spice
STARZ! - encore 8
STARZ!2 - encore 8
Student Film Network
Sundance Channel
TBS
Telemundo
The Box
The Crime Channel
The Disney Channel
The ECOLOGY Channel
The Family Channel
The Filipino Channel
The Golf Channel
The History Channel
The Idea Channel
The Independent Film Channel
The Inspirational Network (INSP)
The Learning Channel
The Movie Channel (TMC)
The Music Zone
The Outdoor Channel
The Travel Channel
The Weather Channel
The Worship Network
TNN: The Nashville Network
TNT (Turner Network Television)
Total Communication Network
Trinity Broadcasting Network
Trio
Tropical Television Network
Turner Classic Movies (TCM)
TV Asia
TV Food Network (TVFN)
TV JAPAN
U Network
Univision

USA Network
UVTV/KTLA
UVTV/WGN
· UVTV/WPIX
ValueVision: The Brand Name Channel
VH1 (Music First)
Via TV Network
Video Catalog Channel
Viewer's Choice
WorldJazz
WSBK
WWOR/AEC Service
Z Music Television

## PBS — How It Works

Beats me! I have produced 6 one-hour specials for PBS over the last 20 years, and it continues to be a mysterious process. Even those who work within PBS find themselves in a labyrinthian landscape.

One of my specials, *Dolphin*, was independently financed by private investors outside the PBS system. We took the special to one of the dozen or more "stations of entry" — usually one of the larger producing PBS stations such as WGBH, WQED, KQED, WNET, KCET, WETA — and searched for underwriting. For *Dolphin*, we received a $25,000 licensing fee from Atlantic Richfield, the sponsor, of which $17,500 went to us.

Five of my programs (the Lifeguides series which included *Diet for a New America*) were produced and funded by KCET internally. We developed the concepts, pitched the shows, gained funding, and produced, using the station's production, distribution, and marketing resources. KCET funded each program with budget ranging from $60,000 to $188,000 per hour. I was paid a producer's fee and had a profit share of revenues after breakeven which turned out to be meaningless. (They cross-collateralized the programs so that even though two were profitable, the overall series never saw a profit. Regardless of our contract, they quit reporting video sales after about 2 years even though sales still continue.)

I recommend that if you have a PBS-type program you contact one of the larger PBS station's programming or development director. If there is interest in your show, ask for the name of producers that the station has worked with recently and see if you can partner with them. While you may share 50% of your project's revenues and fees with another producer, you will gain entry much faster partnering with a known entity.

Having a known coproducer is only half the battle. The other is financing. The development departments at the PBS stations compete not only with their own projects but with other PBS stations as well who are all going after the same sponsors and underwriters. It is extremely competitive so your project must have great appeal for the sponsor, a quality which is difficult to prejudge since you don't know the corporate sponsor's agenda.

If you produce a show with private financing and then take it to PBS, be prepared when they offer to broadcast it for no or very little money. You can however craft other deals with PBS, such as premium deals, which allow you to keep creative and financial control, and yet still reach a national audience building awareness for your title.

## PBS

Producers frequently say, "My project is perfect for PBS." Most of the time this is a statement of hope, not one based on reality. The reason for this is that they do not understand how PBS operates, what it is, nor how it obtains its programming.

Before approaching PBS (and below I will give you several ways to do this) you need to be sure you are meeting PBS's needs. Get the schedule magazine from your local PBS station and study what is being aired when. Notice that the "core programming" times of 8 p.m.-10 p.m. are already filled up with national programming. See what appears on the weekends and in fringe time. Try to understand why they program what they do. See if you can learn what the mission statement and objectives of the local PBS station are. Do they focus on public affairs programming, arts and music, or multicultural programming? Only, once you've done your homework can you say, "My project is perfect for PBS." Do not put your head in the sand and neglect to study your potential buyer (and this goes for any buyer not only PBS) or you will be admitted to the not-very-exclusive club of other producers who've received "we pass" form letters from PBS.

## Points of Entry for PBS

There are three major points of entry for licensing your films and documentaries to PBS. Study each method and decide which can be most effective for the kind of program you wish to create.

*Independent Television Service (ITVS)*
http://www.itvs.org/

ITVS was created by act of Congress and sets aside about $6 million a year for programming. Jim Yee, the managing director, lives in San Francisco. ITVS supports and funds the work of independent media in all categories, both fiction and nonfiction, and distributes the work through the PBS system. On rare occcassions they will get a program on "The American Experience," or more often on POV series or as stand-alone program. The "United States of Poetry" and "The Trip" were both highly visible shows that originated through the ITVS system.

Grants can be as high as $200,000 to $300,000. They want to fund highly visible programs in their entirety. They receive thousands of proposals a year and select a few dozen for funding. They have a reputation for being very filmmaker friendly. Their primary reason for existing is not to make money but to support independent work. They will take some percentage of income from a project to help cover their investment, but this is not the motivating force for their support.

*POV Series (American Documentary Consortium)*
http://www.pbs.org/pov/

POV is based in New York City and focuses on supporting independent documentaries. Each year they receive hundreds, if not thousands, of documentaries and from these choose 12 to 15 and broadcast them in the summer on Tuesday nights at 9 p.m. (sometimes filling the slot when "Frontline" is off the air). Their documentaries are winners of many awards, Emmies, and Academy Awards. They do great promotion and have attracted large audiences for documentaries. The PBS stations around the country support the series because POV has done a great job of organizing a presentation for them.

ADC was created by a spin-off from the board of directors that ran American Playhouse (which consortium of stations includes WNET, KCET, WGBH, and formerly South Carolina ETV). They have been around for 10-11 years and achieved great relationships with filmmakers and audiences alike with shows such as "Silver Lake Diaries." Their deal is a straight licensing deal of around $1,000 per minute (everything is negotiable). Mark Weiss is executive director and has an office in New York City.

## Major Producing Stations

There are three tiers of producing stations categorized by how prolific they are in producing programming. The first tier is WNET (New York) and WBGH (Boston) which account for about 60% of the total PBS schedule. The next tier is KCET (Los Angeles) and WETA (Washington, DC). The third tier includes assorted others like Maryland Public Television (Owens Mills, MD), KQED (San Francisco), KTCA (Minneapolis), KCTS (Seattle), Dallas, Philadelphia, etc.

Producers who approach these major producing stations are in essence getting a representative or a broker. In some rare cases the stations will help nurture along a project, but this is extremely rare since they are hard pressed to find an economc reason to do it. Any show that producers take to them should be fully packaged. The best use of a producing station is to get their support to promote the program to the general audience and to the community of other PBS stations across the country.

In exceptional cases they might take on your show (or proposal) and seek underwriting. Like a sales rep or a broker, they will take a commission of 5%-35% of the license fee or whatever is raised. Everything is negotiable. Here they play the role of an agent or a rep more than a distributor.

What you need to keep in mind is that they've got a lot of product themselves so they are looking to supplement their product. Very few stations can make a business of solely representing the programs of independent producers. An exception, I'm told, is South Carolina ETV, which has a reputation of being very hands-off and producer friendly, but they do not have a lot of "oomph" in the PBS system.

This route to getting your program on PBS is a less likely scenario than ITVS or POV/ADC.

Many PBS stations are underfunded and understaffed and so even considering your pitching your project to sponsors for underwriting becomes another speculative venture. One scenario that may work is to enroll them a little at a time in your project. Report in and share with the new developments as your project takes shape (before enrolling them), let interest and momentum build so that they become emotionally and passionately involved. This may make all the difference in getting them to partner with you.

## PBS/CPB Approach

*PBS*

Here is another approach. PBS itself has money to license programs if they like them. Although they license very few programs (maybe less than six a year and these tend to be with known quantities like Ken

Burns), it the most direct route. Their focus, however, is not on marginal filmmaking but on creating broadcasting events. They want hits. They want visibility. They want ratings. Thousands of projects are turned down instantly each year because they don't meet this criteria. If you have something that is innovative and can fill the gap, then apply. If not, don't waste your time. Remember that most core broadcasting time (8 p.m. to 10 p.m.) is taken up by "NOVA," "Masterpiece Theater," "Nature", "Mystery," etc. By the time a show gets a slot, it tends to stay there.

*CPB (Corporation for Public Broadcasting)*

CPB accepts general solicitations which go before a review panel three times a year. They fund a couple dozen independently produced programs per year. The proposals can come from independents or through a station acting as a broker. CPB prefers the programs come from stations as they want to see the community of broadcasters come together. It is a slow and agonizing process. Write CPB, 901 E. Street, NW, Washington, DC, and ask for an information kit. They too receive thousands of submissions.

## National Endowments for the Humanities (NEH)

For grant consideration, the NEH requires that you write a huge textbook with academic credibility. Grants are given to programs that deal with history, literature, the humanities, and the study of culture. Selection is through a panel which receives hundreds of proposals a year; a dozen are accepted. KCET's *The Great War* got its seed money from NEH which does provide development money for a lot of projects, but you really have to work hard to get their money. First time filmmakers probably shouldn't start here; it's simply too difficult and you will need to establish academic credentials.

*All Other Options*

Sometimes "Frontline" might buy one program a year from hundreds of submissions. They tend to work with producers they already know, but it's worth a shot.

A&E and Discovery Channel pay around $60,000 to $80,000 per hour and demand to own all the ancillary rights. The programs also have to be designed to fit into their niche. It's tough to make a show for that and earn a producing fee!

What you should keep in mind is that most organizations do not finance programs altruistically; there is usually an economic factor driving the decision. PBS is perhaps the only place left which is sort of in-between the commercial and noncommercial world; however, as government funding is getting tighter and tighter, PBS is more than drifting towards commercialization of their programming.

**Sponsor-Driven Proposals**

*What if I bring in a sponsor?* If you have already identified a sponsor who is willing to fund your show, you can go to PBS. They will naturally be suspicious of the sponsor's agenda. (PBS hardly funds programs without an agenda. *What does the sponsor really want?* they'll ask themselves. *What are they getting out of it? How are they profiting?* If there is some way they are profiting, PBS will reject your sponsor. This happened to me. I went in with a sponsor willing to put $200,000 into a documentary budget, but the local PBS station felt the content of the show was too directly related to the business of the sponsor. Even though this was not the case, PBS rejected the sponsor. No sponsor, no show.

If you have a sponsor, then PBS becomes your distribution channel. You can go to PBS directly or to one of the sponsoring stations.

**On-Air Offers/PBS**

You have probably seen the on-air home video offers that follow a program on PBS. Videofinders manages PBS on-air time (among others) and charges 58% of your gross revenue for the service. You supply the packaged videos. This is a large fee for the service. In addition, PBS must not only give approval for on-air offers, but they also must approve the copy for the offer, which is always very low-key and without hype.

## How to Do PBS Premium Deals

In 1996 we created a series of half-hour videos on the Internet. The most successful and popular one was *Kids on the Internet*. We made a license-free deal with PBS through their Washington, DC, office to air the program during pledge week. Pledge week occurs several times during the year and during these long breaks between programs, viewers are pitched to become "members" of their local PBS station. As an incentive, higher level of pledge commitments ($50, $100, $200) are rewarded with higher levels of merchandise such as books, CD's, videos, or bundles. In our deal PBS could, free of any licensing fee to us, broadcast the half-hour program during pledge week throughout the country. In return, they would order the pledge giveaways (videos, books, magazines, etc.) directly from us.

Here's how the deal worked.

1. First PBS required some editorial changes where we had to remove any *Futurekids'* logo which appeared in the show. (*Futurekids* is the computer learning center where we shot the video.) On PBS, the program content cannot provide any opportunity for anyone to "profit" from the broadcast. (Beware: if your program features commercial entities too close to the subject matter your program will be rejected. When I asked PBS to please explain how Black and Decker was allowed to sponsor *This Old House*, there was silence on the end of the phone.)

2. From February through September, PBS could air the show during pledge periods.

3. The deal was nonexclusive. We could license the show to cable television or other broadcasters.

4. We would receive a "performance fee" based upon the gross dollars raised from the pledging on all participating stations. The performance fee was $10,000 for every $100,000 earned up to $500,001. The fee was capped at $60,000. ( I had asked for a flat 10% of the pledge income, but it was refused. They wanted a threshold structure

so it would not appear that we were "profit participants" in the fund-raising drive. (Let us not forget that they were raising money around a program for which they did not pay either any production costs nor a licensing fee.)

5. We fulfilled orders and shipped the premium products to the individual stations. They in turn sent new or resubscribing members the premiums which included magazine subscriptions, software, a book, and our videos. (We were able to obtain limited quantities of the other products for "free" because of the publicity value to the company of being exposed on PBS during pledge breaks.)

6. PBS distributed or offered a "feed" to all the stations after announcing its availability and terms of the pledge deal via fax and email to all 300+ PBS stations. We were responsible for taking orders and fullfilling the orders with the individual stations.

7. We offered various bundles of products:

**$40 Pledge Gift**

| | | |
|---|---|---|
| *Kids on the Internet* Video | Retail $ 14.95 | |
| Free Computer Class | 25.00 | |
| Total Retail Value | $ 39.95 | |
| | | |
| Selling Price to the Stations | $ 4.00 | |
| | | |
| Our Actual Cost | $ 1.30 | |
| Profit Per This Item | $ 2.70 | |

If they accept your premium for pledge, PBS pays 1/10 of the "value" of the premium to the producer. So if a single video is offered to people to pledge and become members for $50, then they will pay the producer $5 for the video. For the premiums above, we received $4 for a bundle valued at $39.95. We netted $2.70 profit per item. A tough way to make a living unless you sell a lot of them. The stations paid shipping costs so this expense was a wash or provided a slight profit.

**$120 Pledge Gift**

| | |
|---|---:|
| *Kids on the Internet* video | 14.95 |
| Compuserve's *Internet in a Box for Kids* | 49.95 |
| *Livin' on the Net* video | 29.95 |
| Free Computer Class | <u>25.00</u> |
| Total Retail Value | $ 119.85 |
| | |
| Selling Price to the Stations | $ 13.00 |
| | |
| Our Actual Costs | $ 2.30 |
| Profit Per This Item | $ 10.70 |

On-Air Offer to Viewers: $130.00

Because of funding cutbacks, PBS is becoming more entrepreneurial in its search for profits. If you can design an offer or project that will produce income for them, you have a much better chance of getting your program made and aired on PBS.

If pledge items become successful, more and more PBS stations will want to use your premium. This is rare. Programs featuring John Tesh, The Three Tenors, and Deepak Chopra are recent PBS examples of successful pledge offers.

# Corporate & Industrial video Markets

## Institutional/Corporate Markets

There are many markets for videos outside the so-called home video marketplace that can be extremely lucrative with the right combination of product and promotion. These are not movies but videos, intended not for the consumer market but the corporate or industrial markets.

What follows is an example of a fictitious training program intended for the industrial or corporate market that focuses on the step-by-step considerations that go into its program design, casting, pricing, marketing, etc. It doesn't matter whether the video is for the consumer home video market, the educational or school library market, or the corporate market. If you don't do the homework and really examine the assumptions for your whole project (from concept to marketing), you may be sadly disappointed by the results.

The institutional markets (think Fortune 500 companies) can be a lucrative market for well-produced, highly informative, instructional or training programs. Here's the rationale: a corporation will pay thousands of dollars to have top speakers come in and give a presentation. Or, they may purchase a video tape instructional package for $1,000, gain the valuable information for use on video at any time, but not have to bring in expert speakers. (It's the same motivation you had when you bought this book. It looked like what you needed, right now, to make decisions. The price was very low for the information that you needed.) Same thing here. Put yourself in the end user's or buyer's shoes.

A well-thought-out marketing plan is the key to financial reward in this market. Too frequently producers get caught up in financing and production issues and overlook how their program will be brought to the market.

## The Program Objective

If you expect to be a player in this market, here are some of the considerations and challenges you will be faced with. First, what should you produce? What concepts and issues facing today's workplace are the most crucial? What information will the marketplace pay top dollar for? Why? What else is out there? Is there a hole in the market that you can fill?

## Your Team

You are the producer. Someone else will supply the content and perhaps be an on-camera spokesperson. Who are your partners? What's the business arrangement? Do they get a fee, a deferment, participation in net profits? Who holds the leverage? Are your partners highly visible and known to the business and corporate markets? Do you have a Tom Peters on your team?

If you are the producer, who is the distributor? Have you entered into discussions with the distributor about the program format and its marketability? Have you been careful in shopping around your idea so that it won't be co-opted by someone more experienced?

## The Product & Pricing

What's the product? A single video? Or a package? What's in the package? Could be an hour-long management video, an hour-long employee video, five employee guides, five management guides, and one 100-page trainer guide.

What's the pricing: $1,000? $1,295? Maybe a single management or employee tape with guide is $795 each. Extra guides are an additional $2 to $5 each, depending on the quantity ordered. You should think about a secondary back-end sale item. One corporation might purchase the tape and then order 5,000 guides!! Run the numbers.

## Price Justification

What about the price point? How in the world can you justify a $1,295 price point? If you think you are selling someone a videotape, you can't justify it. However, if what is being sold is value-added courseware that allows the buyers to really solve their critical problems, then the price might be appropriate.

For several thousand dollars, you could hire experts to speak to your managers and employees for one day. But then they are gone. A video training course enables employees to benefit all year round. In addition, the experts you may want have very busy schedules. Clients can either wait in line until they are available, or purchase the training tools and use them tomorrow. The corporation must provide someone to take on a leadership role — like a committed manager or human resources person — and adapt the training tapes for the company's needs. The training manual that accompanies the videos provides clear assistance in this regard.

## Target Audience

Who is the target audience? Where have your experts lectured or consulted in the past? That's the beginning of your mailing list. What are other similar companies with the same needs. Even if you only have several thousand names, selling tapes at $1,000 a package adds up. A mailing or outbound telemarketing campaign to your primary list might yield a very high response rate (10%, 20%, or more!).

Buy other lists. Say your training program will appeal to human resource directors. If so, there are 70,000 buyers throughout the United States!

## Competition

If this kind of money can be made on single subject training video packages, why isn't everyone doing it? Because it's not as easy as it sounds. You need a great concept and high profile experts, well known within the corporate world, to make these numbers. Plus you have to find a subject area that either hasn't been done, or hasn't been done well. You have to do your homework and scout the earth for anything similar to the idea you have in mind. Do not put your head in the sand. You need to find out as much as possible about what may already be out there before you invest time and money in production and marketing.

## Program Concept

Your experts have a body of knowledge. As a producer, your job is to maximize that information and carve it up into video programs. Are you designing a one-hour course, a two-hour course, or a half-day seminar on video? The buyer receives videos and course books which help him or her use this body of information. By carefully looking at the publishing requirements and consulting with potential buyers you can determine the correct formatting for the body of knowledge. Know how the buyer is going to use your program. Go talk to him or her before you start production.

You will also need to bring in an instructional design writer since the creation of the program is quite different from any other form of video. Your writer too needs to understand the marketplace and determine how the product is going to solve the problem. How does it work? It is small bits of information that are reinforced by personal and interpersonal communication that comes after the viewing of the video. Where does the "value-added" aspect come from? Perhaps what's most important is the audience interaction and interpersonal learning that happen after the video is turned off so that the video is a catalyst for interaction. It may be a different use of video than a simple instructional "step-by-step" program.

## Production Elements

What are the production elements? How do they interrelate? What's the link between video and printed material and audience interaction?

There are three production elements with interactive linkage between the video and printed manuals that could appear in your program and format.

1. The scenarios: about a dozen "slice-of-life" vignettes staged in the workplace. These are little windows — about 90 seconds long — demonstrating aspects of the "problem" or "solution." They are deliberately designed to address the client's needs. They also reflect the cultural diversity of today's workplace.

2. On-site trainers conduct a simulated training session with a diverse group of people in an imaginary corporation. As a viewer, you may identify with and share some of the perspectives of a shop manager, sales manager, an operations person, etc. As an audience member, your support group is worked into the video. This "kick–starts" the discussions following the tape viewing.

3. There is the information, the content, the facts. This can be presented with graphics, documentary style techniques, or with on-camera presenters.

These elements facilitate the interactivity and discussion of the real-life viewing audience. The real learning and understanding take place during the discussion, not the video viewing. (This is different from most conventional videos. If you can make this case, the value is greater than a run-of-the-mill video.)

### Packaging

A handsome leatherette binder that commands respect contains all the videos and printed materials.

### Distribution Channels — Release Strategy Assumptions

*Level One.* You telemarket to a small preferred group of existing clients (approx. 500) already aware of your client's work. From the first 150 calls to this elite, highly motivated buying group, 20 programs were sold. A 13 % response rate!

Not only are these people buyers, but they will tell others. Sometimes they are distributors or buyers themselves and will generate referred sales. Naturally you want to launch a product to the class of trade that will generate the most and buffer your cash expenses.

*Level Two.* You send a direct mail solicitation to 70,000 human resource managers. This list is tested to a list of 3,000 names before a mass rollout. It is expected that a sale will be made to 1 to 2% of that population, generating between $700,000 and $1,400,000 in gross revenues.

This answers the burning question all producers ask themselves: *Is there a market for the product and how can you reach it?*

## Impressions for Success

You can't just market in a vacuum. Marketers know that you must have at least five impressions before a sale is made. Production is the fun part and is over relatively soon. Marketing requires a sustained and focused effort to succeed.

Impression #1 is telemarketing to the priority client list;
Impression #2 is a review or publicity;
Impression #3 is a direct mail piece which goes out 60 to 90 days after the telemarketing. (The direct mail piece is a four-color brochure which costs a little more than $1.)

A 1% response rate costs about $100 per order per mailing which is still only a 10% marketing cost. Three mailings would cost 30% of the gross revenues, which by direct mailing standards is still quite low. This model works because the product is high-priced and can support these margins. Obviously this marketing model will not work for $19.95 home videos. The margins simply aren't there.

## Free Trial

To further stimulate sales, maybe you send your program out on a free trial basis for 30 days. If, after 30 days, it isn't returned then it becomes a purchase. Here you are relying on your buyer's desire to have the product, and their ability to understand that its value is that it can be used again and again by employees. It's not just a one -shot video program.

## Telemarketing Video

An article in *Time* magazine demonstrated how large the telemarketing industry really is. In the nineties, telemarketing has reached over $300 billion. With the price of postage rising faster than telephone rates, marketers can reach people by phone for about one-third of the cost by mail. In telemarketing you only need a 1% to 2% response rate for success. The higher the price point, the better. Over 80% of telemarketing revenues come from sales to business.

There is no reason why these marketing techniques cannot be applied to selling video programs. Of course, the economic model must work. In this case, the telemarketers' cost is about $10-$15 per hour. They can make 75 calls per hour. Many are, of course, hang-ups, busy signals, or no answers. The average sales call takes about two to three minutes. This means they may talk to 10 or 15 people per hour, or 80 to 120 people per day, resulting in one or more sales per day. In this model, the cost of one sale is about $120 for the salesperson, plus the cost of the calls and overhead. Marketing costs are about 15%-20% of sales.

## Follow-Up

As sales are made, follow-up calls can analyze the end user's result and collect testimonials for future marketing efforts. The marketers will learn what content is the most successful and can focus sales efforts on those newly discovered marketing elements.

## Line Extensions

It is very valuable for you to determine if there are line extensions or series of related products that can be created in the event the first is successful. Why create only one product and walk away from a market you've penetrated?

Once you've exploited your primary market you may want to "customize" the program for special corporate clients. Or do a version that you can sell at a lower price once sales have peaked with the higher priced version.

## Catalogs

You may find third-party distributors who send exclusive catalogs to specific markets in other countries. Other English-speaking territories like Australia, Canada, and the UK could be potential markets. Third-party distributors take a 10% to 20% fee ($129 to $258) for marketing.

## Splintering Markets & Strategy

It is to your advantage to determine as many markets as possible for your product. However care must be taken not to create confusion in the marketplace by having too many people offer the same product to the same market at different prices. The various distribution strategies must interlock and there must be coordination between sequential marketing to various markets. Naturally you will want to sell to the higher-paying customers first and work your way down to the lower price markets after first selling into the priority markets.

## Marketing Environment

Producers need to pay attention to the mood, atmosphere, and intellectual mind–set of the market they are selling into. A bundle of hypothetical programs we've discussed here only makes sense if your buyer needs the information. If you can deliver high–value information to a targeted audience for a high price point, you can have a real business on your hands. Success means understanding every aspect from program concept and design through the economics of direct marketing.

# Short Film Distribution

## An Exercise

So often I hear filmmakers say that when they finish their short films they are "going to show them in the theaters." Is this a statement of reality or fantasy? Let's examine how it works.

This year we rereleased *Hardware Wars*, our short film parody, to coincide with the *Star Wars* opening. It played a couple of weeks in West Hollywood and Boston with *The Empire Strikes Back*. There were lines around the block. The theaters were packed at $7 a seat. To make the math easy, let's say the theater sold 500 seats for 20 shows a week grossing $70,000.

The Big Question: *What is the total weekly rental you would expect* Hardware Wars *to receive?*

| | |
|---|---|
| A. 25% of the Gross = | $ 17,500 |
| B. 10% of the Gross = | 7,000 |
| C. 5% of the Gross = | 3,500 |
| D. 2% of the Gross = | 1,500 |
| E. None of the above. | |

Take a guess.

The answer is E. I deliberately misled you. Short films are rented on a flat-fee basis regardless of gross. Percentages have nothing to do with it.

The rental per week was $75. "Outrageous," you say? Audiences love to see shorts. Why then don't we see more of them in theaters?

The reason is economics. A theater will pay film rental of about $50 to $75 for a week's run of a short film. A distributor's fee is 50% which returns $25 to $37.50 to the filmmaker. The filmmaker may be responsible for paying for the prints, or the cost of the prints will be deducted after the distributor's share. Prints can cost $200 depending on the length of the short.

And there's more bad news: The shorts and trailers before the feature are at the head of the reel where the most torque is put on film as it goes through the projector. This means more wear and tear on the film print resulting in scratches and torn sprocket holes. Under these conditions a film print may only last for 100 showings before it is unusable. A week's run of a short could have 5 shows per day x 7 days = 35 showings per week. So, in about 3 weeks of screenings you need a new film print. The filmmaker's share for three weeks is $112 which does not even buy a new film print. It's a no-brainer to see that the math doesn't work. The longer a film plays, the more money the film-maker loses!

There are only about 600 theaters that show art and independent films in the U. S. Of these only a few dozen show shorts. Why? Handling costs. I'm told it's a lot of trouble for a projectionist to splice the short film onto the main reel and then after the showing splice it off and ship it to another distributor which surely is not the distributor of the main feature.

In addition, as you are probably well aware, theaters show as much as 15 minutes of trailers before features which can be 2 hours or longer. Exhibitors like to "turn over" the house as frequently as possibly in order to get in as many showings per day. Adding a short film to their schedule will accumulate so much additional time onto the schedule that one showing of the feature could be lost and possible revenues as well. They do not want to do this. In the sixties and seventies there were still several hundred theaters that showed shorts. Even then there was no theatrical short market to speak of, and now, even less so.

## Shorts on Pay Cable Television

When cable television began there were not enough programs to fill the enormous amount of air time available. Many broadcasters such as HBO, Showtime, and Nickelodeon sought out independently produced short films which they used as "interstitial" or filler material. They paid perhaps as much as $100 per minute. And although this was not a significant amount of money it did give independents a new source of revenue and exposure. The situation has changed considerably.

In a move to give cable networks their own look and at the same time save money, almost all of the pay cable systems now produce their own interstitial or short programming. Few short films are licensed by basic and pay cable.

I suppose if you contacted many of the new start-up cable networks you would find product-hungry buyers and could negotiate deals for your short films. However, as soon as possible, the broadcasters will want to produce their own material leaving no room for independently produced shorts.

If you want to produce short pieces, there are lots of opportunities for on-staff producers at the cable networks in their on-air departments. I worked for Showtime/The Movie Channel in the early eighties and oversaw the production of 1,200 on-air segments ranging in length from a few seconds to 15 minutes. Most basic and pay services have their own in-house, on-air division that creates original, short programming. This is an excellent place to produce a lot of work and learn new skills.

## Portfolio Piece

Outside of festivals where do you see short films anymore? Here and there on cable, once in a while in an animated theatrical package, but they are virtually extinct. (I saw more shorts at Sundance in one week than in the last three years altogether. And for many, this may be the only theatrical exhibition they will ever have!) That should tell you something about the exhibition of shorts in this country: there isn't any!

This is a shame because many stories are not big ideas and are perfectly suited for the short film format. Regardless, because of economics, short films are made in almost every film school. They are the student's resume pieces with which many hope will be their calling card to the film industry.

To keep your expectation intact, it might be best to simply consider your short film as your "portfolio piece." Nothing wrong with that.

There are hundreds of festivals here and abroad that show short films, give out awards and occasionally cash prizes. (Contact the AIVF in New York for their guide book to film and video festivals.) Even if you win all the awards it probably won't pay the cost of your film, but you'll have a track record and certainly something which may get you some attention.

The ultimate experience with a short live-action or animated film would be to receive an Academy Award nomination. However, despite the highest award that Hollywood bestows, this glory will quickly fade and not be the fast-track to the end of the rainbow. To friends of mine who've been nominated, I recommend that in the month before the awards they visit Los Angeles and meet as many people as they possibly can while they are a "nominee" — right up to the awards ceremony itself and the parties afterward. Even if you win, the buzz dissipates very quickly and your "15 minutes" are over. Be sure to have other projects that you are ready to talk about since a nomination or award does provide a terrific window with which to market yourself and your new project. But time is limited.

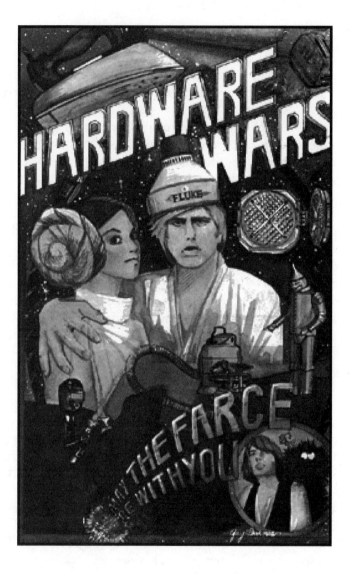

*HARDWARE WARS*
*Original Theatrical Poster*

## Breaking the Rules — *Hardware Wars*

Sometimes you get lucky. Real lucky. This case study is an anomaly. It's happened to me once, and with a short film at that. This is an example of a short film that was both a critical and financial success. It shouldn't be too hard to determine why this short film worked.

In 1977 Ernie Fosselius (writer/director/actor) and I (producer/cinematographer) made *Hardware Wars* which is a 13-minute short film parody of *Star Wars*. Our total budget was eight thousand dollars (yes, $8,000). We entered it in every festival we could and won 15 first-place awards.

Pyramid, a nontheatrical educational distributor, sold and rented 16mm film prints mostly to schools, libraries, and institutions. We received 25% of all sales and rentals, and then 30% when the gross surpassed $100,000. The film was also licensed to HBO, Showtime, and every other pay cable station imaginable; it was blown up to 35mm film and was shown in 50 theaters with *The Wilderness Family* in Australia! (Go figure.) We even had showings on the same screen as *The Empire Strikes Back*. We licensed MCA the videodisk rights and Warner Bros. Home Video the video rights. It showed on PBS, on ABC's Dick Clark's show, and we received a contract from NBC's "Saturday Night Live."

The film earned about $500,000 in the various markets, making it one of the highest grossing short films of all times. After distributor's fees and the recoupment of expenses we (Ernie, our investor, and I) split about $150,000; not bad for an $8,000 investment.

When George Lucas announced "The Force Is Back" and added new special digital effects to *Star Wars*, I announced that "The Farce Is Back," added some 20 new digital video effects, and rereleased *Hardware Wars — The Special Edition* in video packaging that parodies 20th Century Fox's campaign. However, by 1997, the market for the film had changed considerably. No longer was there an educational market nor do cable networks have slots for 13-minute shorts. Even video looked like a tough sale that we'd have to do ourselves.

Nevertheless we plowed ahead and assumed that there would be an audience for a cult classic that didn't run 60 minutes or even 30 minutes and that it was special enough that we could obtain a retail price of $9.95. Through a special promotion with Musicland, *Hardware Wars* was stacked alongside the *Star Wars* videos. We had reviews and special features in all the major *Star Wars* magazines and websites with news of our film. Princess Android resurfaced and did video signings at computer and comic book conventions. We held special event screenings of the original *Hardware Wars* and sold videos in the lobby. We focused on the *Star Wars, Star Trek* comic book and computer conventions. We got absolutely no coverage from *Variety, Hollywood Reporter,* or any of the trade magazines (except *Videography* but then I am a contributing editor for the magazine so that doesn't count). The video did reach #27 on *Video Business Magazine's* Best-Selling Video Charts above the original *Star Wars* for one week! Imagine that.

We act as our own distributor (which also means we pay for publicity, promotion, advertising, marketing, and duplication and take both the inventory risk and the risk of returns). As of this writing, the reissue (*Hardware Wars — The Special Edition)* has been out about 6 months and the wholesale video gross is over $200,000 making the accumulated gross since release around $700,000. Video sales are still going strong.

**Summary**

We were very fortunate to have a breakthrough situation for our little film which rode for two decades in the *Star Wars* slip stream. (Thank you, Mr. Lucas!) Whenever there was a new *Star Wars* our short would be remembered and sales would spike up again. *Star Wars* was our marketing campaign. We didn't know when we parodied *Star Wars* that it would become a worldwide phenomenon. "The Farce" was with us. (Free million dollar idea: *Titanic* anyone?)

You should not expect similar results. However, short filmmaking provides a wonderful opportunity to experiment, to tell short stories, and to actually accomplish the mission of making a film. It does not require the enormous resources of a feature and enables filmmakers to gain the necessary experience. An end result is a portolio piece that will help lead you to your next film. The real rewards are in the process of making the film itself and being responsible for every aspect. When it's finished you get to say, "We did that."

*HARDWARE WARS video box for the rerelease*

# SELF–DISTRIBUTION

## Why Self–Distribute?

When a filmmaker cannot find distribution for his or her film, "self-distribution" becomes the only available option. Some filmmakers are quite good at it. They make multiple copies of their film or video, package it, write press releases, flyer copy, and talk to the press. They are proactive and make numerous phone calls to associations, organizations, and film festivals that may be willing to screen their works. They become the spokespersons for their film and travel around the world ensuring that their work is seen. This is commitment! This is the filmmaker's job. If you think that making a film is simply the shooting and editing of it and that from that point on the film will take off in some magical way by itself, you are sadly mistaken.

So often producers complain about how distributors promote their films. Or that no distributor will even take their films. As they say, *If you want something done, then do it yourself.*

Self-distribution means that you distribute the film yourself. You order prints from the lab, place advertising, do promotion, book screenings, invoice customers, ship prints, maintain records, and so forth. In short, run a distribution business. If you are also trying to make films, then you've got a lot on your plate. But, if you can't find a distributor it may be the only way to go.

My approach to distribution has been to find the best distributor for each market and then let the distributor do the job he knows best. And rather than give all rights to one distributor, I have suggested that you find the most powerful distributor for each of the rights in the "pie." While it is a lot of work, it is not really self-distribution because you are not handling direct sales to each customer. You are putting together your own "consortium of distributors" that will market your film. They do the actual distribution. But, sometimes, you may wish to hold onto some rights and self–distribute.

Many independent films will not interest a traditional distributor. There may be many reasons for this, ranging from the subject matter being "too specialized" or difficult to market, to the film being inappropriately designed for a distributor's target audience.

Years ago, I made several films that did not find distributors or didn't like the deal. Since I wanted the films to be seen I had to self-distribute them. It was a lot of work, and every time I'd sit down to work on the next film I'd be interrupted by an order or an interview request. For most documentaries and experimental works, very little money is to be made through self-distribution. You'll be lucky enough to cover your expenses, let alone make money for new films. There is, however, great satisfaction from knowing who is watching your film throughout the country, and it feels good when you hear an audience somewhere liked your work.

Another reason for self-distributing may be that you know you have a large audience. You know who they are and how to get to them. You might have a video and (even though many distributors want to distribute it) you decide you want to market it yourself. Therefore, if (1) you want to expend the energy it will take, and (2) you think you could do a better job than a distributor, (3) you want to make more than what's left after a distributor deducts his fees, and (4) you want to determine your own destiny—then self-distribution might be the way to go.

## The Avenues of Self–Distribution

There are many areas where you could distribute your own work; it's just a matter of whether you have the time and money to treat this like the business that it is. Every area of distribution is a potential area for self-distribution. You could release your film theatrically by renting your own theater. You could make flyers and send them directly to the video stores, hoping for sales. You could use television, catalogs, mailers, and magazine advertising to sell copies of your video. You could seek out corporate buyers who may want your video as premium and buy thousands of copies. You could solicit PBS, the independent television stations, and cable broadcasters in the U. S. and abroad. You could sell stock footage from your film. The list goes on. You have to seriously ask yourself if this is the business you want to be in and something you will be managing five, ten, or twenty years from now because that's how long it will take to develop the necessary relationships, contacts, and experience to be successful. In the meantime, what happens to your producing career?

### 'Four-Walling' Theatrical Documentary Features

Very few theaters book documentary features. Those that do, show 35mm prints. To release *Dolphin* theatrically we "four-walled" a theater (that means that we rented the four walls of the theater). We paid a flat fee to rent the Palace of Fine Arts in San Francisco. While the San Francisco Film Festival is held here, it is not generally used throughout the year for film; therefore, ushers, stage lighting, a lighting man, projection equipment and projectionists were all extra. You can rent halls similar to this (and equip them with what you need) or you can rent theaters.

As a very rough rule, theater rental, including projectionist, for a commercial theater is about $2 per seat per day. But this rate will vary greatly depending on how busy the theater is, the time of year, location, and size of the theater. When you four-wall you pay all the costs, theater rental, advertising, etc. When you take this great risk you get all the ticket money. The theater keeps the money from the concession stand, which can be 30% of the gross ticket sales! (Some theaters claim they wouldn't exist at all without this income.)

To four-wall, you must be very certain your film will have an audience because it is a very expensive venture with high risk. The first week of advertising could cost $10,000, or much more, although once the film gets going and there is word of mouth the ad budget may be reduced.

Dolphin *1/4 page newspaper ad promoting five theaters.*

If you have a film that has an audience you might book a low–cost small theater and run the film for as many weeks as you can, relying on minimum advertising and maximum word of mouth. Spend six weeks or more publicizing your film in every way you can, with the reviews, articles, and interviews to appear a week before the film opens. If it is a good film and people talk about it, you can build a larger and larger audience.

If you are fortunate enough to find an exhibitor (theater operator) that thinks your film will draw, you may be able to work out a deal. When we four-walled the Palace of Fine Arts, we also booked four other theaters around the San Francisco Bay area to maximize on our advertising and publicity which included newspaper ads, newspaper and local magazine reviews and feature stories, radio interviews, television interviews, and extensive use of posters.

With repertory or art theaters you may negotiate their fee to be 35%-50% of the gross receipts. Often they will want a minimum guarantee to cover their "house nut," which are their basic overhead expenses. The theater provides the theater, projectionist, box office person, and sometimes minimal advertising (like inclusion of your film on their monthly calendar). You provide any other advertising such as newspaper ads. The more publicity you do, the larger percentage you are entitled to.

The best way to get an idea of what is involved is to play some "what if" games with budgets and projections. List your anticipated expenses and income before proceeding. You may find you do not have a large enough audience to pay back the distribution costs. Sometimes the numbers simply don't make sense and you are forced to abandon the project. Many times I discover ways of slimming down costs or increasing the potential market by adding some element to the project. It is valuable to do your own "paper study" before leaping in.

To self-distribute you will need capital over and above your production costs. If you are planning to self–distribute, you should include this in your prospectus as part of your business plan for production and distribution. With the high volume of movies coming from the studios and the independents, nowadays it will be very difficult to four–wall all but a few independent theaters. And the costs will be high. You may look to alternative venues such as community centers, churches, music clubs, etc., to "premiere" your home-grown independent movies. However, non-movie theaters are not only hard to equip for good picture projection and good sound quality, but people are unaccustomed to going to them to see movies. You should find a location that is both an acceptable "movie house" (after all you are showing a movie) and has the equipment to do so. You can also look to traditional theaters at strange hours when they normally do not show movies (e.g., before noon or after midnight). The Landmark Theaters in Los Angeles frequently show independent films (one-showing only) on Saturday mornings. Not the greatest slot, but these screenings will draw people interested in independent films. Midnight movies are another venue for the late–nighters. The scheduling of your film must also match your target audience's waking hours. Every now and then some independent successfully four-walls their theatrical film. But not often.

## Self–Distributing Video

Several years ago I interviewed and wrote about the Kantola brothers who are a focused and profitable small company that produce and distribute their own videos. Self-distribution has led their company to $3 million in sales. They've mastered the business and by studying what they've done, you can cull principles to apply to your own work.

With the plethora of low-cost production technologies available, there are a lot of producers who feel they could market and distribute their own programs. Everyone has thought of doing this at one time or another. You may have created something that no distributor will take, or feel that you could do a better job marketing your video title. Maybe you want to make more than the traditional video royalty.

For some, it's the right move. For others, the constant attention to customer service, marketing, promotion, duplication, and shipping may be enough to drive them right back onto location. For Kantola Productions, self–distribution was definitely the right move.

Steve and Rick Kantola formed the video production and marketing company that bears their name several years ago in San Francisco. As a two– (now seven–) person operation, they took destiny into their own hands and produced one video program followed by a line of them — creating a quiet but successful distribution company. How did they do it?

Here are some principles that may help you in your own distribution efforts. Think about whether or not this is a viable route for you.

*1. Start Small, Have a Strategy, and Bootstrap Your Way to Success.*

The Kantolas produced a video titled *Toastmasters Be Prepared to Speak*. Rick was the researcher/writer and worked with an organization known as Toastmasters to develop the script. Steve served as producer and is now marketer/distributor of this and an entire line of Toastmasters video programs. Toastmasters was not paid any fees during development or production. They do, however, now receive a royalty on tape sales. The Kantolas self-financed the $50,000 budget and worked with an experienced production team to produce the first half-hour program.

*2. Make the Owner of the Content and Core Audience Your Partner.*

The "how to" nature of learning how to speak in public is ideal for video because you can see how–and how not–to give a speech. It's informative, entertaining, and dramatic. Toastmasters had both the content and the core audience.

*3. Be Sure the Content Works Well in Video.*

Viewers go through every step of learning how to give a speech, from speech writing to practicing and delivering their words. The video is a comprehensive approach to the art of how to give a speech; this is a skill needed by almost every businessperson today.

*4. The More Needed the Skill or Information, the Greater the Market.*

The initial program was sold at $79.95 and sells today for $89.95 with a 32-page study guide. When the tape was first produced, there were only a few similar tapes on the market, and those had higher price points.

*5. Research Similar Titles–Look Before You Leap.*

Today there are several $29.95 "speech" tapes in the marketplace, but the producers have inappropriately selected consumer distribution. This is a very tough way to go because (1) there are many movie titles competing for shelf space, and (2) the producers must sell at a low price point when actually the market will bear a higher price. The consumer-oriented "speech" titles have had little success.

*6. When You Get a Hit, Create Sequels.*

Once it was clear that *Be Prepared to Speak* had found an audience, the Kantolas developed three new titles that could be marketed to the same buyers. These included *Be Prepared to Lead*, *Be Prepared to Sell*, and *Be Prepared for Meetings.*

*7. Pick the Right Channels of Distribution.*

Through Steve Kantola's efforts, 60,000 units of their program have been sold. And, as they get better at opening up channels of distribution, sales increase each year.

*8. Keep Working Your Title.*

Steve emphasized that they are "very careful" and "give full attention to all the details." He says, "When we started we were undercapitalized and had to be very careful. If we had started with all the money we needed, we probably would have made expensive mistakes early and been out of business today."

*9. Start Small Until You Learn the Business.*

The good news for producers, then, is that in most cases they have to start small. Lean and mean is a great teacher, because you must be innovative and employ low–cost guerrilla marketing techniques. You can't buy an ad in *People* magazine, so you have to get customers in clever and effective ways. The Kantolas started small, "in a low-profile office and without much of a phone system," and have built a very successful small business.

*10. Self-Distribution Means Do It Yourself.*

The two-person operation must go through all the steps from brochure design, copy writing, getting it printed, buying lists, and doing the mailings. (The Kantolas also hire graphic artists to tweak their designs and employ a mailing house in Oregon to do the mailings.)

*11. Hire Professional Help When Needed.*

They also do their own order fulfillment. When testing a mailer or sales offering, they may select as few as 2,500 names from four or five lists. Strangely enough, Steve says, "Tests do better than rollouts and no one knows exactly why." So even though you may identify a strong list, you may not get the exact percentage return as the test. Once the test is successful, then all the names from the list will be used. Lists that do not perform well will not be used any further.

*12. Tests–Walk Before You Run.*

Mailing pieces, in quantities of 10,000, may cost $1 each, or a total of $10,000. A 1% return would be 100 sales. For an $89 tape, the mailing would gross $8,900. A half-percent return would gross less than $4,500. Subtract other costs, such as duplicating, shipping and handling, overhead and program production, and you quickly see how little is left as "net profit." This emphasizes the importance of testing. The difference between the right list and the wrong list is the difference between success and failure.

As the business grows and you gain confidence in mailing hundreds of thousands of flyers at a time, the price for an eight-page color mailer can fall to 30 to 60 cents. Thus your cost per order will fall accordingly. A strong list and high volume mailer can increase your profit margin.

*13. Identify as Many Distribution Channels as Possible.*

Besides selling directly through the mail to individuals and corporate buyers, the Kantolas also sell through distributors—mostly catalogers

—who feature videos in their own direct-mail catalogs. The catalogs buy the videos at a 40% discount.

Self-distribution works best once you discover several different channels of distribution. You then begin to market to each, gaining larger and larger entry into those channels. Kantola Productions videos are sold through these channels: 20% through display ads; 10% through catalogs/distributors; and 10% through joint venture and newsletter.

*14. Know Your Buyer, and Market to That Buyer.*

It is important to identify your buyer and find ways to communicate directly and effectively to that buyer. The more you sell, the more you will come to know who the buyers are. And in doing that, you can refine the copy and design of your mail piece and improve your ability to communicate the benefits of your program. Kantola has found that his video buyers are both middle– and upper-level executives ("given the benefits, it's not an expensive product"), university professors, high school professors, or "anyone who teaches public speaking."

*15. Produce Programs That Have a Long Shelf Life.*

It's cheaper to work out your ideas on paper before you start shooting. Don't be seduced by ideas during your cappuccino rush. Wait. Think about the criteria of your product. Is it a short, fad-type subject that in two years will be of interest to no one? Or is it "evergreen," and will be used for a long time? If your subject is of general interest, all the better. If it has a prepromoted name, subject, or celebrity attached, all the better again. There is nothing wrong with producing a tape on a "hot" subject, but you must have a marketing and distributing channel that can get the "hot" tape out before it turns "cold."

In the Kantolas' case, they selected an "evergreen" subject that will be of interest all year long, for many years. Basically, the content (public speaking) is timeless. The only thing that may need to be updated from decade to decade is the clothes his subjects wear.

The secret to the whole operation, according to the Kantolas, is to stick to the basics. For them, that is (1) a name product (Toastmasters), (2) a title with great general interest, and (3) a low price point (in comparison to what a professional seminar consultant would cost).

### 16. Select a Marketing Partner.

Select a strategic marketing partner that can help you start off strongly. This partner may have access to content or proprietary information (for development into video) and to a mailing list, magazine, or newsletter to get to a large target market. "Toastmasters," says Steve, "is a great organization. They helped develop the program. They wanted the exposure, and it was a good thing for their 170,000 members. They helped us bring the video to the market in the beginning."

### 17. Build a Database of Your Buyers.

Building from a core audience, Kantola began developing a mailing list of individuals, educators, and businesses interested in his videos. As he developed new and similar titles, he could go back to his previous customers. He is always expanding his database. Now he sends out 1.5 million mailings per year. A 1% return would yield 15,000 orders or gross revenues of $1,335,000.

### 18. Develop Customer Loyalty.

Kantola has focused on the kind of information his customers want. Experience has taught him who his buyers are so that he can send his mailer to the right person in the corporation.

### 19. Master One Line Before Going On to Others.

From the experience of developing one successful line, Kantola has also produced four business training videos in cooperation with the Wharton School of the University of Pennsylvania. The Kantolas are applying what they've learned to new lines of video product. Kantola Productions is just one of many quiet success stories. Yours could be the next.

## Direct Mail

One way to sell your special interest video programs is through direct mail to targeted mailing lists. Sometimes you may have a program with a very specific audience where a mailing would generate a 5% return or better. Other times, no mailing list in the world is going to get to the audience you are trying to reach and therefore it will not be worth the time and money buying lists and testing.

The best place to research and test potential video buyers is through mailing lists. Remember, however, like the Kantolas, you need to have a price point high enough to justify this. Our consumer video, *Hardware Wars*, is simply not priced high enough ($9.95) to cover the mailing costs.

You will get many ideas about markets just by studying mailing lists. Each list gives the total number of names so you can determine how many potential buyers you may have. Even if you don't self-distribute your video, these lists will give you a sense of whether or not your video is marketable. It is a good idea to do this research prior to production and include it in your prospectus. The market potential (based on mailing list totals) for a video on working with handicapped children might look like this:

*End Users/Teachers*

| | |
|---|---:|
| Medical College Teachers-Senior College | 3,672 |
| Physical Therapy | 751 |
| Occupational Therapy | 410 |
| Nursing-Senior College-Dept Heads | 423 |
| Nursing-Junior College-Dept Heads | 472 |
| Special Education-Dept Heads | 2,399 |
| Intro to Learning Disabilities | 2,067 |
| The Disadvantaged Child | 1,596 |
| Introduction to Audiology | 909 |
| Speech Pathology | 1,151 |
| Speech & Hearing in Public Schools | 796 |
| Teacher Aid Education | 296 |
| Computers in Education | 792 |
| **Total** | **15,734** |

*Potential Buyers*

| | |
|---|---:|
| Libraries-Colleges | 2,948 |
| Audio-visual | 164 |
| Business | 947 |
| Medicine | 2,344 |
| Public Libraries | 8,798 |
| | |
| Elementary Institutions w/video | 6,392 |
| Regional Media Centers | 853 |
| | |
| Public Elementary Schools w/MediaCenters | 51,005 |
| Junior Highs w/Media Centers | 9,996 |
| High Schools w/Media Centers | 14,631 |
| Hospitals | 7,015 |
| Medical Schools | 53 |

Total 105,146

Some lists will look like better possibilities than others. This might be your "A list" from which you'd pick several categories and do test mailings to determine which would yield the best results. No sense sending out a huge number of solicitations only to find out that the list doesn't work. Wait for strong results, then remail to the entire list.

## Mailing List Sources

There are mailing list companies which sell every kind of list imaginable. For video sales, these business, health, and educational mailing lists are the most appropriate.

For educational institutions:

> CMG Information Services, 187 Ballardvale Street, Suite B110, P.O. Box 7000, Wilmington, MA 01887-7000. (800) 677-7959, FAX (508) 988-0046.

Market Data Retrieval, 16 Progress Dr., P.O. Box 2117, Shelton, CT 06484-1117. (203) 926-4800, FAX (203) 926-0784.

For organizations and individuals:

American Business Information (was formerly Zeller Letica)
15 East 26 Street, Suite 1711, New York, NY 10010
(212) 685-7512

Dunhill International List Co.
1951 NW 19th St., Boca Raton, FL 33431
(561) 347-0200 /or NY office at (212) 686-3700

Some mailing list firms also sell subscriber lists from magazines and journals which help you target interests even more.

## Video Catalogs

Another channel of distribution is through catalogs. Some are devoted entirely to video and others carry a wide range of products. PBS-type titles and documentaries can be found in these catalogs:

Signals/WGBH Educational Foundation, P.O. Box 64428, St. Paul, MN 55164-0428; phone (800) 669-9696 or fax (612) 659-4320.

Wireless, Minnesota Public Radio, P.O. Box 64422, St. Paul, MN 55164-0422; phone (800) 669-9999 or fax (612) 659-4320.

The Video Catalog, P.O. Box 64267, St. Paul, MN 55164-0428; phone (800) 733-2232 or fax (612) 659-4320.

You can contact them directly about whether or not they would be interested in carrying your title. It should have played on PBS, however, or is similar to that kind of programming. Terms are usually 50%-60% off retail. The producer supplies the fully packaged video. They will place your video in the catalog and send you orders as they receive them. Prices in catalogs are sometimes slightly higher than the normal retail. The cataloger wants to maximize profits for the precious space they are allocating to the video titles; that is, they prefer slightly higher prices for high quality titles (e.g., $14.95 rather than $9.95, or $39.95 rather than $29.95). Yes, it does cause some confusion in the marketplace, but some people would rather just buy the video when they see it in a catalog and not bother trying to find it or order it from a retail store.

You might also look through the book *Catalog of Catalogs*, which lists all kinds of catalogs. Pick the ones that might carry your special interest video title and contact them.

## Summary

Self–distribution to the theatrical market may be one of the hardest undertakings ever while self–distribution of your videos may be much more achievable, especially if it covers a topic where a high price point may be charged. The greatest thing about self-distribution is seeing and knowing that your work is getting out into the world. Beware, however, since it is a full–time job and your ability to produce may be severely hampered while you are launching your distribution business.

# MARKETING YOUR FILMS & VIDEOS

### The Marketing Food Chain

Every step of the filmmaking process involves marketing. Whether you like it or not, become conscious of this fact and then use your creative powers to enhance the possibilities for your film's success.

Here are the different groups to which you will need to market. Each requires a different presentation as each has different needs.

Marketing Your Idea and Yourself

1. A screenwriter (or book author)
2. A producer
3. A director
4. Actor(s)
5. Crew
6. Financiers
7. Bank
8. Completion Bond Company

Marketing the Finished Film

1. Distributors/Broadcasters
2. Exhibitors
3. Your target audience

You will communicate your vision to various constituencies to enroll their participation (as either co-contributors or viewers). You will know that you have to position your film differently for each group, appealing to their desires and needs. Marketing is being conscious of this process and acting intelligently to gain the results you need. Different people have different needs. Your job is to meet those needs to get participation and financing from these groups.

Stars

When you are trying to interest stars in your film, what are their needs? Most actors like parts which could win them an Oscar. Actors love to play crazies, famous historic figures, saints, martyrs, serial killers, and fish–out–of–water characters. They like roles that stand out and are memorable — where they can do something that they haven't done before. Does your script provide this opportunity?

Directors

Directors like dark, film noir, downbeat movies that could win them recognition and Oscars as well. They want to do films that will enhance their visibility and position in the world of filmmaking. They want far-out characters and exotic locations. Does your project provide this opportunity?

Distributors

Distributors like movies that are easy to market: buddy movies, romantic comedies, action adventures, and with highly sympathetic characters and "up" endings. They want movies with bankable actors and directors. They do not want the dark movies that the stars and directors want to make. If you have a dark drama with two guys, pitch it as a buddy-buddy movie. Use language that they understand. Be appropriate in your pitch to the buyers. Give them what they want to hear.

What you are trying to do is pull investors, stars, directors, and distributors together even though everyone has a different agenda and needs. Not impossible but you should know what you are getting yourself into and the differing needs that you will have to encounter.

In my seminars I have the attendees pitch their projects. We role-play. I play The Fat Man, a very busy rich guy with a short attention span who owns a chain of bowling alleys. He makes movies that make money. The seminar attendees pitch The Fat Man knowing that he is looking for commercial hooks.

For those attendees with documentaries, I am a program director at a large PBS station who buys programs for a documentary series. Sometimes I am a corporate sponsor who is pitched on underwriting a television program for PBS, or buying video premiums. The attendees learn to pitch according to the needs of the buyer.

## Who Is Your Target Audience?

Let's start with the last group, the audience. If you can clearly identify this group, you can easily work backwards. As you develop your ideas make sure that you know who your audience is. Too frequently producers say they are making something *for everyone*. What that really indicates is that they probably haven't thought very hard about their audience at all. You can't afford to market to everyone. One of the first questions distributors will ask is, *Who's your audience?*

Imagine yourself sitting around a campfire telling your story. Who are you talking to? That's your audience.

When you make a programming decision, you are making a marketing decision. Who are you telling your story to? From the answer, a distributor's marketing staff will know how to craft a campaign to appeal to that target audience. They will know what exhibitors to pitch and what theaters to book. They will know what media to buy to reach the targeted audience.

Whether I am executive–producing, producing, or directing, or whether I am creating a book or video, I always ask myself and collaborators, "Who are we making this for?" because that will determine the design of the program itself. It will determine your movie poster art and through what marketing channels the film will be introduced to your audience.

## Existing Distribution Channels

When you can identify your target audience, then you can determine how to use existing marketing and distribution channels to deliver your movie. This is the job of the distributor; however, the more you learn about marketing and distribution, the better you can craft your movie for success.

The trick is to marry your film or video with an existing distribution channel. It is risky to come out with a new product for a new audience because not only is the product (e.g., movie) untested but there may be no distribution channel for that movie. You cannot market a movie to an audience that you cannot reach.

For example, one of the PBS specials I produced was on adoption. There are 10 million people who want to adopt in the U. S. We made the show, it got good ratings, but then we found we could not find the audience for the home video. People who want to adopt do not belong to a club, subscribe to a specific magazine, or meet in the auditorium down the street. You can't find them, so you can't market to them.

If you have a very targeted audience, like people who own horses, and you are marketing a horse grooming video, you can readily reach them through horse magazines, horse shows, tack shops, and mailing lists. It's easy. Hence, the importance of knowing your target audience and matching it with existing distribution and marketing avenues.

The big question is, *Will your movie find its audience?* If you have made a genre film, that is, an easily recognizable and marketable genre (e.g., erotic thriller, horror, action adventure), then there are established ways (and distributors) to market these films to audiences. There are readily identifiable images and icons and ad copy that sell these films to audiences that can be reached through traditional methods (newspaper advertising, posters, reviews, etc.). If it's an offbeat drama, it's much harder.

The principle bears repeating. If you learn nothing else about marketing, know that <u>when you make a programming decision, you are making a marketing decision</u>.

## Market Research

It is critical to find out whether your ideas, once made into films, will have a market.

This is probably the most important but neglected aspect of the whole filmmaking process. For years I avoided studying marketing. I felt that by dealing with such commercial concerns I would somehow compromise my creative and artistic efforts. This was simply not the case. It is critical to find out whether your ideas, once made into films, will have a market. It is a matter of survival.

I guess I was afraid that I might find out (and later did) that many of my ideas were not in fact marketable. They were good ideas but too limited to have much of an audience. That's fine, but if you want to make those films it's best to raise the money through grants or contributions and not through investors who will expect to be paid back.

Once you get an idea for a film, research how the film will be used. What will be the most successful markets for your film or videotape idea? What similar films or videos have been made? Can you use these as models?

Try to answer these basic questions in depth. Then present your findings in your prospectus under "market research," "trend indicators," or "income projections." Without knowing answers to these questions, you are not only fooling yourself about your film or videotape's potential but you may be misleading your investors and collaborators as well.

*1. What, specifically, is the subject of the film?*

Once you have determined the purpose of your film, this question will be easily answered. While you are at it, you might brainstorm on

176

other related ideas around your main subject area. You may be surprised to find a wealth of other ideas, spin–offs or other media that you could produce at the same time, thus economizing and creating additional income through other sources. Perhaps your one idea will lead you to a series. In the end, you will need to clearly identify the primary subject of your film.

## 2. *What is the length of the film?*

The answer is not "as long as it wants to be." That is a fine way to make personal and artistic films but not media that someday will be bought and sold in commercial marketplaces. If, for example, you are making a television program, then you must stick to the standard times. If you don't, you'll surely come up with an unsalable "white elephant." Commercial prime time is different from non-prime time. A television half-hour could vary between 22 and 26 minutes. A PBS hour is 58 1/2 minutes. International television hours are different still. If you make a film with an unusual length you'll have great difficulty in selling it. You must adhere to the standards for your particular target markets. It's best to know your exact running time before scripting your project.

## 3. *What formats will be required?*

Should you shoot on film or video? If your film can compete in the marketplace and sustain a theatrical release (and you can afford it), then film is probably the way to go. If your markets are television and video, then you can shoot in video. Some filmmakers shoot in 16mm and blow it up to 35mm. Some filmmakers shoot in digital video and transfer it to film, or give it a Filmlook® to enhance their movie's salability. How sophisticated are your buyers and what image quality are they willing to accept? It may not be economical to shoot in film. This depends entirely on your distributor's expectations and what the market requires.

If you expect foreign distribution, then don't forget to make a "music and effects track" ("M and E" track).

*4. Who are the distributors that may potentially distribute your film?*

There are about 45 or 46 companies that release films. Some are micro-distributors and may only release one or two films. The audience for American independent films is expanding, particularly in television. There is great interest in American culture throughout the world.

Many of these distributors and other buyers are listed in the back of this book. This will give you a healthy start in exploring possibilities for your films and tapes, even if they are only in the idea stage.

You may find similar genre films or videos already in distribution. By identifying their distributors you may find a home for yours as well.

*5. What are the influences on the buyer?*

What will make your audience want to see your film or rent your video over other movies and videos? You need to be able to answer this question to determine how to compete in the marketplace. You will need to create feelings, expectations, and images for your potential audience to attract them to your movie. If they are only going to see one movie this weekend, and 20 are playing, why are they going to drive across town to see yours?

If you are selling information in a corporate training video, then price may be a factor. How can you increase the buyer's perception of the value of your video? (Recognizable names is one way.) It's wise to look into the markets you are interested in before leaping. Many small educational distributors are going out of business. The school and library market has dwindled and can no longer support many distributors. The corporate training market has its own needs.

Another influence on buyers is advertising and promotion. The more ways they come into contact with your program, the more likely they will buy (or rent) it, particularly if they derive some benefit or value (information, entertainment, etc.).

*6. Do you have any competitors? Who are they?*

If you are producing informational programming, who are your competitors? By going through distributor's catalogs you will find programs similar to yours. Don't despair. View these videos; they could be very different from yours. When you find a distributor that you think could market your program, call him up. Learn everything you can about his business. Act as if you are already producing your program. Most distributors aren't producers and will be glad to help you design new programs which they can distribute. Don't work in a vacuum. A distributor is closer to the market than you are. He can suggest ways to make your program more marketable before you spend money. Speak with foreign television distributors who can give you insight into the international market.

Listen closely to what the distributor says. The distributors know their markets. They know what sells and what doesn't. And since they may someday handle your film, they should be very willing to discuss your project with you. This free information can help you immeasurably in the planning stages. If you are afraid to explore these areas, you may limit your chances for success. This does not mean that you should go and tell everyone about your idea. Just the contrary. Keep your ideas and thoughts to yourself; don't dissipate your energy and focus. But what you can do is learn about marketing and establish valuable distribution contacts for later.

*7. What share of the market do you expect to reach? Of this market, how many do you expect to sell to? How will you reach them? What will it cost? Why will they buy?*

Is theatrical distribution a reality for your film? Really? Examine other independent films that made it to the big screen. Remember that of approximately 4,000 films that are made each year only about 400 are released theatrically. Will yours be one of them? Why? And if it will, do you think it will gross $1 million or $10 million at the box office? Why? If your film will only generate $1 million at the box office, then your budget should be adjusted accordingly. You should not overspend on your film unless you can demonstrate that the money will be returned from the various markets.

You will need to do your income projections and really determine what the real (not hoped–for) market for your film really is. If you are producing a video, the same exercise applies. How many videos do you think you can sell? To whom? Why?

8. *What is the retail price to the consumer? Is the program competitively priced?*

If you are producing a consumer home video, then you know that the sell-through prices are very low. It is not unusual to find movies and special interest videos priced between $6.95 and $19.95. Can you really make the numbers work at these low price points? Can you produce cheaply? Can you get distribution to sell enough copies to break even? To make a profit? These are hard questions that must be addressed with critical eyes. Don't gloss over this exercise in your passion to produce.

## Festival Strategies

The more you can glean from talking with and listening to distributors, the better your understanding will be of how exhibition and distribution work. It's not enough to know your own needs; you have to know a distributor's needs and whether or not your film can fill those needs.

Here are some strategies I picked up at an IFP (Independent Feature Project) panel held on November 17, 1997. You could learn similar things by attending these kind of events. Remember, you are hearing the opinions and the needs from distributors. You also have to read the subtext behind their words. Sometimes distributors on a panel will tell audiences what they think they want to hear. Distributors also want to dictate how films are presented to them. (For example, they say they would rather not get involved in bidding wars at Sundance and want to screen films before Sundance. No kidding! Eliminate the competition and not have to pay higher prices to acquire films.)

Two scenarios were discussed on the panel.

> Scenario #1: Create heat at Sundance, hold off showing your film to distributors. Sell to the highest bidder. (Common wisdom among filmmakers.) The counter argument:

> Scenario #2: Show your film to the distributors in advance. Go to Sundance with a distributor. Let them handle the publicity (which they'll do better than you) at Sundance. (This eliminates competitive bidding.)

A third scenario, hybrid strategy, that emerged in 1998: filmmakers have some screenings in Los Angeles and New York immediately prior to Sundance but do not make their deals until Sundance. Hopefully this will create some buzz, some advance offers and interest, and can raise the bidding at Sundance. Distributors try to see as many movies as possible before Sundance. If they can't see a film they think they may want, distributors may employ sneaky tactics by acquiring a script or querying a sound mixer (since people who do the postproduction see films first).

Most agreed that, in many ways, Sundance (or any festival, but particularly Sundance) is an awful environment to gauge your film. The audience is made up of industry-savvy, hip professionals whose tastes are not those of the general moviegoing public. Nevertheless, Sundance audiences love films and distributors use the "buzz" generated at the festival to select their films. They check the word of mouth on films, then get the candid opinions of reviewers and critics (because this will help or hurt their publicity efforts later). Distributors will, if they can, wait until a month or so after Sundance to buy films when the filmmaker is in the dumps and expectations have crashed. It's then that the distributor can make a better deal (e.g., pay less money) than in the heat of Sundance.

Tom Bernard, of Sony Pictures Classics, one of the top independent distributors, expressed a desire to hear from the filmmakers. *Come in and tell us about your movie. Set up a formal meeting. Don't just send it in. Why did you make it? What's it about? What were you trying to do?*

181

*Who it is for? Share with us how you can promote the movie. Don't screen it without being with it.* Others on the panel agreed and also said to have a producer's rep pitch your film to them. These distributors want all the help they can get to find marketing angles but when it comes to business they want to talk with the producer's rep and not emotional filmmakers.

Miramax sends an army of acquisition people to festivals. A phenomena, lovingly called "festival helium," sets in at festivals where there is a frenzy to acquire movies. These staffs hope to find the next hit movie. They buy as much as they can, only to realize back at corporate headquarters that they may have made a mistake when the marketing people cannot find a hook necessary to sell what they've bought. Or, as in the case with *House of Yes*, there was great festival buzz, the picture was bought, but then it got poor reviews and performed poorly (under $1 million at the box office).

Gramercy's president, Russell Schwartz, said when they go to Sundance they see four to seven movies. Most they've already seen in advance of Sundance. (Distributor mythmaking?)

What often happens is that filmmakers have very high expectations for their films. They've just finished a film (barely) and come to Sundance with a "wet print" fresh out of the lab. They haven't screened the film for an audience yet and they've built up all this hype. What often happens is that the film doesn't play as well with an audience as it could because it's the first showing, so the filmmaker hasn't really assessed what is and what isn't working with a real audience, nor has he had the opportunity to trim it down based on audience response. Sundance is not the place where you want to test the audience. It's not unusual for a first-time filmmaker whose work has been picked up by a distributor at Sundance to have to cut 5% to 20% of the film's running time because it isn't playing well.

Distributors don't like the film appearing in festivals everywhere because the film gets reviewed in the local papers. When the film is eventually released the newspaper will not run the review again. So too much prerelease exposure can hurt a film's publicity in the long run. Some distributors expressed the feeling that showing in too many festivals gives a film a "used goods" feel. If you are going to show at festivals, pick the ones that will give you the most industry exposure such as Sundance, Toronto, Berlin, Cannes, the AFI Festival, or the L.A. Film Festival in Los Angeles. (Smaller regional festivals are not advisable without a distributor, they say, because it dilutes publicity efforts later.) Others say that you should show wherever you have the opportunity to spread word of mouth without using up the precious ink of film reviews that you will need later. Some festivals have agreements with local newspapers not to run the reviews until a film's release.

Strand's copresident Marcus Hu said that since they are a small distribution company and cannot afford major advertising campaigns, they rely heavily upon publicity and critical reviews for the release of their films. They also have specialized in gay-oriented films to tap into a wide array of media contacts in the gay community.

Most distributors want to see finished films although a few uncompleted films—*El Mariachi, Clerks, Go Fish,* and *Brothers McMullen*—were sold in screenings and distributors put up the cash for completion. Sometimes filmmakers will negotiate music clearance fees but not pay them until they know they have a distributor. (From a negotiating point of view it's better to buy your music before you have a distributor as a distributor's name could easily raise the cost of the music.) You can get "festival waivers" for a small fee from record companies so that you can show your film with music although you haven't, as yet, licensed it for other media.

Bert Manzari, Executive VP of the Landmark Theater Chain (150 screens, mostly art house/independent theaters), said that his theaters will, a few times a year, hold screenings for filmmakers whose work has been overlooked by distributors. They don't do this more frequently because filmmakers usually haven't prepared the marketing materials (posters, ad slicks, trailers, etc.) that are necessary for a theatrical release.

He also said that there are about 600 solid art theaters in the U. S. that run independent feature films. For all movies, the top ten markets draw most of the theatrical revenues.

All the distributors emphasized that you need to know what you want from your film deal. What do you need? Naturally all filmmakers want as large an advance as possible, but it probably pays to think deeper than this. How can you use the release of your first film to get your second film off the ground? How can a distributor help you broaden your career? Will you go on a press tour with your film? Is that of value (or just a pain)?

*Release Strategies*

Distributors take six months to a year to launch a film. It is a large commitment on their part. Besides wanting a crate full of money you should tell your prospective distributor what kind of advertising (P & A) commitment you are looking for. Ask about the marketing strategy they plan to utilize. There are various release strategies. Here are two simple platform scenarios:

> #1: Platform in N.Y. and L.A. in week one, roll out to 10 other cities thereafter and see how the film does.

> #2: Platform in N.Y. and L.A. in week one, roll out to 20 theaters in week two, 40 theaters in week three, 250 in week four, and 400 in week five. (The *Trainspotting* model.)

The second requires a much larger advertising commitment than the first which is a "wait and see" strategy and to some degree makes good business sense. How can a distributor tell you what they will spend on your picture until it goes out in front of an audience? Good performance will motivate a distributor to capitalize on their investment and roll out a film to more and more theaters. Poor performance may send the film quickly back onto the shelf or into the ancillary markets.

It is to the distributor's advantage to release a film as widely as it possibly can. Most distributors have output deals with home video companies and pay cable broadcasters. The greater visibility the film receives in its theatrical launch, the greater the revenues from home video and pay TV to the distributor.

Filmmakers can study the different modes of operation among the different distribution companies to see if their film fits the release history of the company and if they have marketed similar films in the past successfully. Miramax, for example, markets "sex" in the selling of many of their movies. Try to meet the marketing people and see if your ideas are in sync.

While most of the independent distributors will not put money into your new or incomplete film, they also don't want you to sell off the home video rights. Naturally they want these rights to cushion their downside should the film not perform well theatrically, so they don't want you to come to them if you've sold off the home video rights. There is not enough upside in most films for just theatrical distribution alone. On the other hand, you have to raise the money for your movie however you can and that may mean selling off the home video rights.

*About Direct-to-Video Movies*

Foreign language and independent films direct-to-video sales have fallen off about 50% since 1995. The falloff has been even greater among direct-to-video action adventure films. What's happening is that the video store buyers are so inundated with product they can't possibly keep up with one film over another, so they tend to buy only those films that have performed well over $10 million in theatrical grosses. This cuts out most independently made films from the video store rental market. It's also a shelf-space issue. When you buy 50 copies of *Men in Black* there's not much room for the smaller movie.

*Director as Showman*

Many distributors look to the filmmaker to help with marketing a film. A filmmaker who is charismatic, charming, intelligent, and funny can do a great deal to explain the motivation for making the

185

movie to the press. If the filmmaker has an attitude, is rude, or shows up for interviews drunk and late, this will negatively influence the publicity the distributor is trying so desperately to get. Since most independent films have no stars, one of the few publicity hooks a distributor has is the filmmaker and his or her story. Keep this in mind as you develop your own "myth"; whether it is the Rodriquez (*I made my movie for $7,000*) or the Robert Townsend (*I made my movie on credit cards*) story, you'll need to find fresh ideas to help the press retell your story and promote your film. The *I made it for no money* is a tired and overworked approach. Don't use it. It is the filmmaker's job to help with the follow–through on the marketing of your film and to express to the world how you want the movie to be taken.

### What About a Hit Sound Track?

All the distributors agreed that the sound track music is wildly over-rated by filmmakers. A sound track album adds to the marketing value because now potential moviegoers may be exposed to the sound track album first, but it really isn't the reason people go to films. A good film attracts viewers. A bad film, no matter how great the score, doesn't.

### Misrepresentation

The distributors suggested that some independent filmmakers get upset when they see the marketing campaigns for their films and feel they misrepresent their films. What distributors do is deliberately exaggerate an aspect of the movie to draw in viewers. "That's why it's called marketing," one of the distributors quipped.

### More Notes

An audience member said that there seems to be a trend, at least at Sundance, toward the more provocative films and asked, "Is this what distributors need to sell a film?" The distributors answered that "Yes, controversy is always good and having a provocative film helps but not to the point where it may be a turn-off." One distributor said that filmmakers should concentrate on making emotionally involving films on whatever subject challenges them. Additionally, filmmakers should ask themselves, "Is there a bottom cap in terms of audience numbers for what you are distributing?" A film with gay sex, for example, might only have audiences in the top ten cities.

*Budgets*

One of the most recent independent hits was *Chasing Amy* which was made for $240,000 plus another $20,000 for music and finishing costs. It drew in $12 million at the box office.

There is no correlation between a film's budget and what a distributor will pay for a film (as an advance). A distributor only looks to answer the question, *Can I sell this film? And for how much?* It is irrelevant to the distributor what the film cost to make.

*Using Producers' Reps*

Independent producers' reps know the distributors, the financiers, and what films may be worth in the marketplace. They know who has deep pockets and who doesn't, who is facing bankruptcy and who has too much product. They can help steer a producer to a distributor and help make a deal. They take a percentage of the sale of the film which can range from 5% to 8%. It's all negotiable.

Producers' reps for independent films include:

| | |
|---|---|
| Ira Deutschman | 803-849-1174 |
| Jeff Dowd | 310-576-6655 |
| David Linde/Good Machine | 212-343-9230 |
| Arthur Manson | 212-832-2806 |
| Gary Meyers | 510-644-9131 |
| John Pierson | 914-424-4235 |

*Publicists*

Publicists may be another way to get to distributors. They know the distributors and have often worked for them. They may be able to help you submit your film.

## Who's Who Among Distributors?

Now that you have a general sense of the attitude of distributors of independent films, it is very useful to study who's who, what they've released, and what they are looking for. Each has its own individual tastes and marketing abilities. These are thumbnails of the distributors as of August 1997. You should update your own lists and do your own research.

### Gramercy
Owned by PolyGram Filmed Entertainment. They release many films from Working Title, Propaganda, Island Pictures, Def Pictures, Jodie Foster, Alan Parker, and Interscope Communications. Very stable company. Hits include *Fargo* and *Dead Man Walking*. Release around 17 films a year.

### Miramax
Owned by Disney. Also includes Dimensions Films (genre films). Large executive turnover. Release about 35-40 films per year. Release films with budget ranges from $300,000 to $15 million. Hits include *Cop Land*, *The English Patient*, *Trainspotting*, *Sling Blade*, and *Chasing Amy*.

### Dimension Films
Miramax genre label. Release about 7 films a year. Grows titles in house. Films include *Scream* and *The Crow*.

### New Line Cinema
Owned by Time Warner and is a division of Turner Broadcasting. Fine Line Features is the art-house label. Films include *Michael*, *A Thin Line Between Love and Hate*, *Set It Off*, *Rumble in the Bronx*, *Austin Powers*, *Boogie Nights*, and *One Night Stand*. Release about 14-16 films per year.

### Fine Line Features
Subsidiary of New Line. Release about 6-10 films per year. Budgets are in the under $5 million range. Films include *Shine*, *Crash*, *Gummo*, and *Deconstructing Harry*.

*Sony Pictures Classics*
Falls under the Sony Pictures Entertainment banner. Also acquires foreign rights for films which are distributed through Columbia Tri Star International. They release about 15 films a year. Films include *Lone Star, Welcome to the Dollhouse, Manny & Lo, SubUrbia, The Myth of Fingerprints, Fast, Cheap and Out of Control,* and *Men with Guns.*

*October Films*
Sold 51% of the company to Universal. Averages about 10 releases a year. Picks up films with budgets from $200,000 to $12 million. Films include *Secrets & Lies, Breaking the Waves, Lost Highway, Career Girls, Kicked in the Head,* and *Kiss or Kill.*

*Fox Searchlight Pictures*
Owned by 20th Century Fox and distributes and markets its own art-house fare. Releases about 10 films a year with about 3 or 4 as in-house productions with budgets between $3 million and $13 million. Outside acquisitions budgets range from $500,000 to $2 million. Releases include *She's the One, Smilla's Sense of Snow, Girl 6, Star Maps, The Full Monty,* and *The Ice Storm.*

*Artisan Entertainment (formerly Live Entertainment)*
A private company without studio ties. Releases 10-15 titles per year. Films include *Trees Lounge, Wishmaster, Critical Care,* and *Permanent Midnight.*

*First Look Pictures*
Parent company is Overseas Filmgroup, a global film distribution company. Releases 6 to 8 films per year. About 1/3 are acquired for U. S. distribution only, 1/3 for foreign sales, and 1/3 in which they invest in the production. Budgets range from $1 million to $6 million. Released *Antonia's Line* and *Mrs. Dalloway.*

*Trimark Pictures*
Once a home video company, it has recently shifted to

features. Releases 10 films a year with both acquisitions and productions in the $1 million to $12 million range. Released *Kama Sutra, Spring, Meet Wally Sparks, Eve's Bayou,* and *Blackout.*

*Metromedia Entertainment Group*
Acquired Orion Pictures and Goldwyn Entertainment. Released *Big Night* and *Rough Magic.* Releases about 15 films a year.

## Distributors by Market Share

It is also useful to get a big picture of the distributors' ranking among themselves. The big guys will release several films a month while the smaller ones may only release a few pictures a year. Here is the U. S. market share of box office from the top 11 U. S distributors in 1997:

| Company | Number of Films | % Market Share |
| --- | --- | --- |
| Sony | 37 | 20.3 |
| Buena Vista | 35 | 14.2 |
| Paramount | 29 | 12.3 |
| Warner Bros. | 28 | 10.8 |
| 20th Century Fox | 22 | 10.3 |
| Universal | 14 | 9.9 |
| Miramax | 34 | 6.8 |
| New Line | 31 | 6.0 |
| MGM/UA | 18 | 2.9 |
| DreamWorks SKG | 3 | 1.7 |
| Gramercy | 14 | 1.2 |

*Under $37 Million in Gross*

Metromedia Entertainment Group (Orion)
Sony Classics
Fox Searchlight
October
Metromedia Entertainment Group (Goldwyn)
First Look
Republic
Warren Miller Entertainment
Northern Lights Arts
Strand
Kit Parker

*Under $1 Million in Gross*

Zeitgeist
Legacy
Artificial Eye
Filmopolis
FM Entertainment
Manga
Discovery Channel Pictures
Seventh Art
Savoy
Gotham
Greycat Films
Concorde
Cabin Fever Entertainment
Arrow
In Pictures
GGT
Troma
Tara
Tree
Farm
Hemdale

## Overall Top-Ten Home Video Companies

The market share of video sales by the top 10 home video distributors for 1997:

|  | Market Share |
|---|---|
| Disney | 19.8 |
| Warner Home Video | 18.4 |
| Fox | 10.6 |
| Universal | 9.4 |
| Paramount | 9.1 |
| Columbia | 8.9 |
| Anchor Bay | 2.7 |
| Sony/Sony Wonder | 2.6 |
| Live Home Entertainment | 2.5 |
| Polygram Home Video | 2.0 |

Source: *Videoscan*

## Current Trend

The film business is cyclical in nature and changes over time. At present there are too many films in the marketplace competing for screens and screen time. Many more films are being produced and released by the majors which means fewer independent films are being picked up for theatrical release. A huge number of independent films (403) were represented at the 1997 IFFM (Independent Feature Film Market). Marketing costs (television and newspaper advertising particularly) are skyrocketing. Buyers are generally much more cautious. Like everything, this too will change.

After a big surge for the independents in 1996, in the first six months of 1997 independent films accounted for only 1.3% of the domestic box office, down 50% from each of the prior three years.

The two largest audiences are ages 15-25 and 40+ (baby boomers). Young audiences are looking for films which address their concerns of alienation, finding purpose and meaning in their lives. Baby boom audiences are looking for more adult-themed, intelligent fare.

International independent sales are surging due to the expansion of new theatrical and television markets worldwide.

## Film Festivals & Markets

Audiences come to film *festivals* to see new works. Filmmakers show their works at festivals because they want to have their films seen and reviewed. Distributors only attend a half-dozen key festivals. It is hard to get shown in a festival because they are competitive and few films are selected.

Film buyers and distributors come to film *markets* to buy the rights to new films for their own territories. Anyone can display their film in a film market. Filmmakers show their works at markets to find distributors and sell rights. It is not hard to get shown in a market: you pay your money, you get a suite and a screen.

Unfortunately though, it's not quite as clear as my description may indicate because some festivals are also markets where distributors come to buy films. A filmmaker must ask herself if she wants exposure or a distributor. The answer will indicate what strategy to employ and what film festivals or markets to attend.

Film festivals have grown considerably. It appears that almost every major city has a film festival. There are hundreds of festivals for films and videos. The best guide to festivals is The AIVF/FIVF Guide to International Film and Video Festivals.

In the early days when I made short films I entered every festival I could. Beware of entry fees; they can cost more than your film!

The good news is that your work is shown. The bad news is that may be the last time your film ever sees the light of a projector. Festivals do not necessarily bring you a distribution agreement although they could. That's the golden ring all independent filmmakers are looking to grab onto.

There has been so much publicity centered around the Sundance and Telluride Film Festivals that it would appear that all you have to do is enter your film and whammo, Miramax will be wining and dining you. Not so. The competition for screen time is fierce. Although many festivals have concurrent screens running with hundreds of slots, there will always be more films than there are slots. Over a thousand films are submitted to the most prestigious festivals; perhaps less than 10% are actually screened and less than 10% of those screened find distribution. It is not the best films, but the more marketable films, that find distribution.

Depending on when your film is finished, you should submit it to the most prestigious festival possible and hope for the best. Attend the festival if you can afford it and meet as many people as you can. For a few days you'll feel like a player mixing with other filmmakers, distributors, and reviewers. Be open and listen and the experience will be very rewarding. Understand, however, that your film may be seen by very few people, that distributors and reviewers may well walk out in the middle (to catch a few minutes of some other film), that the projection may be poor (out of focus, poor sound system, bad seating, etc.). You've now done all you can; you finished your film and took it to a festival. If you designed your film well and did everything you could to get the distributors and reviewers to see your film, then you've done your job. If you don't find distribution, at least you've learned something and can employ this experience in your next efforts.

For filmmakers of shorts, festivals are about the last bastion that will exhibit shorts. Festivals may be the last opportunity for audiences to see some very fine work and for short filmmakers to have the pleasure (or terror) of seeing their films with an audience.

When Steven Arnold and I finished our student film *Messages*, no theater in San Francisco would show it. I took it to New York where Salvador Dali held a premiere for me in the ballroom of the St. Regis Hotel. Back in San Francisco, we took matters into our hands and rented a theater for one night to show this 25–minute, black and white experimental film! Two thousand people showed up. As a result of that showing *Messages* was shown in the San Francisco International Film Festival and was seen by the director of the Cannes Film Festival who invited it there for Director's Fortnight, a prestigious, noncompetitive section of the festival. I was not able to attend so I have no idea of the response. By the time the film was shown we had a distribution contract with a nontheatrical distributor (which was extremely onerous. It was our first film. What did we know?).

*Hardware Wars*, a short film parody of *Star Wars* which I made with Ernie Fosselius in 1978, received over 15 first–place awards in film festivals. Festivals helped launch and sustain the reputation of the film which, to this day, generates revenues. Probably the most valuable festivals were those that were attended by media center buyers. When you win an award, lots of orders for copies of the film or video follow.

## Festival and Market Timetable

| | |
|---|---|
| Sundance Film Festival | Late Jan. |
| Slamdance Film Festival | Late Jan. |
| Rotterdam Intl. Film Festival | Late Jan. |
| Berlin Intl. Film Festival | Mid–Feb. |
| Cannes Intl. Film Festival | Mid–May |
| Telluride Film Festival | Early Dec. |
| Venice Film Festival | Late Aug.-Early Sept. |
| Toronto Intl. Film Festival | Early Sept. |
| N.Y. Underground Film Festival | Mid–March |
| Independent Feature Film Market | Mid–Sept. |
| Montreal World Film Festival | Late Aug. |
| New Directors/New Films | Late Mar.-Early April |
| Locarno Intl. Film Festival | Early Aug. |
| London Film Festival | Mid–Nov. |
| San Francisco Intl. Film Festival | Late April |
| Munich Film Festival | Late June |
| Seattle Intl. Film Festival | Mid–May |
| Deauville Festival of Amer. Films | Late Aug.-Early Sept. |
| Mill Valley Film Festival | Early Oct. |
| Natl. Educ. Media Competition | Late May |

The most prestigious festival is Sundance. Competition is heavy since this has become "the" festival for American independent films and is attended by studio and foreign buyers.

## Sundance Pickups

Here are the films that were bought at Sundance in 1997, their buyers, the price, and the rights acquired (if known).

| Film | Distributor | Price | Rights |
|---|---|---|---|
| Hurricane | Mayfair Entertainment Intl. | $ 1.0 | Intl. |
| Star Maps | Fox Searchlight | 2.5 | All rights |
| Going All The Way | Gramercy | ? | U.S. Rights |
| | Polygram | 1+ | U.K./Germany |

| | | | |
|---|---|---|---|
| *Box of Moonlight* | Trimark | 3 | U.S. rights |
| *Dream with Fishes* | Trimark Intl. | ? | Intl. x U.S. |
| *I Love You...* | Alliance Communications Corp. | ? | Intl. xU.S./Can. |
| *Don't Touch Me!* | Metromedia/Goldwyn | | |
| *In the Company* *of Men* | Alliance Communications Corp. | ? | World |
| *The Last Time* *I Committed Suicide* | Roxie Releasing | ? | U.S. |
| *House of Yes* | Miramax | 1.9 | U.S. |
| *Fast Cheap and* *Out of Control* | Sony Classics | | |
| *Dream with the Fishes* | Sony Classics | | |
| *When the Cat's Away* | Sony Classics | | |

1996 Sundance Pickups                    *Advance/ U.S. Box Office Gross*

| | | | |
|---|---|---|---|
| *The Spitfire Grill* | Columbia/Castle Rock | 10.0 | 12.4 |
| *Slingblade* | Miramax | 10.5 | .2 |
| *Swingers* | Miramax | 5.0 | 4.3 |
| *When We Were Kings* | Polygram | 3.0 | ? |
| *Big Night* | Goldwyn | | 11.3 |
| *Shine* | Fine Line Features | 2.5 | 10.6 |
| *Welcome to* *the Dollhouse* | Sony | | 4.5 |
| *Bound* | Gramercy | | 3.8 |
| *Angels & Insects* | Goldwyn | | 3.4 |
| *If Lucy Fell* | TriStar Pictures | | 2.4 |
| *I Shot* *Andy Warhol* | Goldwyn | | 1.8 |
| *The Celluloid Closet* | Sony Classics | | 1.4 |
| *Walking and Talking* | Miramax | 1.0 | 1.3 |
| *Looking for Richard* | Fox Searchlight | | 1.3 |
| *The Flower of* *My Secret* | Sony Classics | | 1.0 |
| *Manny & Lo* | Sony Classics | .75 | .5 |
| *All Over Me* | Fine Line | | .5 |
| *Lost Highway* | October | | 5.0 |

Previous Sundance Films

| Film   Intl. Sales/Distributor | | Intl. Gross | /Domestic Gross |
|---|---|---|---|
| Before Sunrise (1995) | Castle Rock International | 5.8 | 5.5 |
| The Brothers | | | |
| McMullen (1995) | Fox Searchlight | 9.1 | 10.2 |
| Clerks (1994) | Miramax International | 1.3 | 3.1 |
| Kids (1995) | Miramax International | 12.1 | 7.4 |
| Miami Rhapsody (1995) | Buena Vista Intl. | 5.0 | 5.2 |
| My Family (1995) | Majestic Films & TV | .4 | 11.1 |
| Reality Bites (1994) | UIP | 20.0 | 20.9 |
| The Usual Suspects (1995) | Polygram/Spelling | 43.6 | 22.5 |

Source: *Variety & Screen International*

Berlin is a monster festival, showing more than 400 films and attended by nearly 8,000 industry and press people.

The Independent Feature Film Market (IFFM) is the largest and most important American independent film festival with screenings of more than 400 features and documentaries. There are sidebar events for shorts, scripts, and works in progress. It is the festival for first features.

The New York Film Festival is held at the prestigious Lincoln Center. It shows only a few American films which means a review in the *New York Times* and lots of attention if your film is selected.

For independent features the top festivals are Telluride, Toronto, New York, and Sundance. This is where you want to be. If you aren't accepted you try the other festivals. Where you hop on the cycle is dependent on when you finish your film. You may submit an answer print and rough sound mix (often on VHS cassette) for entry purposes, but you should definitely have a finished film to show at a festival. Better to miss the festival than show an unfinished work that could get creamed by audiences and reviewers alike. You are only going to get one shot. Make it your best.

## Total Market for Independent Films

Independent English-language films collected a record–breaking $1.84 billion at the international box office in 1997 according to the American Film Marketing Associations (AFMA), and the number has been growing ever since reaching $1.656 billion in 1996.

*Total International Sales for Independent Films in 1997*

| | |
|---|---|
| Television | $ 798.7 |
| Video | 461.1 |
| Theatrical | <u>565.5</u> |

$ 1.84 billion

The reason continued to be the home video and television growth in international markets and new Eastern European markets. It is expected that 1998 will not see such stellar performances with the Asian markets in disarray.

## Summary

You are always marketing your idea, script, or finished film to someone and should give serious consideration to how to position, market, and publicize your script or film at every stage in its making.

This chapter encouraged you to know your target audience and focus on existing distribution channels for your films and videos. It is vital to find out the interests and needs of your intended audience or buyers. Learn everything you can about potential distributors before approaching them. Since most independent filmmakers use festivals as their primary marketing tool to distributors, you need to study what others have done and model your approach on their successes.

For every situation, have a clear understanding of who your audience or end user actually is. Producer Lynda Obst would say, "Have a purpose and agenda for every meeting. Know what you want."

# PROMOTION, PUBLICITY, & ADVERTISING

## What Are Your Hooks?

If you've followed some of the principles suggested in the early chapters of this book and brought prepromoted elements into your film's design, then you should have a number of publicity hooks already identified for your film. And having done so, you've probably thought of a lot of things you can do to promote your film once it is done.

If you've just gone out and made your film, then you may have to come up with marketing hooks. Find all the positive points of your film and bring them to the public's attention. Create a desire for people to see your film. Hopefully, your publicity and marketing plan are not something that just happens but, like the production of your film, is a carefully choreographed plan. Maybe a few big stories break and you get lucky. Most films will need all the help they can get in the very competitive marketplace. The more prepared you can be, the better your chances for success.

## Promotion and Publicity

Promotion is all the things that you do to generate publicity for your film. You do not pay directly for promotion as opposed to advertising which you do pay for.

Hyping a film before, during, and after production increases its value among distributors. Creating "the buzz" is an important aspect. The acquisition buyers at the distribution companies seek out films based on the buzz. The buzz is created by special screenings, one person telling another how great the film is, and carefully placed tidbits in newspapers and magazines. It is a delicate art. You want to get out there with your film but not so much that it's old news by the time your film is ready for release.

Promotion and movie marketing create word of mouth which is by far the most powerful of the persuasive mediums. Don't you go to see a movie based on the advice of a friend over reviews, ads, and television spots? That's the power of word of mouth. The more stories you can get in the trade papers, the greater awareness, the higher the fees which you can obtain from domestic and foreign markets. You are creating perceived value for your film or video. You need to develop an ongoing strategy for publicity and promotion.

An in-depth study of publicity is beyond the scope of this book, however. I recommend that you read the case study of *Dirty Dancing* in my book, *Film & Video Marketing*. Publicity and promotion are carefully designed and orchestrated so that there continues to be a build of press which crescendos just before the release date. While this is the job of your distributor, you need to promote and publicize your film to the trade before you even get a distributor. Here are just a few things that are commonly done:

*Preproduction*

In the early stages of your project, you will announce the book you have bought or the life story rights you have optioned. When the financing is in place, this becomes an announcement in the trades because now the film is real. Every name star that is cast becomes a press announcement. Promotion is part of your ongoing marketing campaign which starts with an early announcement in the "Films in Development" section of the *Hollywood Reporter* and continues throughout the domestic theatrical release, during the home video release, and again when the film is on television. The cycle is repeated overseas. You are always promoting your film. News and feature stories can come out announcing the film, the story, stars, director, producer, and location; they help elevate the film to the trade's and public's awareness. It is the publicist's job to come up with every conceivable angle on the film. Press releases are sent out on a regular basis. Interest will grow among distributors, exhibitors, and film buyers.

*Production*

Filmmakers overlook the value of promotion during production because they are so busy getting their films made. Hire a publicist or assign someone to oversee promotional activities while the film is being made. The day principal photography commences there are press announcements, and often magazine writers and TV interviewers are invited to the set. Your publicist handles these activities so that they will not disrupt the actual filming. Directors and producers have little patience as they are occupied with the real business at hand: making the movie. At the same time, everyone realizes the value of ongoing publicity.

Some films, like the *Star Wars* films, maintain great secrecy around production, while others are delighted to generate press over just about anything. Hopefully, there will be many interesting scenes, locations, and promotable hooks during production that can be exploited through magazine articles, photos, and interviews.

Most interviews will occur while the film is being edited. Since there is really not much news on the film during postproduction, the publicist can send out stills, bios, and press releases.

*Release*

When a distributor picks up the film, this is yet another press announcement. Once the release date of the film has been set, the publicist can schedule TV and radio interviews and magazine articles for specific times.

Promotion could be a tie-in with a fast food vendor when the film is released. It could be a tie-in with a theme park. A magazine. Your film's premiere could be a fund-raiser for a charity. Your video could be a premium (*free gift with purchase*) or bundled with another product. The objective of any promotion is to create awareness for your film or video. Get as creative as possible and see everything as an opportunity to promote your film.

Your distributor will spend a large amount of money for a major blitz of promotion, publicity, and advertising weeks before the film hits the theaters. This is a moment of greatest risk for the distributor because he may spend 70% of a movie's marketing dollars before the film proves itself in the marketplace. Scary. Very scary.

Often gimmicks are used to promote a film. One of the most talked about promotional gimmicks was a crystal ball that you turn over and snow falls, except this time the scene was the murder site in *Fargo*. It was sent to Academy members after the film was nominated for the Oscar. Sending a clever gift like this keeps the film fresh in the voters' minds. What can you do to keep your film fresh in the minds of buyers, the press, distributors, exhibitors, and all the people you will depend on to help launch your film? Good publicists (and producers) ask themselves this question every day. It could be something as simple as a postcard teaser announcing your film.

## Publicity

When I started making and promoting my first independent films in the early seventies, there really weren't that many films being made and so it was not terribly difficult to get press coverage. Today it seems everyone is making a film so it's harder to get publicity. The good news is that independent, specialized films get more press attention than ever. (Over 500 media journalists attend Sundance each year.) The bad news is that there are more independent films vying for attention, chasing too little print and television space. How will you position yourself and your film to attract publicity?

The major studios do major media blitzes and junkets for the press. It's the top stars that the journalists want to photograph and interview. This is not the case with many independent films since they do not have stars. However, those that do cover independent films usually write much lengthier, in-depth, face-to-face interviews and profiles. Many believe the *I made it against all the odds* kind of independent story is over, so look for other angles on which to build your story.

Promotion can make the difference between your film's being successful or not. It's not enough to have made an absolutely brilliant film. People must know that it exists. Without promotion, your film may not find its audience. And although it may be distasteful to many filmmakers, it is a job that must be done and done well. No promotion, no audience.

## Paid Advertising

Paid advertising applies primarily to newspaper ads which are placed in local papers during your showings. Some marketing strategists buy larger ads to get the reader's attention when the movie first opens. Once the public is aware of the film the ads can be reduced in size in the following weeks because, hopefully, word of mouth has started. Unfortunately, without a good-size opening ad the public will presume it's small potatoes. Studio advertising has set the precedent: bigger is better.

When we self-distributed *Dolphin* we were competing with full-page ads for James Bond in *Moonraker*. And, even with a 1/4–page ad in the Sunday entertainment section, 70% of our audiences came to the theater because they saw the ad. (How do we know this? We polled them at the theater.)

To buy advertising effectively you must know how your audience gets their information. Teenagers, for example, do not get their movie information from newspapers; adults do. Teenagers listen to radio, television, and surf the Internet. Your media advertising must be designed to reach specific audiences. There is no such thing as the "general public." Every film has its own audience and marketing plan based on the most promotable aspects of the film. A film can have a very broad or a very narrow market. Distributors select theaters by audience demographics. *The English Patient* would not play in the ghetto.

Study the marketing campaign, ads and publicity, for films similar to yours. Build on their successes and failures. Read through old issues of *Variety* to see what theaters have been selected for similar films. See if the box office was strong or weak. You will see that marketing films is a very calculated business. The more precise you can be in your marketing, the better chance you have of attracting an audience that will enjoy your film. If you attract the wrong audience or build expectations that cannot be met, you will create a "negative word of mouth" that will endanger your film's future.

Posters are also a form of paid advertising that, when well placed, will bring out an audience for particular kinds of films.

When designing either posters or newspaper ads it's important to select a log line, hook line, or single image that best represents your film. It could be a review quote. The graphics should be powerful and immediately recognizable. The copy should be inviting, exciting, and tease an audience into wanting to see the movie.

Hardware Wars
*a spectacular space saga
of romance, rebellion, and household appliances.*

If you have a sufficient advertising budget, you can make several different versions of ads and test them. Market researchers use "focus groups," a group of 12 people who reflect the interests and tastes of your target audience in age, income, education, sex, neighborhood, etc. The focus groups help determine which design to use for theater trailers, posters, ad copy, and even titles. You can do successful market research on a smaller scale and produce results that will benefit your film's marketing strategy. Why not do your own focus groups and test your title, trailer, and ad campaign with your target audience?

You are looking for a strong reason for people to want to see your film. You are looking to build an expectation or desire in your audience which your film will fulfill. You are trying to find the best way to communicate to your audience why they should see your film. All forms of media, radio and television spots, theater trailers, posters, or newspaper ads have this objective. They must give the audience a compelling reason for seeing your film.

Radio spots increase awareness but they are not effective for all films. Sometimes you can do promotions with rock stations: give them free movie tickets in exchange for on-air announcements. This is a no-cost way to get free publicity and advertising.

You can also produce radio spots to pitch your film. For example, if you're promoting a horror film you can use a scary, gravel-voiced announcer and blood-curdling screams. For a family film you can use a warm voice with a smile in it. For a comedy you might use actual dialogue comedic "bites" from the film itself. If you have a music or dance film, then you will certainly use the music and release what you believe will be the hit single six weeks before the film opens. Whatever you do, you must design your promotion to appeal to your target audience. Some films design different campaigns for different audiences: i.e., teenage girls, female adults. *Titanic* was sold as an event, as a love story and a special effects, action film. It has even reached cult status where numerous people are seeing the film over and over. Notice that they weren't shy about promoting their huge budget either.

A well-coordinated advertising and promotion campaign will take on an energy of its own. Add good word of mouth (which is impossible to buy) and you've got a successful campaign. As the word of mouth increases, the expensive forms of paid advertising may be reduced to increase profits. When you track the weekly grosses of movies notice which fall off quickly and which increase. You are seeing the power of word of mouth.

## Press Kits  Clip Reels/Electronic Press Kits

A studio will spend an enormous amount of money on thousands of press kits. These slick packages contain a dozen or more stills, biographies of the stars and director, feature stories, and story synopses.

Video press kits are sent to television shows and contain clips from the movie and behind-the-scenes interviews. Some studios even produce "Making of..."' featurettes that either play in their entirety on television or are edited by the TV shows to fit their own programming needs. Many films prepare video clip reels for the press which include scenes from the film. Frequently there are also interviews with stars, with the questions asked off-camera so that local television hosts can ask the question and go to a cutaway of the star answering the question. It looks like it was the local host's interview.

## Press Screenings

If you have a distributor, they will set up press screenings for your film. If you are self-distributing, you will try to get the press to come to your screening. Press screenings allow movie reviewers to see the film and hopefully write a good review the day before it officially opens. Obviously you will want the very best screening room you can find with excellent projection and sound, and comfortable seating. (Most cities have them for rent.) Publicity kits are handed out to the attending press. This screening should be the most pleasant showcase possible for your film. (It certainly doesn't hurt to provide the press with good coffee and Danish for a morning screening, and wine and cheese for an evening screening.) Sometimes several screenings must be scheduled, because the press inevitably won't show even when they say they will. It's best to call the most important reviewers and arrange a convenient screening time for them and then invite the "lesser" radio and TV critics, rather than book a time and then find the "heavies" cannot come.

## Summary

If you've thought about your film while you were conceiving it, you will have many ideas about how to publicize the film. You will have already added as many marketing hooks within the design of your film so that publicity, promotion, and paid advertising will have a synergetic effect, create multiple impressions, and bring people into the movie theaters with a great desire to see your film. More information creates more interest. That is the goal of publicity campaigns. While you're thinking about publicity, take out your yellow pad and write down all your inspirations for publicizing your film. You'll need all these hot ideas later.

# Financing Sources

## Financing

Financing your film is considered by many the most difficult aspect of filmmaking. No one likes to go out and ask for money, but if you are a filmmaker this will be a necessary part of your life and skill you must develop. Accept this, get on with it, get good at it.

Although financing can be very complex, it can also be simple and straightforward. In this section we will look at the complexity and wide range of financing sources. You will probably not use these sources for your first films. You will probably use a Limited Partnership which is described in the next section. If you want an overview of many financing forms read on. If you want to learn about how most first-time filmmakers finance their films, then skip to the next chapter.

This chapter will give you profiles on a wide variety of ways to finance your film or video project. It is far beyond the scope of this book to present in-depth coverage of each form but once you've identified a strategy that is appropriate for where you are in your filmmaking career, and identified a financial structure that is appropriate for your project, then you can discuss this structure idea with your entertainment attorney.

Certain aspects will be more useful than others. Seize those and make use of them. If you really want to make your project, and are smart and passionate about it, you'll get the money.

Filmmakers complain that there aren't any sources of money; however, attorney John Cones' book, *43 Ways to Finance Your Feature Film*, certainly breaks the scarcity myth. My own book, *Film & Video Financing*, goes into the subject much deeper than I am able to cover here. Media arts guru Morrie Warshawski's excellent special report, *Where's the Money?* (800-833-5738) covers how to get foundation and grant money.


## Industry Financing

Studio filmmaking is an insider's game. Yes, occasionally a Spike or Quentin becomes hot (by making one of those profitable outsider films) and then they can play with the big guys. Many other producers shuffle around the studios, spend years in development, and never get anything made.

Studios are in the business to make movies, so for many, this is the first stop on their hit list. Although for neophytes, let alone seasoned pros, it is a very tough pathway. You pitch your project to the studio (not as easy as it sounds because you must get in the door through an agent or through a relationship). If they like the idea, they will attach a writer (whom they approve) to write the script. You will do your best to stay "attached" to the project as some sort of producer. Eventually you hope to get bought off. (Is this filmmaking?)

Your entertainment attorney will try, as best she or he can, to protect your title (associate producer?), profit participation (yeah, right!), and compensation. You will pour thousands of dollars out in legal fees and hope that you can actually make a deal. It is not a game for the weak at heart and you'd better not quit your day job until you have a successful independently produced film to showcase your skills.

From this point, the studio and/or agency tries to attach actors and a director to the project. If they succeed in getting bankable actors, then the film may make it to production. At any number of milestones the studio can (and often does) pull the plug and the project is dead. It is hard to resurrect it anywhere else or even get the property back since the studio has paid for its development. If the film does get made, the studio will distribute and market the film as they see fit. If it fails its test screening or opens poorly, they will take it off the screens immediately to cut their losses.

Until you've demonstrated your ability to make commercial, studio-like films you will not be taken very seriously. The studios receive thousands of scripts a year (many from experienced producers), but only a few hundred go into development. Only a handful of these go into production. The odds are not in your favor. I would rather get something made — a book, a video, a low budget movie, or a one-act play — rather than be "in development" for years on something that never gets made.

For many beginning producers, this message will not get through. I heard a similar speech, but at 26 years old you just don't listen. I spent a few years running around to the studios with projects. Since no one wants to give you a no (because they think that someday you may be in a position of power), they keep the smiles going while never intending to produce your project. I thought I was really getting somewhere. After all, I was meeting with heads of studios, heads of production, and heads of the story departments. Very little money flowed into any of these projects. My options expired, I spent everything I'd earned, and had to abandon the projects.

I had what I thought were great projects but I really did not know (1) how to play the game, (2) how to develop the right relationships, and most important, (3) how to really have something commercial that the studios wanted. I also wanted to make films and not just sell ideas. I hadn't enough experience on the learning curve. My scripts had potential so no one wanted to say no: they wanted to see what else I could come up with. "I won't pay you, but I'll encourage" you drama can go on for years until you say, "No more!"

It is the producer's job to put together the package for the studio. It is not about how great your idea is; it is about how marketable your package is. The executives want to say yes to you. It is their job to find projects, but it is not their job to do the work until you bring them the salable elements. Put together a package that's hot and you'll get attention. This is a path that very few readers of this book will follow.

## Independent Producer Production-Financing Deal

In this scenario the producer comes to the studio (or distributor) with a finished script and package. It is highly commercial. It is not a low–budget art film. The producer is not looking for development money. The package consists of a script, a budget, a schedule, and commitments from stars and a director. The studio or a distributor likes the package and wishes to produce the film so they sign a pro-duction/financing/distribution agreement with the producer. The studio acts like a bank and loans the money to the producer. The studio will demand and have approval over the script contents, budget, producer, director, actors, start date, total running time, rating, etc. The film will be owned by the studio.

Different from the development deal, the producer will receive a higher fee because more work and money went into developing the script, preparing a budget, and attaching talent. And the producer is bringing a much more tangible asset as opposed to an idea or just a script. There is still the problem of creative control. In most situa-tions the Golden Rule (my father's favorite saying) applies: He who has the gold makes the rules. If a studio puts up the money, they will vote. In addition, there is the problem of creative accounting. It is very unlikely that the picture, even if it makes a lot of money, will ever be "profitable" by studio accounting practices, and therefore the pro-ducer will never see any profits. (Attorney John Cones says film audi-tors report that only about 5% of profit participants see any money from net proceeds from major/studio films!) "Net profits" are mean-ingless in a Hollywood contract. That is why the bankable stars insist on "gross participation" definitions in their contracts.

It is highly unlikely that any first–time producers would have the clout and resources to develop a script and assemble actors and a director that a studio would approve. The career pathway described above is a fairy tale for most independent filmmakers. (Read Lynda Obst's *Hello, He Lied* and Julia Phillips' *You'll Never Eat Lunch in This Town Again* for a real gritty eye–opening experience in the studio producer's game.)

## Independent Distribution Financing

Besides the 15 to 25 films that each studio releases a year, there are hundreds of films released by the smaller, independent, non-studio-related distributors. These include New Line (owned by Turner), First Run, Concorde, Miramax (now owned by Disney), and numerous others.

Many of these smaller distributors are unable to obtain screen time in the U. S. for their genre, art, and exploitation films so they rely on foreign distribution in all media to recoup their investment. Most do not fully finance films but they may cofinance low budget films for the rights to the film in certain territories. A producer will then have to find about 50% of his or her financing from other sources. Few of these companies are large enough so that a bank will lend money against a "negative pickup" deal (which we'll discuss in a moment).

These smaller independent distributors are clearly more suitable for small, low–budget films than a major because the distributor, having fewer pictures to release, will give it more attention and also have the marketing know-how for a specialty film. A distribution deal with an independent distributor might also be less onerous than in dealing with a studio; however, the ability of the small distributor to collect revenues from the theaters is considerably less than that of a studio. Independent distributors generally only have about a 5% to 10% market share of box office revenues.

This is the route for many independent producers.

## Loans/Banks

Films are frequently financed through bank loans. (Studio deals are structured very much like bank loans with very high interest. Hence the difficulties in ever seeing any net profits.)

The good news about loans is that they generally do not include equity participation. You borrow the money. You pay it back. The bank does not share in the net profits generated by the film. Nor does that bank have any creative control in the film being made. Banks will always want some kind of collateral either in the form of tangible property or, in the case of a film, the film itself and all its rights. The bad news is that loans are not investments and have to be paid back. If your distributor (in a presale situation) defaults, you are left holding the bag and your film and personal assets may be at risk.

In a presale or negative pickup agreement a distributor agrees to distribute the film. (I'll pay you x dollars when you deliver the film.) You get a contract which you take to the bank to get a loan. The bank may or may not also require repayment from the signer of the loan as well. The money the bank loans will be discounted, or less than what the distributor agrees to pay upon delivery.

Bank rates and terms will vary. Here are some banks that do motion picture financing.

| | |
|---|---|
| American Film Services | (310) 472-5858 |
| Bank of America | (213) 312-9000 |
| Bank of California, L.A. | (213) 243-3000 |
| Bank of New York | (310) 996-8650 |
| Banque Paris | (310) 551-7314* |
| Chase Securities | (310) 788-5600 |
| City National Bank | (310) 888-6209* |
| Comerica Bank California | (310) 824-5700* |
| Daiwa Banks, L.A.* | (213) 623-0060 |
| Film Finances | (310) 275-7323 |
| Films (Guernsey) Ltd. | 011-44-171-434-0340 |
| The Films Group | 44-171-434-0340 |
| Fuji Bank, L.A.* | (213) 680-9855 |
| Guinness Mahon | 011-44-171-623-9333 |
| Imperial Bank | (310) 281-2400* |
| Lewis Horwitz Organization | (310) 275-7171* |
| Merchantile National Bank | (310) 282-6708 |
| Natwest Markets/Coutts & Co. | (213) 624-8555 |

| | |
|---|---|
| Newmarket Capital Group | (310) 858-7472 |
| Silicon Valley Bank | (310) 786-8640 |
| Stone Canyon Investments | (310) 553-7920 |
| Sumitomo Bank | (213) 623-6832 |
| Union Bank, L.A.* | (213) 972-5200 |
| Yasuda Trust & Banking, L.A.* | (213) 243-1850 |

Most of motion picture lending banks are in California, New York, or London. Those marked with an asterisk (*) will do "single picture" financing. You can contact the officers of the entertainment divisions at any of these banks and ask for more information.

Here is a list of what you'll need to have before a bank will consider loaning you money.

**Required Documents**

> Budget
> Cash flow details
> Script and synopsis
> Completion guarantee
> Production insurance
> Service agreement with the producer, director, and principal cast
> Distribution agreement(s)
> Summary sheet which should include:
>> Project title
>> Writer
>> Principal Actors
>> Director
>> Producer
>> Completion guarantor
>> Sales agent
>> Legal representation
>> Details on borrowing entity, usually a single purpose nominally capitalized company (limited partnership, corporation, limited liability companies, etc.)

Additional Documents That Will Also Help

E&O (errors and omissions) insurance
Chain of title documents
Sales agent agreement
Assignment of copyright
Corporate documents including board of resolutions approving execution of the loan agreement, certified memorandum articles of association/by laws, certificate of good standing, certified certificate of incorporation
Laboratory pledge holder's agreement
SAG subordination agreements
Cross-collateralization agreement
Production timetable
Drawdown schedule
Presales estimate sheet
Copies of all contracts/deal memos/agreements
Biographies for actors/director/producers


## Completion Bond

A bank or a lender will usually require a completion bond which is like an insurance policy on your film's completion. If you run out of money, the completion bond (insurance company) will cover the overages but also may take over control of actually completing your film. The cost for a completion bond is high (about 3%-6% of the budget) plus you must add a 10% contingency to your budget.

Think of the completion bond company as an insurance company that guarantees to your bank, distributor and/or investors that you will not go over budget, and if you do, they will take care of any overages. If I was an investor, I'd want to see that the producer had a completion bond on the film. On the other hand, if you are making a film under $1.2 million you may not be able to get a bond.

When you have a completion bond, you will also have a "bond man" or production manager from the bond company assigned to your film.

The bond man will work with you during preproduction and go over every deal you make with talent, crew, licenses, and insurance to assure that you stay on budget. These are very savvy guys. They know what things should cost and there's no monkey business with your budgets. If you start to get into trouble they will first warn the director that "No, you can't do six shots of this scene, you are going to have to do it in two setups." They don't care about artistry, they only care that the picture gets finished on budget. If the director is not able to bring the picture back on schedule, which they will monitor through daily reports, the director will be replaced and the picture will be finished by the completion bond company. Not a pretty picture. In the movie business, having a completion bond take over your picture is a black mark on the reputation of the producer, line producer, director, and others.

Here are the documents that you will need to obtain a completion bond:

For the Preliminary Requirements-Production Analysis

> Shooting script
> Detailed production budget
> Shooting schedule w/boards
> Resumes of key personnel (Producer, Line Producer, UPM, Production Accountant, Director, AD)

> Balance of Requirements — Documents Analysis
> Projected cash flow schedule
> Rights and underlying rights agreements in regard to the script and copyright reports and screenwriter's agreement
> Director's agreement between the production company and the director
> Key crew agreements
> Production agreement, financing agreement, distribution agreements
> Evidence of insurance coverage which includes guarantor as an additional loss Payee/Named insured

    Principal artists contracts
    Postproduction schedule (as soon as possible, but no later
    than two weeks before the end of principal photography)
    Location agreements
    Music agreements
    Sound laboratory agreements
    Film laboratory agreements
    Special effects agreements (if any)
    Other applicable agreements

The two primary completion bond companies in Los Angeles are Film Finances, Inc. (310) 275-7323, and International Film Guarantors (310) 208-4500.

## Negative Pickup

Negative pickup refers to a contractual agreement by a distributor (foreign or domestic) with a producer to license his film for a specific price when the film is completed. Many distributors will ask for all rights, foreign and domestic, in their negative pickup contracts. The contracts are usually very tightly woven so that the distributor gets the picture he thought he was getting. For example, they will demand that there be no changes in principal cast, director, key production people, production technical quality, maximum running time, rating, or any deviations from the script. Some of the contractual clauses put forth by the distributor, such as script deviations and a film with a specific running time, put additional creative limitations on the director. (The producer should be as diligent as possible in removing as many of the distributor's possible outs or contingencies for refusing the film after it is finished. The more "out clauses" that are deleted by the producer's lawyer, the easier it will be to find a lender.)

The negative pickup contract is taken to a bank (mostly New York- or Los Angeles-based) or lender and it is discounted so that the producer receives perhaps 70% of the negative pickup license fee. If the price is $1 million dollars, the bank may loan $700,000 which may be used for the production of the film. The bank will have legal fees and points as well as interest that it will charge for the loan. Producers need to discuss the procedure and fees involved with their banks so they can anticipate how much money they will need to raise to make their film. (This should include the cost of a completion bond as well.) The negative pickup is a form of presale.

If you are producing a low budget film, you may not be able to get a completion bond because of the highly perceived risk by completion bond companies of low budget films. Perhaps 30% of the major studios' films are made through negative pickup deals.

While you may not be able to raise all the money you need from a bank loan through a negative pickup deal, you are in a much better position to be able to obtain the rest of your money from investors because not only do you have most of the money needed, you also have a distributor willing to pay a licensing fee and distribute the film.

There are many variables in a negative pickup deal. The distributor has less risk than developing a script which may or may not turn out well. In a negative pickup deal he doesn't have to pay until he sees the final film and it meets his requirements. A producer may or may not get a cash advance upon signing. A producer may or may not get an advance on delivery of the film (some negative pickups are only for distribution and do not include a license fee). The producer may or may not get a minimum guarantee license fee from the distributor nor participation in the revenues from distribution.

Since the negative pickup license fee is usually based on what the film actually costs (unless there is great competition for the film script), the producer has to look to sell other rights or territories after the film is finished to generate profits. Or, as some advise, do not tell your distributor the actual budget of the film but rather say, it's under a million, under $10 million, under $20 million, when it might actually be $400,000, $7 million, or $14 million. I am not sure how practical this is because the distributor, the bank, and the completion bond company all want to see your budget if you expect a deal. If you have finished your film through independent financing then there is no reason why you have to reveal your budget. In fact, you probably should not. Hopefully it will look like it cost more than it did and you will receive a higher licensing fee.

The point that should be emerging by now is that the "money talks." The more financing you can obtain independently, the better deal you should be able to obtain from distributors. When you ask for money from a distributor or through foreign presales (which we'll discuss later), you are giving up some of your upside because you are asking someone else to risk his cash. Whoever takes the risk expects to be rewarded. Distributors will also try to obtain as many rights (theatrical, home video, television, both foreign and domestic) as possible to "compensate their risk"; however, if a producer gives away too much, there will be no upside left, and possibly no remuneration other than his production fee.

It is usually very hard for producers to hold onto additional rights unless they have some leverage such as a hot property, actor, lawyer, or all of the above in their corner. Distributors will try to get as much as they can for as little as they can. A distributor is not at risk in a negative pickup situation. If the film isn't delivered, it's not the distributor that has to repay the bank or deal with the completion bond company. The distributor can walk away with no financial liability. Meanwhile, it's disaster for the producer. If the film is finished, and the distributor decides he doesn't want it and finds some "out clause" (e.g., the picture deviated from the script), he can walk away. Distributors do not care whether producers go broke making their pictures. A good lawyer experienced with negative pickups is required for these deals. It's even better if you can find a lawyer who has done negative pickups before with the same distributors as he will be familiar with their contract, their reputation in these matters, and their negotiating style.

Obtaining domestic (U. S.) distribution is key to getting foreign distribution in place as well. It is often the milestone for many foreign deals. (If it played in the States, we want it.) Since most independently financed films do not get domestic distribution, most producers sleep better at night knowing the film they are about to produce will actually be distributed. However, they also know that by entering into a negative pickup deal they are giving up most of the financial upside in the domestic rights (theatrical, home video, television) to the distributor. But the film gets paid for and is distributed. This makes most producers happy since they will not have to chase private investors for financing.

A negative pickup deal is unobtainable unless the film is substantially well packaged (actors, director, script, etc.). Once again, the marketing elements included in the package are key to getting this kind of deal. Distributors only want to obtain films that they believe are marketable.

Negative pickups are probably outside the realm of most new independent filmmakers.

## Presales

Presales are the licensing of rights in a film by the producer to a distributor in a specific territory (Japan, South America, etc.) and for a specific media (theatrical, home video, television) before the film is finished. They are similar to a negative pickup. A reputable foreign distributor, known to a bank, gives the producer a contract which is bankable. Or a presale agreement may involve a cash payment by a film distributor, television buyer, or a video distributor.

Some rules

Rule #1: Foreign buyers only want to buy films that will have a U.S. theatrical release. Why? Because of the publicity value, plus the attitude, why should we buy it if you can't even sell it in your own country?

Rule #2: If the film is salable in their territories, foreign buyers don't care if it doesn't have a U.S. release. A contradiction? Yes. Both are true. It depends on the film and on market conditions. In your discussions with presales agents you will hear both rules and get very confused.

If you can raise your money entirely from foreign presales and hold off on selling the domestic rights, so goes the common wisdom, you are in a much better position to get a higher price from a U.S. theatrical distributor if he wants your film. So some producers try to finance their films through foreign presales without a U.S. release in place hoping for a big domestic sale after the film has premiered in Sundance, Cannes, or Toronto.

Only about 15% of U. S. released films utilize foreign presales. One reason is loss of upside. The more you need to raise from distributors prior to finishing your film, the more upside you give away. Presales buyers are buying something before it's made and in doing so offer less money for something unseen. However, producers need a presale commitment to raise the money from a bank to make their movies. In taking the money, they give away the upside margin to the buyer. Producers may have to sell all the foreign and U. S. rights in their film to cover their budget and may see no revenues beyond the presale.

Presales are a form of "split-rights" deal strategy. That is, the rights are split between U. S. domestic and foreign. A producer splits the territorial rights between U.S. and foreign and first tries to obtain a distribution deal for the U. S. Once done, he sees how much of his budget he still has to cover; then he makes his foreign rights sales make up the difference. Hopefully there will still be some unsold territories that he can sell (for a higher price) when the film is finished. That's the upside. Perhaps the producer sells the U. K. and Japan rights to cover his budget. He makes his film. All other world territories he can sell when the film is finished and possibly make more than if he presold it.

## Getting Foreign Sales Agents

To sell foreign rights, the producer contracts with a foreign sales agent who knows the foreign markets and can negotiate on behalf of the producer and his film package. The sales agent may get a 10%-25% cash deposit when he makes a presale deal plus a minimum guarantee when the film is delivered. He will also get a letter of credit from the distributor which the producer can take to a bank for a loan against the distributor's guarantee. Banks will only make loans on contract from credible distributors. A presale arrangement with a nonbankable distributor does not give you the cash you need to make the picture because no bank will honor their contract. In a worst–case situation, a bank gives you a loan based on a distribution contract. By the time you make your picture the distributor goes bust, there is no cash on delivery, but you still have to repay the bank loan. Banks obviously don't like to be in this position and are justifiably cautious. Other groups have appeared that will loan the money on nonbankable distributors, but they will want equity in the film's profits for taking the risk which is exactly what the producer has been trying to avoid by getting bank loans that have no profit participation strings attached.

Sales agents will receive a 10%-25% fee for obtaining distribution contracts only and as much as 30% to 35% when they secure a cash advance, bankable contract, and letter of credit from distributors.

Discuss your project with a foreign sales agent as soon as possible because he will be aware of trends in the marketplace. These agents are especially savvy about actors that bring value in the foreign territories. They cannot sell anything until your package is contractually locked in place, but early conversations can be very beneficial in getting you to think about packaging for the world market. Not all genres travel. Comedy is far more difficult than action-adventure which is considered a universal genre. (The less dialogue the better.) The writer, producer, director, and script are the marketable elements for the sales agent. Hopefully, your creative team has made successful commercial films in the past. The foreign sales agent cannot successfully sell your project unless there is a finished script and committed actors, which might mean a "pay or play" contract is in place. If the picture doesn't proceed, the actors still get paid.

The sales agent will need sales materials such as posters or key art work, stills of the actors, a synopsis and script, background information on all the principals, letters of commitment, budget, and any and all other information that will help entice a foreign buyer in committing to the film. All the selling materials that you provide prior to production as well as after postproduction should be included in your budget, such as M & E (music and effects) tracks, and E & O (errors and omissions) insurance. This can cost as much as $50,000 or more.

A film's revenue may be equally divided between U. S sales and foreign sales, so presale deals may bring in a significant amount, if not all, of your film's production budget. The largest markets are Japan, France, Germany, the U. K., Australia, Spain, Italy, and Sweden. These territories account for about 85% of the average film's revenues. Depending on your budget and your expected revenues from each country, a financing strategy starts to emerge. You try to sell off the least valuable countries first (where your upside potential is limited) and not presell those territories that have the most value. By doing this, you reserve the potential of greater profits. On the other hand, look at the odds—very few films make a profit for the producer.

If your expected revenue is close to your production budget (I hope it's much more!), then you will have to sell every country just to finance your film. If you can, look at your project objectively and really see if it's got widespread commercial appeal. If it doesn't, presell whatever territories you can and don't expect future revenues. Make your film, take your fee, and if there's money left over, there's your profit. End of story.

Making your film through presales takes the producer out of the committee process of the studio and away from many of the bureaucratic restraints. The bank or financial lender will still want the producer to have a completion bond. Do not think that by preselling rights you will have a bag full of money and carte blanche creative control.

## FOREIGN PRESALES MINIMUM ESTIMATES

$3 million budget

| Territory | Asking Price | Gap Basis Non-Presale | PreSale Expected |
|---|---|---|---|
| **Eng. Speaking** | | | |
| United States | 1,125,000 | 600,000 | |
| Eng. Canada | w/US | w/US | |
| Fr. Canada | 35,000 | 22,500 | |
| UK | 490,000 | 175,000 | |
| | | | |
| **Australia. N.Z.** | 175,000 | | 105,000 |
| South Africa | 75,000 | 28,000 | |
| East Africa | | 1,000 | |
| West Africa | | 1,000 | |
| West Indies | | 1,000 | |
| | | | |
| **Europe** | | | |
| Germany/Austria | 750,000 | | 425,000 |
| France | 300,000 | | 190,000 |
| Italy | 265,000 | | 165,000 |
| Spain | 225,000 | | 130,000 |
| D. Benelux | 112,500 | | 52,500 |
| Fr. Belgium/Switz. | 22,500 | 7,000 | |
| Scandinavia | 245,000 | 150,000 | |
| Portugal | 37,500 | | 17,500 |
| Greece | 15,000 | 7,500 | |
| | | | |
| **Far East** | | | |
| Japan | 750,000 | | 375,000 |
| Korea | 550,000 | | 337,500 |
| Taiwan | 75,000 | | 45,000 |
| Singapore | 37,500 | 15,000 | |
| Malaysia | 30,000 | 15,000 | |
| Indonesia | 50,000 | 30,000 | |
| Phillipines | 30,000 | 5,000 | |

| | | | |
|---|---|---|---|
| Phillipines | 30,000 | 15,000 | |
| Thailand | 30,000 | 15,000 | |
| India | 30,000 | 10,000 | |
| Pakistan | 12,000 | 5,000 | |
| China | 15,000 | 5,000 | |
| Vietnam | 3,000 | 1,000 | |
| | | | |
| **Arg./Par./Uru.** | 75,000 | | 37,500 |
| Brazil | 187,500 | | 112,500 |
| Mexico | 75,000 | | 37,500 |
| Chile | 40,000 | 20,000 | |
| Columbia | 25,000 | 15,000 | |
| Venezuela | 30,000 | 15,000 | |
| C. Amerca | 3,500 | 1,000 | |
| Ecuador | 3,500 | 1,000 | |
| Peru/Bolivia | 3,500 | 1,000 | |
| Dominican Rep. | 3,500 | 1,000 | |
| Pan-Latin Am. Sat. | 50,000 | 30,000 | |
| | | | |
| **Middle East** | | | |
| Mid East/Egypt | 40,000 | 20,000 | |
| Turkey | 40,000 | 20,000 | |
| Israel | 30,000 | 15,000 | |
| | | | |
| **East Europe** | | | |
| Bulgaria | 5,000 | 2,000 | |
| Czech | 30,000 | 12,500 | |
| Hungary | 30,000 | 10,000 | |
| Poland | 35,000 | | 20,000 |
| Ex-Yugoslavia | 30,000 | 15,000 | |
| CIS | 40,000 | 20,000 | |
| Rumania | 10,000 | 5,000 | |

| | | Gap Basis | Presale Expect |
|---|---|---|---|
| | Asking Price | Non-Presale | Major Territories |
| **TOTALS** | **6,271,500** | **1,307,500** | **2,050,000** |

| | | |
|---|---|---|
| **Total Expected** | **$** | **3,357,500** |

The best position to be in is to have a film that every studio and every foreign buyer wants. In this scenario you can splinter the rights, presale the foreign territories, and still make a domestic only distribution deal. Why? Because the studios will take U. S. only rights (including home video and television) since you have a great script, a hot director, and stars. However, it is highly unlikely for a first-time producer to be in this position. More likely what will happen is (1) the studios won't be interested, (2) preselling will be tough, and (3) the producer will be forced to look for independent financing and hope domestic and foreign distributors pick it up after it is made. If you look at the statistics, you'll see that very few independently financed films find distribution. Those that do, unless they are really terrific, don't get much of an advance or ever make back their money. Why? Because, unless the film is hot and there is a bidding war, the distributor holds all the cards. Plus there are hundreds of unsold films looking for distribution. The marketplace is very crowded. The filmmaker is desperate to get distribution and is forced to take any deal to do so. The distributor will make money (they wouldn't distribute it otherwise), and the film's investors will stand little chance of recouping their investment. This is not negativity but reality. You need to look at independent filmmaking, for a minute, as a business. Nearly a thousand independent films (film as art) are submitted to Sundance (the leading independent, non-genre-driven, film market and festival.) Of the hundred shown, only a handful find profitable distribution through distributors that control only 5%-10% of all box office revenues? It should be very clear to you that this is a high risk, high stakes business where failure is the norm. What keeps it going are independent filmmakers' hopes to replicate those few moments when an unexpected film breaks through, is widely shown, critically praised, and profitable, sending its maker into the spotlight and on to a glorious filmmaking career. Is it worth the gamble? You bet! (But remember that you are also taking investors, family and friends, with you to the high stakes craps table.)

While the formula for presales is a well-known director + stars = bankable project = presales, at the AFM you will see hundreds of films that you've never heard of. The good news is that although 80% of what is being sold at that market is unknown to you, there is still an interna-

tional market for these films. The bad news is that the genres are usually not the kind of films that most independent filmmakers are interested
in making (e.g., exploitation, thriller, T&A, action/adventure). Every
year you see the same posters filled with guns and breasts selling the
same kind of movie. This is the bread and butter of the movie business.
These are not Hollywood high concept movies. These are not quirky
independent features with a twist. These are give 'em what they want,
buy low, sell high, go home and make another movie kind of business.
Art filmmakers need not apply. Go to this festival one year for an
eye–opening experience to what much of the world thinks moviemaking
is all about. You won't find any Ingmar Bergman films here.

## Presale Meets Private Investors

Some producers obtain distribution agreements through presale
arrangements and then take these to private investors as collateral,
thus avoiding the whole bank approval/nonapproval business. The
investors still have to be compensated for taking the risk, but now the
producer is not paying a large fee to the sales agent nor to the bank
for interest. In this case, the producer does not sell every territory but
just enough territories to give the investors some assurance that their
money will be returned when the film is finished. The producer then
keeps all the other territories open until the film is finished which raises the upside potential, as better deals can be negotiated when there is
demand for a finished film.

## Deal Points With Your Foreign Sales Agent

When searching for foreign sales agents, you should interview as
many as you can. They will all tell you what you want to hear. What
you want to find out is: Have they sold the same genre as your film?
Same budget range? Do they have relationships with banks? (Talk to
the banks. Ask about their reputation.) Which ones? What producers have they represented? (Call the producers. Were the sales agent's
projections accurate? Were sales made in a timely manner as expected?
Any problems?)

Picking the right foreign sales agent is vitally important because it's his job to sell your film and help you make up any deficit you have in your financing. If he can't do what he's told you they can, you may have a serious problem with the bank, your investors, and others.

You can find foreign sales agents by going through the special issues of *Variety* that cover the Cannes, MIFED, and AFM festivals. Study the films listed for sale. You'll get an idea whether these sales companies are "A" players with studio product or "B" players with exploitation (action/adventure) films Find the ones who are suitable to sell your picture. Finding the right match between your product and the experience of the presales agent is the key to not wasting everyone's time.

The fees you will pay them on the monies they collect are negotiable. If you give them a finished film and pay for all the sales materials you may be charged 10% on the low end. If you need them to do presales, then you may expect to pay 30% or more. If you provide sales materials, trailers, etc., you may be able to reduce the costs they will deduct after their fees.

Say you are the producer and anxious to get into production. Your foreign sales agent says, "Yes, we've sold the territories." And by this you believe that your budget has been met and you start spending money. Danger! Don't. Don't spend a cent until you see signed contracts from the presales agents. Many producers jump the gun (because the start date is quickly approaching and the sales haven't really been made) and start spending their own money for preproduction. If the sales don't really go through, you don't really have your budget, and end up spending all your own money. If the production stalls and fails altogether, you are left holding the bag, your savings are spent, the film is unfinished. It's happened.

## Gap Financing

If you can cover 40% of the budget through presales and your foreign sales agent can show projections that exceed the additional 60% of the budget coming from expected sales, then a bank will loan "gap" financing to cover the balance of the budget. The foreign sales agent must be reputable and a known entity to the bank. Sometimes the foreign sales agents will recommend banks that they have relationships with for the producer to contract.

Gap financing lends against the unsold rights and territories as collateral. Gap financing lending is at high and unfavorable rates to the producer. Banks are now much more aggressive than ever before and even read scripts! Some banks charge high points (3%) for the loan and may even ask for a back-end profit participation position. Gap financing is probably only feasible after the producer has made five or more films.

Producers are often surprised when suddenly their $2 million budget rises to $3 million because of the various bank fees: point, gap interest, interest reserve, the foreign sales reps' fees, the costs of "deliverables" (i.e., sets of prints and video masters), bank's attorney fees, completion bonds, etc.

I attended a financing seminar presented by the Imperial Bank, a large motion picture lender. Other guests included producers with modest to high-budget films. By the end of the presentation I calculated that 25%-30% of a film's budget goes for the financing vehicles, loans, lawyer's fees and documents, and does not appear on the screen. A low-budget independent filmmaker could make a handful of films on the banking fees alone for most major motion pictures. For independent filmmakers, this is not a route to even consider.

## A Financing Strategy

You should think about the financing strategy you will use to raise your money. As we've discussed, much of the business operates around Catch-22 situations. For example, you can't get stars without having the money to hire them, but you can't get the money until you have the stars. So what do you do?

Here's a strategy for a $5 million film.

1. Put together a list of the stars you want and their expected salaries.

2. Take your terrific script to a foreign sales agent and the list of the stars. Get their recommendations and sales estimates based on your question: what if I had this actor?

3. Go to private investors for an equity investment of $2.5 million which you will use as "pay or play" money to get the stars. (This assumes that you also have a director with whom they will work.)

4. Go back to the foreign sales agent with committed actors and your script. They sell some foreign territories and get $4 million in contracts. They take their sales fee of 20% off the top.

5. Go to a bank and get "gap financing" based on foreign sales commitments. By the time you get the money and after bank fees, you receive $2.5 million.

6. With the $2.5 million investor money and the $2.5 million bank money you start production.

7. When your great film is done you sell the U. S. rights and any unsold foreign territories. You pay back your investors and are in profits!


## Private Investor Financing

Most people start making films and videos as sole proprietors. They self-start their company with their own funds, open a bank account, register their company name (with the county clerk and d/b/a: "doing business as" company name) and hope that they'll make profitable films or videos. The company will sometimes borrow money (using the owner's credit line or collateral) or enter into limited partnerships to develop or produce their products.

I started this way as did just about everyone I can think of. In the beginning you don't notice that you have no "corporate shield." You just start and hope that there are no problems for which you'll be liable. You make all the creative decisions, and there are no hassles with studio executives or anyone else for that matter. You pretty much do what you want. Your neck and money are on the line.

It can be difficult to raise funds when you are a sole proprietor (as opposed to being a corporation) because your investors (or the bank) are relying on your financial ability to bail out a project if it goes over budget. The only real asset is yourself. If you don't have the personal assets or cash to protect your investor's investment (and most of you won't), then your investors will have to rely on good fortune and your charming personality to get you through. It is difficult to establish the very necessary lines of credits with suppliers (labs, equipment rental houses, postproduction facilities, etc.) if you are not a corporation. It's not a terrible situation but eventually you'll want to incorporate and begin building tangible assets for the corporation (equipment, personnel, expertise, relationships, contracts, a film or video library, real estate, etc.).

As a sole proprietor all the contracts will be in your name and signed by you. You will be the financially responsible party and liable if anything goes wrong.

## (Active) Investor Financing

We should be so lucky to find one investor to fund our entire project (or production company), but it does happen. Usually the investor is involved in the management of the project and so it's called "active investor" financing. He or she will get a credit in the film (sometimes as executive producer). A standard deal would give the investor 50% of the producer's net profits (or 25% of the film's net profits) after first paying back the investor (all of the investment plus, sometimes, some interest as well). An active investor will see a greater profit participation than a passive investor.

The investor will sign an investor-financing agreement which will describe his or her activity on the project or in the day-to-day

231

management of the company. Sometimes these agreements are written just for the development of a script. While this is the simplest document for a lawyer to prepare because there is only one other individual and there are no requirements for complying with federal or state securities laws, it is vitally important that the investor actively participate in the business activities of the project. They cannot be passive investors. If you do not heed this warning you could find yourself in serious trouble with the Securities and Exchange Commission (SEC).

## Joint Venture Financing

A joint venture is a general partnership, but it is set up for one specific purpose which is restricted and clearly defined in the joint financing agreement. A general partnership might exist for a company to be in the candy-making or film-producing business. A joint venture financing agreement would be prepared if you want to produce chocolate-covered almond candy, or a specific horror film.

This is not the same as a limited partnership because if you have several investors in a joint venture they all must be active, and not passive. The investors must take a role in the business activities. They may be involved in creative filmmaking decisions or have approvals over various stages of the production. In a joint venture set-up to produce a film, one partner could contribute the script, another the talent commitments, another lab facilities, and another the financing. Here, they are all active and everyone is financially liable (as in a sole proprietorship).

## Corporations

A corporation is an entity that has the ability, just like a person, to enter into contracts, take out loans, and pay taxes, but it is distinct from any of its owners. It is truly a bizarre concept but one which is obviously very popular because it protects the people who run corporations. It also enables you (the president of a corporation) to provide profit-sharing plans for employees, pension plans, group insurance, and other employee benefits. The corporation can own buildings, cars, and deduct business expenses.

You can set up a corporation with a group of investors. The initial founding shareholders would be on the corporate board and maintain an active role in the corporation's activities. It is not advisable to first set up a corporation and then seek to sell stock because of the time and cost involved in registering a securities offering. If you can identify all your investors beforehand, bring them together at the very beginning, you are much better off. A corporation may act as a general partner in a limited partnership which can help protect the liability of the corporate members.

I set up my first California corporation by following one of those self-help books. It was not difficult. These books exist for nearly every state. Essentially you write an "article of incorporation" which you file with the secretary of state in the state in which you plan to operate your business. Shortly after sending in your papers you get approval from the secretary of your articles. Your name is also registered and you get a certificate of incorporation. At this point, you hold a meeting of your shareholders and name a board of directors. (A single person can hold all the positions in a corporation and own 100% of the stock.) You then take your articles to the bank and set up a bank account. There are business stationery services that will sell you kits for about $100 that have sample bylaws, minutes, share certificates and a corporate seal which you use to squeeze an impression on your stock certificates. (It's extremely exciting to see your stock certificates with your company name on them!)

You could also have a lawyer set up your corporation ($500 to $1,000) or go to one of the legal services firms that are found in most major cities and which offer corporate setups, divorces, or deeds ($275).

You also let the Department of Corporations know who received the initial shares and how many. The procedures are clearly laid out in any number of "set up your own corporation" books, or you can have your attorney do it. The minimum franchise tax for a California Corporation is $800 which must be prepaid each year.

Once you've set up your corporation you can sell stock to shareholders (passive investors). This can be an expensive proposition with legal fees ranging from $5,000 to $50,000. You must print and bind documents which disclose the business of the partnership (very much along the lines of a business plan with income projections and financial statements). You will need to pay accountants for their expert opinions and to provide financial pages. You may also need to pay brokers who may want to be paid up front (in case your stock doesn't sell) plus their expenses to market your stock sales.

If you are creating a production company that will be ongoing (as opposed to a single project like a film or a video) and that needs capitalization, then a corporation is the route to take. It is much easier to do business as a corporation than any other kind of business structure because it's widely recognized. The stockholders are not liable for any more than the stock they purchased. The corporation, being its own "person," is responsible for its debts and to its stockholders. It is generally easier to sell stock than limited partnership shares, but consult your lawyer on this and other issues as there may be significant state to state differences.

The board of directors decides when to pay dividends on the stock and how much the dividend will be. These payments are based on how much stock is held by each stockholder and paid on a pro-rata basis.

The only downside is that corporation is taxed by the IRS on profits and shareholders are taxed on their dividends which can be double taxation; once for the corporation and again for shareholders. This, however, can be avoided by using an S Corporation or Sub Chapter S Corporation structure.

**S Corporation**

The Subchapter S Corporation or S Corporation is taxed differently than a regular corporation, and it pays no federal income tax at the corporate level. Instead, the taxation occurs at the shareholder level on all income whether or not it is actually paid out to shareholders. You can change your regular corporation into an S Corporation by filing at specific times at the beginning of each year. Ideally, you decide what kind of corporation you want at the outset to avoid long waiting periods. You can only have 35 shareholders in an S Corporation and they must be U.S. citizens. No corporations or partnerships may be shareholders (whereas a corporation may be a general partner in a limited partnership).

If you have an ongoing production business where you can take the earnings out each year and disburse them, then an S Corporation makes a lot of sense. You will only be taxed at the shareholder level. If you need to reinvest the earnings to keep the business going, then it is better to have a regular corporation. Since the earnings are reinvested there would be no double taxation because there was no disbursement to stockholders.

If you have an S Corporation and you need operating capital for the first part of the year, you may be able to borrow funds to bridge any cash flow problems.

Have a discussion with your attorney and/or accountant to advise you on the best business structure to support the business you have in mind. Decide whether you want to create an "ongoing business" such as a production company, a development company, a distribution company, a consulting business, or a "project business" such as a single video or film project. If you know going in what you want to accomplish, you will not waste time and money choosing an inappropriate structure.

I have not touched on a whole range of public offerings because (1) they are extremely expensive and complex to launch, and (2) it is the rare independent filmmaker that would even consider using them.

### Foreign Financing

In my *Film & Video Financing* book, I discuss "blocked funds" which are monies in foreign countries earned by banks or corporations that, because of local laws, are blocked from being removed from the country. (The country wants the profits used in their country and not taken out.) If you are producing in a foreign country like India, Ireland, Brazil, Yugoslavia, or Russia, then you might be able to purchase the blocked funds in local currency at a discounted rate. A U.S. $1 may buy $2 of local currency. You can use this currency in the indigenous country for below-the-line expenses (hiring local actors, crews, and equipment, lodging, transportation, production facilities, etc.).

If you are a really good negotiator with a track record of making profitable films, then maybe you can talk the corporation with the blocked funds into giving you their local currency (blocked funds) to make your movie and in exchange give them a profit participation in the film. This is an extremely complex area to even research since many corporations keep this information quite private. You may need to hire the services of a producer's rep to find foreign blocked funds situations and negotiate deals for you. The fees you pay for this service may eat up some of what you hope you'll save. Look how extremely creative producers have become in financing their films! Just because it's not in this book doesn't mean it can't be done. You may find your own creative ways to finance your film. Here are a few more.

## International Coproductions

American-based independent filmmakers are significantly behind their European counterparts in utilizing coproduction structures to finance their films. Why? Because they haven't had to. The American market, until recently, returned the largest proportion of revenues. Now, the foreign markets can account for 60% or more of the revenue stream for many types of films. Instead of financing the entire film in the U. S., especially if there are international elements in the film (actors, locations, etc.), why not go to international producers and have them contribute cash (or services) in exchange for the film's right in their own country? Half of the films produced in France last year were made with coproduction partners.

The simplest approach is to give your partners the domestic film rights in their own country and/or share revenues from worldwide distribution.

The filmmaking industry is underwritten by the governments in many foreign countries. The good news is that foreign producers have a lot more government grants for filmmaking than the U. S. The bad news is that because of this, foreign producers are not very good at marketing, nor in many instances, identifying well–structured screenplays. They neither have to write a great script nor come up with a marketable film to get financing. If you can partner with one or more foreign producers (and if your film elements qualify for their government subsidies and grants), you can get far more cash value on the screen than by pre-selling your rights or through distribution later. It is a very tricky business to get your film to fit the requirements of several countries to qualify for their cash grants, but this is exactly what foreign producers are very good at doing. American producers with expertise in story and marketing (and access to the one worldwide territory that brings in 40%-60% of a film's revenue) should be able to leverage a very good position. Coproduction is an underutilized area that American independent producers should learn. Go to the Cannes, MIP, MIFED, or AFM (American Film Market) film markets and meet foreign producers. Get yourself an attorney well versed in international coproductions. The legal and financial issues are enormously complex and there are openings here for creative producers and packagers.

## Grants

Ahhh, grants. They are wonderful when you get them. Awful when you don't. After nine years of writing proposals to the AFI (American Film Institute), I finally received a grant in 1976. It was tough then, and tougher now. We published Morrie Warshawski's excellent book *Shaking the Money Tree*, which is now out of print because many of the sources that he wrote about have dried up. His book is now a special report called *Where's the Money?* (800-833-5738).

Grants are the way to go if your film is noncommercial and has no hopes of ever earning back its cost. But expect to spend a lot of energy and many months waiting for an answer. It certainly doesn't hurt to apply for every grant you can because you have to write budgets and proposals anyway, but you should be well aware of the odds. (See the section in this book on PBS for some of the current grants available to documentary filmmakers.)

## Summary

There are a whole range of ways to finance your film. Be as creative as possible. Select a form that you feel most comfortable with, which will most likely not be any of the above.

Equity financing (through a limited partnership) is the route that nearly every independent filmmaker goes. Why? Because the first-time filmmaker's resources are mostly family and friends, and not the traditional sources of film financing. An independent filmmaker who tries to go the traditional industry financing routes (as described above) may spend three or four years trying to package actors, get pre-sales made, find distribution, banks and completion bond companies, get embroiled in the seemingly endless Catch-22 situations, and end up exhausted, broke, unable to realize his vision in a reel of film.

Obtaining investments from family and friends, and supplementing this with their credit cards, is how the great majority of first-time filmmakers get independent films made. The budgets are in the $50,000 to $100,000 range. Your first film becomes your portfolio piece to prove that you can do it. Since you don't have the money, you will have to rely on your passion, your negotiating skills, and a fabulous script to attract name actors to your film.

While this chapter has been an overview of many of the financing structures for films, the next chapter explains the structures that most independent film- and videomakers will use to finance their films.

# THE LIMITED PARTNERSHIP

## The Limited Partnership

This is one legal form that is used to finance business ventures of all kinds. The purpose of this section is to describe the basic aspects of a limited partnership structure and not, in any way, to provide legal counsel. Please consult your lawyer to determine whether this business form is appropriate for you.

## Preparing Your Package for Investment

Simplicity rules. If you have a well-thought-out plan that's easily understood by investors, then you are in great shape. Be as creative in financing your film as you are in your script writing, your directing, your production design, or your lighting. Financing is not a cookie-cutter process, nor is filmmaking. There are numerous creative approaches to every deal. Be aware of this and feel free to adopt, change, modify, and reinvent the wheel.

There are seven basic elements that you will need to have before you can raise your financing. (There are more, but these form the spine of your business plan.)

- a commercially viable film concept
- a great script
- experienced (or if not, passionate and communicative) director
- strong, recognizable cast
- appropriate scale budget and production schedule
- income projections
- a limited partnership agreement

Most of the independent feature films that were accepted to be shown in the Sundance Film Festival had concepts that had some degree of commerciality. That simply means that the filmmakers came up with themes and casting that would appeal to a specific, albeit limited, audience. Without a specific audience in mind a film cannot hope to attract an audience, let alone a distributor. If you can't attract a distributor, your entire business plan (let alone your dreams and aspirations) will plummet to the ground.

Once you have your film concept you need to write (or have written or obtain) a script that has a unique sense of place, great dialogue, compelling characters, intriguing plot, and an unusual filmic style. In short, a great story and the ability to show it well.

Many films are funded based on the abilities of the director. If you are a first-time director, then you really have to demonstrate your unflagging willingness and persistence of vision at every turn so that investors will be compelled to support your efforts. If this is not the case, then, as a producer you will need to find a director that can "bring it on home" and that you can stand behind to get the job done. If you are the producer, then it's your job to find the story and get a good script written which will attract a good director. A good script and a good director will attract the cast. Everyone wants to work on fabulous material, but it all starts with the script.

Clever directors and producers who are just starting out find ways of telling their stories for very little money. The more you are able to do for less, the easier it will be to attract money. Investors want to minimize their risk. When they see a project that is well designed and can be simply but uniquely shot, they may be willing to invest. (Investors are not only private individuals but also distributors who advance monies to filmmakers.) Therefore, your project needs to have enough money for you to accomplish your mission, but not so much that you will never raise it. I've seen projects from first-time directors that have had huge multimillion dollar budgets for special effects. While some of the concepts have been quite good, none of these projects was ever able to attract that kind of money. You have to show that you can make a tremendously creative film for not a lot of money when you are just starting out. The money will follow if you can make your first few films work.

This may mean that you will have to defer your fees until the film goes into distribution. Or perhaps defer all cast and crew fees as well, or pay partial fees. The more resources you are able to garner together for little or no money, the more likely it is that you will be able to finish your film.

If you know your intended audience, you can realistically compare it with recent, similar genre independent films. By studying the performance and sales records of these films (which sometimes means you have to call the producers), you can begin to project the markets into which you will be able to license your film. Perhaps there will be a limited theatrical run, then a cable and home video sales. Your income projection pages will describe to what degree these distribution avenues return income to your investors and when. If your budget is low, and you are able to make sales in the U. S. and abroad, you may be able to show your investors that the film will make a profit. If you can truthfully and realistically demonstrate that your film will make money, you will find investors.

Do not go out looking for investors until you have thought through your entire project and assembled the above elements including the legal document: a Limited Partnership Agreement. This legal document describes how the money will be raised, and spent, and how the business of the partnership will be run (by you and perhaps your cocreators). Many filmmakers actually find potential investors before they have their legal documents, which is foolish, because by the time their lawyers draw up all the necessary papers, the investors change their minds. You have to strike while the iron is hot and not come back months later saying, "Remember when we talked about my movie and you said you might like to invest?" Too late. The momentum is gone.

You will have to do a great deal of preparatory work before you can even start to raise money. Keep that day job for the time being. This is difficult but not impossible. Every year, hundreds of filmmakers just like you raise money in just this way and make their films. Not all of them are acceptable to Sundance, but they did get done and some of the filmmakers are going on to make their next films. You can too. It's a matter of preparing everything you need in a very organized, step-by-step manner.

To do this, you have to be committed and approach your work in a professional manner. There is too much to do to be sloppy or careless about how you proceed. This will take time, possibly two or five or ten times longer than you originally planned. But you can do it and get your film made.

Think about your budget. What resources do you really think you can raise? $30,000? $50,000? $100,000? $300,000? Whatever the number, think for a moment—can you find 30 people to put in $5,000 each? If so, your resources will bring in $150,000. What kind of film could you do for $150,000? This is called "backing into your budget" or "reverse engineering." Know your limitations and plan accordingly.

Your entire plan, from script synopsis, marketing plans, budget, income projections and more are written up in legalese and included in your limited partnership agreement. You must know what you are doing in great detail before you begin to prepare your legal documents.

## The Limited Partnership

The way most filmmakers raise money for their independent films is through the limited partnership. It is the simplest and easiest of all legal structures to set up and understand.

Limited partnerships are a very common business form for funding all kinds of projects. Most lawyers are familiar with them; however, producers should only work with experienced entertainment attorneys in preparing their documents. They can cost from $1,000 to $3,000 or more depending on the complexity of your project.

In a limited partnership there are one or more general partners (you and your partner) who run and oversee the management of the business. There are also limited partners who are "passive" and do not participate in any creative or management decisions. They are limited in their liability to only what they have invested, nothing more. If the production goes overbudget they are not responsible for contributing more money. If the film loses a lawsuit, they are not liable to pay settlements. The general partners assume all the liability. (If the general partner is a corporation, some of the personal exposure can be eliminated. Consult with your lawyer on this.)

Come up with a name for the partnership and file it with the secretary of state in your own state ($50-$100). Your lawyer or accountant can do this for you.

The limited partners invest monies which are spent on the film's budget. In exchange for this investment they receive a percentage of profits (and losses), usually in proportion to their capital contribution; the greater their investment the greater their percentage of profits.

Once the film is in distribution and begins earning income, the investors start recouping their original investment. Once the original investment is repaid in full then profits, if any, are shared between the investors (the limited partners) and the producers(the general partners).

You can structure the deal anyway you like, but usually the limited partners (investors) are paid back their investment first and then receive 50% of the net profits. There are no rules and you can be as creative in designing a "win-win" situation for yourself and your investors. With *Hardware Wars*, we knew it had tremendous upside, plus we were virtually working without pay, so we gave the investor 35% of the film's profits after repaying her very low investment. She made incredible multiples on her money. In another instance, I was unable to close a deal because the investor wanted two times the investment recouped before profit sharing and wanted the general partner (me) to receive only a 30% share of the film's profits. The acceptable range for both the investor and the producer (general partner) is somewhere between these two extremes.

243

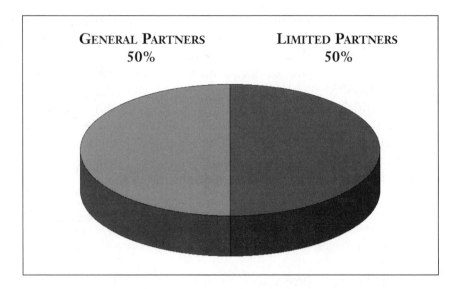

GENERAL PARTNERS
50%

LIMITED PARTNERS
50%

A producer (general partner) can also be a limited partner. Say, for example, that you've invested $10,000 actual cash in developing your project. Instead of paying yourself back from the budget you decide that you will become a limited partner and receive a proportionate share of profits like any other limited partner. Often investors will ask, "How much of your own money is invested in the film?" The idea being that if you really believe in the film you'll put your money where your mouth is. I don't necessarily agree with this reasoning (because the producer may have put in years developing the project), but I understand it from an investor's point of view.

**Creative Spins**

To further motivate an investor you might offer a recoupment of 110%, or 120% or 130% before the profit sharing starts. A 130% recoupment means that if someone invests $10,000, they will receive $13,000 before the general partners (producers) share in profits. Since it can take several years for recoupment to occur, even when a film is successful, this additional 30% is an enticement to the investor. Of course, this is only an incentive and doesn't mean anything unless the film actually earns money.

Or, rather than increase the recoupment, you might give investors a 55% or 60% or 65% share of net profits instead of 50%.

Or, you could allow the investors to recoup their investment and then receive 70% of the net profits until they double their investment and then flip-flop the profit share to 70% to the general partner and 30% to the limited partner (or nothing to the limited partner at all). Anyway you want to creatively set up the deal is fine as long as you are able to secure investors. I prefer to keep it similar.

I have seen other producers' partnerships only let the investors participate in film revenues (and not ancillary such as video, toys, merchandising, novelization, etc.). I figure that since the investors are taking the risk, they should share in as many revenues streams as possible. Isn't that what you would want if you were an investor?

Before you start giving away "points" or large percentages of net profits, I suggest you carefully consider for a moment that besides cash the one thing you can give away to others (partners, actors, directors, writers, etc.) is profit participation.

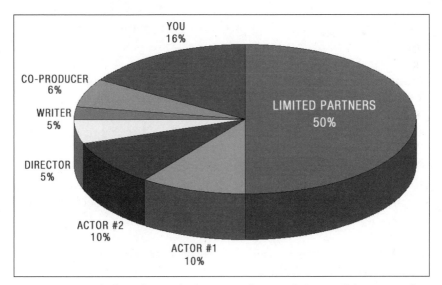

*It is pretty good if, as the producer, you end up with 25% of the net profits.*

You may think that 50% is a lot for you (general partner) to receive until you realize that large chunks of this 50% may be given away as compensation to others. An actor might want 10% or more of net profits. What if you have two actors and they each want 10%? Then there's the director. The writer. Will you be giving them profit participation as well? Do you have a coproducer who is expecting to split everything with you? It is pretty good if you, as the producer, can end up with 25% of the net profits after everyone else's participation. Sometimes you can do better than this, sometimes not as well. It all depends on the project and your negotiation skills.

## Partnership Rules

Study a limited partnership agreement. Take notes how it applies and doesn't apply to your own project. Discuss any changes in how you'd like to run your partnership with your attorney so they can document it in the agreement. You are pretty free to do what you want in running the partnership as long as it benefits the partnership. You are now running a business on behalf of other people who've invested their money and you are expected to keep their best interests in mind as well as follow the rules and procedures as described in the partnership agreement.

Warning: depending on how the partnership is set up, a majority of 70% of the limited partners can reappoint a new general partner if they feel the current general partner is not operating the partnership in their best interests.

The partnership will last as long as it is set up to run, which is generally the life expectancy or income-producing years of the film or video which could be ten years. If the film fails to meet its expectations, the partnership can be closed earlier.

The partnership does not pay federal or state income taxes. These taxes are paid by the limited and general partner in relation to their capital contribution. Sometimes general partners will have contributed capital in order to get the partnership going.

Any losses are treated like ordinary losses. The tax shelters of the past were done away with by the 1986 Tax Reform Act. Now, losses in the partnership may be written off over the life expectancy of the film. Limited partnerships are no longer marketable to people who need losses on their income taxes. (In the past you could write off more than your cash investment! In some foreign countries you still can.) If the film is less successful than you expected, then your investor's tax loss write–off may be accelerated. Discuss this with your accountant. The accounting procedures will be determined in advance and described in the Limited Partnership Agreement.

Sometimes you will hear that you should not use the limited partnership format because too many people have been burned by it in the movie business. It's not the limited partnership form that causes people to get burned. It's unrealistic expectations. It is films that don't perform or making deals with less than credible people. I have been using limited partnerships since 1976 and they work just fine. They give the producer (the general partner) the greatest freedom to operate the business and get the film or video made with the least interference from the investors. So it's not the form that matters, it's how well conceived your project is, how timely, and whether distribution channels can be exploited for your project by reputable companies.

## Attorney Costs

The range of costs for a lawyer may vary from a low of $75 to around $375 for a top–notch entertainment attorney. Some will want a flat fee plus an hourly fee, others will bill hourly. Call several entertainment attorneys in Los Angeles or New York who have had considerable feature film financing and distribution experience, and discuss your needs. Some work independently and others are partners in large firms. You can interview attorneys without incurring any fees. You will then be expected to sign an agreement with your attorney. If it is a law firm then you have the advantage of having several lawyers who specialize in different areas such as securities and financing, performer's agreements, guild negotiations, and distribution agreements who are available to work on your project as needed. You will be charged on an hourly basis for how much work each lawyer does. Sometimes filing forms is done by junior lawyers or paralegals and you are billed at a low $50 per hour rate. Naturally, what you want to do is establish a relationship with a lawyer or law firm that is highly experienced and can represent not only your current project but future projects. If this is your intent, make this clear in the initial meeting. Some large law firms will not want to take on small projects. The fees are just not great enough for them.

Some lawyers may write a limited partnership agreement for you on a "deferred" basis. That is, you pay them a partial fee of one or two thousand dollars and ask them to defer the rest until the project is financed. If it is not financed, then you don't have to pay the deferral. You should make this clear. Sometimes they will want to be paid the deferral regardless. Discuss with them whether you need them to handle all the other legal aspects of your project as well as such talent agreements, distribution contracts, footage and music clearances, sponsorship deals, insurance, copyright clearances, corporate setups, etc.

You cannot do the legal work yourself so find a lawyer as soon as possible. I have found lawyers that have not only worked on "spec" but, because they believed in me and the project, invested as well! It does not get any better than that! When your lawyer has invested, it sends a very strong message to other potential investors. His lawyer invested cash, and he knows more about this business than I do. Sign me up too! Lawyers may also point you to prospective investors. In this case they expect to be compensated. I put aside a set amount as a "finder's fee" in the budget. It is based on the size of the budget raised. For example, if the project's budget is $500,000 I might put aside $10,000 for those who lead me to investors. If two people (say one of them is my lawyer) leads me to someone who invests $250,000, then they each get $5,000. They may or may not receive a very small percentage (1/4% to 1%) of the producer's net profits as well. It's all negotiable!

Sometimes lawyers will prepare all the documents necessary for your film for 5% of the budget. I always run the numbers and see whether this is appropriate or not. Sometimes it is, sometimes it isn't. It all depends on what your needs are and how much representation you will need.

If there are a lot of investors and you are raising money from a number of different states, you must file and pay fees ($50-$200) in each state and pay the paralegal fees to make the filing. If there are a lot of distribution agreements or rights agreements to negotiate (and make interlocking), it can be a considerable amount of work for an attorney. If it is more straightforward, then they have most of what you need already on their computer and it just has to be customized (but takes less time).

## Ongoing Business of the Partnership

Developing and making the film is one thing; getting it marketed and into distribution is another. When you set up your limited partnership, have 5% of gross revenues flow back into the production company's bank account for distribution and marketing expenses. (Even though you have budgeted these expenses you may discover that you forgot to include trips to festivals, lodging, car rental, prints, video dupes, sales materials, phone, fax, office overhead, publicity, etc.) If you don't include a contingency for this in your budget and provide for future income to help cover these costs, you'll find yourself in a demoralizing position. You've finished your film but have no money to market your film to distributors. Everyone always runs out of money at the end of a project.

Allow up to 5% or 10% of the budget to go to repaying your development costs. Or you can simply itemize these costs and make sure that they are included in production budget so that you can be reimbursed for start-up costs.

It is your responsibility (as a general partner) to provide income statements to the limited partners each year. (Your accountant will help.) Tax returns show each partner's capital account and profit or loss for the year and are sent to the limited partners. To keep on your investors' good side, send their tax statements to them as soon as possible after the close of each year, as they must include this information in their own tax reports.


**Summary**

The Limited Partnership Agreement describes how the business will be conducted. It describes your responsibilities and what will happen if you die, neglect your responsibilities, encounter a limited partner who wants out, and other sobering thoughts. It states what method will be used to return the initial investment to the investors. It is a good idea to have your accountant and lawyer consult with one another when writing up the Limited Partnership Agreement so that the best legal and accounting practices can be integrated. Since the agreement states how business will be conducted, you may refer back to it from time to time for procedural matters.

This document should be prepared before you begin raising money. You will give the Limited Partnership Agreement only to those who are seriously interested in investing in your project. They will probably have their own lawyer and accountant read it before they will invest.

Your lawyer will advise you to number each copy of the agreement and to record whom you give it to and what the relationship is between you and the recipient (friend, acquaintance, relative, etc.). By law, there are restrictions on how many limited partners you may actually have as well as how many people you can approach for investment (35 investors in California). Ask your lawyer how to proceed. A limited Partnership is not a "public offering" and cannot be advertised, nor can you mail out limited partnership agreements to just anyone.

Make it clear to potential investors that films are a tremendously risky investment and that there is a great likelihood that they could lose all their money. While it is very exciting to think your project may be the next *Shine*, the real possibilities are (1) the film will never be finished, (2) it won't find a distributor, (3) it won't have wide distribution, (4) the public won't like it, (5) the theater will cheat the distributor and not report all ticket sales, (6) the distributor will cheat you, (7) the check will get lost in the mail on its way to you, or (8) all or none of the above.

It is better to be very conservative in your estimates of profits than raise everyone's expectations. You can print the horrible truth about movie investing in bold type in your prospectus and Limited Partnership Agreement so no one can say you didn't warn them of the risks.

If the project fails, your investors will lose everything and you will not be indebted to them. I've made films that have not fully repaid their investors, and even though I legally do not owe them any money I still feel responsibility to them. They believed in me, in the film, and it failed to make money. This has made me even more sensitive when preparing new projects for investment and has dampened my boundless enthusiasm when it comes to painting bright vistas for would-be investors. Unlike some producers, I just can't (as they said in *Shogun* after someone died a violent death) karma, neh?, turn and walk away. So, if you're like me, be forewarned.

You want to do everything to see that your investors do not lose their money. That means choosing the right projects, conducting market research, preplanning and careful budgeting, striking good distribution deals, and continuing to promote the film well into your old age. If the film is successful (which could be defined as simply returning the original investment), your investors may be willing to reinvest in your other projects.

On the other hand, if your project fails you could find yourself in a lawsuit regardless of how hard you worked making the movie, how well you communicated with your investors, or how much you struggled to secure marketing and distribution for your project. If investors do not make the money they hope they will make, they can get very mad, and lawsuits, even unfounded ones, aren't out of the question. This means that you must either (1) fight and spend money with lawyers to prove your innocence, or (2) settle, that is, pay money, to make it go away. Imagine how you would feel if you spent years working on a project that you believed in, but it wasn't that successful, and still you had to settle with investors who were suing you. It happens.

Raising money from other people is not something to engage in lightly. It is a very serious contract between you and "the money people" and you'd better be as certain as possible that you'll be able to do what you say you will do or suffer the consequences.

# OTHER CREATIVE FINANCING MODELS

## Limited Liability Companies (L.L.C.)

This is a new form of structure that combines the best of the limited partnership and corporate structures. I have heard a lot about them over the last few years. They are relatively new to California; a limited number of other states (Colorado, Florida, Kansas, Texas, Utah, Virginia, Nevada, Wyoming) allow you to use them. This is a structure that is used in Europe frequently. The L.L.C. has managers who are like the board of directors in a corporation and like the general partner in a limited partnership. There are also members who are like shareholders or limited partners who have invested and have shares in the company. Both the managers and the members have limited liability (which is what everyone likes about this structure), although there must be a general partner who does not have limited liability. Creative control issues can be streamlined as well. They may be handled by a single individual, several individuals, or a board.

The L.L.C. files with the secretary of state in those states which allow this structure. The L.L.C. is not taxed like a corporation but like a limited partnership (or S Corp.) where the profits and losses flow down to the members. So the L.L.C. provides both tax benefits (like a general partnership) and limited liability (like a corporation).

The L.L.C. is still relatively new to many lawyers. Some swear by it. Others do not. Some issues are still untested in the courts so there is some uncertainty about how well it actually protects the liability of its members.

## Mini-Deals That Can Help Make Up Your Budget

I frequently say to producers, Why pay for something when you may not have to? Why put yourself through all the effort of raising a cash budget when you could go directly to the source of what you need and get it for equity or profit participation instead of cash?

Facilities are a perfect example of this. There are many studios around the country (California, North Carolina, Florida, Texas, and Tennessee) that are without production for many weeks and months during the year. These studios might be approached to contribute below-the-line goods and services in exchange for equity and profit participation in your film. This might include sound stages, production offices, production equipment (cameras and lights), crew, locations, and postproduction facilities. You might calculate what percentage of the total budget the contribution could provide in exchange for a prorated participation in the profits of your film. In essence, you treat the facilities' contribution as if it were the same as cash. You need to convince a facility that not only will they benefit from doing your project, but it may bring them future work as well.

## Facilities' Deals

There are film and video rental houses whose equipment is not rented every day. There are film laboratories with down time. There are postproduction video editing suites sitting vacant at night. It is to your advantage (and to the facilities) to see if you can work out an arrangement to use a facility during nonpeak times in exchange for profit participation in your film or video. Here's how it can work. The facility looks at your budget and agrees to give you $50,000 in services. You treat this $50,000 just like cash; like a cash investment. When revenues come in from the film, like the other investors, and at the same time, the lab recoups the $50,000. Once the film has recouped the investor's contribution in full the facility receives profit participation in a pro-rata proportion. (The facility is not a limited partner.)

Sometimes a facility will argue that they have some real, hard costs which must be paid. You might agree to pay them 30% of the facility budget in cash and get the additional 70% as an investment. You are still tremendously ahead and you don't have to raise cash for this portion. How many other budgetary items could you treat in the same way? I met a no-budget producer in London who claimed that he could get every single budgetary item for free or in exchange for equity! (To test this premise I produced a no-budget movie. You can do it.)

**Below-The-Line Deals**

If you shoot a large portion of your film in an Eastern Bloc country they may, in exchange for the Eastern European rights, provide up to 70% of a film's below–the–line costs (the hard fixed costs, not actor's, writer's, producer's, or director's fees). This is another example of not having to come up with all the cash. However proceed with caution on this one because the difficulty of working with a foreign crew and equipment may outweigh the apparent advantages. If the provider of these items wants to exert creative control on the film or the business of making a film, they may become an "active" investor which may require you to rethink your financial structure form.

**Deferrals**

Another approach that producers commonly use to make their films and videos is the "deferral." The producer goes to the actor, coproducer, director, and any other crew member or provider of services and asks that either all or part of their fees be deferred. Since most films do not make back their investment, those who defer usually see little or none of their fees. However, with some first-time filmmakers (and their first-time actors and crew), everyone is willing to defer in order to get the film made. You have to start somewhere.

Since getting a deferral is as good as getting cash from an investor, it is an approach well worth looking into. A few years back I produced a very profitable health-oriented infomercial. The company that financed it made a lot of money. Our production company received excellent fees and some small profit participation. Had we also financed it, we'd be in hog heaven. So we decided on the next production, we would finance the infomercial ourselves. I went back to everyone who worked on the first show (and with whom I wanted to work again) and said, "As you know, our last infomercial was a big hit. We want to do another, except this time we'll finance it and share in the profits. Here's the deal. I'll pay you the same fee I paid you last time, in cash, or you can defer your fee, and we'll treat it like an investment, the same as cash. If the project is successful you'll be paid your deferral at the same time as the cash investors and then share in profits on a pro-rata basis." Everyone I talked to deferred either all or most of their fee. This added up to about 25% of the budget. It was much easier talking to people who knew me and what we wanted to accomplish than finding, meeting, and talking to new investors about giving cash to someone they'd just met, for a project they barely understood. When it was time to meet potential cash investors, I could proudly state that I had already raised 25% of the budget (even though it was in deferrals).

## Development Funds

It does cost something to develop an idea. You have to find a writer (or write a screenplay yourself). You have to do research. You have to live while you are assembling your package and cover expenses. Some filmmakers are so excited about their grand idea that they want to get development money. You could go to a studio but the competition is fierce and by the time they get through with you, you won't know what happened. Your writer will get a little money and you'll lose control of your project.

But that still won't stop some independent producers from seeking development money anyway. This is the most risky investment of all for investors. They are investing in a script which may never be sold. Remember, out of 70,000 scripts written each year only a few hundred get made. Not great odds. An investor is going to want a tough deal to take the risk (unless it's Uncle John who just wants to see you make your movie).

If you feel you must raise money to develop a script (which I do not advise), then here's a starting point on the kind of deal you can offer an investor.

They put up $10,000 (or better yet $1,000 or $5,000). The smaller the better. This goes to a non-guild writer to do a finished script. It does not go to the producer. When the script is finished and money is raised, the investor will recoup their investment plus a 50% return on their money, stop, end of deal. They do not participate any further.

Or, you might offer them a return of 100% or 200% or 300% of their money. You might have to. Their risk is that great.

Or, you may tell them that instead of getting their money back in cash they can reinvest it and have equity in the movie and a profit participation twice as good as any other investor. So if a normal investor's $10,000 would get 1% of net profits, then the development money investor's $10,000 would get 2% of net profits: twice as much for taking on the risk of development of the project.

An investor may or not accept this deal. I've never made a deal like this and don't plan to. It's too risky. Not only is there no guarantee you'll ever make the movie, but if you do, you'll end up giving away too much to the investor. It's better to develop it yourself even if it takes longer.

### Money Finders/Brokers

Set aside a line item called "finder's fee" in the budget. The finder's fee is based on the amount of money to be raised. For example, if the project's budget is less than $500,000 I might put aside $10,000 for finders who lead me to investors. If two people (say one of them is my lawyer) lead me to people who invest $250,000, then they each get $5,000. They may or may not receive a very small percentage (1/4% to 1%) of the producer's net profits as well. It's all negotiable!

The rule of thumb for money finders is that their fees for raising money range between 2% and 8% depending on what they actually do for you. Money finders may only lead you to brokers willing to underwrite and raise money for your project. In that case they would get a small negotiated fee.

In regard to brokers, The National Association of Securities Dealers (NASD) limited the broker/dealer expenses and commissions to 10.5% of the offering proceeds. This means their fees also cover any printings, mailings, phone, etc., and should not be billed as separate expenses. Once I, unknowingly, paid 18% to brokers for raising money for me on a project. I also paid a fee to a money finder. This was money that was not seen on the screen and money that you have to raise.

Money finders can work within the sales and deal term parameters that you establish. They are intermediaries that help you raise the money. Rules and regulations about money finders vary in each state so you might do some local research to understand how to best use them.

Normally here are some of the deal points you might consider in working with money finders:

1. They agree to pitch to third parties to lend, finance, or distribute the film.

2. They agree to a six month or one year term.

3. They receive 5% of the funds raised, not to exceed $45,000. (Again this depends on the size of your budget, of course.)

4. If the finder raises more than 90% of the budget, then they get an Executive Producer credit on the title.

5. The finder is not paid his or her money until the producer has the right to use the money (or when escrow breaks). You don't want to pay a finder's fee if the full amount of the money isn't raised and the investor's money has to be returned.

6. The producer doesn't have to take any deal that the finder offers.

You must be careful. Once I worked through a securities firm who were licensed brokers. I pitched their sales folks on my project. They took notes and immediately set to work calling people on their "accredited" investor lists. (To qualify as an accredited investor you must have a yearly income of over $200,000 per year and a net worth of $500,000. This is to supposedly provide assurance that the investor can afford any losses and has some sophistication when it comes to investment.) The broker's salesmen called their accredited investors and sold out the limited partnership units. Terrific!

The project unfortunately failed and only returned a fraction of its investment.

A few years later, one of the investors called me and asked for her money back. I told her that it was a risky investment and that the partnership was now closed since it had no capital whatsoever. I explained that I was sorry for her loss but that everyone (ourselves included) had sustained losses.

A few years after this she sued the security firm, the partnership, the general partners, and me personally claiming that the brokers had said her investment would make triple its money in a few months, that it was a perfectly safe investment, and she could take her money out at any time. In the meantime the securities firm, who indemnified the partnership against any claims like this, had gone out of business. It is possible that the salespeople did misrepresent the project, but I have no way of knowing whether they did or not.

It was very clear on the front cover of the prospectus that this was an investment and that you should not invest unless you were able to bear the burden of complete loss of your investment. Inside the document were several pages warning why the project was particularly risky and might not succeed.

The investor claimed that she had not read the document. She found a lawyer willing to take the case on spec (he would receive 30% of any award or settlement). To defend myself I hired a lawyer and made a settlement with the investor. These are called harassment and nuisance suits. Even though the partnership committed no wrongdoing and as its general partner, I lived up to my complete obligations during the production and operation of the partnership, the partnership and everyone remotely involved was named in the suit. The lawyer told me it would cost me $30,000 to $50,000 to go to court to simply prove my innocence. It was cheaper to settle and pay her and her lawyer to go away.

When you raise money, you do so on people's heightened expectations which can lead to disappointment if the financial projections are not met. Regardless of the legal documentation and notifications, regardless of the fact that there was no wrongdoing on the part of a general partner, lawsuits can still occur to your detriment. You can choose the best partners, brokers, and financial managers. You can do everything by the book, but if you are going to be out there producing films with other people's money, it is very likely that sometime in your career you will run into unfair situations where you will be challenged. Know it. Be aware of it. And move forward with as much integrity as you can.

### Film Lab Deals

You need to have your film developed and prints made. Perhaps there is a lab willing to come in as an equity partner. They provide the developing, workprints, coding, sound editing, negative cutting, optical transfers, dupes and internegatives, and film to video transfers plus release prints (depending on the deal you make with your distributor) in exchange for profit sharing. Or perhaps they will defer half their fees until your film is in distribution.

### Summary

There are a myriad of deals limited only by your imagination. Every step of the production process requires experienced people, goods, services, and materials. Why not make these people your partners and reduce your budget at the same time? Smart producers do just that. It doesn't take a genius to spend money. It does take a genius to figure out how to make a movie for nothing. If you can do that, you are worth your weight in gold to production companies and studios everywhere. Think about it.

Sit down with veteran Internet explorer and future thinker HOWARD RHEINGOLD, (Editor, *Whole Earth Millennium Catalog*), as he shows you how to transform your life and career on the super information highway.

This is the first video series to help you find Internet treasures fast—without wasting your valuable time. This and the other videos in the series will introduce you to the smartest people and take you to the coolest places in no time. You'll learn how to download text, graphics, and even movies. You'll learn how to publish on-line, hunt and gather information, send and receive e-mail, and join virtual communities. As you gain insights from Rheingold's vast experience and wit, you'll soon become a player in on the most exciting networks of the new communications age.

*The cover of a business plan which later became the*
*"Living On The Net" video series.*

# The Business Plan/Prospectus

## The Business Plan/Prospectus

There are two things that you will need to do to inform investors about your project. The first is prepare a written prospectus or business plan which goes into great detail about every aspect of your project but focuses on how and why the film will be commercially viable and generate profits. Secondly, armed with copies of your prospectus and your limited partnership agreement, you will need to do live presentations, either one-on-one or to groups, for investors. You cannot send out a prospectus without talking to the prospective investor and hope that you will get a check by return mail. Nor can you do a presentation without a business plan or prospectus to leave behind. You need to do both. This chapter discusses the business plan or prospectus—the written presentation.

The business plan is the document where you present every aspect of your business so that partners, investors, banks, and others may get a clear idea of what you intend to do to create a profitable film(s) or video(s).

It is really necessary to create a limited partnership agreement before looking for financing or talking with any investors. (If you talk to investors without signing documents, and they are interested, by the time your lawyer prepares the documents the investors can easily have changed their minds or invested elsewhere. Get them while they are hot!)

Much of what is in your prospectus is information that you will need to assemble anyway such as synopsis, stills, key credits, budget, etc. The business plan or prospectus is really a description of your film and the entire business around it, from financing through distribution. It is written in language that unsophisticated investors (family, friends, and friends of friends) can understand.

Here are the elements that go into a business plan. You may follow my "rules" or not. I offer them only as suggestions since there is no one way to do this. The goal of the prospectus is to make your project understandable and appealing so that the readers will wish to invest.

## The Elements of a Business Plan

Executive Summary
Introduction (Overview)
State Independent Filmmaking
Management Team (biographies of key players)

The Proposed Project
Synopsis/Treatment
Status of Rights
Comparable Box Office Performances
Production Aspects
Budget/Use of Capital
Summary Budget
Distribution Approach
Income Projections
Funding of the Picture/Cofinancing
General Company Description

Exhibits
Lead Actors
Resumes
Production Schedule
Marketing Analysis
FilmProfit® Projections
Letters of Intent/Agreements
Industry Articles
Press Coverage
Contact Information

Include other relevant documents in the exhibits section such as a title report, copyright search, copyright assignment, options, distribution agreement, completion bond letter, rating certificate, insurance document, etc.

Consider attaching tabs to each section of the prospectus and labeling them. This way investors can quickly flip to "income projections," for example.

Some producers will use the business plan to find "active" investors who will not only invest in the project but also participate in producing the film or running the business. This business plan is intended as a nonlegal document. On the cover I write for informational purposes only. Anything you may say, imply, or promise in the prospectus is not binding. When I write the prospectus I have to be careful that the project is not misrepresented in any way. I then go over the prospectus with my lawyer. From my document he prepares a "Confidential Summary" and a "Limited Partnership Agreement," which are binding legal documents. They restate much of the information in the prospectus, but do so in a legalese and a nonpromotional manner.

The prospectus, on the other hand, is written in a user-friendly, easy to read, visually interesting format. There are pictures and graphic headings in a well-designed format. My lawyer is not pleased that I use my own document because of possible liability issues. However I feel that filmmakers must use whatever tools they can to create a good impression. I want to give the potential investors a document that is exciting and fun to read (but also accurately represents all aspects of the project. It is better to be extremely conservative in your income projections, otherwise you may open yourself up to litigation down the line: You said it would make just as much money as *Pulp Fiction*!

The business plan is as complete a picture as you can possibly give of all the aspects of your project. This includes the organization of the business, distribution market, income projections, product and program descriptions, financing structure, and more. You do not go out to raise financing until your business plan is in place. This means you must carefully pull together as much information as you can, which may require consulting with lawyers, accountants, and your creative and business partners.

I will use as examples of the prospectus, my proposal for a film I am preparing to do in Indonesia titled *Bali Brothers*. This is a work-in-progress. When I gather new elements for the movie, I update the proposal. The prospectus is a sales piece.

Here is, start to finish, the examples of some of the elements that go into a business plan. I generally put them in this order but you don't have to. The point is to be clear and precise so that investors get all the information they want, and they don't have to flip around to find it.

**Style and Layout**

Don't make your document wall-to-wall words or no one will read it. Use bold headings for each section and each paragraph. Lay out the pages in an interesting fashion with lots of white. Do not try to overwhelm with content, but make each page inviting with a balance of graphics and text. You can use hanging paragraphs to pull out or emphasize the content of each page.

Use clear, informal language that is inviting, and not too much industry jargon. Don't assume your investor knows what you know about the movie business. Give definitions and explanations of how various markets differ, for example.

**Cover**

Contrary to the advice of many books on business plans, your cover should have a stunning, provocative graphic. After all, it's a movie we're selling! It should grab attention. When your prospectus is on a desk or a coffee table it is selling through its evocative cover. The cover could be your key art and title treatment for your movie.

You should have a strong title, and names of any well-known actors, writers, or directors. There should be a copyright notice and a disclaimer (either here on on the first inside page) that says this is for "information purposes only." I don't know whether this lets you off the liability hook or will quell your lawyers' concerns, but it's a start.

# Bali Brothers

### A Film by Michael Wiese

# Bali Brothers

*"Bali Brothers is a touching and frightening story of what happens when two opposing moralities encounter the overwhelming beauty of Balinese culture, and the powerful forces beneath it."*

## TABLE OF CONTENTS

2

## Table of Contents

Next is a clearly organized table of contents. Organize your material in whatever fashion best suits your project. Each project is different, and you want to display all the aspects of the project in their best light.

## Executive Summary

The first page is a summary of the entire document where you make a compelling argument why this project is worthy of investment. You might talk about the boon in independent filmmaking and how profitable it can be. You can briefly describe the market and your marketing hooks. You state why your film is unique and exactly how much financing is sought. My summary extends into describing the various markets for the film and the average return on investment that our past projects have garnered.

## The Project

Next comes all the aspects of the project itself. You can mention casting, provide a synopsis of the film, its target audience, and status of literary rights. The synopsis is very brief. Sometimes it is only a paragraph long. (The investors can always read the script if they like.) Here you give just the essence of the project.

Most filmmakers say their film is for everyone, but that's never the case. You can get an outside market research group or consultant to analyze your script and provide a marketing report. That's what we did with Jeffrey Hardy and the market research firm Big Horse Productions (415-431-5143). He prepared several pages of analysis which we include in the appendix of the prospectus. We also discuss how our film is similar to another and our financial expectations.

Unless you are producing a straight genre picture (action/adventure, horror), it may be difficult to match your film with another. Nevertheless try to find something similar, in the same genre, budget range, target audience, and with similar elements with which to compare your film. It should be a film that neither failed nor was wildly successful.

Investors like to look at numbers so the two movie's budgets are as similar as possible. Include P&A and the grosses in the U.S. and internationally if you can find them, the assumption being, if someone else with a similar film achieved these numbers, then you should be able to as well. (Naturally that's not necessarily the case, but you've got to start somewhere.)

To further drive home the point that high profits can be made from low budget films I show the ten best cost-to-return independent films. Give the readers a little something to dream on. But if you overemphasize *Sex, Lies and Videotape* or *Pulp Fiction* (which were both anomalies and not the norm), you are pushing your credibility window too much. We are making the argument that, because the budget is low for independent films, when there is an upside it can be tremendous.

We all know that for every film that is successful there are another eight or nine that fail; however, there is no value to overly stressing the downside in the business when the goal of the prospectus is to raise money. (The limited partnership agreement will be loaded with warnings of doom and gloom in the risks section. Here everything that can possibly go wrong will be stated so that the investors are fully informed of the downside possibilities.)

# Bali Brothers

## EXECUTIVE SUMMARY

The overwhelming success of independent films in 1997's Academy Award nominations reveals an expanding audience for dramatic adult films. The U.S. aging population of moviegoers are turning to independent films with engaging, heart-felt stories with compelling performances by up-and-coming actors such as BALI BROTHERS.

This proposal seeks financing for an independent feature film budgeted at $5 million.

BALI BROTHERS is a touching and frightening story of what happens when two opposing moralities, represented by two brothers, encounter the overwhelming beauty of Balinese culture, and the powerful forces beneath it. The story will be particularly appealing to today's "baby-boomer" audience as well as "teenagers" who make up a significant segment of the moviegoing audience.

According to a marketing analysis of BALI BROTHERS film script there are many reasons why a film with its theme and story will be of interest to audiences:

*"This independent film is being produced by filmmaker Michael Wiese who for the last 28 years has been a frequent visitor to Bali."*

• **The romantic aspect** of the story—one of the young men falls in love with a village girl—will be an outstanding marketing hook for both male and female audiences.

• Older audiences idealize <u>Bali as a tropical paradise</u>; a time when life was simpler.

• Young audiences identify with **the young adventurers' search for meaning and purpose.**

This film is being produced by independent filmmaker Michael Wiese who for the last 28 years has been a frequent visitor to Bali. His appreciation of the Balinese culture is expressed in his novel *On the Edge of a Dream* which is the basis for the screenplay.

During his career Wiese has produced numerous films, videos, television programs and books. His short film *Hardware Wars* has returned over 100 times its original budget and has recently been rereleased.

Wiese's most successful infomercial had a 860% return on investment. The *Shirley MacLaine* video which he produced and directed returned a 456% return on investment. **Wiese's average return has been 242%.**

3

271

# Bali Brothers

### Target Audience: Baby Boomers* and Teens*

MWP contracted Big Horse Productions to complete a marketing analysis and income projection of the film. According to the market research firm, BALI BROTHERS will appeal to two very large audiences.

The first is the "baby boomer" audience which is the largest segment of the U.S. population. They are educated and frequent moviegoers. The film's story takes place during a critical, formative time in this audience's memory. Its theme, setting and place will evoke a "want-to-see" desire among the "boomers." The second audience are the teenager and "twenty-somethings" (18-34) who will be attracted to BALI BROTHERS to see the two young adventurers search for personal growth and explore new relationships of friendship in a larger world.

| | Age Groups | Percent of Group | # of moviegoers |
|---|---|---|---|
| * | 18-24 | 82% | 21,924,916 |
| * | 25-34 | 70% | 30,013,200 |
| | 35-44 | 68% | 26,705,640 |
| * | 45-54 | 58% | 14,629,390 |
| | 55-64 | 40% | 8,459,169 |
| | 65-74 | 34% | 6,156,230 |
| | 75-96 | 19% | 2,495,702 |

### Status of Rights

A final draft screenplay has been written which is based on the novel, *On the Edge of a Dream: Magic and Madness in Bali* by Michael Wiese. The work is wholly owned by MWP. The rights are readily transferable to the Partnership.

### Comparable Box Office Performances

Marketing analyst Jeffrey Hardy, along with the chief financial officer of LucasFilm created FILMPROFIT, an income projection software package which has become an industry standard. While there is no sure-fire method to project income from unreleased films, one approach used by Mr. Hardy is to look for films with similar international appeal.

Mr. Hardy compares the film *Sirens* to BALI BROTHERS which was also an off-shore production utilizing Australian crew, exotic in nature, with sensuous characters and settings. Mr. Hardy thinks the film has similar international appeal and is a good target for the "break-even" model.

*"Wiese deftly recreates that magical and all too brief moment in history when Bali stood poised between her past and her touristic future, with old demons and new ones coming face-to-face across the frontier of myth."*

Lorne Blair,

Author,

*Ring of Fire*

5

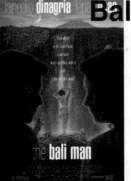

# Bali Brothers

BALI BROTHERS' negative cost is $5 million with less spent for cast. Prints and advertising are projected at $3 million to yield a U.S. box office gross of $9.6 million. International net revenue is projected at $3.9 million. Video sales in the U. S. are projected at 58,000 units.

| | Budget (mil) | P&A (mil) | US (mil) | Int'l (mil) | Video (units) |
|---|---|---|---|---|---|
| Sirens | $ 7 | 5.5 | <8 | <7 | 90,000 |
| BALI BROTHERS (break-even model) | $ 5 | 3.0 | 4.8 | 6 | 58,000 |

In recent years there have been several independent films that have seen a significant return on their investment. Here are some examples of the top 10 best cost-to-return. They represent the high returns that can result from independent film production and distribution.

**Ten Best Cost-To-Return Independent Films**
(in millions)

| | Budget | World-Wide Gross |
|---|---|---|
| The Brothers McMullen | 0.2 | 13.4 |
| Muriel's Wedding | 9.0 | 176.8 |
| While You Were Sleeping | 7.0 | 181.9 |
| Kids | 1.5 | 14.0 |
| Before Sunrise | 2.5 | 22.5 |
| The Usual Suspects | 6.0 | 51.0 |
| Shallow Grave | 2.5 | 20.5 |
| Friday | 3.5 | 28.1 |
| Bridges of Madison County | 24.0 | 175.2 |

*Pulp Fiction* cost $8.2 million to produce and had a $200 million box office gross since October 1994.

Last year's independent film, *Spitfire Grill* was produced for $4 million (plus $2 million in deferments) and was sold at The Sundance Film Festival for a $10 million advance.

*"SPITFIRE GRILL was produced for $6 million and was sold at The Sundance Film Festival for $10 million."*

6

## Production Aspects

There is great value in knowing and communicating who your intended audience is. Here we indicate the large core audience we expect for the film with a more detailed analysis to follow.

## Comparable Box Office Performances

We are not doing a "me-too" film but this information helps the investor to imagine that "they did it, so can we." Find a film that is similar in budget range, locales, and genre to the one you will make.

## Production Aspects

Because our particular film will be shot in an exotic location, we discuss the production aspects that have come together to date. As you continue to develop your film, you continually update this and other pages. This is not the place to go overboard with what you intend to do technically and artistically. Remember the business plan is supposed to be as concise as possible about the project you expect to make. More is not better.

A touch of the technical process is useful to show you know what you're talking about. Too much is not interesting to most readers.

## Progress to Date

This page you will update frequently as people come and go from your project. This is a kind of snapshot of what's true at the moment: a running account of the people involved with the project. It shows there is already great support for the film and that you are moving forward. There is also a disclaimer because none of the people have signed contracts with the production company. Do not represent someone who will actually work on the film unless it is contractual.

# Bali Brothers

### Production Aspects

After 7 weeks of preproduction on location, filming commences for 6 weeks in Bali (on a 6 day per week schedule.) The best times for filming in Bali are after March and before November. [See Production Schedule.]

Additional location scouting and casting trips will occur before the anticipated principal photography date mid-March 1998. The exquisite landscapes—from beaches to terraced rice fields, village temples to volcanoes—will leave an indelible impression of a South Seas paradise in the viewer's mind.

The head of Pengosaken has granted us permission to film in the in village which will include some 10 days of temple ceremonies, rituals, and performances during the Balinese new year.

Most key crew positions will be filled by Australians who are experienced in working in tropical situations. Besides a favorable foreign exchange rate between the U.S. and Australian dollar, the close proximity of Australia to Bali offers further cost savings in the area of travel.

There are few digital special effects and stunts in the film. Some of the filming will use Steadicam rigs which will allow for a higher speed of production.

The cast size is approximately 30; the Australian/Indonesian crew is about 50 people.

Most of the equipment will be rented in country from Sammy's, a reputable equipment house in Jakarta, which saves on transportation and import taxes.

The film will be shot in 35mm and transferred to video for non-linear editing on the AVID (a computerized editing system). After a final cut is complete, the original negative will be conformed and printed, resulting in 35mm theatrical exhibition film prints.

*"I am fascinated by the courage and success of the two American young men especially because they did not come as tourists but tried to live within the customs of the Balinese people. . . extremely visual and, most of all, inspirational."*

Soetomo
Gandasoebrata
Former Dean of
Indonesia's National
Film School,
and esteemed
cinematographer

7

# Bali Brothers

**Progress to Date** (as of 6/1/97)

• The script has been rewritten as a contemporary piece and not as a 60's period piece as was originally contemplated. This brings about a savings of nearly $500,000, and will reduce the number of shooting days significantly without affecting the power of the story.

• Lee Zlotoff (writer/producer of *Spitfire Grill*) has consulted on the script. His film was made for $6 million and sold for $10 million at the Sundance Film Festival.

• A budget by Australian production manager Brigitte Zeisig and Michael Wiese was completed after a two-weeks of location and research in Bali in April 1997.

• Pengosaken village will be the site of much of the filming. They will also supply hundreds of extras, musicians, temples, village compounds, and construction support. Eighty percent of the locations have been found.

• The Park Royal Hotel provided fee and low cost lodging for the recent scouting trip to Bali. They have agreed to provide lodging for cast and crew and will also set up a production center for us with a dozen incoming direct phone lines.

• Lawrence Blair, internationally known on-camera presenter for the TV series "Ring of Fire" has agreed to play the part of Great Scott, a mentor to the young adventurers. He appears as host in a promo video tape for the film.

• Paquita Wijaja, an Indonesian actress/pop singer, is interested in playing the part of Great Scott's girl friend.

• I. Wayan Wija, Bali's most popular shadow puppeteer, has agreed to be in the film.

• I. Dibia, PhD. (dean of Bali's performing arts college, dance, music, drama consultant, author) and Njoman Sumandhi (director of the performing arts high school of Bali, shadow puppeteer and dancer), and Andy Toth (ethnomusicologist and music consultant) will consult on the dance and musical aspects of the film. Dibia will play a role as well.

• U. S. based-Australian production and set designer Bernard Hides (*Casualties of War, Farewell to the King, Jag*) is interested in the project.

• Geoffrey Burton ACS, Director of Photography (*Flirting, Wide Sagasso Sea, Sirens,* and *The Nostradamus Kid)* has been sent the script. He was the cinematographer for the comparable film *Sirens.*

8

# Bali Brothers

- Several presales companies are reading the script.

- Investors have been contacted in the U. S. and Indonesia.

- In April and May 1997, Wiese made another scouting trip to Jakarta and Bali to arrange financing, interview cast and crew, and scout locations. Two more trips are expected before principal photography.

- Fireman's Fund Insurance will review the script and budget for insurance estimation purposes.

- Film Finances Co. will review the script and budget for completion bond consideration.

- Two Indonesian based companies (Katena and BaliVideo) have offered to assist with the production and local permits.

- Cinema 21, which has over 300 first-class theaters (a virtual monopoly), is interested in the film.

- Marketing Consultant Jeffrey Hardy of FILMPROFIT has prepared a marketing analysis of the film and FILMPROFIT income projections.

- Casting Director Laura Schiff has assembled a preliminary "wish list" of actors which will be culled and reviewed in the coming months. (See Lead Actors in the Exhibits section.)

- Editor Stephen Cohen (*Blood and Wine*, Oscar-nominated *Rambling Rose, Lost in Yonkers, Angie, Three Wishes, No Man's Land)* has helped prepare the editing budget. Time available, he is interested in this film project.

- Film Laboratories AtLab in Sydney and Crest National in Hollywood have bid for the film processing work.

- City National Bank (Beverly Hills) is prepared to handle the Escrow Bank Account for the Partnership.

Note: The people and companies herein have been in discussions with the producers. Many have read the screenplay. Some have worked on the development of this presentation. Schedules permitting, most of these people are willing to participate in the film. No contractual agreements have been entered into as yet. No representation is being made here that all of these people will actually participate in the production.

### Budget/Use of Capital — Summary Budget

On the following page is the summary budget for the film. The budget is approximately $4.5 million.

9

## SUMMARY BUDGET
## "Bali Brothers"

| | | | |
|---|---|---|---|
| A. | STORY & SCRIPT | 131,627 | |
| B. | PRODUCER'S UNIT | 245,490 | |
| C. | DIRECTOR'S UNIT | 175,360 | |
| D. | PRINCIPAL CAST | 158,210 | |
| | **Total Above the Line** | | **$710,687** |
| E. | PRODUCTION UNIT | 1,024,279 | |
| F. | FRINGES, PENSION & WELFARE (included above)) | 0 | |
| G. | OTHER CAST & EXTRAS | 61,029 | |
| H. | MUSIC | 130,000 | |
| I. | WARDROBE & MAKE UP | 57,552 | |
| J. | SETS & PROPS | 123,761 | |
| K. | FILM & LAB | 205,298 | |
| L. | SOUND | 123,170 | |
| M. | CAMERA EQUIPMENT | 156,636 | |
| N. | RENTALS, STORAGE & EDITING | 84,441 | |
| O. | TRAVEL & TRANSPORT | 107,133 | |
| P. | HOTEL, LIVING & CATERING | 477,100 | |
| Q. | INSURANCE | 85,000 | |
| R. | PUBLICITY | 36,000 | |
| S. | OFFICE EXPENSES | 37,787 | |
| T. | OTHER PRODUCTION COSTS | 3,822 | |
| U. | FINANCE & LEGAL | 84,885 | |
| V. | COMPLETION BOND | 237,500 | |
| W. | CONTINGENCY | 514,728 | |
| X. | BROKERAGE/UNDERWRITING | 200,000 | |
| | **Total Below the Line** | | 3,750,120 |
| | | | **$ 4,460,807** |
| | less Bond Rebate (2%) | | 95,000 |
| | **TOTAL BUDGET** | | 4,365,807 |

## Budget

The budget is stated and a summary budget enclosed. Investors will want to see how the money is going to be spent.

## Distribution Approach

There are several strategies. Whatever you choose you must be able to support it intelligently. Most independent films will not have a distributor before they are made. There are usually not enough saleable elements to get a distributor. *Shine* is a prime example. The producer received 39 rejections from the majors, minors, and everyone else. There was no known cast and a first-time dramatic director. Tough, but most independent projects will fall into this category.

If you do have some saleable element and are able to make a presale in some country or to pay cable, then you should tout this in the prospectus. That someone has already committed to distribute or broadcast your film gives investors great comfort. Plus, now the entire budget does not have to be raised.

In this section you describe the distribution approach. For most independent films without significant cast this will be an open issue filled with hopes. We hope this, we hope that. If you do not have names in your cast, you cannot presell.

# Bali Brothers

### Distribution Approach

Our film is free of studio overheads and large star salaries. **Its cost is 9% of the budget of the average Hollywood film.** The exotic locations and favorable foreign currency exchange rates should give the film a look of 2 or 3 times its actual cost which should help during the selling process.

Our marketing strategy is to use publicity to "create heat" around the film's production and elements, then later screening it at prestigious film festivals like Sundance, Toronto, Cannes or Berlin. **It is our expectation that a number of worldwide distributors will wish to license the film for advances which will not only recoup the investor's $4.5 million investment but also yield a profit.** In addition, it is expected that there will be additional ongoing revenues. The income projections describe this scenario in greater detail.

*"We expect to license the film to U. S. and foreign distributors at the most advantageous times for the Partnership."*

Besides the traditional studio distribution arms (Disney, Warners, Sony, Universal, Paramount, Fox) there are other US distributors, including Miramax, Sony Classics, Trimark, October, Fox Searchlight, Gramercy, New Line, MGM/UA, Lakeshore, and Savoy who attend the film festivals and markets to buy independent films. Foreign distributors also attend as buyers. Uncompromised and unencumbered by the studios, independent producers make the best films they can and sell them to the highest bidding distributor.

We expect to license the film to U. S. and foreign distributors at the most advantageous times for the Partnership. This licensing could occur immediately before principal photography before the buyer has seen the film and when interest may be especially high. Or licensing could occur once the film is finished and premieres in festivals. We do not expect to show the film during editing as we want to build up a "bidding war" for the completed film.

### Income Projections

The spreadsheet on the following page shows three different levels of performance for the film ( "break-even,, "medium," and "high") and the subsequent return of net profits to the investors.

11

# Bali Brothers

The income is returned to the limited partnership investor over the "life" of the film which could stretch for a decade or more. However, about 80% of the film's revenues are expected in the first three years which is what is projected in the tables herein.

These are the income projections from all markets worldwide over a three year period. Excluded are merchandising and television syndication. In addition, it is possible to obtain better deals from distributors than are indicated here, such as a 25% or 30% home video royalty rather than 20%. **Instead of making high projections we have taken a more conservative approach in regards to the available distribution markets and more favorable deal structures.**

Here is an explanation rationale for the "break-even," "medium," and "low" income projections on the previous page:

### U.S. Distribution

*"Instead of making high projections, we have taken a more conservative approach in regards to the available distribution markets and more favorable deal structures."*

We assume that $9.6 million is received from the box office. A distributor's share is approximately 50% or $4.8 million. From this, a distributor will deduct 30% as a distribution fee and then what they have spent for film prints and advertising. Ideally, as a film rolls out, the distributor will spend less and less on marketing in relationship to the gross revenues brought in. That is why—at the "high" projection—a distributor spends $10 million to net $17.5 million from film rentals.

### Non-Theatrical Rentals

These are the revenues collected by the distributor from film rental to universities, colleges, and other institutions. There is minimal income from these markets.

### Pay/Cable

A U.S. pay cable network, such as Showtime, The Movie Channel, HBO or Cinemax will license the film for broadcast following the theatrical and home video release of the film. The better the film does at the box office, the greater its preexposure and worth to a pay television buyer.

### Television & Syndication

The final ancillary market is licensing to network television and syndication. **Sales are not shown in these projections because they occur well after the three year period projected here.**

# Bali Brothers

### Home Video

For a finished independent film the distributor is not entitled to a distribution fee from home video. A royalty of 20% (or more) will be paid directly to the producer. Sometimes a large portion of the anticipated royalty is paid out as an "advance" prior to distribution and before actual sales are made. Assuming a retail sales price of $100, and a wholesale price of $62, a 20% royalty would yield $12 per unit. In the "break-even model" a sale of 58,333 units (at a 20% royalty) would generate $700,000 in revenues. In the medium scenario, a 20% royalty would generate $2.5 million in revenues. Usually, the better the theatrical performance, the better the home video sales, but not always.

### Sound Track Royalties

Similar to a home video advance, a record company would pay an "advance against royalties" for the rights to distribute the motion picture sound track on CD or audio cassette. Assuming a retail price of $15.00 and a wholesale price of $9.00, a royalty of 10% ($.90 per unit.) on sales of 77,000 units would generate $700,000. A sale of 444,444 would generate $400,000. **The sales of the sound track to foreign record companies have not been projected.**

### Foreign Distribution

A foreign distributor will license the rights in each media (theatrical, home video, tv, pay/cable) to the territories throughout the world. Often these are "advances" from which the distributor will deduct a 35% distribution fee.

### Foreign Film Rental
These are the revenues generated by theatrical exhibition of the film worldwide. Foreign theatrical markets may return revenues equal to, or greater than, the U.S. box office rentals. **Conservatively, we have projected that the foreign film rental is either less or equal to the U. S. box office rentals.**

### Foreign Television License Fees
These are the net license fees for the foreign television rights.

### Foreign Home Video Royalty
These are the net license fees for the foreign home video rights.

### Foreign Pay/Cable
These are the net fees for the foreign pay television and syndication rights.

14

*"BALI BROTHERS' budget is 9% of the cost of the average Hollywood film."*

## Income Projections

This is the most important page in the prospectus. Every investor will flip here within moments of receiving your document. From most presentations that I've seen, this is by far the weakest page. Most producers are quite adept at coming up with all the other information that we've discussed but when it comes to the numbers, the wild assumptions and bad math make the most important page fall flat. Then the proposal and project lack credibility.

I recommend that you do three projections. "Break-even," "medium," and "high".

The break-even shows the investor how the film has to perform in order to return their money. If your budget is too high, then the film must work even harder to make its money back. Not a compelling investment.

Next pick an average expectation. Would it be bad to earn 20% a year return on your investment? Heck no. What would your film have to do in all the various markets to hit this target? If it looks realistic and there's not too much "blue-skying," it will give an investor comfort.

Lastly, do a "high" projection. Here you want to "blue-sky" but not to the *Star Wars* or *Pulp Fiction* level. You want to dream a little, but not too much.

All your assumptions in the income projection page must be supportable and documented in the prospectus. It's very easy to do high projections but substantiating your claims is another thing. In actuality it's all fantasy. The film could bomb or it could have spectacular results. You just don't know, but you have to write a plan as if you do. Remember, this is a selling and promotional document. This is not the legal document. You are not making any promises, only doing your best to project.

| | | "BALI BROTHERS" | | |
|---|---|---|---|---|
| | | **Income Projection Summary** | | |
| | | Over a 3 year Period | | *Prepared 1/6/1998* |
| | | | | |
| | | | | |
| **U.S. BOX OFFICE:** | | **$9,600,000** | | |
| | | | | |
| | | **BREAKEVEN** | **MEDIUM** | **HIGH** |
| **U.S. DISTRIBUTION** | | | | |
| US Film Rental | | 4,800,000 | 9,000,000 | 17,500,000 |
| Nontheatrical Rentals | | 80,000 | 150,000 | 200,000 |
| Pay/Cable | | 400,000 | 750,000 | 2,750,000 |
| | | 5,280,000 | 9,900,000 | 20,450,000 |
| *less distribution fees* | *30%* | (1,584,000) | (2,970,000) | (6,135,000) |
| *less Prints & Advertising ('P&A.)* | | (3,000,000) | (5,000,000) | (10,000,000) |
| | | | | |
| | | 696,000 | 1,930,000 | 4,315,000 |
| | | | | |
| **HOME VIDEO ROYALTY** | | | | |
| *no distribution fee* | | 700,000 | 2,500,000 | 5,000,000 |
| | | | | |
| **SOUND TRACK ROYALTIES** | | | | |
| *no distribution fee* | | 90,000 | 200,000 | 400,000 |
| | | | | |
| **FOREIGN DISTRIBUTION** | | | | |
| Foreign Film Rental | | 3,900,000 | 9,000,000 | 15,000,000 |
| Foreign Television License Fees | | 600,000 | 800,000 | 2,500,000 |
| Foreign Home Video Royalty | | 900,000 | 1,600,000 | 5,000,000 |
| Foreign Pay/Cable | | 600,000 | 1,700,000 | 2,500,000 |
| | | 6,000,000 | 13,100,000 | 25,000,000 |
| *less foreign distribution fees* | *35%* | (2,100,000) | (4,585,000) | (8,750,000) |
| | | 3,900,000 | 8,515,000 | 16,250,000 |
| | | | | |
| **GROSS REVENUES TO PARTNERSHIP** | | **$5,386,000** | **$13,145,000** | **$25,965,000** |
| | | | | |
| Film Cost | | 4,500,000 | 4,500,000 | 4,500,000 |
| | | | | |
| Deferments | | 0 | 0 | 0 |
| | | | | |
| **Net Profit to Partnership** | | **$886,000** | **$8,645,000** | **$21,465,000** |
| | | | | |
| **Investor's Share** | | **$443,000** | **$4,322,500** | **$10,732,500** |
| | | | | |
| | Return on Investment | 10% | 96% | 239% |

*Note: These are hypothetical projections for information purposes only. No guarantee of net profits nor return of income can be made.*

## State of the Industry

Although 1996 was an unusually good year of critical acclaim for independent films, it is discussed nevertheless and the reader is reminded how so many of the Academy Award® nominated films were from independents. In the next section this is backed up with actual revenue as well.

## Expanding Foreign Markets

Describe the expanding marketplace for independent films and the trend of independent filmmaking as much as possible and support it with numbers throughout your document. To say it's one thing, to back it up with numbers from credible sources is another. Investors want to feel that your project will reward them financially and they are willing to dream with you, but you have to show them the facts.

# Bali Brothers

### State of the Independent Film Industry — An Overview

There are two ways to produce a film in America. The first is through the traditional Hollywood studio system in which the average film costs $39 million and has an average marketing budget of $19 million. For this reason, Hollywood finances only large "event" films with mega-stars and high concept themes for mass audiences.

The second route—and the one we shall employ—is through independent financing outside of the studio system. We shall produce a smaller, lower budgeted film with an adult-theme for a more specialized audience.

As Hollywood films get bigger in scale and budget, a significant market is emerging for the more serious, story and character-driven, independently produced film. This trend began eight years ago with *sex, lies & videotape* which was the first commercial hit to come out of the film festival world. Since then, independent films have generated $735 million in yearly box office sales in North America alone. The total box office gross for independent films has risen from 5% in 1992 to about 14% in 1995.

*"Our film's story, unique characters, spectacular locations, and stunning photography is well positioned to generate profits. . ."*

These independent films appeal to the burgeoning baby-boomer audience who are looking for more intelligent, story-driven fare.

In 1995, three of the five 1995 Oscar nominations for Best Director were for small pictures (*The Postman, Leaving Las Vegas* [made in 16mm for $3.5 million], and *Dead Man Walking*). These independent low-budget films not only reached wide audiences, but were profitable.

The 1996 film critic nominations for the Best Film, Actor, Actress, and Director Awards demonstrate that the **critics clearly favor independent films.** Of the 35 nominations, **independent films received 83% of the awards.** Hollywood films are clearly losing the critical battle to well-made, smaller scale films that appeal to both younger and older audiences.

### Greater Financial Upside

Independent films cost less money and therefore have a greater opportunity to recoup their investment and return profits to investors.

A Feb. 2nd, 1997, *New York Times* article says, *"Hollywood has embraced independent films as never before. . . a huge middle ground has emerged (for independent films)."*

16

# Bali Brothers

### Expanding Foreign Markets

According to the American Film Marketing Association (which represents the non-major distributors) **independent English-language films collected a record-breaking $1.656 billion at the international box office in 1996.** Experts say this number will grow.

Total Foreign Sales for U.S. Independent Films in 1996
(in millions)

| | | |
|---|---|---|
| Theatrical | $ 501.3 | 30% |
| Pay TV | 250.5 | 16% |
| Video | 418.1 | 25% |
| Free TV | 485.7 | 29% |

### Funding of the Picture/Cofinancing

We expect to fund the film through sales of units in a Limited Partnership. We will simultaneously seek presales from selected pay cable and international markets at appropriate times to raise production money. Sales to the remaining territories and markets will occur after the film is finished.

The budget of the film is approximately $5 million dollars. The budget will be raised through a Limited Partnership. **The Limited Partners will retain 50% equity in the net profits (and losses) of the partnership after first recouping 100% of their investment.**

The Partnership's gross revenues shall be obtained by licensing the film's theatrical, pay television, free television, home video, and music rights in territories throughout the world.

If one or more individuals are responsible for raising and/or contributing a significant budget amount, then he or she shall receive an "Executive Producer" credit on the film.

An Escrow Account will be set up at City National Bank in Beverly Hills. Investments will be made into an interest-bearing account until such time as either the amount necessary to begin is raised and the production commences, or the money is returned in full with interest.

There will be various milestones that must be met before a percentage of the budget will be released to MWP, the production company:

| | |
|---|---|
| • PreProduction | 15% |
| • Prior to Principal Photography | 45% |
| • End of Principal Photography | 30% |
| • Laboratory Work is Complete | 10% |

17

287

## Funding

Here is a discussion of the amount that shall be raised, how limited partners will participate, the setting up of an escrow account, and budget milestones. It is a very brief overview of the financial structure and requirements.

## General Company Description

A key question from investors will be about the company that's making the film. Or the filmmakers. What is the history of the company? Its longevity? Its past experiences? Relate your background to the project being pitched. Include your history as an independent, your experience in distribution and marketing. In my proposal I present both my production and marketing background and drop names of well–known organizations that investors may recognize. Do not be modest. If you have a great credit or story to tell, use it.

Track records are also important. In my proposal I averaged the return on investment on ten projects that I produced. I threw in a few that bombed; I did not include the largest hit as I wanted to come up with an average that looked good, but not outrageous. I found that my return on investment averaged about 242%. In truth there is no telling what will happen with your current project. The investor is looking for this to be your next hit so you should position your current project in a positive light.

Help them dream and expect high returns, but at the same time show you are realistic and conservative. Even cautious. Do not overly hype the project. Am I talking out of both sides of my mouth? In a way I am. It's a delicate balance between stating what you think will happen and what you hope will happen. You do not want to raise unrealistic expectations. If you've put together a great project with highly promotable elements, then you really do have a chance for success. Say that.

### General Company Description -
Michael Wiese Productions (MWP)

Michael Wiese Productions (MWP) was founded in 1976 and incorporated in California in 1990. **In its 20 year history, it has produced films, videos, infomercials, and television programs.** It utilizes a small staff and relies on an extensive free-lance staff for its various projects.

Michael Wiese Productions also operates a book publishing company with a line of best-selling professional film software and film books, eight of which Wiese has authored.

As a producer of independent short and documentary films, Michael Wiese Productions was very active until 1981 when he left California for New York City where he held several high-level corporate careers.

Wiese's corporate careers:

- DHS Films (an agency producing political television commercials)
- Showtime/The Movie Channel (a pay television broadcaster)
- Vestron Video (a home video and independent film distributor)

Wiese has also worked as a consultant to:

- National Geographic Television
- The Smithsonian Institution
- Republic Pictures Home Video
- Hanna-Barbera Home Video
- King World Television

### About Michael Wiese

Wiese began making films in the mid-1960s. During his career he has produced a prodigious number of media products: from films to television, from books to videos.

Michael Wiese has his share of hits and misses. The hits have been very profitable; the misses disappointing. It is Wiese's belief that **the more quality programs you create, the greater the opportunity for profitability.**

*"The more quality programs you create, the greater the opportunity for profitability."*

18

289

# Bali Brothers

### As an Independent Producer

MWP has produced a wide array of media products ranging from films to videos, from television programs to infomercials. Of the 10 projects shown in the "Past Performance" page, **the average total return on investment is 599%.** This is unusually high because of the phenomenal success of HARDWARE WARS, a *Star Wars* parody which was released in 1977 and is in rerelease now, some twenty years later. If HARDWARE WARS was not included in this chart, then the **average return on investment is 242%.** In keeping with Wiese's past average performances **our "high" income projection does not exceed a 210% return on investment**.

### As a Corporate Executive

While Michael Wiese was vice president at Vestron Video from 1984-1988 where he developed, produced, and/or acquired over 200 programs, **more than 94% were profitable** for the company. Here isa sampling of titles which Wiese acquired or executive-produced (e.g., oversaw production). They have **an average return on investment of 741%.**

While it is impossible to forecast future profits from BALI BROTHERS, the attached income projections anticipate accumulated sales in all media to **yield a return on investment of up to a high of 210% over a three year period.**

Wiese's three career phases:

- independent producer      1965-1981    16 years
- corporate media executive    1981-1988     7 years
- 2nd independent period     1988-1998    10 years

Having first been an independent producer, Wiese later worked "inside" for various commercial producers, pay/cable broadcasters, and home video companies. Learning about market-place distribution and marketing, Wiese has returned once again to the independent arena with these skills.

*"Having first been an independent producer, he later learned about distribution and marketing."*

19

290

# Bali Brothers

### Past Performances

Wiese's student film was invited to the prestigious Cannes Film Festival making him perhaps one of the youngest filmmakers to ever have a film shown there. **His first big hit was _Hardware Wars_, a parody of _Star Wars_. It has returned over 100 times its original budget** and is still going strong. After 20 years, the film is currently in rerelease and it is expected that many more multiples of net profits will be achieved.

Over 200 videos were produced, acquired, and/or marketed by Wiese while he was an executive at Vestron Video. He achieved an extraordinarily very high rate of return. He founded Vestron's original program business and gross revenues from his division exceeded $80 million. **Nearly all of the videos released under Wiese's regime were profitable,** some making more than 10 times their investment.

As an independent, Wiese produced and directed _Shirley MacLaine's Inner Workout Video_ which was **on the best-selling charts for over a year and returned 456% of its investment**. Wiese produced and directed several profitable informercials, including _The MacDougal Program_ (an 860% return). **He also has had some complete failures where the entire investment was lost.** Independent production depends on a strong well-packaged product, strong marketing, and a timely release into the marketplace, the latter being impossible to control.

The chart on the following page shows the return on investments on various Michael Wiese projects.

_"His student film was premiered by Salvador Dali and received a special invitation to The Cannes Film Festival."_

20

**Production Team Bios**

Here you list your team. This is another page that will be expanded as the project develops.

It can include producer, director, cast, screenwriter, director of photography, production manager, production designer, associate producers, executive producers, marketing consultants, distributors (if any), casting agent, composer, publicist, photographer, entertainment attorney, financial consultants, accountant, banker, production insurer, completion bond company, etc.

Make a note as to who is contractual and who is not. Investors will want to know what rights are in place and what binding contracts already exist.

The previous pages are the core of the prospectus. The pages that follow are included in the exhibits or appendix section.

**Cast Hit List**

This prospectus was written before casting had begun, therefore we included a four page list of our cast "wish list"; the actors we'd like to see for the parts. No actors had been confirmed when the prospectus was written. If you have committments from recognizable actors then obviously this element is played up at the very beginning of your proposal.

# Bali Brothers

### ProductionTeam (Bios)

### Producer/Director
Michael Wiese was vice president at Vestron Video where he developed, executive-produced, and/or marketed over 300 programs including *Robin Williams, Billy Crystal, Whoopi Goldberg, Arnold Palmer, National Geographic,* and many others. His credits include *Shirley MacLaine's Inner Workout* (Producer-Director), *The Beach Boys: An American Band* (Executive Producer), *Hardware Wars* (Producer-Cinematographer), *Dolphin* (Producer-Director), and *Diet for A New America* (Executive Producer). He has written many best-selling books covering independent filmmaking and a novel about Bali on which this film is based. Wiese has lived and traveled in Bali over the past 26 years and has developed extensive personal contacts.

*"Wiese developed, produced and/or acquired over 200 programs. More than 94% were profitable. . ."*

### Production Manager
Brigitte Zeisig has been a production manager and line producer since 1979. She was line producer on *Trackers* and is currently production manager for the Television Unit at Murdoch Media on two new dramas. Her credits include the Australian films *Sons of Steel, The Girl From Steel City,* as well as television specials and series including *German Democracy* (National Geographic Special).

### Production Designer
Australian production designer Bernard Hides (*Casualties of War, Farewell to the King, Jag*) has overseen a number of high budget Australian and American feature films and television series.

### Associate Producer
Ken Lee is vice president, Michael Wiese Productions, and has overseen the management of all production and publishing operations for the last 6 years. He previously worked in advertising agencies and in corporate media production.

### Marketing Consultant
Jeffrey Hardy is the president of FILMPROFIT which has developed and commercially markets a software program for projecting income returns from motion pictures. He is also the head of the marketing group which analyzes feature films' marketing potential.

22

293

# Bali Brothers

### Casting
Laura Schiff is president of Laura Schiff Casting. She has cast numerous low-budget films for Roger Corman's Concorde-Horizon Films.

### Publicity Photography
Geraldine Overton was a chief photographer for CBS Networks for nearly 20 years. Her photographs of hundreds of television and film stars have appeared in entertainment and mass market magazines in the U. S. and abroad.

### Publicity
Joe Dera and Associates will manage the publicity surrounding the film. Joe Dera was formerly the head of the office for Rogers and Cowan in New York City. His clients include Paul McCartney among others.

### Entertainment Attorney
Edward Labowitz, Esq., is a partner in Alexander, Halloran, Nau & Rose, Los Angeles. He has represented numerous film producers in developing their projects, arranging financing and distribution. He has represented MWP in various projects over the last 5 years.

### Financial Legal Services
Bruce Vann, Esq., is a partner in Meyer & Vann, Los Angeles. He specializes in motion picture financing. He has prepared Limited Partnership Agreements for MWP in the past.

### Accountant
Steven Salant, CPA, formerly worked for Michael Neidorff & Associates, a leading Los Angeles entertainment management firm. He has prepared partnership tax returns for MWP over the last 7 years.

### Banking
City National Bank in Studio City has been MWP's bank since 1989. The Beverly Hills branch has previously managed MWP's Escrow production accounts.

### Production Insurer
Fireman's Fund in Los Angeles has provided production insurance to MWP productions in the past.

### Completion Bond
It is expected that the partnership will obtain a completion bond from the Film Finance Bond Co.

23

## Production Schedule

This page can go out of date very quickly so you will probably be updating it frequently. (No one starts his film when he thinks he will. It takes a long time to finance your film.) Sometimes I use headings on this chart which read "first month," "second month," etc., meaning that the production process begins the first month from when all the financing is actually obtained.

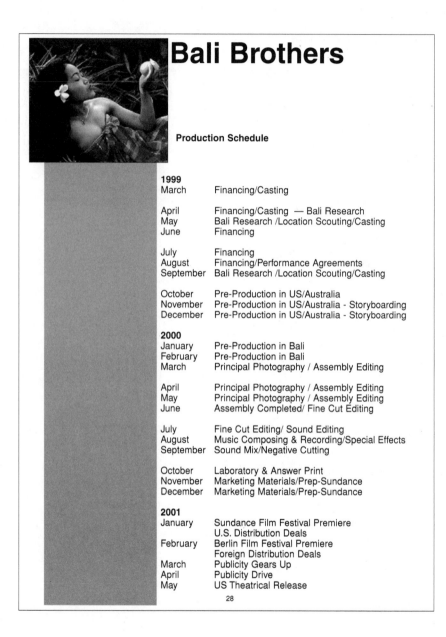

# Bali Brothers

**Production Schedule**

**1999**
March       Financing/Casting

April          Financing/Casting — Bali Research
May           Bali Research /Location Scouting/Casting
June         Financing

July          Financing
August     Financing/Performance Agreements
September Bali Research /Location Scouting/Casting

October    Pre-Production in US/Australia
November  Pre-Production in US/Australia - Storyboarding
December  Pre-Production in US/Australia - Storyboarding

**2000**
January     Pre-Production in Bali
February   Pre-Production in Bali
March       Principal Photography / Assembly Editing

April          Principal Photography / Assembly Editing
May           Principal Photography / Assembly Editing
June         Assembly Completed/ Fine Cut Editing

July          Fine Cut Editing/ Sound Editing
August     Music Composing & Recording/Special Effects
September Sound Mix/Negative Cutting

October    Laboratory & Answer Print
November  Marketing Materials/Prep-Sundance
December  Marketing Materials/Prep-Sundance

**2001**
January     Sundance Film Festival Premiere
              U.S. Distribution Deals
February   Berlin Film Festival Premiere
              Foreign Distribution Deals
March       Publicity Gears Up
April          Publicity Drive
May           US Theatrical Release

28

## Marketing Analysis

I was fortunate to have Jeffrey Hardy prepare a detailed marketing analysis for me. Using outside counsel to give their opinion about the market potential and target audience for the film is a very useful exercise. Too often filmmakers focus more on the making of their movie than on whom their movie is for. A marketing consultant can help focus the thinking on the best markets for a particular film.

# *The Bali Man*

## FilmProfit Market Positioning Report

prepared expressly for

## Michael Wiese Productions

January, 1997

# THE GENERAL MOVIE-GOING AUDIENCE

### *Who Goes to the Movies?*

According to the Motion Picture Association of America, 67 percent of all Americans over 18 years of age go to the movies. Which means approximately 124 million of us are heading for the Bijou, and buying the tickets that generate this industry's annual gross revenues of $5.7 billion in ticket sales in 1996. Naturally, some of us attend more often than others as you can see from the charts below:

*Percent of yearly movie admissions by age of movie-goer, 1992*

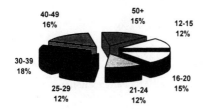

source: Harold L. Vogel, Entertainment Industry Economics

Ticket Sales by age for 1992, as reported by the Motion Picture Association of America, reveal the spending power represented in each of these groups.

- **15%** of all tickets were sold to the **16-20 year-old** market, which spends approximately $810 million annually,
- The **40-49 age group** represents **16%** of the overall market.
- The **30-39 year old market** commands the highest portion of sales at **18%**, representing approximately $826.2 million at the box-office.

### *Frequency of Attendance Among Adults 18 years and over*

| | | |
|---|---|---|
| At least once a month | 24% | 44.42 million |
| At least once every 2-6 months | 32% | 59.23 million |
| Less than once in 6 months | 11% | 20.36 million |
| Never attend | 31% | 57.38 million |
| Not reported | 2% | _3.70_ million |
| | | 184.09 million |

(total US pop. of adults 18+)

MPAA 1995 Almanac; 1992 figures/184 million adults is population according to 1990 census

### Analysis of Movie-Going Audience by Age, Education and Income

#### An Aging Audience

Looking at the general movie-going audience by demographic factors such as age, education and income reveal several emerging trends, that can be used in developing a marketing strategy and to identify a highly efficient target market for *The Bali Man.* Let's first examine the National Endowment for the Arts survey of over 12,000 Americans * which indicates movie-going propensity among different age groups:

| Age Groups | Percent of Group | # of movie goers |
|------------|------------------|------------------|
| 18-24 | 82% | 21,924,916 |
| 25-34 | 70% | 30,013,200 |
| 35-44 | 68% | 26,705,640 |
| 45-54 | 58% | 14,629,390 |
| 55-64 | 40% | 8,459,169 |
| 65-74 | 34% | 6,156,230 |
| 75-96 | 19% | 2,495,702 |

Source: U. S. Bureau of the Census, and Arts Participation in America: 1982-1992, NEA Research Division Report #27

* 1992 Survey of Public Participation in the Arts, conducted by the U.S. Bureau of the Census lists the mean movie attendance as 59% among those responding yes or no to "During the LAST 12 MONTHS did YOU go out to the movies?"; differing from the MPAA 68% figure due to the SPPA inclusion of the oldest age segment (75-96)

Here we can see how movie attendance rapidly declines after age 55, but as the largest segment of the population - the baby boomers - age, we are seeing their demographic muscle shift the profile of the general movie-going audience.

Ticket Sales by age for 1992, as reported by the Motion Picture Association of America and represented in the chart below, reveal the spending power commanded at the box office for each of these groups. Representing 15 percent of all tickets sold, the 16-20 year-old market spends approximately $810 million annually, close to the 40-49 group, representing 16 percent of the overall market. While the 30-39 year old market commands the highest portion of sales at 18 percent, representing approximately $826.2 million at the box-office.

Traditionally, the motion picture industry's primary marketing axiom maintained that 17-year-olds determined the success or failure of movies because of their high attendance at the crucial first weekend release. Since the late 1960s , teenagers have been the most reliable moviegoing audience. But the drive-ins of those days are now bygone relics turned to swap meets, and the teens of that time are now middle-aged baby boomers. As this comparison chart shows, today, teens and young adults are vastly outnumbered by older boomers. And the movie tastes of these groups are very different, as are their reasons for attending a film. This represents an opportunity for *The Bali Man* and it's dramatic themes of coming to terms with friendship and with one's self.

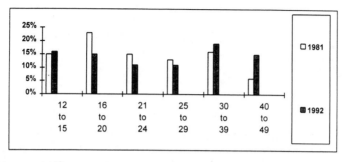

### An Educated Audience

Adults with at least some college education are most likely to attend movies, and this crowd wants more sophisticated fare than they can find on television.

According to the NEA 1992 Arts Participation Study, 81 percent of adults with a graduate degree attend movies, and 77 percent of those with Bachelor's degrees attend. Whereas only 54 percent of high school graduates indicate attending. Falling in line with this trend, 71 percent of those with some college education indicate attending movies. Interestingly enough, average hours of daily television viewing trend in a similar manner, with those holding graduate degrees viewing the least (2.1 hours), and those with some high school viewing the most (3.7 hours). Targeting a college educated audience is extremely efficient, both as a core audience and as the opinion leaders others count on in selecting films.

As of 1995 calculations based on Census Bureau surveys of the 168 million Americans aged 25 or older, 23 percent indicate having some college (including associate's degrees), 15 percent hold a bachelor's degree (25.2 million), and 8 percent have completed graduate degrees (13.44 million).

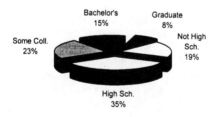

### A Well-Heeled Audience

Household income figures indicate a clear trend in movie attendance:

| HHI level | percent attending movies |
|-----------|--------------------------|
| Under $5,000 | 43% |
| 5,000-9,999 | 35% |
| 10,000-14,999 | 44% |
| 15,000-24,999 | 53% |
| 25,000-49,999 | 67% |
| 50,000 and over | 76% |
| not ascertained | 58% |

*1992 NEA Arts Participation Study, Research Division Report #27*

According to the 1990 census, of the 94.3 million total U.S. households, 18.5 percent households earn $15,000-24,999 annually, with the majority of 35.5 percent of households in the $25,000-49,999 income range. At the extreme ends of the income scale, 25.5 percent of households earn under $14,999, and 20.4 percent of all American households command an income of $50,000 or more. High income is a strong predictor of attendance, but in large part due to its connection to education.

### Tailoring Efficient Target Audiences for The Bali Man

Positioning for *The Bali Man* will be strategized to take advantage of an aging audience as well as a secondary target of teens to establish first weekend box office. Marketing angles that will resonate with the older audience are the story's sixties setting, the search for self and a peacefully close community, as well as Nick's ultimate act of sacraficing his freedom for a friend in need. As the generation that embraced the Peace Corp they will also appreciate the exotic locale. Highlighting the adventure of two friends taking off to explore the wider world together, and growing up in the process, will appeal to the teen segment. Each of these audiences are explored below.

### Cashing in on Boomer Behavior

Sixteen years ago, 24 percent of total yearly admissions to movies were to those aged 16 to 20, according to the MPAA. By 1992, only 15 percent of admissions were for those aged 16 to 20. Attendance of 40-49-year-olds rose from just 6 percent to 16 percent during the same period. This is while not forgetting the 30-39 year old market, which commands the highest portion of sales at 18 percent, representing approximately $826.2 million at the box-office. No doubt about it, attendance of middle-aged adults has jumped in each of the last three years, and this trend will continue for the next decade. Since aging boomers are making up an increasing part of the first-run audience, and just beginning to reach their peak earning years, as frequent movie-goers, educated and monied boomers are a prime target to build *The Bali Man* audience. As boomers are the largest segment of the population, the net can be cast quite wide to capture this group.

According to Fred Pampel, professor of Sociology at the University of Iowa, his studies show these older adults are attracted to a greater mix of movies than are teenagers, resisting stories of teen angst and those with the goriest of violence. They appreciate films with adult and timeless themes, and selectively attend those that appear to be popular, entertaining, and original. Certainly the story of *The Bali Man* and it's themes of search for personal growth and negotiating relationships of friendship and a close community—in the Bali village where Nick and Eddie settle—is speaking to the tastes and interests of this grown-up audience. In selecting a film, older adults respond most often to critical acclaim and to recommendations from friends.

It would be advisable to utilize film festivals, where the picture will be exposed to critics and opinion leaders, as well as utilizing PR aimed at the prime portion of this target -- 30-49 years-old, with some college and household incomes of $15,000+ -- to generate the enthusiastic word-of-mouth and critical acclaim necessary to draw these targeted boomers to the theater. Further narrowing this target definition by concentrating on those households with children under 18 at home will also be an efficient tactic.

### *"Kids at Home" as an Indicator of Movie Attendance Among Adults*

Adults with children under 18 living at home attend movies more often than adults with no children at home according to the MPAA. Of the total 98 million U.S. households, married couples with children under 18 represent 26 percent in 1995, and single parents represent 9 percent. Certainly many of these adults are accompanying children to family oriented films, but just as surely they are attending movies as a perfectly timed respite from the kids, and this is when they enjoy more adult-themed fare.

Consider the comparison of movie attendance figures of adults <u>with</u> children to that of adults <u>without</u> children: Of adults who attend movies frequently (at least once a month), those with and without children are fairly even, but among those adults attending movies occasionally (at least once in 2 to 6 months) there is a dramatic difference between these two groups. Whereas 40 percent of the 78 million adults with children under 18 in the home occasionally attend, only 28 percent of adults without children attend at the occasional level. Childless adults are less likely than average to go to the movies, to the extent that **38 percent of adults without children *never* attend films**.

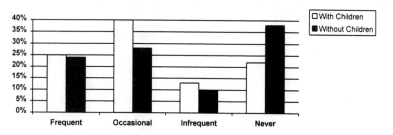

While the older audience is growing, teens still are a powerful movie-going segment.

### Strategies to Approach Teens

Today, nearly half of teenagers go to the movies at least once a month, compared with just one in four adults. Because teens (those 12-20 years of age) make up such a large share of opening week audiences, they continue to be a prime target for movie marketers, representing 24 percent of all movie admissions in 1994. Movie makers are now targeting a prime segment of the teen market to gain entry to the entire teen audience, New Line Cinema, Disney and MGM have conducted focus group discussions among urban youth. This particular segment has been deemed key in developing the cultural cache not only needed to address American youth, but teens in overseas markets as well with forces such as MTV globalizing teen style and taste.

*"If a movie develops good word-of-mouth among urban teens, it is practically destined for success."* --- Ivan Juzang, President MEE Productions, a research firm doing focus groups for Hollywood studios including Disney.

Teens will attend a movie without advance word-of-mouth if they see it addressing their lifestage issues. But, especially amongst urban teens, a good soundtrack can be a clincher. Developing a soundtrack for *The Bali Man* will find a good match between contemporary popular music trends; sounds of the sixties are alluded to in many of top alternative and rap hits, as are culturally diverse "ethnic" sounds finding their way in to the mix. So much so in fact that Depeche Mode, a successful contemporary band, is being now sued by a Thai man whose chants they included—without his knowledge—in a 1996 chart topper. While Paul Simon has been exploring this for years, and David Bowie's most recent hit "You Little Wonder," uses a Trinidadian drum band as a backdrop, utilizing younger bands will better attract the younger audience.

### A Growing Indie Audience

Over the last decade, independent films and independent directors have been achieving increasing monetary success and recognition. According to Goldman Sachs Reports, in 1983 41.9 percent of U.S. movie release were major studio products, whereas in 1993 the number of pictures released by major studios had shrunk to capture only 34.7 percent of the market share. During this same period consumer expenditures on filmed entertainment have more than doubled, reaching $40 billion in 1994, according to Standard & Poor's analysis.

The growth in the numbers of film festivals and attendance at these festivals over the last 20 years is indicative of the increasing sophistication among movie-goers. While Hollywood has tried to address this sophistication, independents rely on their more daring artistic vision to infuse fresh angles into telling a story. Recent pictures without Hollywood size budgets, such as *The English Patient*, Shine, *Big Night, Breaking The Waves,* just to name a few, have drawn successful box office audiences to stories with a more independent viewpoint. And it should be noted that independent pictures with smaller budgets can have very attractive cost-to-return ratios. Witness *The Wedding Banquet,* the picture with the highest cost-to-return ratio of 1993.

Where there's an audience, there's money and this growing indie audience is now being courted by Hollywood as a revenue source. Studio executives, agents and development people are now regular attendees of film festivals, as they hunt for material and talent. Hollywood is not the only corporate structure to show an interest in this expanding audience, The Independent Film cable channel is also now in the process of being launched, which will give independent filmmakers an additional vehicle for their pictures to be shown.

## Film Profit®

FilmProfit® is an extraordinary program designed to give extremely detailed income projections for investors. In our prospectus we ran very detailed spreadsheets for all three income projections (break-even, medium, and high). Each report runs seven pages. However, this is far more detailed information that draws upon a great number of factors. Using the software you make assumptions about the return in each market, you describe the rollout period for theatrical exhibition, the distribution fees, and the program does the rest.

```
                  Michael Wiese
        FilmProfit       Michael Wiese Productions
LN      DISTRIBUTION PLAN  The Bali Man
#       SUMMARY REPORT    HIGHLIGHTS OF PROJECTED RESULTS

101   Film Project            The Bali Man          Total    % to
102   Primary Distributor     N/A                     $    Negative
103   Projected Release Date  Jun-98                         Cost

104   Producer's Gross Profit                        7750     155%

105   Production Negative Cost                        5000     100%
        --less--
106     Interest-Bearing Advances/Loans                 0       0%
107     Noninterest-Bearing Presales/Grants             0       0%
                                                    ------   ------
108   Other Funds Needed for Production              5000     100%

109   Domestic Box Office Gross                     18000     360%

110   Total Distributor Revenue (all markets)       31269     625%
        --less--
111     Gross Participations                            0       0%
112     Total Distribution Fees                     -13890    -278%
113     Total Domestic P&A                           -5500    -110%
                                                    ------   ------
114   Producer's Gross                              11879     238%
```

SUMMARY OF DISTRIBUTOR REVENUE AND DISTRIBUTION FEES

| | ------ Revenue ------ | | | ------Fees------ | |
| --- | --- | --- | --- | --- | --- |
| | Total $ | Dom % | Total % | % Rev | $ |
| DOMESTIC | | | | | |
| 115 Theatrical | 9000 | 51% | | 30% | 2700 |
| 116 Video- | | | | | |
| 117   Wholesale Share | 6135 | 35% | | 100% | 6135 |
| 118   Royalty | 1534 | 9% | | 0% | 0 |
| 119 Pay TV | 850 | 5% | | 30% | 255 |
| 120 Public TV | 0 | 0% | | 30% | 0 |
| 121 Network TV | 0 | 0% | | 30% | 0 |
| 122 All Other | 250 | 1% | | 30% | 75 |
| | ------ | ------ | | | ------ |
| 123 | 17769 | 100% | 57% | | 9165 |
| | | | | | |
| FOREIGN | | | | | |
| 124 Total Foreign | 13500 | | 43% | 35% | 4725 |
| | ------ | | ------ | | ------ |
| 125 Totals | 31269 | | 100% | 44% | 13890 |

307

## Book Flyer/Articles

In this section you will put any other additional material that supports the project. Our strategy was to publish the novel first so we could say we were doing a film based on the novel. This is one of the mailers for the book.

I also include xeroxes of articles from the *Hollywood Reporter, Variety, Premiere,* and the *Wall Street Journal* that are relevant to independent filmmaking (and of course have positive news to share).

In January *Variety* publishes the top box office performers for the year. Based on the three income projections for our film, I took the box office grosses and inserted our title in bold in the box office performers' list. Investors look at the list and see where, in relation to this year's movies, our film might land if we hit our projections. Since they see films in the list that they will probably recognize, this is another way to get the investor to dream with you.

## Contact Information

Be sure to have contact information on your cover page as well as the last page in the prospectus. Investors will need to know how to find you. You'd be surprised how many people leave this off their prospectus. Having it on a cover letter isn't enough because the cover letter often gets separated from the prospectus.

Give this prospectus to investors when you do presentations. It is an excellent talking piece. I often go through it page by page with investors so they feel that everything they would ever want to know about the project is covered.

# Bali Brothers

**For Further Information Please Contact:**

Michael Wiese
Michael Wiese Productions
11288 Ventura Blvd., Suite 821
Studio City, California 91604

(818) 379-8799
(818) 986-3408 fax
mw@mwp.com
www.mwp.com

## Summary

Be creative in designing your prospectus. Make it represent the project. Use graphics and pictures to keep the image of the film before the readers. In the prospectus you are trying to make it real in the readers' minds. Everything you say needs to be grounded in reality and, at the same time, you want to give the impression that no matter how you look at your project, it is fated to succeed wildly.

# PRESENTATIONS

## A Dream Come True?

Many years ago it looked like my dream would come true.

I never wanted to go out and find money for films. I just wanted to be a filmmaker—an artist. I wanted someone else to raise the money and leave me to the creative chores. (Don't we all?) Finally, I met him. His name was Gene. He'd made millions selling real estate. He could sell anything. He liked my film idea. He said, "How much do you need?" I told him. He said, "No problem. One or two people I know could fund the whole thing. Leave it to me. You be the artist. I'll raise the money. Go shoot your film and when you get back all your money will be in the bank."

I couldn't believe my good fortune. I agreed to pay him 10% of what he raised. I went out totally psyched! I ordered film from Kodak. Got my crew together. Flew to location. We stayed in hotels which I put on my credit cards. And for several weeks we shot our film. (You already sense the outcome, don't you?)

When I got back Gene hadn't raised any money. None. Nada. Zero. Zip. I had big time credit card bills coming due, a lab that was threatening to throw away my negative if I didn't pay them, and mutinous crew members outside my office door. That's when the horrible reality sunk in. I would have to get out there myself and raise the money.

I had never done it. I didn't know how. I would have to learn. I would have to find investors, figure out what they want, and get myself out there and pitch. And you know what? Nothing changes. Today is no different. Whenever I want to make a new film or video, I must go through this whole process again.

## Marketing Yourself to Investors

We've discussed this before, but a review is in order. The entire process of filmmaking requires that you constantly market yourself to everyone: writers, coproducers, cast, crew, banks, investors, distributors, the press, the public. Everyone!

The marketing of your project is crucially important every step of the way but possibly most important when dealing with investors. If they don't invest, you don't make your movie.

The key ingredient is you and your enthusiasm. If this film is your passion, if you can demonstrate that it will be profitable, then your chances of finding investors are heightened. If you further demonstrate that you are responsible and competent, then the chances increase again. You must have a winning, positive attitude, and be the embodiment of success in the way you dress and present yourself (even if you aren't).

Your main skill (and goal) is to get commitments from other people. You do this by talking a lot; by communicating. If you can't close, if you can't get people to say, Yeah, count me in, then you have no business trying to produce movies or videos. In getting commitments you are building a critical mass. If you can get a great script or a star or a known director interested in your project, that's critical mass. You use these elements to attract more elements and you get your movie made. If you don't have the clout to attract names and top material, you still need to build critical mass. Except this time you do it more slowly, a step at a time. Like chopping down a tree (I hate that metaphor); by gathering your resources, the tree eventually falls and you get to make your movie.

A track record or portfolio of work helps immensely. It gives investors (and others) confidence that you've been down this road before and can complete a successful film. If you don't have a track record, you partner with people who have the experience and resumes to prove it. You build critical mass with every element in your package starting with a great script, recognizable cast, and a reputable distributor. A package like this is irresistible to investors, and you will get your film made.

Most important is your belief that you can do it. Filmmakers are part dreamers, part doers. Put the two together and it's the magic of manifestation. Filmmakers make their dreams real.

Before you hit the streets you need a prospectus, a packaged project, limited partnership agreements, and an unstoppable, unbeatable, inexhaustible mind-set that you are going to make your movie! Do not cross the starting line until you are absolutely ready. You don't get second chances with investors.

### What Investors Want to Know

You are quite aware of what your need is. Money! Your need is with you constantly. You wake up with it, you go to sleep with it, you dream about it. But by being so focused on your needs it's often possible to overlook the needs of others, especially investors. If you don't meet their needs, you won't get funded. So for a moment, put aside your needs (don't worry, you can take them out again in a moment), and when you go to your meetings with potential investors to pitch your project, try to listen and sense what their needs might be. If you can do this (it's also called mind reading), you will be very effective at selling your film and securing financing.

In dealing with investors over the years I've come up with a list of questions that they will probably have. Some questions they will express directly. Some questions they don't even know that they have, but when answered by you, will help them feel more secure in investing. Some questions are obvious, some are not.

1. Will you be able to complete the film?

Investors will be scanning into the very depths of your soul to see if you follow through on things. If you don't finish the movie, they will lose everything. That is why banks, distributors, and investors require a completion bond. This insurance policy protects the investors. If the producer overspends, goes over schedule, or runs into other difficulties, the completion bond company will rush in with funds and expertise and guarantee completion of the film. As a producer you must demonstrate with all your facilities why you will be able to complete the film because you won't have a completion bond for your low budget film. You must show that you've thought of everything in your desire to protect the investor and get the movie made. You are organized, you are responsible, you have the best people working with you, you know what you are doing, etc.

2. Will it return my investment? When?

In your prospectus or business plan are income projections. A quick look at these spreadsheets and an investor can see how much money is expected, when and from what sources. If you can successfully support and provide rationale for how you came up with these projections, and really understand how the business works and the money flows, you will be well on your way to answering perhaps the most important question an investor will ask.

3. Will it make money?

This too will be answered in the income projections. Investors will see what happens once the film's investment is repaid, how profits are shared among the various participants.

These are the obvious questions. You've probably already anticipated them. However, lurking within many investors' brains are other questions which you will miss answering if you are too caught up in your own needs to get the money. Be sensitive and let the investor do much of the talking.

4. Do you (the filmmaker) have integrity? Will you do what you say you will?

You need to find out how, through your words and actions, to demonstrate your deep commitment to your film. Answering the question has to do with how you are perceived. If you believe in what you are doing (and yours is not a "get rich quick scheme"), then your integrity will be seen in everything you do and say. One way to demonstrate this is to follow up quickly with answers to any of the questions they may have that you aren't able to answer right away. If you say you will get back to them with an answer, do so.

5. What are the social, emotional, or spiritual values of the film?

This may best be communicated by you indirectly. As you tell the story of your film the theme will be apparent. Or if you are doing a documentary, its cause will rise to the surface. If the investor supports it politically and socially and also feels how important it is, you will gain their investment. The meaning and value of what you are doing will need to be first discovered by you so that you can communicate it. If you did the mission statement exercise, you will already have a firm foundation.

Most investors do care about getting their money back on their investment. But they often want something else. They want to do something worthwhile, something that contributes to others, makes a statement, sends a message.

A film I did in the seventies returned less than half its investment. The investors did not get all their money back. What surprised me was that of 32 investors, only two really cared that much about the money! They told me they thought the film was great, that I did everything humanly possible to get them their money back. Overall they had a good experience with me. Two people were ticked not to get their money back . I learned that it's not just about money. This isn't to say you should go into your endeavor expecting to lose your investors' money, just that there are other deeper reasons than a profit that will influence people to invest in you and your film.

6. How can I (the investor) participate in the project?

Investors want to participate, but they don't always articulate this desire. Sometimes they are not even fully aware of it themselves. Whenever you meet a potential investor, look for this need somewhere in their dialogue. When they see you are doing something that they've always wanted to do, they may identify with you and "make their film" through you.

There are a variety of ways that you can create a sense of participation for your investors without it interfering with your film. They can come to investor meetings and meet actors and crew members or visit the set on an easy day when their presence won't upset things.

Stay in communication with them. Every few months, or whenever you have news, send out a letter about the progress that is being made on their film. When you hire that special actor or composer, or finish your music, or when you have made your first distribution deal, tell them about it.

Invite your investors to the premiere (reserving the best center seats) and the party afterwards. If the film will be on television, let them know when so they can tell their friends. Send them clippings, reviews, and copies of film festival awards. By sharing with them your sense of excitement as the film progresses, you can give them a sense of participation that they will truly appreciate.

People invest in movies for all kinds of reasons. At present there are over 100 people who have invested in one or more of my projects. Once I thought that if I could come up with a "personality profile" of my "typical investor," then it would be easier to find them for future projects. It didn't take long to discover that there is no one type of investor. People invest because they want to make money, or they believe in what the film is trying to say, or because they know and respect the filmmaker's previous work, or they just like the excitement and want to be part of it.

**Too Much Participation**

Once I was invited by Frank Sinatra's orchestra leader to see the show in Las Vegas and then we'd discuss the orchestra leader's interest in putting $500,000 into a film about the Sea of Cortez that I wanted to do. Sound good? It did to me too. After sitting around his pool, dining in a nightclub (accompanied by a harpist on a floating boat), and touring the casinos, his hidden agenda became clear. What he really wanted to do was (a) take a tax write-off on his new sailboat on a film project (he had not yet learned to dock the boat successfully), (b) bring his wife and daughter along on a vacation, and (c) compose a musical score for the film.

Now if he wants to take a vacation on his new boat with his family, okay, fine. But, having worked on the ocean with film crews, I am not about to take along anyone who is not working. It is too hard and dangerous. Having his wife and teenage daughter wander about the boat in bikinis and distract my sea-worthy crew was a formula for disaster! When he played me some of his bouncy compositions I realized a better use for them would be in a dance number rather than in a nature documentary. So, as much as I wanted his money, the strings attached were detrimental to getting the job done. I told him I would be glad to have him as an investor but that I couldn't use his boat, the extra passengers, or his music. Bye bye money!

I am not against including someone who may also be an investor in other aspects of the film, but there has to be a real fit. Do not compromise the film for the money. Don't create more problems for yourself. The investor's other skills must also add to the filming process. Do not allow an investor to buy his way into your film if it's a bad match. Once you determine the investor's needs in regard to participation, you have to tell yourself the truth about whether it makes sense or not and then act accordingly.

There are two types of investors. The first type are the circle of family, friends, dentists, doctors, and professionals that are likely to invest in your project because they know and like you. The second type are more sophisticated and have knowledge of film investments.

Most likely, your investor will be unsophisticated (family and friends) because (1) they will be the investors you can get to, and (2) your film won't have the high profile packaging elements (script, director, stars) that a sophisticated investor will require. Realizing this will help you enormously. Do not waste time on industry or sophisticated investors. Go for the people around you.

What Unsophisticated Investors Want to Know

1. Can you complete the film?
2. Will the film return my investment?
3. Will it make a profit?
4. Will you do what you say you will do?
5. What are the social/spiritual values in the film?
6. How can I participate?

What Sophisticated Investors Want to Know

1. Is there a market for your genre film world-wide?
2. Do you have a competent, reputable distributor?
3. Do you have a favorable distribution agreement?
4. Is your budget too high or too low?
5. Will the film recoup its investment?
6. Will the film go into profits?
7. Will the film provide a high return on the money invested?
8. Does it have bankable stars and a director?
9. Is there a great script by a proven writer?
10. Is a completion bond in place?
11. Is it easily marketed?
12. Do your creative participants have substantive track records?

Once you've made your breakthrough film, then you may approach sophisticated investors. Until then, it is a waste of time trying to meet them. You simply cannot compete with the Academy-nominated producers, directors, and writers who are courting the same people. You can however partner with a producer, writer, or director that can provide entry to this level of financing. Most independent filmmakers have to find independent, nonindustry financing sources.

## Thirteen Steps to Successful Pitching

1. Know your buyer. Is this person really a potential buyer for your film or video?

2. Make friends with the secretary or assistant who is the gate keeper to the inner sanctum. Enroll their support. They won't be secretaries forever. Someday they may be producers or executives. If they knew more about you and your film, perhaps they'd campaign within the company. (Sometimes the bosses trust their young assistants' instincts more than their own!)

3. Dress appropriately.

4. Arrive on time.

5. If possible, get a glimpse of the office where you'll be pitching. Maybe you can do this before the meeting, or maybe you can sit where you see into the office before you enter. This way you can prepare yourself for the environment. This will ground you as you need to be fully in your own power (and not the other person's) in order to make the most effective pitch.

6. Small talk when you first enter the room is okay. Find something in the room that you can respond to and help draw the other person out. Show that you are interested in this person in some way. Find anything. You've got to make a connection before you start pitching.

7. Do not pitch until you've got the other person's full attention. Wait for the phone call to end, for the person to stop reading, or whatever he or she is doing. Get the person's attention and then pitch.

8. Start your pitch with a hook. It could be a question. A provocative statement. Maybe it relates somehow to the small talk you've been making so you can provide a smooth transition.

9. Be prepared to make your pitch in one minute. That means you

will reduce your film or video to a one- or two-sentence *TV Guide* log line. State the title of the film, the genre, and the conflict. It's an action adventure about two half-brothers who go to Bali and compete for the affections of a village girl. They should be able to "get" the concept right away. If it takes you minutes to pitch, you are in trouble. Most people are very busy. They've heard pitches and business proposals all day long. They respect brevity.

10. After the short pitch wait for a response. Be sensitive to them. Listen. This will indicate what to do next. If they are intrigued, then you can give an outline of the story; this does not mean tell everything that happens in the story beat by beat but rather give the two-paragraph synopsis. You are drawing them in. You are revealing new information which is increasing their interest. Only when asked do you tell the whole story. Or maybe you just entice them to actually read the script themselves.

11. You want to start a dialogue. Everyone wants to be creative. They want to respond and participate. If they do, then things are going well. They like you. They like your project. You can explore how you may work together. (Are they interested in investing, being in your film, distributing your film?)

12. Graphics are a great tool. Make a mock-up of the movie poster or the video box. The more real you can start to make your dream, the more they will share your vision.

13. Be confident. Show your passion for the project and your enthusiasm for seeing the project to a successful conclusion. Be aggressive to the degree it's not offensive. You need to demonstrate that you are going to get this project done through your personal power. How you conduct yourself in this meeting is of great importance.

## Things Not to Do

1. Cop an artistic attitude. Do not play the artist outsider. Do not bear a grudge. Show how appreciative you are that the other person is meeting with you.

2. Don't wing it. Practice your pitch so it rolls off your tongue. Try it out with friends.

3. If you are nervous, that's okay. Say you are nervous. Don't try to hide it.

4. Don't have closed body language. Use your hands and posture to express your enthusiasm for the project while pitching. Make eye contact. Be confident in the way you express yourself.

5. Do not leave without making some agreement for follow-up, getting a referral, or in some way enlisting them. Ask if you can call back in a few days. Find some other information they may need, promise to get it to them, and then do so a few days later. Leave them with a gift that ties in with your project. It doesn't have to be big and expensive. Maybe it's a hardbound copy of the book on which your script is based. Or a small knickknack that relates to the project. That something will then do the work for your after you are gone. Use graphics on the covers of your prospectus because it's selling long after you are gone while it's sitting on the coffee table.

## Four Quick and Easy Pitch Exercises

Individualize your pitch based on its intended recipient. The tone, manner, and style of the pitch must be designed to fit the needs of the person you are pitching to. Get into the mind-set of the receiver.

Here are several techniques to use before a pitch.

1. Feel Your Feet on the Ground. What can happen before a pitch is that you go into your head. All your energy is focused in your brain as you nervously think about the upcoming pitch. What you need to do is get back into your whole body so that it will serve you to express yourself . Stamp on the floor, walk around and feel the earth under your feet. Focus your attention back in your body so that you will be present when you are giving your pitch.

2. Previsualize Your Audience. It doesn't matter whether it is one person, a small group, or an entire audience. Previsualize people looking at you, smiling, asking questions, getting enthusiastic themselves, investing and supporting your project. When you have to give a presentation to a large group of people, go to the room before anyone arrives, stand at the front of the room, and imagine all the seats filled and all eyes on you. When you do this, and then actually come in front of a room full of people, you are prepared for it and will not be thrown by all the energy coming your way.

3. Relax Your Voice. The last thing you want is to go in front of the room, be overwhelmed by all the people, and in your first sentence have your voice crack. The stress from all eyeballs on you can restrict your throat so that your voicebox doesn't work properly. When you do speak, you squawk and immediately feel even worse. Do a simple exercise before speaking. When driving in your car, do some low chanting (think Tibetan monks) to loosen and stretch your vocal cords. It sounds funny, but it sure relaxes your throat. Your voice will then serve you well when you speak.

4. See Yourself Successfully Delivering Your Message. Similar to the exercise in the front of the book, this one allows you to see yourself giving a terrific presentation. See the room, the look on people's faces, see them laughing, interacting, participating, and writing you checks. If you are able to evoke these images, your body will be energized and actually appear to others as successful. You will create, in reality, exactly what you visualized.

Try these four simple exercises to prepare for any presentation, large or small.

## Pitching to Investors

Before you pitch review your mission statement and get focused on who you are and what you want to accomplish. Tap into the deepest and most committed place in yourself. This is where you pitch from. When people see and hear you, and realize that this is what you are meant to do, it is irresistible. This is called finding someone "ready to pop." That's you. You are ready to realize your dream; you've pulled all the resources together. This is very attractive to investors.

Investors run to abundance and away from scarcity. In your presentation you must appear successful. You must have a winning attitude. A "starving artist" attitude does not attract money. Money attracts money. (Ever notice how willing the bank is to give you a loan when you don't need it?) Investors want to sense that the project already has momentum.

Getting the first money is the most difficult because no one wants to be first. However, if you get deferrals from cast, crew, and for other budget line items, add them all up and then you can truthfully say, We have $ x already committed. You have your first money.

You will talk to dozens of people. Know that. Expect that. Realize that you are going into a period where you will spend many days on the phone and many hours giving presentations. Selling is part of a filmmaker's job.

You will as you move through your day get lots of no's. That's all right. It's not personal. My ratio is something like 1:5. Of every five people that I ask, one will invest. Not bad. However I could go through twenty no's before getting five yes responses. When people say no, I don't get discouraged. I thank them. Because with every no I am getting closer to a yes. And that's true.

## Where to Find Investors

Drive to Redmond, Washington. Rent an apartment near Microsoft's headquarters. Learn where the thousands of millionaires that now work for Microsoft live, eat, and play. Only kidding! But maybe not. High-tech millionaires have today supplanted yesterday's doctors and dentists as independent film investors. Go get 'em.

Filmmakers tell me that they do not know where to find investors. Filmmakers tend to look "out there" to find investors when they are much closer to deep pockets than they think. Investors are all around you.

As you drive down the street you see building after building filled with products. Someone thought all these businesses were a good idea and so they invested in them and in all the stuff that fills these stores. If they could all find the investment, capital, and resources to start their business, why can't you?

Your investors are not the rich fat cats of your imagination. They are real, accessible, friendly people. If this is your first or second film, your financing will come from your family, your friends, and your friends' friends.

People say to me, Well, I don't have rich friends. So? Neither did I. That shouldn't keep you from finding backing for your film or video-tape. It's time to find them. Think for a minute. Who do you know that knows about money? Who has a small or large business? Who owns a house or works for a large corporation? Do you know a doctor, a dentist, a lawyer, a retired businessman, a young entrepreneur? All you need is one, and you're on your way.

Go to him or her with your idea (prospectus). Or invite several people to a presentation. Enlist their help. Although they may not invest, get from them no less than two more names of their friends who may be interested. Ask if you may use their name when you call their friends. You will soon have a long list of people. This should not be difficult. (Even if friends don't invest, they still may be willing to help you find other people who will.) If they do invest, then you should also ask them for referrals. And now your pitch to the person your friend referred will be even stronger because their friend has invested.

You will be very surprised when you find investors. They will not be who you expect. Many people may have some savings or resources or trust funds that you never knew about until you asked them to invest. Not only that, many people will be genuinely delighted that you

324

thought to include them in your film project. It's flattering to be thought of as an investor!

I am frequently asked if I have a list of people who invest in films. No, I don't. I have a list of people who've invested in my films over the years. I've always found that these people came through people I know because what you are selling is yourself and then your project. So, in the beginning, most of your investors will come through friends of friends of friends.

## How to Give a Successful Presentation

Before you can make a successful presentation, you must know what you want. You must have a result you want to produce. Without actually setting a goal or objective for yourself, you will have no way to measure your results.

The main purpose of a presentation is to raise money for your film or video project. Once you tell yourself and the prospective investors the truth about what you want, you stand a much better chance of getting it. Your objective for the presentation is to "get someone to invest." If they do, your event has been successful. If they don't, it's only been a party, and doesn't matter how much fun people had. It was not successful because you didn't achieve your objective. You need to be very clear about this to get the real results you desire. Treat the presentation as seriously as you do your film. Write a script for the presentation with a good beginning, middle, and end.

## Visual Impact in Presentations

If you know how you come across to people, you can accentuate your strong points and cover your weaknesses. Since human beings are primarily visual creatures and receive most of their information through sight this is the first judgment that will be made by an investor. If you remember this and can work not only your own visual appearance but visual aids into your presentation, you will be able to make the greatest memorable impact.

325

People are also influenced by other factors. A classic study done at Yale revealed that people are influenced in various ways but that sight is predominant:

55%   Visual  (What is seen.)
38%   Vocal   (What you say; the content.)
7%   Verbal  (How you say it.)

(If your presentation is made on the phone, then it is 85% vocal and 15% content.)

Another way to understand this is to realize that the impact of a presentation comes through "style" and not "content." Sad, but true. It is "personality" that sells a project. Your presentation needs to be very visual and have a style that expresses your project. Substance is important but the first impression is visual.

**Personal Appearance**

The audience of investors, whether it be 50 people in a room or two people over dinner, will only get what you give them. So you need to be aware of that which enters their conscious and unconscious minds. Their eyes will fall on you first. Within seconds, you will be judged and evaluated solely on your appearance, before you utter a single word! Therefore, you must be dressed and groomed in a manner appropriate to the tastes of the people you will meet. Unfortunately, many filmmakers with wonderful projects never get funded because they are more interested in making a statement with their appearance. If your appearance separates you from other people, then it's probably time to make a change. What you are trying to do is connect with people, to communicate your ideas, not to create distance between yourself and others through your appearance.

In my experience, appearance and personal style is one of the most frequent barriers to fund-raising that I've seen among filmmakers who have come to us for consultation. They go to endless lengths to make their films look great and then neglect their own appearance and presentation, thinking that somehow they are not that important. The question goes back to your objective: do you want to "be you" or do you want to get the job done and raise money for your film? Do you want to get on with making your film or would you rather sit around with your friends over cappuccino complaining about how misunderstood your genius is. I don't have much patience for the "starving artist" attitude. You can find support for anything you are doing if you will allow it.

Position your project (and yourself) in its most favorable light so that it has every conceivable chance of being accepted. An inappropriate appearance may disqualify you in the first few seconds.

In addition, you need to have a project that stands a chance for commercial success. Commercial, in the sense that a lot of people will want to see it and a distributor (theatrical, television, or home video) will want to distribute it. That doesn't mean that your program won't have artistic integrity or a meaningful theme or be done in an innovative style. It means that somewhere along the line you decide that you want people to fund your work and to see your work. These two things are not mutually exclusive: they go together. If an investor or distributor thinks a lot of people will want to see your work, they will give you the money to make it. If they think people will not be interested in your script or video idea (noncommercial), then they won't fund it. But you already know this, so let's get on with it.

## Presentation Space

This is your show. Control the space. Pick a location that is familiar to you and fully supports your objective. The room should be clean, well lighted and have comfortable (but not too comfortable) seating. It should be in a part of town that is safe and easily located. Include a map along with your invitation.

**Screening Rooms**

Screening rooms are good for presentations because you may want to show film clips. Investors can see the screening room's sound recording equipment and mixing console. Since most people have never been in a professional screening room, it is very exciting for them to see where movies are made. It gives them a sense of being part of the moviemaking world and establishes credibility. Screening rooms can be found in most major cities and rented by the hour.

If the screening room is located in an unfamiliar part of town, position someone outside to let people know they are in the right place. Post signs along the route to show the way. You want to make things easy for attendees. You do not want them coming into your event after being lost or having difficulty parking their car. Treat the event as if it were a production because it is and requires the same attention to detail. Put yourself in their shoes and visualize the event from their point of view. You have a terrific opportunity to impress your investors with how together and detail-oriented you are. You can make a great impression and raise a lot of money at the same time. How you produce your event says a lot about how you will produce your film. Don't think there is no connection.

Make people's total experience as pleasurable as you can. You want them to feel that you will take as good care of their money as you have of them, so be conscious of these small details. It is one of the easiest ways to let people feel your sense of style and grace. All of this happens before you've said a word about the project you want to do. The enrollment process has already begun.

**Private Homes**

If you use private homes for presentations, you can prepare (in advance) your sample film clips and transfer them to videotape. Rent a videotape player, plug it into a television set, and the private home can serve the same function as a screening room. Take full control of the room. Remove anything that is distracting and does not support your purpose. The worst thing you can do is have a clock or distracting art work on the wall behind you.

Take the theatricality of the event as far as possible. It will be to your benefit. Light the room, by moving lamps or ceiling track lights around, so that there are no dark spots where investors may sit and become drowsy. Arrange flowers, lay out a wine and cheese table, open a portfolio or a prospectus on the coffee table. You may want to have your friends (assistants) greet people. Make people feel as comfortable as possible. Make them feel special and cared for. Introduce people to one another so they can relax. What you are doing is building agreement among a group who will invest and support what you are doing. You must do this very quickly, from the very moment they walk in (actually long before they walk in), to make a great impression.

### Restaurants

When you do presentations in restaurants make sure you will have minimal distractions. It should be quiet so that you can be heard and leisurely enough so that you can sit and talk after eating. Survey the restaurant before meeting there. Talk to the manager about any special requests you may have. Tell her what you are doing and maybe she'll have some suggestions as to table, menu, or extras that can be provided. Since you cannot completely control the environment, you must be very careful in your selection. You may only get one chance.

### Group Dynamics

Groups of people create a synergetic effect. If you do a very successful presentation, it will be even more so. People who were on the fence about investing will be swayed because of the enthusiasm in the room. They will sense it is a good investment and want to join in. If, on the other hand, the presentation is awkward and goes poorly, then the audience as a whole may decide not to invest. Stack the odds in your favor by being conscious about your purpose, projecting a personal style and creating a supportive environment in which to do your presentation.

329

Groups communicate something else. If you can put together an investors' meeting of 20, 30, or 40 people, you can certainly handle a crew, a press conference, and the other group tasks associated with filmmaking. If you are not good at presentations, then team up with someone who is. Not everyone's personality is suited to public speaking. If the thought of getting up in front of a group terrifies you, practice until you can do it easily. If it still terrifies you, then get someone else to do it.

## The Wise Guy

I don't know where they come from but there always seems to be one at every presentation. They show off by challenging you with questions. They want you and everyone else present to know that they are smarter than you. I suppose they would rather be the one making the film. But they aren't. Whatever their motivation, they can be a real bother. Worse yet, if you aren't prepared for them they can throw you off, which you certainly don't need. You want to look your best. (For mock-ups a friend can role-play the "wise guy." It will help you to be firm and keep the presentation on track.)

If these wise guys ask questions that you don't know the answer to, simply say you don't know and go on. Don't totally ignore them. Give a courteous answer and then move on. Do not let them dominate the situation. Do not give away your power. It's your presentation.

When you set up investor meetings, try to weed out people that you think might be problematic in groups. Don't invite them to be with a group; see them one-on-one.

## 'Inner' Environment

Once you have created a pleasant and supportive "outer" environment, it's time to work on your "inner" environment.

What is your overall attitude? How are you expressing yourself psychologically? Where are you coming from? Try to locate your own point of view and make sure it is conducive to the job at hand. You do not want to be nervous or high-strung. If you are, convert that energy to enthusiasm and passion. Push yourself to meet everyone as they enter as if they were already your friends. Your attitude will subtly influence your communication to your investors.

Many independent producers are coming from "survival"; living hand-to-mouth, day-to-day existences, never knowing where the next job or bit of money is coming from. That's okay. That may be your reality, but that is not the reality that you want to impart when you meet prospective investors.

If you come from survival the tone of your presentation says to the investor, Please help me. Without your money, I can't do my film. (Or, I need you to survive.) Hey, who needs that? An investor does not want to keep you boosted up as well. He just wants to invest. He doesn't want any more responsibility than that. If an investor feels that you can't do your film without him, then it may frighten him off. It's too much burden. If you were an investor, would you have a feeling of confidence in the filmmaker?

Investors want to know that, with or without their backing, you are going to make your movie. When they feel this, they are much more willing to invest. You must exude confidence and place no responsibility on the potential investors. You simply want to know if they'd like to invest.

## Cold Calls

Someone you don't know is about to answer the phone. It's the cold call. In a few seconds the tone and content of your voice must capture the attention of someone who may be interested in your project. Think of it as an adventure.

Although you may never use these exact words, the tone of your first telephone call to a potential investor may sound like this (you may even write a script or some notes that you can follow):

"Good morning. How are you? (captivating) John (or his friend's name who recommended you call) suggested I give you a call to tell you about the film I am making. (Present tense, not we "will" make this film, but we "are" already making it.) (Here's where you do your short, succinct pitch.) The film is called _____ ; it is an _____(genre) about _____(the log line which has conflict in it). We've been working on it for ___ months. What we have accomplished so far is .... We expect to finish in .... months at which time we hope to show it in _____ Film Festival. We expect an independent distributor to offer us an advance and pick up the film for distribution. We have sold ___ shares and raised $ ___ . We need to raise $ ___ more. Does this sound like something that might interest you?"

The style is very straightforward. It shows the potential investors that you are moving forward, that you have already accomplished something and you know where you are going. It provides enough information for them to know (and for you to ask them) if they'd like to hear more. The information takes less than two minutes to deliver, during which the potential investor can decide to attend a one hour group presentation or to meet with you in his or her office, or over lunch, to gather more detailed information.

## 'Maybe's '

What if someone says, maybe they will invest in your film? You probably don't want them. Maybe's drive you crazy. At least with a "no" you know where you stand. With a "maybe" it is unresolved, incomplete, and psychologically draining. You want to find out if someone is going to invest. If they don't want to, go on. Life is too short. Some people like to hang out with filmmakers. It makes them feel creative and important. Lunch after lunch goes by. But enough is enough. You are not there to socialize but to raise money. Make that clear.

If you haven't provided enough information for them to make a decision, do so.  If you have, then it's time to have them give you an answer. Get yourself off the hook and onto new prospects.


## Sometimes You Need to Say No

I've been telling you all along how to get someone to say yes and invest money in your project.  But sometimes you don't want their money.  Even though you've courted them, wowed them with your intention, if ever that little red light goes on in your brain, then pay close attention.  You do not want this person involved with your project.  Stop.  Stop everything.  Call it off.  Do not take his money. Maybe you get a little egg on your face, but that's better than having an investor who may turn out to be a troublemaker.  Do not be so desperate that you think you have to take all the money that's offered to you. You don't.  There's more out there.  A bad investor can cause you immeasurable grief.

These know-it-all types bring nothing but trouble and wasted time. Don't get me wrong. I am not talking about investors who are accomplished in business and can truly help your endeavor.  I welcome investors like that.  I am talking about these yo-yo's who think because they've invested a few thousand bucks in your film that they have the right to mess with it.  They don't.  They are limited investors. Nevertheless they will try if you let them in.

Just say no!  Not only is it a great boost to your power, but you'll prove to yourself that money isn't scarce.  Don't take it just because it's there.


## Another Reason Not to Take the Money

If prospective investors want to fund all or most of your project, then they could negotiate with you.  Maybe they want a greater payback than their initial investment, or a greater share of the profits.  It may be to your advantage to just have one or a few investors, so it might be worth it to you to negotiate. On the other hand, it's your project and your dream, and hence a fair share of the rewards should also be yours. Do not be bullied into giving away a greater percentage of ownership in your project than you are comfortable with.

Investors are support. They are supporting you with money (physically) and emotionally. Each investment carries with it an "intention" that goes into the film as well. You will feel their support through phone calls, letters, e-mail, clippings, etc. You can sense they are thinking about your film all the time as you are.

### You've Got to Ask

If you want someone to invest in your project, you've got to ask. Many filmmakers are afraid to ask for what they want. You may be having a great time with someone over lunch and feel you don't want to spoil it by asking for money. What's the point then? You are really wasting your time. You need to make it clear in the beginning why you are meeting. Do you want to make your film or not?

### Presentation Budget

Have money to live on while you are fund-raising. Give the appearance of being successful.If you are to attract money, you have to look like you don't need it. You must already look like a "success" on your way to another success.

It will cost money to create a presentation. Perhaps a few hundred dollars, maybe more. You need to be aware that you will have these costs and include them in your budget under "preproduction" or "presentations." It costs money to raise money. It is a legitimate business expense. Among these expenses are screening room rental, slide shows, equipment rental (slide projectors, videotape players, projectors), printed invitations, color Xeroxes, typesetting, legal fees, copying and binding proposals, flowers, wine, cheese, and travel.

334

## Invitations

As you call friends, friends of friends, and make "cold calls," you can list all those people that you have invited to the group presentation. Some will be invited to lunch. It is up to you to be selective. Some people you will only invite to a group presentation. Let them know that you will be discussing the film, its marketing, and why you think it will be successful. Let them know if you will show clips from your work-in-progress and how long the presentation will last. (I suggest no longer than 1-1/2 hours. Then stick to your time limit!) Tell them that refreshments will be served.

You can also send invitations. I usually have an artist prepare calligraphy on good paper. I also include a detailed map of the location. I ask that they RSVP (or I confirm their attendance with them a day in advance). This way a guest list can be made up and you will know when everyone has arrived. And you can begin to memorize names.

First and foremost is the presentation itself. Every moment is planned in advance. All the equipment is tested. All visuals such as slides, film clips, flip charts, and graphs are readied. Prospectuses or business plans are xeroxed and bound. Be sure you have enough for everyone. The room is booked and "dressed" as necessary. Friends and associates are asked to assist. Their responsibilities are carefully defined (help with parking, greet people, take people's coats, hand out prospectuses, serve wine, collect enclosures, etc.).

## Rehearse Your Presentation

To find investors, cast and crew, do publicity and the many other duties associated with filmmaking, you are going to have to do a lot of talking. Those who talk inherit the world. If you sit on the sidelines, the world (and people who could support you) will pass you by. You have to talk, you have to do presentations, you have to get out there.

Give presentations—big ones and little ones in all kinds of places. Most people are not comfortable speaking in front of groups. That's okay, take that nervousness and that uncomfortable feeling and use it to fuel your presentation so that it actually helps you. Many cities have public speaking experts. Take a class from them. There are self-help books and tapes. Practice speaking in groups whenever you get the chance. You will survive. You might even enjoy it.

Videotape it. Nothing clears up bad presentation style faster than seeing it yourself.

Do your presentation for friends and have them critique you on the following:

1. Being there. You need to really "be there." Be present, right here, in present time, not off in your head thinking about anything else than what you are doing right now. If you know what you want to accomplish, then that will get you through. If you are not clear about what you want to accomplish, then your mind will flit around and you'll lose connection with your audience. In turn you will get nervous as you sense that you are losing them. If you are passionate about achieving your objective (get the money, make a great film), you will make sure that you are connecting and the whole event will spiral upwards. People will connect with intention. You'll accomplish your objective.

2. Eye contact. Your eyes should not dart nervously side to side. They should connect with each and every listener. Eye contact gets the attention of your listener. Your eyes reveal everything about you. When you are sure of your project, eye contact will convey that confidence better than any profit projections chart. If you are not prepared, your eyes will communicate that.

In groups make eye contact, first with one person (for about 5 seconds), then move on to another (5 more seconds). By meeting as many eyes as you can, you will keep the people interested and receptive. Each person will feel you are speaking directly to him or her. Sometimes I move from side to side in a room during a presentation to "wake up" the energy in the direction I am moving. I continue to keep eye contact. It's amazing how you can feel the energy rise in that part of the room you address.

3. Awkward movements. Your friends will notice if you clench your hands in a nervous manner. Your hands can be expressive and complement what you want to say with graceful, expansive gestures appropriate to your own style. They should not be distracting. Get loose. Have fun with your presentation. Let your hands open up your body language as well. If you're having fun, they will have fun. You want to get your audience enthusiastic about your project.

4. Voice. Record your voice during a rehearsal. Many people are pleasantly surprised when they hear what they sound like. Any "ummms" or "ands" can be deleted from your presentation. Learn to generate enough energy to project your voice out into a large room. The people at the back of the room will have to hear you over the air-conditioner and the trucks in the street outside. If there are more than 50 people, use a microphone.

5. Smile. Your smile is very important. It expresses goodwill. If your presentation is lively and naturally humorous (without being a comedy routine), it will relax your audience.

Your dress, posture, voice, hand gestures, movements, and particularly your eyes communicate a lot about you to your potential investors. There are many ways you can use these things to help rather than hinder you.

Know your material before you do a presentation, especially since there will probably be a question-and-answer session at the end. When you know what you are talking about, you automatically exude confidence and enthusiasm. You've got the dream in your head, bring your audience into the process, enjoy the moment. Let them feel that it is coming together as you speak and they are part of it. Then they will be. . .and that's what you want.

## The Presentation Structure

The presentation starts when the guests enter the room. (Actually it starts when you meet them or speak to them on the phone.) You might invite them to the wine and cheese table first. You may hand out prospectuses or you may wait. Whatever you do, start the presentation on time.

Keep in mind that your talk is a "conversation" with the group. Do not read it. Speak it. It is not a lecture. Use note cards if you like, but do not depend on them. Memorize your presentation so the cards are just a reminder. Your talk is a relaxed and fun sharing of information. Its purpose is to sell yourself and your project.

## The Beginning

Like any good book or film your presentation (and prospectus) will have a beginning, middle, and end. After saying hello and making some brief, informal remarks, begin with something bold. A thought provoking statement or a startling fact, something that gets their undivided attention. You might flash a strong image on the screen and leave it there for the first few minutes.

Preview your point of view and intention, but keep it short and get to the heart of your talk. (Let people know they may ask questions at the end of the talk. If you don't do this, they may interrupt you and break your concentration.)

## The Middle

The middle of your talk should expand the group's understanding of your project. You may wish to hand out the prospectus during your talk. If you do, be sure to tell people that you will cover everything in the prospectus. Tell people they may take the prospectus home with them. This will allow them to relax and not feel they have to read it during your talk. Sometimes it's possible to follow the same order as the information in your prospectus. If you make it clear to your audience that this is what you are doing, then they may feel that everything is being covered. This may help to speed up their decision making process. The danger with handing anything out during your talk is that people may read it rather than have their full attention on you.

Develop your points in a clear order with one thought leading to the next. Don't jump around. Be sure all your points support your purpose. (Motivate people so that they will want to invest.) But don't be too serious about it. Keep it light. Don't be afraid to make a joke or have fun (when appropriate). You may weave in personal stories, analogies, experts' opinions, and fascinating details to emphasize your main points. Feel free to use colorful graphics and flipcharts to illustrate your points. This can be anything from cartoons to graphs as long as it is appropriate. When you rehearse your presentation, ask your friends to tell you what was boring and what was fascinating. Discard what didn't work. Find ways to make your talk forward moving and fresh. Your enthusiasm and energy are selling points.

## The Ending

The ending should be crisp, clear and, most of all, memorable. End with a bang! Review your main points, which support why people should take action (that is, invest). Again, don't get serious, keep it consistent with the rest of your talk. Finish with confidence. This is what they will remember most about the evening.

## Questions and Answers

After you do your formal presentation with a group or a single person, allow some time (keep it brief) for questions. Be so well prepared that you can answer anything they might ask. (When you do your mock-up presentation for your friends, have them ask difficult questions.) Do not give a presentation until you are prepared and have a prospectus with budgets, market research, and income projections prepared. You will also want to have a first draft of your script completed. Make it as easy as possible for someone to invest. The legal documents should already be prepared by your lawyer so that all that is required of an investor is a signature and a check. You will already have an escrow account set up with your bank so you can deposit the money. You're real. You're happening. You're ready to go. Nothing speaks more of your professionalism than being prepared.

If you don't know an answer to a question, for heaven's sake, don't lie or make something up. Write it down and tell them that you will get the answer. Then do so and call them back. If it is a financial or legal question, ask the person if he/she would like your lawyer or accountant to call. (Be sure your accountant and lawyer are willing first!)

Answer your questions in a way that expands and supports your own point of view and involves your entire audience, not just the person asking the question. Address your answer to everyone so you don't lose the whole group's attention. If questions are slow in getting started, then ask a question yourself. "People often ask me ..." When the questions do begin, keep an "open" body posture, arms at your side. Do not cross them in front of you or put your hands in your pockets because (in body language) this is a defensive and guarded position. It will communicate that you are trying to hide something. Most of all, keep the answers short and concise. Keep the same confident and personal tone as in your original talk. At the end of the questions, bring everything together in a concise closing statement which you have prepared.

If film and videomakers put as much creative thought into the process of giving talks and presentations as they do into the design of their works, they would have much more success at raising money for their projects.


## Film Clips

If your project has already begun, you may want to show film clips or videotape. In some cases, it is not a good idea to preview this work-in-progress. Investors are not filmmakers and they may be disturbed by a scratchy workprint or spotty, unmixed sound track or videotape with rough-cut "glitches" (flashes at the cuts between scenes). Because an unfinished work can look so bad, people may assume you are not a very good filmmaker. I've heard people ask if the lines (drawn on workprint to indicate dissolves and fades) would be on the final version! Unless you plan to do a lot of explaining, which makes you look like you are apologizing, you may wish to hold back on showing rough-cut clips.

If you do use a film clip, it should not be too long. It should be like a "coming attraction" and make the audience want to see (and invest in) the film to come. If you do not have footage to show, you may wish to screen other films you or your partners have made. Keep them consistent in style or subject matter with your current project so that they do not detract from the mood of the presentation.

Show the film or videotape early in your presentation because it will act as a "grabber" and set a tone that the evening is about filmmaking.

## Enclosures

Once the presentation is over you will want to find out how you did. That is, have you found anyone who will invest. Since people tend to be uncomfortable talking about their financial intentions in front of others I provide an "enclosure" that can either be slipped in the back of the prospectus or handed out separately. This is a more private method for people to let you know if they will invest. It also asks for their investment in a very direct way.

The enclosure will be filled out by everyone and returned at the end of the presentation. It also allows investors to communicate to you about investing or needing more information. This way, those who say no need no follow-up and those who say yes can be clearly identified and closed. The forms can be gathered and then people may be invited to partake of the refreshments.

## Enclosure Sample

```
Your project's title:_____

I wish to invest in "title."    Amount: $._____.

_____ I do not wish to invest at this time.

I would like some more information about the project.
Please call me.

Name: _____     Phone: _____

Thank you.
```

At this point the presentation is over. People can stay and socialize if they like. You can answer questions privately, but be aware that this can create a feeling of exclusion for others. I say that I would like to chat with everyone afterwards but don't want to answer any more questions about the project.

## Summary

If you have made it to this point in the long and arduous process of being an independent film or videomaker, you have a lot to be proud of. You have overcome the fear of public speaking and introduced yourself and your project to discriminating investors. You have clearly outlined your film's purpose, your distribution plans, and projected the project's future earnings based on your market research. (Consult the chapters that follow.) You have taken a major step towards realizing your goal.

When you look at the returned enclosures, you'll have a pretty good idea of exactly how much you can expect from the investors. Hopefully in the days that follow you will be depositing checks in your limited partnership's bank account. If you are clear, confident, enthusiastic, and you have a project that merits being made (either commercially, emotionally, politically, or spiritually), you will find people who will invest. If you receive any money at all after giving your presentations, you are well on your way in establishing your own independence as a film or videomaker and transforming your ideas into reality.

# A No-Budget Movie: Coyote's Honor: A Case Study

This chapter is compiled of three articles (except Part III) which were edited by Brian McKernan and published in *Videography Magazine*. They document the making of a no-budget digital video movie which I made in the summer of 1997.

As someone who's worked in video and film for most of his life, it's exciting to witness the decline in the cost of ever-improving production tools. If, as French poet Jean Cocteau claims, film will become an art only when its materials are as inexpensive as pencil and paper, then we may well be closer than ever to a revolution in moviemaking. In a world where a consumer videotape format—DV—offers Betacam SP quality at S-VHS prices, old complaints of no one will give me the money, video just isn't there yet, and there really isn't a big market for independent movies become increasingly irrelevant.

I've produced and/or directed scores of film and video projects over the years, including the recently revived low-budget 1977 hit *Hardware Wars*. I'm also a consultant and publisher serving video and film professionals. Last summer a combination of circumstances enabled me to make a no-budget digital-video movie and experience life on the "bleeding edge" of production. Never before has the realization of one's personal vision been as attainable than in today's cost-effective video production environment. Nevertheless, you need to know what you're getting into when planning a professional no-budget, digital video "movie."

This article is the first installment in a series on the making of that movie, titled *Coyote's Honor*, which was shot film-style on a Sony DCR-VX1000 DV camcorder. Although technically very sophisticated, the DCR-VX1000 is essentially made for rich dentists who want an automatic camera. With careful handling, however, it can yield professional results (more on that later). This article focuses on production technique. I'm extremely grateful to Steve Parker (sparker@uiuc.edu), ace cameraman on *Coyote's Honor*, for his insights and comments in this installment. In future issues of *Videography* my "Producer to Producer" column will examine other production aspects of the making of this movie, including scripting, working with actors, legal issues, postproduction, and distribution.

ERIC WIPPO ("Coyote"), JOHN MACLAY. MIKE KUEHL, WILL RANSOM, RICHARD BARROWS,
KELLY COOPER, HEATHER SALINY, EMILY A. PARKS, HEATHER LAMB, DUSTIN WILKINSON

## COYOTE'S HONOR

**Coyote wanted their wine and
women . . . for a song.**

MICHAEL WIESE PRODUCTIONS PRESENTS
COYOTE'S HONOR *Story By* DOUG MCCORD &
MICHAEL WIESE *Screenplay by* DOUG MCCORD
*Producers* RICHARD BARROWS, BOB ROITBLAT
& MICHAEL WIESE *Co-Executive Producers* BRUCE A.
BROOKS DENNIS FEDORUK JOHN THOMPSON
*Director of Photography* STEVEN R. PARKER *Associate Producers* KEN LEE & MARK W. TRAVIS
*Lighting Director* TIMOTHY HARTIN *Editor* BRUCE A. BROOKS *Music Written & Composed by*
STEVE DANCZ, DAVIS CAUSEY, RANDALL BRAMBLETT *Directed by* MICHAEL WIESE

### Part I – Genesis

*Coyote's Honor* and I both have origins in Champaign, Illinois. I grew up there and return nearly every summer from my home in Los Angeles to visit my father. I'd gotten to know actors in the University of Illinois' summer-stock theater a year earlier during rehearsals on a feature film script I'd written about the island of Bali. I soon became friends with this terrific group of actors, whom I found refreshingly uncorrupted by Hollywood attitudes. I made a mental note at the time that I should make a movie with these kids someday.

It was April of this year when I called Rick Barrows, an acting professor at the university whom I'd worked with that previous summer. Let's make a movie with your summer-stock actors, I suggested. I'll give you two weeks to think it over. Barrows immediately agreed, and I hastened to mention that it wouldbe a ton of work. Fortunately, his enthusiasm was undampened.

This hey, let's do a feature exercise had several objectives. First, could we use an off–the–shelf consumer camera that was so low-priced that just about anyone could gain access to the tools of production? Would we continue to be intimidated by the Hollywood insider's myth that only a few can play because "you need millions of dollars to make a movie?" Could we really make a movie for no money? Has consumer video technology really matured to the point where—in the hands of a driven film- or videomaker—a decent piece of work could be produced? Are passion, street smarts, and perseverance really the main ingredients—not money? Lastly, I wanted to throw open the door to participation. Anyone who wanted to work on this movie could have a job—pros and amateurs alike.

Most movies are scripted, then cast. We did just the reverse. Barrows sent me head shots of actors he'd recommended; I put them together in various configurations and came up with some story lines (more about this in a future installment). As luck would have it, Doug McCord, a screenwriter and University of Illinois grad who'd studied with several of our actors, lived nearby in North Hollywood. We talked about story ideas and in less than a week he had banged out bios and back stories for the characters, and an outline and a first draft. By the first week of June I was back in Illinois and in discussion with the actors on their parts.

Basically our story was about a young outsider who impacts the lives of his classmates during the last summer before they all go off to college.

## The Gear

In addition to the Sony DCR-VX1000 we had two TK BRAND wide-angle converters (a .5x and a .7x), a Sennheiser ME88 mic on a boom, and a Shure FP32 audio mixer. The DCR-VX1000 has a color viewfinder, but it's too small to see things like mic booms, so we supplemented it with a five- and 13-inch field monitors. The wide-angle lens converters were crucial for shooting interiors, as there was usually insufficient space to get back far enough with the camera's lens.

Lighting and grip gear was pieced together from everyone, including cameraman Steve Parker and lighting director Timothy Hartin (who's also production manager at WILL-TV, the local PBS station). Hartin is the consummate LD, and he took great pride in lighting each scene. Although both these men were qualified to light and shoot, we decided that Hartin would light and Parker would shoot so that they could focus on their own tasks and not jump back and forth. Dennis Komack (of St. George Productions, Springfield, Illinois), loaned us a two-and-a-half-ton grip truck of assorted lights, reflectors, a dolly, tracks, jib arms, grip stands, and other essential equipment.

Having the proper gear is only half the battle; it's also essential to have a crew that knows how to use it (something that mainstream film-makers know only too well). Our only experienced crew members were Parker and Hartin; grips Chris Dowell and Ralph Roether also knew their stuff. For the most part, however, we had a crew of rookies. Our crew couldn't stow our gear fast enough when a summer shower suddenly hit, and on the second day of shooting it quickly become clear that using the dolly would add hours to each setup. They weren't up to the task of making smooth moves, either. (I have to admit the DCR-VX1000 looked ridiculous on the large dolly.)

Fortunately, after a day or two under Hartin's guidance the crew began to get the hang of what we needed and how to set it up. Most of the outside scenes were lit with reflectors. On the first day of shooting we had about 12 to 15 crew members and assistants. Attrition set in after a few days when people saw how hard a job it really was. By the end of the shoot we had a hard-core team of about 8 crew members.

Shooting *Coyote's Honor* reminded me once again that there's nothing like a good tripod. We had a Mitchell with O'Connor fluid heads, baby legs, and a Steadicam JR, which I used for just one shot (a motor-cyclist's POV of a crash). Parker and I also had small Bogen tripods with mini fluid heads. Since they are light and easy to set up, we used them occasionally. Parker's had a ball-leveling device that makes it even easier to set-up in uneven terrain. The lightweight camera really didn't need much more of a tripod, and we moved very fast.

Parker confides that his "secret weapon" was his bean bag. I pay the rent shooting in documentary and news situations, he explains. This large bag is filled with a couple of pounds of plastic beads, and it became our car mount, high hat, and general all-purpose method of mounting the camera. All we had to do was put the bag where we wanted it, place the camera on the bag, and "smoosh" it around until the framing was right and the camera was steady. Yes, folks, Parker confirms, "smoosh" is a technical term.

*Wiese looks through the VX-1000 with DP Steven Parker*

## The Look/The Approach

I strove for a realistic look that would capture the quality and light of the Midwest (country mornings, old parts of town), and I chose a backlit-look for the story's dream sequences.

For nearly a year I tried to get a demo copy of "Storyboard Artist" from Power Productions (I have a copy of "Storyboard Quick"). It finally arrived in the middle of our shoot. In less than an hour I was able to storyboard an important scene on my laptop. Although I didn't take the storyboards to the set, the process gave me a clearer idea of what my coverage should be and it saved me from shooting things I probably wouldn't have used.

There was no time to establish a stylized "look," as there was only about an hour to set up the lighting for each scene. Even with our skeleton crew and our ensemble group of ten actors, we managed to shoot an average of seven pages a day. Some days had multiple locations. We were damn lucky just to get coverage, most of which was pretty straightforward. There weren't any Orson Welles or Coen brothers angles or lighting on this picture.

Plans to shoot a "making-of" video fell apart due to lack of crew, although we did manage to shoot all of the rehearsals, which helped the actors get used to the camera. I expect I may do a "how to rehearse" video with that material.

Camera planning was more difficult than it might have otherwise been because of our ensemble cast. The story doesn't follow one character, so I had to think about each scene and determine whose point(s) of view should be covered. There were several large scenes (a dinner, an emergency room), where we had enough time to cover three or more points of view besides a master camera position. These scenes were the most fun to cut in editing and really allowed the audience to follow several POVs at once. I'd shoot the wide shots first, keeping the camera and lights in one position with slight readjustments as we went in for two-shots or close-ups, and then do the reverses (if any). When there was no time to do reverses, I staged the scenes so the camera could see most of the faces much of the time.

Little did I know how difficult it would be to get Mini-DV tape stock! I bought the last two boxes at my local Good Guys in Los Angeles, and another box at a Circuit City in Champaign. I tried to get additional boxes from a mail-order house in New York, but despite their promises to overnight it I never received the tape they supposedly had "in stock." I bought a cassette here and there, but we cut it close. Lesson: Buy your DV tape very, very early; it's still hard to find. Panasonic and Sony tape stock is superb; I couldn't tell the difference. Even after viewing the originals once or twice during logging—digitizing once and sometimes twice—there was no noticeable dropout or wear.

We shot about 22 Mini-DV cassettes; some were half-hours, not all were fully used. We shot roughly 15 hours of material for a 1:12 ratio or lower; a great deal of video was run off before each take. The shoot ran for 12 days with several 12- to 14-hour days (including three with record-degree prairie heat, and two days of severe thunderstorms, which made us run for cover while on location).

Costumes consisted of what the actors had in their closets. Makeup consisted of frequent "dab downs." There was one "facial injury" (which I created with a tiny brush and a bottle of theatrical blood). The "injured" actor and a medical consultant did the more elaborate injury makeup for a hospital scene.

## Audio

Audio was our greatest challenge. My attention was riveted on the script, rehearsing, trying to gather up all the necessary resources (both human and material), scouting locations, learning about how to tweak the camera, getting releases and contracts signed, and directing. I did not find an experienced soundman. My fault. Those duties fell to a local musician who had never used a boom mic before but who did his best every day. In retrospect I have to say that you should never underestimate your audio requirements. If necessary, restage your scenes so you can capture good sound.

We were fine when we used a mixer and two lavaliere mics. Our soundman could ride levels. But once this equipment had to be returned (four days into the shoot), we fell back on a single boom mic patched straight into the camera. You just can't ride the levels from the camera (with its tiny dials and buttons) and hold the boom at the same time. If you can't get a mixer, at least get a XLR adapter for the audio. Messing with menus and tiny click wheels is no way to run a camera. Dramatic scenes that have both yelling and hushed conversation were very difficult to record. We spent hours and hours "fixing it in the mix" on a Scitex Stratasphere with editor Bruce Brooks, of Wiz Bang Productions, in Atlanta. Four or five of the scenes with the most serious sound problems were laid off and tweaked by Chris TK using Digidesign Pro-Tools at Oasis Recording, also in that city.

When the audio was recorded well, it sounded great. When it was recorded poorly, it was very difficult to fix. Digital can be very unforgiving with audio.

## Tricking the Camera

As mentioned earlier, our cameraman was Steve Parker. Parker shoots for the University of Illinois' Agriculture Department, and among his accomplishments is the distinction of having shot more cornfield footage than anyone on the planet. He took a two-week vacation to join us. What most impressed me about working with Parker (besides his great eye) was his professionalism; his own comfort was secondary to getting the shot. It wasn't unusual to see him lying in the dirt to get a great low angle. Our production procedure was fairly standard. I'd pick a camera position. Parker or Hartin would then offer suggestions. I'd block the scene with the actors. Hartin would start lighting; even on our largest scenes he probably never spent more than an hour at this (even with his inexperienced helpers). There simply wasn't time.

We'd shoot our master shots first, then move in for two-shots and three-shots, and finally singles and inserts. We did this because we could at least get a master (once when it rained that's all we got!) and it made lighting faster. We never had to go back to lighting a large area, only smaller and smaller areas.

When I first told Parker—who owns a Betacam and several other cameras—that I wanted him to shoot with the DCR-VX1000 , there was silence on his end of the phone. I have to admit that I was more than a little apprehensive about using what is essentially a souped-up Handicam to shoot a feature, he recalls. But now that we're done I think it did a pretty good job. The main problems we had all along were not with the DV format; it performed beyond my wildest dreams. Our problems—or should I call them "challenges"—resulted from the inherent limitations of camera itself. The DCR-VX1000 is capable of producing incredible video. But it must be tweaked correctly, and then extreme care must be taken with the essentials: focus, white balance, exposure, and of course audio.

Fortunately, we had several technical meetings where Parker, Hartin, and I went over the camera. I'd just bought it a month earlier, had taken it to Bali, but hadn't yet tried out all its manual bells and whistles. Parker's advice about the camera was to spend a lot of time getting to know it. Don't expect to be able to shoot with it fresh out of the box. In particular, learn the capabilities of its different modes, and—even more importantly—how to turn them off.

As mentioned earlier, the The DCR-VX1000, although technically very sophisticated, is a prosumer camera with automatic features. Professionals, on the other hand, need to be able to override automatic modes. The main limitations are the lens and the lack of professional controls on the camera, Parker explains. A professional is used to having all the controls at his fingertips, not buried in a menu. The DCR-VX1000, however, assumes that you want to use its automatic modes. The problem with this is that the computer chip really has no idea what you're attempting to accomplish. When I started playing with the camera, I noticed a "gain pump" when panning from light to dark. Instead of staying dark, the video got very noisy. It was the equivalent of boosting the gain. Finally I figured out that this was happening when shooting wide open. When the lens was stopped down a bit, the noise problem disappeared.

The DCR-VX1000 is controlled by a menu system and the manufacturer's supplied manual is next to useless. It's vague, confusing, and at times downright contradictory. Fortunately we got real help from cyberspace.

Parker got on the Internet and found a "Tipsheet/FAQ on the VX1000" at http://www.videouniversity.com/dvcuse.htm, written by John Ferrick (j.ferrick@bibliotech.co.uk). Thanks, John, for the jump start.

In our technical meeting, Steve—armed with a light meter, chip chart, and waveform monitor—started tweaking. Here's what he did:

1. Reset the gain to -3db for normal. This setting produces video with the sharpest colors and least amount of noise. The entire movie was shot at this setting.

2. By shooting various exposures of the chip chart he determined that the auto iris was about one-half a stop hot. He reset the iris through the menu in half-stop increments plus or minus.

3. He determined the "zebra"; setting on the camera and the effective ASA of the system in order to set everything manually. The only way to control the image completely is to go to total manual settings. Turn the auto white, auto exposure, and all the modes off. They just make it more difficult. Use a light meter, watch the zebras, remember your basics in regard to depth of field, and you're in business.

(Zebra is an exposure indicator in the viewfinder that shows up hot spots in the video above a certain IRE. It's important to know when the zebra kicks on so you can adjust exposure and lighting accordingly. The zebra on our camera was set around 80 IRE.)

It's your job to control the image; no camera can do it for you automatically, Parker says, adding that through his testing he established that the working ASA of the camera was 200, which allowed him to light "film style," using light meters.

**VIDEO ASA**

Steven Parker suggests the following procedure for determining your video camera's ASA. This is an edited version of the ASA method found in the fine book *Electronic Cinematography* by Harry Mathias.

You will need:

> Your video camera
> A chip chart
> A waveform monitor
> A light meter

1.  Illuminate your chip chart.
2.  Hook the wave form up to your camera.
3.  Shoot the chart with your camera. (Set iris on manual)
4.  Adjust the iris until you have a full signal. (i.e., Whites are at 100 IRE)
5.  Look at the f-stop on your lens. (Let's say it is 5.6)
6.  Set your meter on the proper fstop, and rotate the film ASA until the proper frames per second line up with the mark. (Use the cine' mark 24fps rather than 30fps)
7.  Look at the ASA for your answer.

You can now light a set without even taking a camera or monitor out of the cases. This is especially useful for scouting. Saves a ton of time on the day of the shoot.

Since this is a "movie," I wanted a film look, which meant avoiding deep depths of fields and flat video lighting. For a shallow depth of field (in order to soften backgrounds and separate the actors from the locations), we lit for f 2.8 inside and tried to get f 5.6 outside. Foregrounds and backgrounds stayed out of focus.

We did our best to avoid overhead and front lighting. I staged as many scenes as possible so that Parker could take advantage of backlighting and throw key light from reflectors (especially when we were shooting outdoors). Sometimes he would set up three or four reflectors through a diffuser on a bright day (a poor man's HMI!). One day he used a reflector to throw light 200 feet onto a paddle boat in the middle of a lake. It worked!

We augmented the existing lens and camera ND (neutral density) filter with an ND.6 (to keep a wide aperture) and those screw-on wide-angle adapters (.5x and .7x) mentioned earlier. The .5x wasn't truly effective because it "vignettes," blacking out the picture around the edges of the frame. You couldn't always see this in the viewfinder or on the monitor, but you could certainly see it later in the darkened editing room. We weren't able to make full use of the widest angle because we would have had to zoom in quite a bit to lose the vignetting. An "ADO blowup" on the digital image in post didn't work because the DV picture simply doesn't hold up. The wide angle was great for our many cramped interiors and for specialty shots where we needed that effect.

Because we wanted to maintain as shallow a depth of field as possible I tried to limit the use on exteriors, Parker says. The camera flares like crazy. It was a common sight to see me crawling around with the wide angle with a French flag as big as the camera clamped to it. Other random bits of camera advice Parker recalled include the following:

Do everything in the manual mode, especially focus. Don't rely on the automatic mode, especially with mixed light. Control exposure manually to influence the shutter and iris controls to get greater depth of field. Turn off the digital zoom (which kicks in at the end of the optical zoom) to avoid getting "grain." Set your own white balance.

Lenses were sharpest at a stop or two down from wide open. The DCR-VX1000 has a color-bar generator; it's a very nice feature. Stop the lens down a bit, which turns off the automatic gain and cuts down on grainy noise when in the manual mode. Forget about putting pull-focus marks on the lens; somehow they shift, and if you try focusing to your "mark" you'll be out of focus. The focusing marks end up in a different place each time. Go figure. Last but not least there's time; get more of it. Plan well. Everything requires time: lighting, dollies, you name it. Fortunately our actors were well rehearsed so they were ready when needed.

As I write this *Coyote's Honor* is being transferred to Digital Betacam. I've been working full steam ahead since late May and it's now mid-September. Three weeks from concept to script, three weeks of rehearsals, two weeks of shooting, five weeks of post.

Now that you know all this, go to that script you've got in your drawer that you've always wanted to shoot. Instead of working for a client, work for yourself and realize your own personal vision. Tell your clients or your employer that you'll be busy for a while realizing your dream of making a movie. Cast some actors. Book your crew. As a video professional you have the knowledge to make it happen. Technology hasn't totally caught up to Cocteau's dream just yet, but we're getting close.


## PART II: Production Begins

The *Coyote's Honor* experience proved that you can shoot a "movie" with a small crew, a prosumer digital camera, and a limited budget. But it's tough work, real tough. I worked full-steam from May through September and only recently solved some vexing audio post problems. Screenwriter Doug McCord, cameraman Steve Parker, DP Timothy Hartin, and many other talented people all worked equally hard at their own crafts to make this movie a reality. No-budget movies aren't easy; sissies need not apply. Above all, you need a good story. But if you've got the passion to realize your personal vision it can be done—and for far less cost than ever before possible.

## Casting

As I mentioned last month, I'd gotten to know Rick Barrows, an acting professor at the "U of I," during previous summer trips to Champaign where I grew up (I live in Los Angeles). I had been impressed by his summer-stock actors, who were young and uncorrupted by "Hollywood" attitudes. Most movies are scripted, then cast. We did just the reverse. In late May of this year Barrows sent me a stack of eight-by-ten head shots of actors who'd be available over the summer. Unable to interview them in person, I put the photos together in various configurations and came up with some story lines. Screenwriter and U of I grad Doug McCord just happens to live near me in North Hollywood. We discussed story ideas and in less than a week he'd banged out bios and back stories for the characters, an outline, and a first draft. Off I went to Illinois, and by the first week of June I was meeting the actors and discussing their parts. Bingo! With the exception of one actor that McCord didn't know, he'd nailed it. The parts he'd written matched their looks and abilities.

## Second Draft Scripts and Rewrites

Originally our story was about high school kids, but within minutes of meeting the actors I realized that they were too old to play them. They'd be college students in the rewrite. Then I met Eric Wippo, who played "Chuck," the "coyote." This six-foot-one yellow-spiked-hair kid with an earring was never going to be the introspective angel the script called for. He's an improvisational livewire (think Robin Williams meets Jim Carey). More script changes were needed.

I told McCord that Chuck should have a "coyote's energy" and be a kind of trickster, a shape-shifter who would have the kind of energy the story required, the ability to change the lives of those around him. He was to have no back story. We wouldn't know anything about him. He'd hitch into town and leave the same way. There'd be no exposition about him. Instead, he'd be some weird kind of performance-artist guy who mooches on everyone's food, wine, and women. Wippo's off-the-wall acting style would bring a much needed levity to our film, which was getting too heavy with too much youthful angst and drama.

*Eric Wippo as Chuck, "the Coyote"*

By mid-June McCord was into the rewrite. We'd talk a couple of hours a day. For half the day I was in rehearsals and improvisations with the actors. The second half of the day was spent on the phone hustling a long list of items that I still had to find in the middle of Illinois for free! Here's a partial list I wrote at the time: some money, a production crew, camerapeople, a lighting director, a sound recordist, grips and gaffers, a makeup person, production assistants, a line producer, a nonlinear editing facility, a composer and/or some music, catering, costuming, a lighting package and grip gear, tape stock, a shotgun mic and boom pole, and—oh yes—a video camera.

The main lesson about this—or any other—production is that it's a step-by-step process. You don't get there all at once. You think big, you build your team, you ferret out resources, and eventually, you hope, it all comes together. For us it had to happen before mid-July when we planned to shoot; by early August we'd lose all our actors.

## Go in With Your Eyes Open

For low- and no-budget projects, you will find you are writing, fundraising, producing, and directing all at the same time. It's difficult to give every function full attention and something has to yield. For *Coyote's Honor* I felt I should put most of my attention on getting good performances. If the performances were strong, perhaps the technical limitations of a low-budget video "movie" would be overlooked. That's been the saving grace of just about every successful independent movie I can think of. Independents don't have special effects or box-office stars. They need an engaging story with great characters and terrific performances. Here's a short list of things to think about as you start an independent feature project. These items will either make you move forward with gusto or stop you dead in your tracks. If you want to embark on such an adventure, you'd better know what you're getting into." Just how committed are you? Are you really ready to put your entire life on hold (job, family, relationships) and focus all your energy and resources on "getting it done"? You're making a personal commitment that you'll see the movie through to the very end. If you ask people to give up their jobs, family, and relationships and work for free, then you'd better be committed to finishing the project for everyone's sake. Nobody gets anything out of it unless the project is finished and seen. Don't start it if you don't intend to finish it.

In my agreements with everyone (which such a project absolutely must have), I left myself an "out" because if the shooting didn't go well, I didn't want to commit to the time and expense of editing and finishing a bad movie. But this "out" was really a cop-out; I knew in my heart that if I was asking people to work for free they'd damn well better get something good and usable out of the experience. This was the exchange. They would work hard for me, and I would work hard for them, make the best movie I could, and finish the project.

* What is that personal vision you want to realize? You need to see the story in your mind first. How else can you communicate to your writers, cast, and crew what it's about, and then muster the support you will need? After you see the story in your mind you have to imagine all the production elements you'll need so you can begin to assemble your resources and ask everyone you know for favors. You need to keep the project constantly moving forward. You keep one eye on getting it done in the moment and the other eye on the future, anticipating every next move. Your vision must also extend to exhibition and distribution, so this will also influence your decisions over the film's title, publicity strategy, collecting production stills and portraits of your actors, and a myriad of other marketing decisions that I'll discuss in a future installment.

* As I mentioned before, such an undertaking is not for sissies. Moviemaking with money? Hard work. Moviemaking without money? Even harder work, not for the faint-of-heart. You must really see every obstacle as an opportunity to get something for free. You must be willing to negotiate, negotiate, and then negotiate some more. This takes time (which you probably don't have). So you'll have to assemble others around you who have this same mind-set.

* Anticipate the snowball effect. Once you commit to your project, and that commitment is strong, you will draw others in. At the beginning of this project I said, "I don't care if I have to shoot the whole thing myself with a camcorder and available light—I'm gonna get it done! If you want to join in and learn a lot, have some fun, and make something really good, climb aboard!" If you promise a learning experience, fun, and the opportunity of doing something worthy, it's hard to be turned down.

* Let the crew members decide their own time commitments. When you're doing a no-budget movie you're not paying your crew. I asked everyone to tell me how many days they could contribute. Some of the crew worked during vacation time, spending two or more weeks on

the project. Others gave us a few days. Some could only work on weekends or at nights. I didn't want anyone to overcommit to a schedule and then not be able to keep to it, or to start to resent it because they weren't able to pay their rent.

* Bear in mind the real costs. Some things will, and do, cost money. No matter how hard I tried I could not make a deal with Kinko's (we needed the scripts fast, and couldn't just use someone's office machine). Also, some restaurants and grocery stores contributed free food, but I did have to pull out the credit card for some cast and crew lunches and dinners. There were also occasional rentals, diesel fuel for the grip truck, burned-out lamps, used gels, gaffer tape, and other expendables that added up. I didn't know until postproduction wrapped what the actual hard costs were, but I did know that I'm the guy responsible.

* Agreements. Since this was a no-budget project there were no lawyers nor agents. I wrote the agreement, so there were no legal fees. When it's time to negotiate a distribution agreement, I will hire a lawyer.

* High risk. We had no insurance. It was the first time I'd done that in over 15 years, and it's very scary to "fly without a net." Even though there's a clause in the agreement that says "everyone is responsible for their own well-being," you can be sure that if an accident did happen lawyers would come after the wallet of the person in charge—in this case, me. If you have a weak stomach for risk, no-budget production is not for you!

* The digital video camera. I had the opportunity to shoot in 16 mm and 35 mm film, but I didn't because I didn't have the time to hustle up the $30,000 to $50,000 in cash it would have required for film and processing. In the end, I will spend this much for a transfer from video to film. Secondly, the film-camera gear I found for free didn't have Arricode (which puts time code on the film for nonlinear editing later) so I would have had to edit on a flatbed. There's nothing wrong with that, it's just that these days I'm more comfortable with nonlinear editing. I also had the opportunity to shoot on Betacam, but I really

wanted to do a "desktop digital movie" using "prosumer" gear, hence the Sony DCR-VX1000. If we could be successful with it, it would mean that anyone with a minimal investment in gear could also do it. Imagine that, the democratization of movies!

## PART III: Agreements With Participants

Agreements are what you need to get in place with each and every participant in the project, whether they are actors, crew, personnel, or people who loan you equipment, houses, cars—whatever. What follows is an example of what I used. This is not a great document, nor do I suggest cribbing it; there are probably inconsistencies of language and style. Besides, you will need an agreement specific to your own needs if you are planning to do your own indy video feature. What I present in this month's column is for information purposes. It's to get you to think about some of the issues you'll want to cover in your own document.

My agreement document was not prepared by an attorney (nor is it 50 pages long). I wrote it based on my experience as a video producer. Again, consult with your lawyer before using this or anything like it. Whatever way you wish to structure your deal with everyone is fine as long as there's an exchange and it's a "win-win" for everyone.

My agreement gives me pretty much total control to do what I want. It's my project. In essence it says, "These are the rules if you want to participate." It was essential I make this very clear to everyone at the start.

What did the participants get out of working on my feature? They get the experience of working on a real project and a credit in their resume and on the feature itself. The time they put in will be valued, and they'll get a deferred fee as well as profit participation.

As we all know, however, most independent films don't find distributors or make money. Since this is the case, you'd better make sure everyone is treated well during production (well fed and appreciated). Make sure they have a chance to learn and an opportunity to contribute.

And lastly, with all your other responsibilities, try to have fun on the set so that everyone works hard and has a good time. Okay? Still want to "do it"?

If so, here is the agreement document accompanied by my comments.

## FILM AGREEMENT

Dated:_____

When signed by each of us, this letter will constitute an Agreement between you and DESKTOP
BROADCASTING INC., d.b.a. Michael Wiese
Productions (hereinafter referred to as
"Producer"), 11288 Ventura Blvd., Suite 821,
Studio City CA 91604 and_____(your name,
address, and Social Security number) hereinafter
referred to as "Participant") for the production,
distribution, and broadcast by Producer of a "no
budget," direct-to-video film ("Film") entitled
"COYOTE'S HONOR" (working title).

An agreement is between two parties. This defines
who they are and describes the project.

    The parties agree as follows:

1. Services: Participants shall perform the
duties in the making of the film as usually associated with the credits that they shall receive.

This is pretty general, but it needs to be. Otherwise you'll have to make individual agreements with everyone. You need something generic, although the entire contract is too long and too detailed for some situations. You may wish to have a much shorter, one-page agreement for people who loan you houses, equipment, or who do walk-on parts as extras.

2. Compensation: Participants shall receive no
compensation for their Services nor shall they be
considered employees of the Producer. (In the
event revenues are generated from the Work and
payments are made to Participants, payments shall
be considered "royalty payments.")

Make it very clear they are not getting paid. Or pay them $1. If they
are employees and receive cash, then you have to pay taxes, etc. I've
tried to set this up so that they will get royalties as their fee. This way
if monies come in I can disburse them as royalties and report it to the
IRS on a 1099 form. We'll see if my accountant agrees.

3. Term: The preproduction and production period
shall be June through August 1997 on days to be
mutually    agreed    upon    between    Producer    and
Participant.

4. Compensation: There will be no cash compensation to participants. The Producer shall, however, account for the time and/or equipment rental,
and/or materials that each person contributes. At
his discretion, he will select a "standard industry fee" to be attributed to each Participant's
service or contribution. Fees that are found in
the   film   budget   in   the   book   "Film   and   Video
Budgets" may be used as reference. If no fee for
that job or material is found, then Producer will
use its best judgment to allocate a fair and just
price   to   that   service   or   material   contributed.
Participant agrees to accept the total fee designated by the Producer in its sole judgment.

This gives me the power to value each person's contribution. Yes, it's
fairly arbitrary and that's why I tried to tie it to *Film & Video Budgets*,
a budgeting guide published by my company, Michael Wiese
Productions. I'm just going to have to be as fair as possible based on
the person's experience, industry standards, and contribution. I didn't
say this was easy, did I?

5. Reverse Budget: By accounting for all the services and materials used in the production, the Producer will generate a "reverse budget" of the total hard and in-kind costs of the production. A profit participation will be a pro-rata share of the total budget. (Example: If a Participant works the equivalent number of days to generate $10,000 in fees, and the total budget is $100,000, then the Participant's pro-rata share of the budget is 10 percent. From revenues (if any) the Participant shall recoup his deferred fees on a pari-passu basis with the other participants. Once the budget has been paid back to all the investors and deferred-fee Participants, the investors and Participants shall receive their pro-rata share of 50 percent of 100 percent of the net profits. "Net Profits" are defined as all revenues actually received by the Producer less investors' cash contributions, deferred fees, and loans to the production (if any). (The Producer may be required to withhold taxes on payments to the Participant, which may be deemed by the IRS to be salaries and/or royalty payments.)

The notion here is that at the end of the project I will do a budget. An individual's deferment will be a pro-rata share of the budget. This pro-rata share will give him or her profit participation in the net profits of the film. "Net profits" as defined here mean: (1) the hard cash must be paid back first; (2) then deferments; (3) and then loans, if any; half of everything that is left is net profits.

Why half? In all of my other projects where the entire budget was raised in cash, the investors are paid back and then we split any other income 50/50. This agreement treats the cash and crew members, and those who contributed equipment, as "investors." Not only do they get paid back for their investment, but they get (as a group) 50% of the profits.

What do I do with my 50%? First off, I should be so lucky to keep 50%. I keep these points as I may need to use them as barter for other goods and services as we go along. At some point I may need a cash investment for a video to 35mm transfer, or for publicity, prints, or a marketing campaign. This gives me something to barter with. Also, should we actually make money from the production, then I too can be compensated for my work. (Be careful and be sure to keep something back for yourself. I've met many producers who've given all profit participation away on their own project and years later when they are still working on it, they resent the whole thing!) I would consider it pretty good if I ended up with 25% profit participation.

But again, no one is doing this project for money or profit. That's the great thing about a no-budget project. It's not about money. It's about the independent spirit and cooperation and doing something together because it's fun! I've also noticed that the other projects like this that I've done have been profitable while the "get rich quick" projects haven't. I think this says something. That's especially why on a no-budget project you should have an agreement that specifies what will happen in the event that it does make money.

6. Credits: If, and when, the film is completed the Participant shall receive a credit in the head or tail credits of the film. Head credits may include writer, director, producer, and others. Tail credits may start with the principal lead actors, secondary actors, production and postproduction team, extras, others, and those who contributed goods and services. The Producer, in his sole discretion, will use best efforts to fairly and appropriately credit everyone for their participation and contributions. Accidental deletion of any names or credits shall not be considered a breach of this agreement. In the event that multiple people perform the same function (such as screenplay writing or associate producing) the Producer will use his best judgment to fairly credit Participant.

Credits are very important to the participants, so be sure you get them right. I keep a list of everyone who has participated and I actually start building the credits list while we are in production. That way, I hope-fully won't forget anyone. Here I again have full power to assign cred-its. I'll do my best to make sure everyone is appropriately credited.

By now you should be seeing that people really have to trust you. You are asking for full creative and fiscal power in the agreement. The agreement in fact gives the producer all the power with no recourse for the participant. People will only sign up for something like this if they believe you'll treat them fairly. Keep that in mind. If you ask for all the power, then you have a great responsibility. If you take advan-tage of the situation, you'll be sorry next time you try to mount a no-budget production again. Make it work, and you'll be hero.

7. Non-Union Picture: Producer makes the material representation that it is not a signatory to SAG, WGA, DGA, or IATSE collective bargaining agreements or any other union or guild agreement. Participant warrants that Participant is not a member of any union or guild, memberships in which would prevent Player from working in this Film.

The unions don't allow their members to work for free. You can't do a no-budget film with union members unless they work under differ-ent names. The most experienced cast and crew people are in the guilds.

8. Creative Control: While the Producer seeks cre-ative input from everyone at every level during the production, the Producer shall have final creative control over all aspects of the production includ-ing script, rehearsals, filming, editing, music, artwork, publicity, marketing and distribution.

This clearly defines where the buck stops. You'll never see this in a studio contract!

9. Editing: Producer has the right, but not the obligation, to use any of the materials filmed during production in his sole discretion, including but not limited to a "Making Of..." documentary. At any time, the Producer has the right to deem the filming unacceptable and may abandon production and the completion of said Work. The Producer makes no warranties that it shall actually complete a Film from what is shot.

This is a "cop-out" line that I wrote before I had either cast or crew. I had my doubts whether we could actually shoot anything of quality in a small town in the Midwest. I didn't know that the cast or the crew would be as good as they were. I was giving myself an out. I'm embarrassed by this but I had to do it. I didn't want to commit to finishing something that I didn't believe in. What you want to do is finish the project. Otherwise there is no benefit to anyone. Fortunately, I think we got some great materials and I did finish the project. I owe it to everyone who worked so hard for free!

10. Copyright: Producer shall hold the copyright in any materials created for the Film. Producer shall solely and exclusively own the Film in whatever stage of completion as it may exist, including, but not limited to, all rights of whatever kind and character, throughout the world, in perpetuity, copyright, production, manufacture, reproduction, transcription, performance, broadcast and exhibition by any art, method, or device now known or hereafter devised including theatrical, nontheatrical exhibition, television, and home video, electronic media.

I hold ownership in the entire project in every medium throughout the world forever and ever! (If I saw this language in a distribution contract I would never sign it!)

11. Name and Likeness: Producer shall have the

exclusive right to use and to license the use of
Participant's name, photography, likeness, voice,
and appearance by any means in and in connection
with the Film and the advertisement, publicizing,
exhibition, and/or other exploitation thereof in
any manner and by any means.

Mostly for the actors. In other words, I can use their image and likeness in the film.

12. Wardrobe and Makeup Furnishings: If the
Participant has an on-camera role, the Participant
agrees to furnish all modern wardrobe, wearing
apparel, and makeup reasonably necessary for the
portrayal of their role.

Actors supply their own makeup and costumes. In this case, most of
the actors were performing in summer-stock theater and were accustomed to doing their own makeup.

13. Promotional Videotapes: The Participant shall
receive two (2) VHS format videotapes of the Film
(if it is completed), which shall be sent to the
Participant's address herein. Additional copies
(not for resale) may be ordered for an "at cost"
purchase price from the Producer.

It's very important to give all participants copies of the finished work.
The actors can send them to agents and producers. I've made it possible for everyone to order (at cost) as many copies as they may need
to help further their careers.

14. Scheduling: Since the production of the Film
requires on participation in a timely fashion, it
is expected that Participant's commitment to the
agreed-upon schedule will be adhered to pending
illness or personal emergency.

I'm trying to make it clear to everyone that their participation is vitally important. And it is—especially for the actors. Since none of the actors had been in films before, it took a while for them to understand that if they didn't show up on their shoot day there'd be 30 people standing around doing nothing! Still, this doesn't really mean much. Either they show up or they don't. In a real contract, there'd be a penalty if they didn't show.

15. Hiring and Firing: The Producer in his sole discretion shall make agreements with Participants. Anyone who has not signed this Agreement is not considered to be part of the Film by the Producer. In the event someone is fired from the production, any days that they worked or any contribution that they made will be noted and, in the event of revenues from the film, they will be compensated on the same basis as everyone else (stated herein above). All rights granted by Participant to Producer as stated herein shall continue for the term of the Agreement.

This is important because not everyone that joins the production may work out. You need to have some way of firing them and still compensate them for any work they may have performed. This also covers people who either quit or simply stopped coming to work. Remember, you will naturally have attrition as your crew people discover what hard work this really is. Still, you want to compensate people for what work they do regardless of whether they make it through the whole production.

16. Insurance: The Film production is not insured. Participants shall assume full and total responsibility for their own well-being during the filming process. If Participants agree to any stunts or physical action they shall do so entirely at their own risk. If Participants operate equipment they shall do so entirely at their own risk. The Producer assumes no liability for any mishaps dur-

ing Production. Participants who wish to be insured
should carry their own insurance.

It's tightrope walking without a net. Even though everyone has agreed
to this paragraph, if someone gets injured they may sue the producer.
There is tremendous liability in doing a project without insurance.
But with no money, what are you going to do?

17. Transportation and Travel Expenses: Filming is
anticipated to take place within 50 miles of the
Champaign-Urbana area. There will be no compensation now or later for mileage, travel expenses, or
meals. Participant shall pay these and other incidental expenses.

Everyone pays their own expenses.

18. Arbitration: Any controversy or claim arising
out of or relating to this Agreement or any breach
thereof shall be settled by arbitration in accordance with the Rules of the American Arbitration
Association; and judgment upon the award rendered
by the arbitrators may be entered in any court having jurisdiction thereof. The prevailing party
shall be entitled to reimbursement for costs and
reasonable attorney's fees. The determination of
the arbitrator in such proceeding shall be final,
binding, and non-appealable.

Arbitration gives you a less expensive way (than lawyers and court) to
settle disagreements. I see now that I should have specified in what
state this would take place.

19. Entire Agreement: This constitutes the Entire
Agreement of the parties and all previous agreements, warranties, and representations, if any are
merged herein.

By signing the spaces provided below, you accept
and agree to all of the terms and conditions of
this Agreement.

AGREED TO AND ACCEPTED:

Date:_____
By:_____
"PARTICIPANT" (Signature)

Print Name:_____
(Print Legibly. This will be used for your cred-
it!)
Address:_____
Telephone:_____

Social Security Number:_____

Additional contact name and number. Someone who may
know your whereabouts should you move:_____

AGREED TO & ACCEPTED:_____
"PRODUCER"
Michael Wiese, President
Michael Wiese Productions

I hope this gives you some ideas about the agreement you will need to
create between yourself and everyone who participates in your project. If you go without an agreement, you are opening yourself to
incredible misunderstandings. Humans remember what they want to.
With an agreementyou sign it, put it in a file, and forget about it. If
there is a disagreement you pull out the agreement; it tells you what
you've agreed to and how to resolve problems that arise.

I think it's essential to have agreements, especially among your best
friends and relatives, where you will be most reluctant to have an
agreement. I've seen friendships, partnerships, and even marriages
break up on film projects where there were no clear agreements. The

areas that cause the most difficulty among people are money, credits, responsibilities (who does what), and profit participation. If you are at least clear in these areas, you'll avoid lots of problems later.

In addition, a distributor or broadcaster will not accept your film if you do not have signed agreements from everyone who has participated. Prepare an agreement, get it signed, then get to work!

*(l-r) Heather Saliny (Sandra), Eric Wippo (Chuck), Heather Lamp ('Becca), and Emily Parks (Julie).*

## PART IV: The Postproduction Process

### Storage and Organization

I had a long-standing invitation to use Dennis Fedoruk's Light Vision Films, in Atlanta, after having consulted with that company some time ago. Halfway through shooting *Coyote's Honor* I called Fedoruk to schedule editing time and learned that another company in his building, Wiz Bang Productions, just bought a Power Mac 7200/60-based Scitex Digital Video StrataSphere. Although the system isn't designed for long-form work, Wiz Bang was willing to work with me on the project. My plan was to send the camera rolls (Mini-DV cassettes) to editor Bruce Brooks, take a ten–day break after shooting ended, and then show up fresh in Atlanta and view an assembly based on the script and our camera logs. Brooks heads up Wiz Bang Productions (Acepic@aol.com) with cameraman John Thompson; the two of them served as Co-Executive Producers on the project, along with Fedoruk.

One of the many lessons I learned in shooting this no-budget project is that the keeper of the camera logs doesn't always show up for each shoot. Our camera logs were only partially maintained. Before driving to Atlanta from Illinois I went through all our Mini-DV cassettes, made a new log, and circled the selects. From this log book we rolled a Sony DVCAM VTR up to the selected takes and output to the StrataSphere. We passed the audio through a Soundcraft Spirit Folio mixing board, adjusting levels as we went.

Our first major postproduction challenge was digital storage space. On the first day we loaded a third of the camera selects onto our initial 16 GB of hard-drives. Loading at 2.8:1 compression gave us only 45 minutes of storage on 16 GB. Although I tried to be conservative in what we digitized, we began running out of space fast and needed more drives. If we'd been more sure of what shots we were going to use, storage would have been less a problem. As it was, however, we sometimes loaded three takes of a master shot to get the best performances.

Over the course of the next several weeks we loaded up the drives as much as we could and then edited whatever sequences had enough footage. It was an erratic way to do things, but since we didn't have enough storage there was no other option. When we finally were able to obtain additional storage towers and drives from both Scitex Digital Video and Seagate Technology, we had 72 GB, which gave us about three and a half hours of high-resolution video.

Robert Major, Scitex Digital Video's Atlanta Service Manager, provided upgrades and tweaked the disk drives. Scitex was also very supportive during numerous tech–support calls. They indicated that they hadn't encountered anyone doing this sort of long-format DV project, and indeed Brooks's previous editing experience was with short-form work.

Management of our clips was a major chore. Brooks originally put everything on one tracksheet (the Sphere timeline workspace), but later divided it into two parts so it would load more quickly and free-up memory to speed editing. His clipsheets (bins) were sorted by scene numbers so they would also load more quickly. There were over 100 scenes in the movie, so we made clipsheet folders for scenes one through ten, ten through twenty, etc., plus separate clipsheets for sound effects, music, and wild sounds. As every editor knows, organization is the key to success.

## The Rough Cut

I'm very impressed with the StrataSphere. It was the first time I spent weeks editing hands-on with one of today's top machines, and I loved it. When I began pulling selects and assembling rough scenes I found that I was quickly able to do audio overlaps, dissolves, titles, color correction, and effects. Brooks and I considered our "tag-team" approach to be a positive one. I'd throw a scene together and then take a break. He'd jump in and fine-tune the cuts, work on the sound, or solve other editorial problems. In this way, the show was always moving forward.

The StrataSphere was fussy in the beginning but once we turned off all the extensions that came loaded in Wiz Bang's new Power Mac 7200/60 and ran Norton Utilities, things worked much better. Backing up our tracksheets on a 1 GB Iomega Jaz drive was standard protocol. Early on, I lost about one day's editing when my sequence didn't save. I never did figure out what happened. I remembered the shot sequence, so it only took about an hour and a half to restore.

## Audio

As we edited, audio inconsistencies cropped up. The StrataSphere fixed the minor problems, as long as they didn't peak, but when they did we found that they weren't fixable. The StrataSphere did not at that time have extensive built-in sound sweetening. Scenes with sound problems were laid these off to Betacam and taken to Oasis Studios (in Atlanta) for correction. They used Digidesign Pro Tools to reduce wind sounds, lower distorted peaks, and provide overall dialogue equalization. The audio was then transferred back to Betacam SP with SMPTE time code. We digitized the Betacam SP tape back into the StrataSphere and re-synced the corrected sections.

During the location shoot we occasionally shot with two VX-1000 cameras running simultaneously. One day the primary camera produced unusable, low-level audio. Fortunately, the second camera had good sound. To my amazement, we were able to lay in the good sound with the good picture and the two tapes stayed in perfect sync for the scene, which was several minutes long. This to me seems like pretty good performance from what are only prosumer camcorders.

## Previews

After a while it's hard to critique an edit on a piece you also directed. To freshen my head and get away from the editing room, we laid off various edited versions to VHS, which I would view in my hotel or Wiz Bang's conference room. This enabled me to discern the overall flow of the show and find any weak points in sound or editing. Then I'd make a list of necessary fixes for the following day.

All the titles and credits were done using the StrataSphere's graphic package, which was fine for our purposes. Its effects capabilities were more than adequate for the occasional sparkles, halos, overlapped motion, still frames, mortises, and mattes the script called for. When we started post, Brooks said it would take three weeks; I figured six. We finished in five.

We scheduled a preview screening of *Coyote's Honor* at Atlanta Intercontinental College with the help of our production assistant, Christine Cafasso, who's a student there. The screening confirmed what I already sensed about the movie, although it's always good to see your work with an audience. Even if you don't get specific comments you can "feel" the audience's response and quickly know what does and doesn't work. As a result of that screening I made some changes to clarify places where people got confused.

## Music

Steve Dancz (sdancz@coe.uga.edu) is an outstanding musician and film composer. Besides his numerous National Geographic episodes, he did the music for several of my PBS shows, including *Diet for a New America*. He lives about an hour outside of Atlanta, in Athens, Georgia. Recently he'd been working with accomplished musicians Randall Brambrett and Davis Causey. The three had already recorded some great tracks that I felt were right for *Coyote's Honor*, so we had the great luxury of using this music (and songs) as we edited. We only had time to give Dancz a rough fine-cut of the "movie," so he gave us various versions and lengths of music cues that we slipped and slid against picture. He also introduced us to Dan Tebor (tebors2@stc.net), who'd written a song which we decided to include. Dancz's final cues were delivered a few days before our editing was to wrap.

*Composer Steven Dancz*

## Layoff

For the layoff Thompson output from the StrataSphere to a Digital Betacam tape, using the "lay it to tape with timecode" feature to match up the end of the first tracksheet to the beginning of the second. Audio went from the StrataSphere through the Soundcraft Spirit Folio to Digital Betacam and Betacam SP VTRs.

When it was all done I flew back home to Los Angeles with a VHS screening dub made from the master, grabbed a bowl of popcorn, and put my feet up. And then I got the shock of my life. The sound track was completely distorted, with sound effects three times louder than the dialogue. Plus there were phasing problems. It was unusable.

I immediately called Brooks and Thompson, and to my dismay they reported that they'd been so confident of a successful layoff they had dumped all our digitized footage from the hard drives. Why we did not go through the very standard process of checking the master through playback, I'll never know.

Since the only thing that was usable was the picture, I realized that we would have to go back and redigitize and re-edit all the sound (the dialogue, the sound effects, and the music). It was like someone kicked me in the stomach. It's hard enough to edit your show once, but twice!

I flew back to Atlanta. It took us about another week to redigitize and re-edit the show. Fortunately I had an Iomega Jaz drive on which I had backed up the tracksheets, so we could at least see where the picture and all sound edits went. But since there was no time code references from the DVX-1000, we had to rely on memory and our shooting logs to know what shots to digitize and reinsert.

Special care was taken digitizing each and every shot so that the sound would be at the proper level. This helped eliminate a lot of the distortion we got during the first edit, which we thought was created during the production sound recording. In the end we got a much better quality sound track.

As chagrined as we all were by this major screwup, it was a valuable lesson I'm glad to pass along. I'm grateful to Brooks and Thompson for their perseverance during that trying time.

## Layoff Take Two

For the second layoff, we decided to create discrete tracks (dialogue, sound effects, and music) that I could remix and lay back in a proper sound-mixing studio. Bob Gillespie, of Oasis Recording, brought in his Tascam DA-88 digital eight-track audio recorder and we made three passes from the StrataSphere, each time laying off the right and left channels of one track. At the end we had six channels of discrete sound.

A week later I worked with sound mixer George Bours at Crest National in Hollywood. He transferred the six channels to Pro Tools, equalized some scenes, rebalanced levels, filled some silent holes, and then laid back the mixed tracks to our Digital Betacam master.

By the way, the latest version of SphereOus 1.5 has a "print to disk" function for the sound. You can mix your sound track right on the hard disk, listen to it, and then lay off. We got the new software a few days before we finished the second edit but didn't have time to use it. You can bet we will next time, though.

The final mix was laid back to both Digital Betacam and Betacam SP. The former can be used for transferring to 35 mm film or for making digital dupes for broadcasters; the latter is for cassette duplication and for festival screenings.

The making of *Coyote's Honor* was a learning experience, to say the least. Granted, in post we could have gone about things in more effective fashion. Nonetheless, I set out to shoot a no-budget independent feature with prosumer DV, and did just that. My years of experience as a producer and director certainly came in handy, but I learned many new lessons along the way. One was that people can shoot "movies" with a small crew, small prosumer cameras, and practically no budget. The other major lesson was that it's tough work—real tough. From preproduction to post, no-budget movies aren't easy. Think about whether you are up to the task. Above all, you need a good story.

If you're contemplating such a project, be aware of what you're getting into. Then if you still think you want to descend into this particular kind of hell, get that script you've been wanting to shoot, tell your clients or your employer that you'll be busy for a while, cast some actors, book your crew, and go get 'em.

## Filmlook

The relative merits of the look of video and film will no doubt be a hot topic of debate for many years to come. Film is, of course, the medium everyone is used to for storytelling; it's what has been exhibited in theaters for more than a century, and it's the origination medium for nearly all episodic television. It's also more expensive than videotape.

These days, however, you can combine the best of both worlds. You can enjoy the speed, efficiency, and relative low cost of originating on videotape, but still end up with what very closely approximates the look of film. I was a skeptic until I tried what's known as Filmlook® on *Coyote's Honor*. Filmlook® (www.filmlook.com) is a real-time digital process available from Filmlook, Inc., of Burbank, California; phone (818) 955-7082.

Robert Faber, president of Filmlook, told me about the many producers who shoot on Betacam SP and use Filmlook® before delivering to their distributors. Among the recent productions that have used Filmlook® are *The Gold Rush* (PBS), *FutureWar* (Discovery Channel), *Reflections on Ice* (HBO), *The Great War* (PBS), and *The John Larroquette Show*, which used Filmlook® for its entire four-year run.

Filmlook® adds tremendous value to the look of video-originated movies, although many producers are reluctant to publicize this "secret weapon." Anti-video snobbery is still a pervasive problem, and program buyers aren't always as willing to pay as much for shows that were shot on tape as they are for film work. Fortunately, most people can't tell the difference between film and Filmlook®. I personally was blown away by it. There are three main ways it achieves a film-like image for video: movement, gray scale, and grain.

• Movement Video plays at 30 frames/60 fields per second. Film is shot at 24 frames. What Filmlook® does is give video's 60 fields per second the look of film's 24 (or in some cases 30) frames per second. It also provides the imperceptible flicker introduced by the 3:2 pull-down effect of film transferred via telecine.

• Gray scale Film has a greater dynamic range than video. There's a greater range of colors and brightness. On film, you can overexpose three stops and still have a great image; it's very forgiving. Video on the other hand has a very limited dynamic range since it is constrained by the characteristics of NTSC and the video display. With video it is easier to accidentally overexpose and underexpose with usually undesirable effects. Differences between the blackest blacks and absolute white are limited in contrast ratio. Despite film's latitude, however, film transferred to video has the exact same dynamic range as video. The effect is illusory and has nothing to do with actually increasing dynamic range. All of film's contrast values and color are compressed into the limited bandwidth of NTSC when it is transferred to video.

Filmlook® purposefully distorts and changes the gray scale and color of NTSC to simulate the gamma curve of film as it goes through the telecine process. Film appears to have more contrast than video because the wide dynamic range of film is compressed into the confines of NTSC. Filmlook® creates film's characteristic gamma curve as well as the medium's perceived warmth and color, electronically giving video a much warmer, fuller look than we usually associate with it.

• Grain Filmlook® also adds a subtle "grain" texture to the image. Grain is a visual characteristic of the photochemical nature of film; video, on the other hand, has noise. In this case, however, the look of grain is simulated, with the "grain" changing every few fields to approximate the look of a film emulsion. On *Coyote's Honor* this "grain" is barely perceptible, although Filmlook® allows you to make your images quite grainy if you prefer (think music video).

## Color Correction

Besides adding the visual artifacts of film, Filmlook® also brings many color-correcting attributes to the process. Filmlook® engineer and colorist Allen Kelly has a terrific eye; he works the Filmlook® console like a video arcade game. I watched as he tweaked every shot in *Coyote's Honor*, amazed that a guy could punch buttons so quickly!

It's important that you color-correct in the final stages of video post in a controlled environment with equipment really designed to do the job. Invite your DP to join you. They rarely get to control the look of what they were going for and will be appreciative of this. It will also make your final product look better.

Besides color-correcting, Allen smoothed out rough edits with color so the viewer's eye wouldn't be disturbed by color shifts. He fixed a shot where the setting was bumped during digitizing; now it's invisible. It's possible that you might have a shot within a sequence that looks too "chunky" at the 24 fps "rate." No problem; Allen can change it to 30 fps, and then back to 24, all within the same shot. The eye can't see the change. Needless to say, the actual video frame rate remains at 30 fps. It's just the appearance that changes.

The goal is to suspend belief and allow the viewer to be drawn into the story unimpeded by technical distractions. The Filmlook® process and the massaging of the image is invisible, seamless, and beautiful, but only if your images were well shot and lit in the first place.

We cannot turn your daughter's birthday party video into *Gone With the Wind*, Allen cautions. You have to be careful how you light, expose, shoot, and stage your scenes.

Also shoot everything at normal shutter speed of 1/60th of a second for optimum results. Higher shutter rates destroy the filmic illusion and the main artifact (the shutter motion of 24 fps), which Filmlook® replicates.

Allen was amazed at the quality of the digital output of the DCR VX-1000 we originated on. "The level of detail, color, sharpness, and contrast values in most scenes is very close to Betacam SP," he comments.

### Mastering

We ran *Coyote's Honor* through Filmlook® onto D-2 and laid back to my Digital Betacam master. I also made a Betacam SP master (for making video dubs), and a VHS viewing copy. Our 73-minute movie took about nine hours. On average, Filmlook® takes about an hour for every ten minutes of footage processed. It depends entirely on the complexity of the job and the requirements of the director. Fortunately, Filmlook® charges by the program's running time and by the hour, so whatever they estimate will be your final cost.

## Filmlook Tips

If you're going to use Filmlook® here are some things to do for maximum quality when you're shooting:

- Use a three-chip camera.
- Record on a broadcast format (Digital Betacam, D-2, Betacam SP,
  or 1-inch). We shot on Mini-DVs but once edited, loaded off on
  Digital Betacam.
- Do not use Hi-8 or S-VHS.
- The more attention you pay to lighting the better. Video can look
  beautiful when lit with the care you'd put into a film shoot. Gels,
  ND filters, and other tools are fine. Use the care and attention to
  lighting for best results.
- Never use the high-speed shutter; as mentioned earlier, use the
  1/60th of a second shutter.
- Do not overexpose whites or crush black levels.
- Don't move too fast with camera pans or zooms.

## Summary

Getting a film look is a very subjective experience. I love the end
result. If you're producing a program that needs to have the warmth
and rich feeling of film (and if you've lit that way to begin with), and
if you intend to go to broadcast, cable, or home video (as opposed to
film projection), then Filmlook® is definitely worth checking out.
Request a demo tape from Filmlook® or have them do a test on your
footage.

## An Update

As of this writing (about two months after the completion of the
movie) a sales agent is offering *Coyote's Honor* to various pay cable networks and home video companies. It was rejected by the Sundance
and Slamdance film festivals. While its distribution opportunities are
very limited (short running time of 73 minutes, and a no-name cast),
it has functioned as a beneficial exercise and portfolio piece for most
everyone involved. The experience has encouraged me and my partners to produce three more low-budget digital movies in Ireland.

# Special Interest Video; Kids on the Internet: A Case Study

This first appeared in *Videography Magazine* and was edited by Brian McKernan.

## Creating a Hit Right Out of the Box

When I create a new video title I double-check to make sure the project has the following seven elements.

Formula for Success

- Addresses a need
- Is first (or second) in the market
- Carries or establishes a brand name and identity, name host
- Plays off a trend or social concern
- Is created as a series or line extension of the program
- Has outstanding packaging
- A number of distribution channels exist

I was pretty successful in establishing the first six items. The last item is another story altogether, which we'll get to. Here are the things we learned in the development of this program.

## Address a Need

The Internet has hit the media like nothing before. Everyone I know is talking about it. The problem is that once you get on-line, what do you do? Where do you go? The learning curve is quite steep. You can waste lots of time on-line. I thought to myself, Wouldn't it be great if you could sit down with a master cyberspace pioneer who'd show you not only "how-to" but "why to?"

## Well-Known Host

I called my long-time friend Howard Rheingold, who wrote the best-selling books *Virtual Reality* and *Virtual Communities*. He is also a founder of Hotwired and forward thinking when it comes to the Internet. We were pals in San Francisco in the late sixties. In a few minutes I'd decided that Howard was that cyberspace master who could host a series of programs about the Internet. The first would be called *Livin' on the Net*. It would be a rundown of the basics but also contain some big "aha's" and empower people with how to use the· Internet to further their personal and professional lives.

## Counter a Trend

Another program that we would produce would address what kids are doing on the Internet. There was so much bad press about the Internet, about censorship, and about the dangers on the Internet for kids that there were two things we could do: (1) agree with it, and play to parents' concerns, or (2) show the great, positive things that kids are doing, thereby alleviating some of their fears. We chose the latter.

We also chose to have kids teach how to use the Internet. They were funny, they were bright, they really held your attention while they told stories about e-mail, building web pages, reading dolphin newsgroups, adopting whales, saving the comic–book life of Superman, and doing their homework. The kids were clearly empowered by the Internet. Surprisingly, the parents and educators that also saw the show loved it. Many did not know much about the Internet and learned from the kids! A teaching strategy we intend to use again in the future as we extend the line.

## Check Out the Competition—Don't Put Your Head in the Sand

At the time we developed the idea for an Internet series, there were only four tapes in the marketplace (and only one–from Canada–which in our estimation was any good). Today there are at least three dozen tapes and probably more by the time you read this. If you think this is a good idea, folks—it was, it's over. The market is saturated. Clearly the Internet video genre is jammed with competitors. You must check out your competition for two important reasons. One, you must determine if there is any room in the marketplace for the type of videos you are producing. Second, you need to make sure you can differentiate your product from the competition's. The dozens of producers we consult with each year continue to overlook this important step. They are so attached to doing their project that they don't want to look at, or hear about, anything similar. And that's a very dangerous way to begin.

## Detailed Distribution Plans

The financial projections for the video included the following markets:

- consumer video
- educational/institutional video
- direct marketing
- broadcast television
- premium sales

Initially we believed that the tapes could be priced high ($49.95), much like the MacAcademy instructional videos. By the time we got to market, prices had fallen (our tapes were not purely instructional), and if we wanted to get into the retail video market, we'd have to price them at $9.95! This, of course, changes the numbers and projections drastically. We expected the majority of sales to come from consumer video, then educational, then direct marketing. In actuality, I didn't even include the premium market (where tapes are sold in volume to corporate buyers as a gift or promotional giveaway) in my financial projections because you can't count on premium sales for revenue. Either they happen or they don't. It's a function of the buyer's needs. But as you'll see, this turned out to the leading source of revenue in the rollout phase.

## Make the Best Deal You Can—for Everyone!

When you've established the viability of the marketplace and how your video can be marketed, then it's time to raise the money. I wrote a proposal which included industry trends and Internet information, budgets, and financial projections. Our lawyer drew up a Limited Partnership Agreement. We would create a series by first producing four videos, and if they were successful, roll the money back into new production and marketing. The investors' original equity would carry over into the entire line, thereby increasing their potential profit participation.

(I had an offer from an investor to sell most of the partnership's shares, but I felt the terms of double recoupment and a 70/30 percent split, instead of a 50/50 split, were too tough so I turned down the deal. )

Because of a breakthrough (next paragraph) I decided to only sell a small portion of the shares in the partnership. We immediately began production on the first two videos. Ken Lee (Michael Wiese Production's vice president and staff producer) produced the shows. I directed and executive-produced. (Ken was also responsible for making numerous marketing deals. )

## Network With Everyone—Sometimes Your On-Talent Expert Has Great Contacts!

Through Howard Rheingold, we made a contact at Compuserve who became very excited about bundling Howard's *Livin' on the Net* video with their successful *Internet in a Box* (software that immediately connects you to "safe" Internet sites through Compuserve). However, they didn't at the time have a product manager and said that it would have to wait a few months. During the conversation I mentioned that we were also doing a show called *Kids on the Internet*. The show had been shot at a Futurekids facility, the nation's largest computer learning centers for kids. It featured a dozen computer whiz kids showing you all the great things they do on-line (homework, games, e-mail, chat groups, web pages, etc. ). Compuserve jumped on this idea, and we made a deal to bundle our video with their *Internet in a Box for Kids* .

Although we had already started editing Howard's show, we immediately switched to the kids' show to finish it by October, the deadline to get it out into the retail market by Christmas. The video was cut on an Avid by Chris Wayne at Crest National in Hollywood. It was posted digitally, and duplicated at the facility as well.

By the end of Christmas, Compuserve had ordered 50,000 units of the video which we sold at a few dollars above cost. This income enabled us to finish Howard's video and do some marketing. (Compuserve later decided against bundling Howard's tape with their browser software—prices had fallen, and there was way too much competition now in the marketplace. In a fast-moving marketplace, the ground literally moves under your feet. )

Futurekids also bought 1,000 units of the video (at wholesale) to distribute to their 400+ franchisees throughout the world. The video was to be used to promote the computer centers but also would be used as a giveaway promotional item if you signed up for a computer course. (Futurekids also wrote a six-week curriculum to accompany the video which we are marketing to educational institutions for $250. )

Futurekids also help us cast the kids, trained them for several weeks before filming, provided a free facility and computers, and were terrific throughout production in anticipating our needs. (David Ullendorff, a principal in Futurekids, formerly worked with me in New York producing political campaign television spots. ) David and his colleagues at Futurekids were very deserving of their "associate producers" credits.

At the first of the year we found ourselves with three 30-minute videos (Howard's video had a Part I and Part II). And some in-kind marketing.

**Every Deal Should Have a Marketing Component**

Besides the sales of units to both Compuserve and Futurekids, the deals also included marketing. Compuserve would include us in all national press releases and press conference events, plus they gave us

$45,000 in on-line advertising so we could advertise on their home page. Futurekids included us in their house newsletter mailings, press announcements, and several consumer magazine ads. As I always tell the producers I consult with, You can never have enough marketing. When you make a deal, be sure it includes marketing. Money is not enough.

## Television

We screened *Kids on the Internet* for PBS who showed it as part of their pledge campaign. Some 45 stations picked it up. We receive a license fee in direct proportion to how much money is raised. In addition, through our fulfillment center, we sell pledge products to the PBS stations and keep the profits. (We solicited many of our strategic marketing partners such as magazines, software manufacturers, publishers, computer learning centers, and others. We told them that we would feature their products during the pledge break in return for "free goods" which we in turn could sell to the stations. Everyone was delighted with this arrangement. ) A PBS station will normally mark up the pledge premium that you sell them 5 to 10 times. So a video that you sell them for $5 is marked up to $25 or $50. Pledge $50 and become a PBS station member and we'll give you the video you've just seen. Pledge $100 and we'll give you this video, magazine, software, book, and a coupon for a computer class.

## Internet Marketing

One of the magazines whose product was included during the pledge breaks also gave us some free ad space in their magazine. Together we did a promotion on the World Wide Web where they gave away our videos and provided a link to our page resulting in thousands of hits to our page (http://www.mwp.com) which featured an order form for the videos.

We are constantly coming up with new things to do on the Internet to promote the videos as part of our ongoing marketing plan.

**It's Not Enough to Be a Producer These Days**

I think by now you are beginning to get the picture. It's not enough these days to just be a producer, to just make something. You have to think creatively about how to sell it and get it to your marketplace. Unless your video has a well-known superstar attached, it will be very hard to get widespread attention for the program without innovative marketing.

**Packaging**

I care strongly about great packaging. We go to extra lengths to make sure that our packaging is the best possible because it must stand out in a very crowded marketplace.

## Forget the Majors

Unless you are producing a movie with a big star, forget about the major home video companies. They are too big and their overheads are too great to help you sell your videos. Most have to sell at least 100,000 units of a special interest video before they will go to the trouble of using their marketing machine for your video. That reduces the number of special interest titles that will be distributed a year to very few.

Plus the major's distribution machines will never get to the nooks and crannies and special markets where the bulk of your sales will come from. They never would have found the Compuserve deal, the PBS deal, or been able to sell into computer stores.

Instead what you want to do is employ as many video wholesalers, direct marketing partners, and catalogers for your video as possible. You want to get into those tiny niches with your line of products. (It is not cost-effective to market a single title in this manner. ) Toward that end we are working with a handful of smaller companies who know how to sell Internet-related products.

As our sales increase and marketing expands, we will produce additional videos from a long list that we've already developed employing the same principles we've discussed above.

## Preproduction

Producer Ken Lee and I knew immediately that we would have to find bright, communicative, funny kids who had experience on the Internet. Not only that, they would have to be kids who could really communicate their excitement about the Internet to other kids. Not an easy assignment.

My first attempt was to log onto a kid's chat group on America On-Line saying that I was a producer looking for kids to be in a video about the Internet. Wrong! Silly me. The Webmaster immediately told me to get out of the chat group. When I responded, he pulled the plug and I was immediately disconnected. (I then went back and read the chat room rules—I had clearly made a big netiquette error!)

Then I found some kids' home pages and started writing them and their parents, but there were just too many hurdles. The parents were suspicious and I had no way of interviewing the kids.

How was I going to find bright kids already on-line? I called David Ullendorff, one of the principals in Futurekids, the international computer learning facility for kids. I explained our interest in developing a video featuring their students as "kid experts" on the Internet. They were very enthusiastic about the video and put the entire support of the organization behind the project. They found the kids and brought in Craig Bach, Ph. D., a Futurekids instructional designer as a consultant.

David offered not only to help us find the brightest kids that attended many of their Los Angeles-area schools but also to train the kids with supplemental classes. He also introduced us to Don Liebson, owner of the Futurekids facility in Manhattan Beach, California, who was kind enough to let us shoot for two days.

In exchange, we offered to include Futurekids signage in the show so that they could derive some promotional value in exchange for their services and to sell them some videos of the show for promotional purposes. We put Futurekids logos on some of the monitors, shot a few Futurekids web pages, and had signage on one of the walls of the facility. We never went out of our way to shoot the signs. They are there and are very unobtrusive. (At least we thought so. When the show was aired on PBS, they made us cut out, or ADO-up, any images where you could read "Futurekids. " It took us a day and about $3,000 to cut this out. )

## Casting

We wanted to find about a dozen kids, girls and boys, ages 9-14, with diverse ethnic backgrounds. About 30 or 40 kids came for an evening of quick 10-minute interviews. It was a kind of open house where we set up a high-band 8mm camera in the corner and interviewed the kids.

The criteria we used in selecting the kids was simple: energy, personality, and the ability to communicate stories about the Internet that other kids would relate to. If we found an appropriate candidate, we stopped taping, notes were taken, and contact numbers exchanged. Sometimes it would take a while to draw out the child and learn what his or her hobbies and interests and level of skill in the Internet were. By the end of the evening, we had about 15 kids that we thought we could use.

Ken Lee (who also wrote the show) matched up the kids' interest to the subject outline that I'd written. He did some additional interviews with the kids and their parents. We also discussed the content with Craig and David who designed a four–week prep course that would further get the kids up to speed on the Internet using their individual interests and our subject matter.

The notion was that by the time we started shooting, the kids would be enthusiastic and able to demonstrate and articulate various aspects of the Internet. The prep paid off!

Their interests included Star Wars, Superman, MUDs and games, dolphins, whales, alternative music, the Civil War, and aliens. Ken easily found a way to have them explore their interests and use the Internet to do so. The results were numerous stories of enthusiastic kids telling us about what they did on the Internet.

The stories surpassed our expectations! Kids were saying that the Internet was better than TV, that they used the Internet for homework, and that they were making friends all over the world.

These individual segments would be held together by intros (and extros) of two kid hosts. We cast two more "Futurekids": a very bright girl—Rachel Valente—with a comedic, expressive boy—Brian Ballsun-Stanton. The "straight man/comedian" combination worked very well.

In conceiving a show I frequently list all the elements that I think the show will have. This way, whenever I get into coverage trouble or want to pick up the pace, I can look down the list and see the "elements" I have in my card deck.

*Kids on the Internet* was conceived to have these production elements:

- kid hosts
- kids on camera doing topics
- screen shots
- title graphics/chapter headings
- B-roll footage
- music found on the Internet
- adult instructor (evolved during the shoot)

We originally felt that we wanted the show to talk directly to kids and wanted to only use kids in the show. No one over five feet tall was our motto.

Early on in casting and in the follow-ups we endeavored to keep the whole process fun, never intimidating, so that the kids would know us, their material, and what to expect. The shoot would take place in the same environment as the casting session so there wouldn't be too many surprises. We wanted it to look like fun so we kept the entire process fun by joking with the kids, encouraging them to cut up, and letting their real personalities come through.

Going in we also knew that we wanted to use music that we (or the kids) found on the Internet. For this we went to IUMA (http://www. iuma. com/IUMA), the Internet Underground Music Archives, which lists and has samples of over 800 bands. They helped us find the bands with whom we negotiated a very small fee and a credit (and home page address) in the show. IUMA's logo was placed on the video packaging in exchange for their help.

## Production

The production was very simple. I directed and did not want or need a large crew. The crew consisted of director, producer, a lighting cameraman, sound mixer, and production assistants. We shot with a Betacam SP (with clearscan so we could shoot directly off the monitors without flicker), a small lighting kit, and a few props. Only when we had two kids on camera at one time did we need to mix two audio sources.

Cameramen Chip Goebert (a frequent shooter for CNN) and Danny Dimitroff put in a day each, and Marco Bird did sound.

If the host got too close to a computer (like leaning on it), we picked up some hum. We also discovered that we couldn't do any long shots of all the computers in the room. They all had different monitors and the clearscan could only correct for one screen at a time. (We had tested the camera on several monitors before the shoot but never on all the monitors in one scene. So we just avoided having all the other computers on. No problem.) Otherwise the production and shoot went very smoothly.

Ken had blocked out up to six hours for the hosts because we needed specific content to be covered. We also spent more time lighting and staging the hosts since they were the most integral part of the show. The other kids came for about one to two hours each. Rarely did we need more time since Ken and Craig had so well prepared the kids in advance.

The script segments were all marked into individual lines or paragraphs. The kids learned the lines on camera and did as much material as they could. It worked very well. The material was fresh and did not have a teleprompter look to it. I felt the kids would do much better doing little pieces at a time. We'd written the show so that no one had to do many long takes.

I got the kids to improvise, to goof off, to shout things in unison— whatever I could to keep them loose and having fun.

We only had one kid who got so nervous that his material wasn't usable, but we had double-booked "content" with some of the other kids so we were covered.

Sometimes something funny would happen on the set so we would rewrite the material or use what the kids came up with.

We hadn't planned to shoot any "adults," but when we saw what a great relationship Craig had with his students we couldn't help ourselves. We shot Craig bantering with the kids and had him cover all the various "chapter" material that we intended to use. It didn't matter if it duplicated the content that we had already covered with the kids. Rather, we found that since it was done in such a different style and free–flowing manner, it reinforced the content. So we thread the large group shots throughout the show as "setups" for the hosts. It turned out to be a lifesaver because the kids' material was shorter than we expected and we needed a way to lengthen the show.

## Stock Footage/"B" Roll Elements

It's always great to draw from stock footage, but how can you get it inexpensively? I made a deal with San Francisco cameraman Michael Anderson (National Geographic) for B-roll stock footage that we needed. The deal was that I would pay his day rate, give him a shot list, and have a nonexclusive right to use the material in our show. I would provide him with a dupe master which he could sell through a stock footage house. Everybody won and I got a lot of B-roll material for far less than if I had to buy individual shots; in addition, it was customized for our show.

Ken also asked the kids to bring home video footage and still shots of themselves which helped develop their characters, background, and give us a better sense of who they are outside the computer school.

To further punch up the visuals of the show we added some footage from my feature documentary *Dolphin Adventure* and short film *Hardware Wars* as little "breathers" between the dolphin and Star Wars newsgroup segments. I made a deal with myself and that was that!

## Postproduction

The material was transcribed by Vic Caplan. The best shots were selected; time code numbers were written next to the dialogue. Then we did a paper-cut edit of the entire show.

We then organized the show within the chapter structure that was originally written. The chapter title graphics are:

E-MAIL IS EASY
WANNA CHAT?
I HEARD IT ON A NEWSGROUP
THE WORLD WIDE WEB
THERE'S NO PLACE LIKE HOME
PLAYING IN THE M. U. D.
WHY DO THESE KIDS LOVE HOMEWORK?
ALIENS IN CYBERSPACE?
SAFETY ON THE NET
SURF TOOLS
THAT'S NOT ALL FOLKS!

The actual subject matter included segments on e-mail, chat groups, newsgroups, the World Wide Web, home pages, multi-user dimension games, homework, safety on the Net, and the equipment you need to get started.

We digitized the "in selects" from the paper cut and edited from a rough cut to fine cut on an Avid at Crest National in Hollywood with editor Chris Wayne.

We originally expected to do a one-hour show, but the material didn't play at that length. A 45-minute version was still too long. So since this was a home video tape program (intended also for PBS), we edited a 28:30-minute version. In order to pad the show even more, we added a minute or so of "bloopers" and outtakes after end titles. It turned out to be very funny. The audience response to "kids being kids" was delightful.

We went back to the camera originals and on-lined the show in Crest's digital room. Chris and fellow editor Mike Fusco were the editors. We colorized some of the B–roll, did deliberate jump cuts and some flips and effects, but really keep the whizbang stuff to a minimum, since the kids are the stars.


## Duplication

Chris Whorf and Wade Lageose of The Art Hotel in Los Angeles did the video packaging from a still I shot of the kids and the hosts. Crest National did the duplication.


## Summary

What would I have done differently? Perhaps made sure that the kids knew enough about each topic so that we weren't caught short later. But in retrospect, an hour show for kids (or anybody) on the Internet is far too much. Too much material, too many new ideas. You really do get Internet overload if you haven't experienced it before.

Had we had more money for the shoot I might have animated some introductory sequences explaining what the Internet is, but once the kids get behind the computers you get it very quickly.

It was really an ideal short sweet shoot that yielded a lot of fun footage. The production was very simple and the results among kids, broadcasters, and educators have been very rewarding. We are already getting e-mail from Australia, Argentina, Greece, and other far corners of the world from fans of the show.

I hope that this case study has inspired you and given you ideas for financing, marketing, and distributing your own special interest videos. Remember, whenever you make a decision about what's in your show, you are also making a marketing decision. Cut out this one sentence and paste it to your computer!

# SUMMARY

## Summary

Sometimes the path will be very difficult. It will appear that no one will finance your film or video. Or that you'll be destroyed by the complexities of the production process. Or that no one will leave your production alive! Or that you'll never find a distributor. But if you somehow remember 1) that this is an adventure, 2) it is a test of everything that you are, 3) "it is only a movie" and 4) to keep a sense of humor, you'll be just fine.

## Manifestation

The process of filmmaking is a metaphysical experience. Imagine us sitting around a coffee shop shooting back and forth ideas for a film. This idea has no weight, no shape, no physical characteristics. Through our ability to attract others to our idea we gather the resources to go into production. A year later, what began as pure metaphysics, is now something that can be shown to millions of people all over the world.

That's why I love this process of starting with "nothing" and birthing it, through filmic alchemy, to a "something." We are magicians. We can use our powers in a playful, childlike manner, where every step is joyful exploration, and we can create something wonderful for each other.

The tools of the manifestation process are what I've described in this book. Like you, I too must go through this process every time I want to make something.

## The Vision

In the beginning you need to have a vision. Maybe not a full-blown, 3-D holographic, surround-sound version, maybe only an inkling of something. This glimpse you nurture and build. You communicate it to others, and the vision strengthens. No matter what you are doing, you will find the people you need that will help you get your project completed.

One of the simplest things you can do is to write your mission statement. It will focus your intention which is the motivating force behind the whole endeavor. Your mission statement acts as a magnet for others, attracting them to you. It also acts as a filter, eliminating what you do not want to do.

It's an exciting time. Now, more than ever, people want to make films. A recent high school survey showed that the most popular occupation among students was to be filmmakers. Filmmaking has replaced writing the great American novel as our national ambition. The convergence of low-cost, affordable technology, such as digital cameras and editing systems, makes this ambition possible. The image quality is fine for television broadcast and can even be blown up to 35mm film for projection. However, all these breakthroughs in technology are rather empty unless you have something to say, as evidenced by the endless fodder on hundreds of cable television stations where there is a lack of meaningful programming. This is a great opportunity for anyone with a unique vision and voice. If not you, then who?

That's where your skills in developing your concept come in. Certainly a great story, a cast who can deliver authentic performances, and a clear genre are all elements that will help your film or video succeed once it is finished.

## A Fair Exchange

Once you've identified these elements in a script, then comes the real-world task of moving your vision into reality. You enroll people to help you by creating win-win agreements and documenting these understandings in contracts. Even if you are making a no-budget or low-budget film there should always be an exchange. You can't pay your actors? Buy them lunch. You can't pay a cameraman? Make sure he gets recognition and attention for his fine work. If you are taking the skills and talents of others to realize your dream, be sure that you also give back something that will further the dreams and careers of your co-workers. Create a great film and everyone wins.

## Understand Distribution

You must also understand the distribution process and how to get your film into all the ancillary markets so that it will be successful. (If you've promised a share of profits to investors, actors and crew, then you'd better understand how all this works so that you can deliver on that promise.)

The industry does a good job in keeping the economics and deal-making aspects of filmmaking a secret. It's taken me years to understand some fundamental things. In a few hours reading, you've learned a great deal and are confident and empowered to negotiate much better deals for yourself and your collaborators.

Distribution is the driving force that makes the whole enterprise work. Without it you have a film sitting on the shelf. There are many ways to splinter the rights and sell to different markets. The more markets, the more revenue streams coming back to you. Now you understand how to make intelligent choices and reflect this information in your business plan.

## Pitching

Empowered with this new knowledge, you have confidence which will amplify everything you do, especially your pitching. You can say with confidence how you expect things to turn out and it should be closer to reality than ever before. If you've done your homework, you'll be able to pitch like never before. And these pitches will not fall upon deaf ears. You will close deals, assemble your team, and bring money into your production's bank account.

This will be easier for you than ever before because you can apply these tools to your own projects. If you forget something, you have this book to refer back to. You understand the steps, you understand what you need to do, and you will waste far less time on unproductive tasks.

You've learned that the principles of good storytelling and filmmaking are the same regardless of the length of the program whether they are shorts, industrials, music videos, documentaries, or full-length features.

The mavericks among you may be thinking about self-distribution and how you can compete in the marketplace. You've heard about the satisfaction from doing it yourself and may be passionate about receiving the rewards of your successes.

## Marketing

By now I've convinced you of the importance and value of marketing, which is the most overlooked aspect of the entire process. When you pay attention to marketing, and when you bring marketing elements into your program design you have a much, much better chance of creating a successfully distributable work.

Some of you may find self-promotion distasteful and difficult. Get over it. When your message is important enough, your passion and commitment strong, you'll put yourself in the service of your film and do whatever you have to to get your film into the world. You'll create opportunities for yourself to talk about your film and find the support you need. You will incorporate marketing elements to appeal to every level of the food chain (from actor, writer, director to distributor, exhibitor, viewer). Everyone needs to be sold on your project and you are the one to do it.

Independent film festivals are but one of the entry points to distributors. Clever producers will create their own opportunities to be seen and heard. Because most don't, you will stand head and shoulders above your competitors if you've already worked on your packaging and marketing.

## Inspiration

Every day you will find new ways to advance your career and project. The more you do it, the more friends you will have and the more support you will find. The seeds you plant in the early years of your career will grow. In a decade or two, these seeds will be mature trees bearing unimaginable fruit. You will have become a real player, an adventurer in media, through your relationships and your ability to create works that people will want to see.

If you enter this art/business with a desire to learn and a not-too-sensitive personality, you will thrive. Sprinkle in some wonder and enthusiasm and a desire to tell great stories, and doors will open to you.

Even at this stage in my career I am faced with new challenges that seem, at times, overwhelming. But there is always an opportunity to push past the "fear of the week" and find new strength. All along the way will be people that will appear at just the right time with just the right information and resources you will need to get the job done.

Keep moving forward. Be consistent. Be grateful to those who help you. Give credit and financial rewards and thanks. There's plenty to go around. Plenty of good ideas, plenty of people who will want to work with you, plenty of people who will want to see your work.

When you fail at something, it means it's time to pay attention. Learn why you failed rather than hide from it or place the blame on someone else. You will learn far more from your failures than from your successes. Both are gifts in the learning process.

The wonderful thing about filmmaking is that you cannot learn it all. There is always another vista. There are always deeper levels you can go as a writer, an actor, a director, or a producer. May the material that you choose to explore be worthy of your time here. May the works that you create be worthy of your audience's time as well.

If you've read this far, it's clear you are highly motivated. Intention alone is the fuel to get the job done. You have the information to go to the next level. Make good use of it. Inspire us. Take us to places within ourselves that we've never been. Reveal to us new aspects of the human condition. Teach us something. Share what you learn with your friends and colleagues.

Now it's all up to you. I know you'll do something really great. Now go get `em.

## THE AGE OF VIDEOGRAPHY:
### Where Do We Go From Here?

(This appeared in *The Age of Videography* edited by Brian McKernan.

Growing up as a child of television who today is a producer of video programming, I have seen the medium move forward, sideways, and into many new and converging forms. My own fascination with video started 30 years ago, in 1966, when I first used a television camera, at San Francisco's KQED. Film school followed, at the The San Francisco Art Institute, after which I was fortunate enough to travel to Indonesia and learn about the shadow play, Bali's archetypal pre-cursor to radio and television. After a stint in Japan, where I saw my first portable video gear, I returned to the U.S. and made a few "save the world" films and documentaries. Then I entered the world of commercial television, and alienated many friends. Assignments included segment producer for a live nightly talk/variety show, pro-ducer of political TV spots, and director of on-air promotion and pro-duction for The Movie Channel.

Unlike my father's career, which lasted 30 years at one place, I went from experience to experience. I was never very interested in having "a job" per se unless it included learning and--hopefully--making a contribution to society. Unfortunately, that wasn't what the job mar-ket called for. My assignments were far from soul-satisfying and only served to fill more video landfills with quickly forgettable program-ming.

A position as VP of Original Programming at Vestron Video enabled me to acquire and produce a large quantity of videos in a variety of genres: sports, kids, comedy, exercise, documentaries, music, and direct-to-video movies. Using this production and marketing experi-ence, I was fortunately able to return to being an independent pro-ducer, and choose only  those video or television projects that I felt were worthwhile. Titles I was fortunate enough to develop and pro-duce included a series of *Lifeguides* for KCET, in Los Angeles, TV specials and videos that included *Diet for A New America* and *Healing Sexual Abuse*. I consulted on launching video labels and series, including PBS' Home Video Line, Joseph Campbell's Hero's Journey, a best-selling video with Shirley MacLaine, and several health-oriented infomercials on vegetarian lifestyles.

Looking ahead, new technologies seem to promise major improvements in human communication. I have my doubts about CD-ROMs at this stage in their development, but the Internet and World Wide Web excite me. That's because nearly anyone anywhere can be a publisher. If you want to express something in text, sound, or images, just upload it. It's not censored by economic forces like other media--at least not yet.

Perhaps our digital media future will enable us to someday synthesize visual and audio elements from anywhere in the world, and then broadcast whatever is created from these images back out into the world. The danger, however, is that technologies will evolve so quickly that people won't be aware of their full effects. The great emphasis on the next wave of tools could take our attention away from the work itself.

We need to ask ourselves if we are really producing the kind of images that enhance and contribute to human life and sustaining the environment? Are we envisioning a positive future with world-wide cooperation, or are we looking to expand our market share at any cost? Are we fueling a desire by what we broadcast into third-world countries to pursue and emulate what we already know are dead-end consumption-addicted lifestyles? Or are we enabling and empowering other cultures to find their own voices, images, and icons that will burst our own cultural bubbles and help make us more knowledgeable about the human condition?

Are we taking responsibility for the harmful, violent, and materialistic trends produced in society by our programs, or do we cop cliched pleas that "It's just entertainment" in the same way others argue that tobacco isn't addictive? Do we really want our population and that of

405

the world, to watch an average of nearly seven hours of television a day? Is that the best use of human life?

When given the opportunity, do we "just say no" when asked to participate in the production or distribution of another mindless sitcom, violent action-adventure mess, or 30-second propaganda piece when we know its value to society is less than zero? And if we don't say no, do we know why?

Can anyone say that television or video has lived up to its potential? Do we know what its potential is? Instead of dumbing down humanity with Beverly Hills/Hamptons cultural values, might there not be other worthy sources and mindsets to inform, educate, and inspire us? Where are the "bodies of knowledge?" Where are the world cultural treasures that will bring us greater appreciation of our place on this planet? Where are the great teachers, who when brought to television, could enlighten our short journey here? Where are the daring programming executives willing to shout "Hell, no, we won't take it any more," and find ways to convert their commercial swords to plowshares?

I'll tell you who they are. It's everyone reading this. It's the men and women who've walked the video path to this point. You've heard all this before. It's nothing new. You know who you are, you've come into your own power in this business, and you have developed the skills. I know that you know it's time now to make a difference. To leave a legacy. Teach the next generation. Each of us wants to find his or her own way to respond to these questions. That's the mandate for the next 20 years of the Age of Videography.

# Delivery requirements

It's not over when the fat lady sings. It's over when you deliver most, if not all, of the following materials to your distributor. Then, per the contract, do you get your advance payment.

You should read this list and fully understand what is required of you. Delivery requirements may add another $50,000 to $100,000 to your budget.

**Delivery materials**

Screenplay

Shooting script

Credit statement (main and end title billing)

Publicity Photos
  Black and white photos (3 sets of contacts)
    portrait photos with subjects identified
    100 production stills depicting scenes of cast
    50 informal or casual photos of principal members of cast and crew
    25 gallery or portrait sitting photos in and out of character
  Color photos with ID's
    150 production color shots of scenes
    50 candid shots of cast and key production team
    35 portrait shots of principal cast

Answer Print

Original picture negative and composite optical soundtrack negatives

Interpositive (IP) 35mm color corrected interpositive

Television cover shots and scenes

Internegative (IN) 35mm

35mm textless background negative of titles

Music dialogue and sound items include:
>  3 or 4 track 35mm magnetic masters with separated mixed dialogue
>  music
>  sound effects
>  mixed music and effects

If Dolby Sound
>  access to original 35mm mag 4 track Dobly stereo master with
>  surrounds
>  original 35mm mag 2 track Dolby stereo master with
>  surrounds
>  35mm mag Dolby stereo music and effects on track (w/o
>  dialogue)
>  35mm mag mono 3 track master

Music Master Recordings
>  a 1/4" or 1/2" mag tape or DAT of all music, or
>  phonograph records

Music Cue Sheets
>  specifying the performer, composer, publisher, copyright
>  owner, affliated rights society, usages, place and number
>  of cues showing film footage and running time for each cue

Agreements
>  one copy of signed agreements composer, lyricist, publishing
>  agreements, sync and performing rights

Music Sheet—original leads sheets

Composer's Original Score

Film and Soundtrack Materials—all film and soundtrack materials

Screen Credits, list of credits

Dialogue Continuity, copy of detailed dialogue and continuity

Laboratory Access letter

MPAA Certificate with rating

Certificate of Insurance for E&O. (Coverage for $1 million/$3 million.)

Residual Information (SAG final cast list, writers, directors)

Title and Copyright
>copy of title report and copyright search report, chain of title documents for all literary materials

Sometimes Required:
>Soundtrack Album Materials
>Work Print
>Outtakes

# Hardware Wars Press Release

Here is the fun and charming press release from New York publicist Joe Dera (Joe Dera Associates) which was used to tout *Hardware Wars* rerelease.

For Immediate Release

HARDWARE WARS: SPECIAL EDITION

They're Back. . . from a long time ago, in a galaxy far, far away. . . Fluke Starbucker, Augie Ben Doggie, Princess Anne-Droid and Ham Salad have once again come to save the galaxy from the evil Darph Nader!

HARDWARE WARS, the unapologetic spoof of STAR WARS, has jumped on the inter-galactic revival bandwagon by rereleasing the film to video. HARDWARE WARS, directed by Ernie Fosselius and produced by Michael Wiese, is the most profitable, independent short film ever made, earning 100 times its budget. Not unlike its big screen cousin, this special edition of HARDWARE WARS has been complete redigitized and includes 20 new special defects. . . er, um. . . effects.

The men who devoted their time and energy to redigitizing and remastering this film are veterans in the field of special effects. Fred Tepper, Andrew Lesniak, Glen Miller, and John Allardice, all of whom are long-standing fans of HARDWARE WARS and work together at Digital Domain, began enthusiastic discussions last year with Michael Wiese Productions after learning about the return of the STAR WARS trilogy to theaters.

HARDWARE WARS: The Special Edition may be ordered by calling 1-800-833-5738. It will retail for an affordable $9.95 and will be supported by a massive national and media marketing and publicity campaign that will include television and print features.

But is the galaxy ready? It sure seems to be with sighting of this hilarious short everywhere. In Baltimore, audiences in local movie theaters were seen howling with laughter while viewing the film. There are even plans to screen HARDWARE WARS at the Mann Plaza Theater (310-208-3098) in Los Angeles on April 4th through 6th as well as a special event at Bookstar in Studio City (818-505-9528) which includes a special appearance by "Princess Anne-Droid." After twenty years, the original actress has resurfaced and will be doing a number of special appearances.

VHS, Color, Approx. 20 minutes, $9.95
To order copies: 1-800-833-5738

Come visit the HARDWARE WARS web site at:
http://www. mwp. com

MAY THE FARCE BE WITH YOU!

# INTERNET NEWSGROUPS

## Internet Newsgroups

The Internet is a rich source for research of any kind. Filmmakers congregate in these various forms and share information. You can ask questions in these newsgroups or start ongoing discussions about filmmaking.

rec.arts.movies.production
   Filmmakers discuss filmmaking and share information.

rec.arts.video.production
   For video/TV makers discuss video production and share information.

rec.arts.movies.announce
   Movie announcements, news of celebrities, awards, film festivals, and box-office charts, etc.

rec.arts.movies.tech
   Information about the technical aspects of movies.

rec.arts.movies.people
   Writing about people in the movie business.

rec.arts.movies.current-films
   Discussions, reviews, and information about upcoming and current films.

rec.arts.movies.past-films
   Discussions about past films.

rec.arts.movies.list+surveys
   Various movie subjects.

rec.arts.movies.movie-going
   Movies in general.

rec.arts.movies.misc
   A mishmash of various information and discussion about movies.

aus.film
   Filmmaking in Australia.

bit.listserv.film-l
   A film list server.

bit.listserv.cinema
   A cinema list server.

misc.writing.screenplays
   For screenwriters and those with screenplays.

alt.movies.independent
   Independent filmmakers share information and discuss filmmaking.

alt.movies.visual-effects
   All about the world of special effects.

# SELF-QUIZ:
# DOES YOUR VIDEO HAVE WHAT IT TAKES?

Ken Lee, vice president of Michael Wiese Productions, prepared this self-quiz for our consulting clients who have video projects. We've found there is great value in asking yourself these questions <u>before</u> going into production. Check it out.

Find out your video's potential for success through this simple evaluation. Learn your project's strengths and weaknesses, and how you can fill in the missing pieces to create a project that is unique, profitable, and attractive to your buyers.

There are five key building blocks for you to consider in evaluating your video concept:

- Program Content
- Marketing Potential
- Budgeting
- Distribution Potential
- The Producer's Bag of Tricks

**Instructions:**

When you take the following self-quiz answer each question honestly and objectively. Your responses should reflect what your project *is*, not what you want it to be.

If you truly are having a difficult time in evaluating your project objectively, make copies for your entire production team of office. Take the quiz separately, and then compare notes. The results could be a real eye-opener!

## I. Program Content

*Please select the response that most accurately describes your project.*

|  | *Strongly Disagree* |  | *Somewhat Agree* |  | *Strongly Agree* |
|---|---|---|---|---|---|
| a) Features a "hot" or current topic which consumers are willing to purchase. | 1 | 2 | 3 | 4 | 5 |
| b) Presents "unique" information (or features old information in a new way). | 1 | 2 | 3 | 4 | 5 |
| c) Produced with a clear and specific genre in mind. (i. e., How-to, Exercise, Comedy, etc. ) | 1 | 2 | 3 | 4 | 5 |
| d) Produced with a clearly defined target audience in mind. | 1 | 2 | 3 | 4 | 5 |
| e) Your target market is large enough to support a new product. | 1 | 2 | 3 | 4 | 5 |
| f) Your project has the potential to be developed into a series or line of programs. | 1 | 2 | 3 | 4 | 5 |

## II. Marketing Potential

|  |  |  |  |  |  |
|---|---|---|---|---|---|
| a) Features a well-known celebrity or star. | 1 | 2 | 3 | 4 | 5 |
| b) You know how to "position" your project to your target market. | 1 | 2 | 3 | 4 | 5 |

| | | | | | |
|---|---|---|---|---|---|
| c) Project has identifiable sponsorship opportunities. (i. e., corporate, co-op marketing, premium sales, etc. ) | **1** | **2** | **3** | **4** | **5** |
| d) Your project is appropriately priced for your particular genre, target market, and distribution channel. | **1** | **2** | **3** | **4** | **5** |

### III. Budgeting

| | | | | | |
|---|---|---|---|---|---|
| a) Your budget is appropriate for your particular genre. | **1** | **2** | **3** | **4** | **5** |
| b) Your budget has been prepared by a line producer with production experience. | **1** | **2** | **3** | **4** | **5** |
| c) You can deliver your project without exceeding your original budget by more than 10%. | **1** | **2** | **3** | **4** | **5** |
| d) Your budget is sufficient to support your daily needs while you pursue your project. (Or, you can support yourself through some alternative means.) | **1** | **2** | **3** | **4** | **5** |

### IV. Distribution Potential

| | | | | | |
|---|---|---|---|---|---|
| a) Produced with identifiable distribution channel(s) in mind. (i. e., Home Video, Catalog, Direct Mail, Cable TV, etc. ) | **1** | **2** | **3** | **4** | **5** |

b) Program is formatted
appropriately for
your selected distribution
channel(s).
(Program Length, etc. )    1        2        3        4        5

c) You understand the
fundamentals of a
distribution deal.          1        2        3        4        5

## V. The Producer's Bag Of Tricks

a) You have real passion
for your project.           1        2        3        4        5

b) You are skilled at
soliciting support
from friends, business
partners, and vendors.      1        2        3        4        5

c) You are skilled at
negotiating reduced
rates from vendors.         1        2        3        4        5

d) You think of your
project as a long-term
goal vs. a quick payoff.    1        2        3        4        5

e) You or your business partners
are skilled at pitching your
project to investors,
distributors, buyers, etc.  1        2        3        4        5

f) You have studied your competition and understand how
your product can be
differentiated.             1        2        3        4        5

## Evaluating Your Score!

Add up all the points and write your total score here _____

This is your **overall score** for your program.

IF YOU SCORED:

• 92 -115 points - Your project has all the earmarks of a hit! Keep moving ahead and close as many deals as you can. If you haven't done so already, you can begin developing a series of videos based on your unique idea. Congratulations on a job well done!

• 69-91 points - Your project exhibits strong potential, but may be weak in a few specific areas. Look carefully at each of the five sections. If you scored poorly in one or two sections, this is a good indication that you may need to build up this weaker portion of your package. A few fine-tune adjustments can get you on the right track.

• 46 -68 points - Your project has good potential but may require some major reworking in order for it to be marketable. In this instance, you will have to determine if you have the time, money, and patience to rework your project; or if you want to pursue other projects with your newfound knowledge.

• 23-45 points - Your project is on the respirator and you've got your thumb on the kill switch. If you haven't started production, you've just saved a great deal of money. If you have already spent a great deal of money, well—it certainly would be a good time to stop spending any more. But, don't despair. Even if it looks like you may not have a hit on your hands, you have learned a great deal and will be ready for your next time at bat.

**Further Diagnosis**

To determine which of the five building blocks you need to work on, calculate your AVERAGE score for each category. To do this, simply add up your scores for each category and divide by the number of questions <u>within</u> each category.

(For example, for *Program Content* you would add up all your points for this category and divide by six).

| Score | Results |
| --- | --- |
| 4-5 points. | Excellent. |
| 3-3 1/2 points | Good. |
| 2 - 2 1/2 points | Fair |
| 1 -1 1/2  points | Poor |

# STOCK FOOTAGE LICENSE

## Stock Footage License

Sometimes you may have shot footage for your production that is unusual or hard to obtain. If so, you may be able to obtain additional revenues by reselling footage from your project to other films and television programs. Some stock footage sells for as much as $35 per second (commercials) or $500 per minute (documentaries) which is shared with the supplier of the footage.

If you do not want to try to sell stock footage yourself, contact a stock footage house. They will take a fee for making each sale for you. This could be a lucrative source of found money for you; especially if you shoot wildlife or nature footage.

Here is an example of a stock footage license for licensing your footage to others.

### STOCK FOOTAGE AGREEMENT

To:  Charlie Millimeter, BEST PRODUCTIONS
From: Michael Wiese

Re: `THE BIG GROSS' January 1, 1998

Dear Charlie:

The following confirms our agreement (the `Agreement') with respect to certain film material (the `Footage') which BEST PRODUCTIONS may select for use in the motion picture tentatively entitled

'The Making of The Big Gross' (the 'Picture'):
1. You (hereafter referred to as 'Owner') warrant that the Footage subject to this license agreement, and described in subparagraph (a) below, is owned by you and that you have the absolute and unencumbered right to grant to BEST PRODUCTIONS all rights granted herein.

(a) Excerpts from 'THE BIG GROSS'

2. Owner agrees to make available to BEST PRODUCTIONS respective positive prints and duplicating material of all Footage designated by BEST PRODUCTIONS. BEST PRODUCTIONS agrees to pay all laboratory charges and duplicating costs in connection therewith and shall be billed directly by the applicable laboratory.

3. Within 60 days, after BEST PRODUCTIONS shall have received an answer print of the Picture, BEST PRODUCTIONS shall furnish Owner with a schedule describing the Footage and the number of feet thereof actually incorporated by BEST PRODUCTIONS into the Picture. Said schedule (Schedule 'A') shall be attached to our respective copies of this license agreement and shall be a pan thereof.

4. With respect to the Footage hereunder actually incorporated by BEST PRODUCTIONS into the Picture, Owner grants to BEST PRODUCTIONS the nonexclusive right forever and throughout the universe to use and incorporate the same into the Picture with the right perpetually and throughout the universe and in all languages to reproduce by any means or method now known or hereafter devised, including film and tape, and to record, perform, broadcast and project without limitation as to the number of times and by any known or hereafter devised method,

421

the Footage in and in connection with the theatrical or nontheatrical television, radio, publishing and any other form or presentation of the Picture in any media and for any purpose and in connection with the advertising, publicizing and exploitation of the Picture. Without limiting the generality of the foregoing, BEST PRODUCTIONS shall have the right to edit, interpolate or use the Footage in any manner whatsoever in connection with the Picture, including, without limitation, the right to synchronize music, voices, sounds, or any other portion of the sound track of the Picture, with the Footage or any portion thereof as BEST PRODUCTIONS in its sole and complete discretion shall determine.

5. Owner will indemnify, defend and hold BEST PRODUCTIONS, its parent, affiliates, subsidiaries, agents, representative, and associates, and the officers, directors, and employees of each of them, harmless from and against all losses, costs, damages, judgments, liabilities and expense (including, without limitation, attorney's fees and costs and any payments that may be due any music publisher, writer, musician, director, actor, union, guild or other party) arising from all claims whatsoever and whenever brought, which may be brought directly or indirectly upon BEST PRODUCTIONS use of the Footage.

6. Upon condition that Owner shall fully perform all of the services required to be performed by Owner hereunder, Producer shall accord Owner on-screen credit, substantially in the form of 'Additional photography courtesy of The Big Gross, a film by Michael Wiese'. No casual or inadvertent failure to comply with the provisions of this Paragraph nor any failure by third parties to com-

ply with their agreements with Producer shall constitute a breach of this Agreement. Owner shall be limited to Owner's remedy at law for damages, if any, and shall not have the right to terminate or rescind this Agreement or to in any way enjoin or restrain the production, distribution, advertising or exploitation of the Picture.

7. In full payment for the rights herein granted to BEST PRODUCTIONS and for the warranty of the Owner herein contained, BEST PRODUCTIONS agrees to pay to Owner and Owner agrees to accept the following: Five Thousand Dollars ($5000.00) for up to eighty (80) 16mm feet of Footage actually incorporated by BEST PRODUCTIONS into the final answer print of the Picture.

8. BEST PRODUCTIONS agrees to make a minimum payment of $5000 (for specified Footage under 80 feet) on or before January 15, 1998, to Owner. Any footage beyond 80 feet shall be charged to BEST PRODUCTIONS at $25 per 16mm foot.

Very truly yours,

AGREED TO AND ACCEPTED:

_____

BUYER:

_____

OWNER:
BEST PRODUCTIONS

*Lines around the block for the San Francisco*
*World Premiere of* Hardware Wars.
*(Photo by John V. Fante.)*

# THEATER CHAINS

## Top 50 Theater Chains

So you made a film that no distributor would take?  Not unusual.  It happens to more than 1,000 filmmakers a year.  But don't let that stop you.  Consider self-distribution.  If you've made 35mm prints, a poster, and a trailer, you could approach these large  theater chains to see if they would venture with you on exhibition.  If not, perhaps you could rent ("four-wall") the theaters and do your own distribution.  Here's a hit list.  Start dialing.

1. CARMIKE CINEMAS
2,780 screens

2. REGAL CINEMAS
7132 Commercial Park Drive
Knoxville, TN 37918
423-922-1123
fax: 423-922-3188
www.regalcinemas.com
2,873 screens

3. UNITED ARTISTS THEATRE CIRCUIT
9110 E. Nichols Ave., Suite 200
Englewood, CO 80112
303-792-3600
fax: 303-790-8907
2,275 screens

4. AMC
106 W. 14th St.
Kansas City, MO 64141-6615
816-221-4000
fax: 816-480-4617
2,248 screens

5. CINEMARK USA7502
Greenville Ave., Suite 800
Dallas, TX 75231
214-696-1644
fax: 214-696-3946
www.cinemark.com
FrontRowJoe@Cinemark.com
1,821 screens

6. CINEPLEX ODEON
1303 Yonge St.
Toronto, Ontario M4T 2Y9
416-323-6600
fax: 416-323-6677
1,740 screens

7. NATIONAL AMUSEMENTS
200 Elm St.
Dedham, MA 02026
617-461-1600
1,177 screens

8. GENERAL CINEMA THEATRES
1280 Boylston St.
Chestnut Hill, MA 02167
617-277-4320
fax: 617-277-8875
1,166 screens

9. LOEWS/SONY THEATRES
711 5th Ave.
New York, NY 10022
212-833-6200
fax: 212-833-6292
screens: 938

10. HOYTS CINEMAS
One Exeter Plaza
Boston, MA 02116
617-267-2700
fax: 617-262-2751
screens: 925

11. ACT III THEATRES
919 S.W. Taylor St., Suite 900
Portland, OR 97205
503-221-0213
fax: 503-228-5032
www.act3theatres.com

12. EDWARDS CINEMAS
300 Newport Center Dr.
Newport Beach, CA 92660
714-640-4600
fax: 714-721-7170
screens: 596

13. FAMOUS PLAYERS
146 Bloor St. W.
Toronto, Ontario M5S 1P3
416-969-7800
fax: 416-964-5839
screens: 555

14. HOLLYWOOD THEATRES
2911 Turtle Creek Blvd., Suite 1150
Dallas, TX 75219
214-528-9500
fax: 214-520-2323
screens: 505

15. CENTURY THEATRES
150 Pelican Way
San Rafael, CA 94901
415-451-2400
www.centurytheatres.com
screens: 500

16. KERASOTES THEATRES
104 N. Sixth St.
Springfield, IL 62701
217-788-5200
fax: 217-788-5207
screens: 476

17. MANN THEATRES
16530 Ventura Blvd., Suite 500
Encino, CA 91436
818-784-6266
fax: 818-784-6749
www.manntheatres.com

18. PACIFIC THEATRES
120 N. Robertson Blvd.
Los Angeles, CA 90048
310-657-8420
fax: 310-657-6813
screens: 320

19. MARCUS THEATRES
250 E. Wisconsin Ave.
Milwaukee, WI 53202
414-272-5120
fax: 414-272-0189
screens: 300

20. GKC THEATRES
755 Apple Orchard St.
Springfield, IL 62703
217-528-4981
fax: 217-528-6490
screens: 260

21. SUPER SAVER CINEMAS
109 N. Oregon Ste. 1000
El Paso, TX 79901
915-532-1943
fax: 915-542-2945
screens: 234

22. WEHRENBERG THEATRES
12800 Manchester
St. Louis, MO 63131
314-822-4520
fax: 314-822-8032
screens: 228

23. DICKINSON THEATRES
5913 Woodson Road
Mission, KS 66202
913-432-2334
fax: 913-432-9507
www.dtmovies.com
downs@dtmovies.com

24. MALCO THEATRES
5851 Ridgeway Ctr. Pkwy.
Memphis, TN 38120
901-761-3480
fax: 901-681-2044
www.malco.com
screens: 200

25. O'NEIL THEATRES
1926-C Corporate Square Dr.
Slidell, LA 70458
504-641-4720
fax: 504-641-5726
cjj@communique.net
screens: 200

26. HARKINS THEATRES
8350 E. McDonald Dr.
Scottsdale, AZ 85250
602-955-2233
fax: 602-443-0950
screens: 183

27. GOODRICH QUALITY
THEATRES
4417 Broadmoor S.E.
Kentwood, MI 49512
616-698-7733
fax: 616-698-7220
screens: 179

28. GEORGIA THEATRE CO.
2999 Piedmont Rd., 2nd Floor
Atlanta, GA 30305
404-264-4542
fax: 404-233-8184
screens: 168

29. SILVER CINEMAS
4004 Beltline Rd.
Dallas, TX 75244
972-503-9851
fax: 972-503-9013
www.silvercinemasinc.com
screens: 163

30. WALLACE THEATRES
3375 Koapaka Street, Ste. C345
Honolulu, HI 96819
808-836-6055
fax: 808-836-6077
screens: 157

31. LANDMARK THEATRES
2222 S. Barrington Ave.
Los Angeles, CA 90064
310-473-6701
fax: 310-477-3066
www.movienet.com
screens: 140

32. EASTERN FEDERAL
901 East Blvd.
Charlotte, NC 28203
704-377-3495
fax: 704-358-8427
screens: 131

33. ENTERTAINMENT CINEMAS
7 Central St.
North Easton, MA 02356
781-341-2800
fax: 781-341-4170
screens: 129

34. METROPOLITAN THEATRES
8727 W. Third St.
Los Angeles, CA 90048
310-858-2800
fax: 310-858-2860
screens: 125

35. CINEMA ENTERTAINMENT
P.O. Box 1126
St. Cloud, MN 56302
320-251-9131
fax: 320-251-1003
screens: 123

36. LOEWS STAR THEATRES
3020 Charlevoix Dr. S.E.
Grand Rapids, MI 49546
616-940-0866
fax: 616-940-0046
screens: 108

37. EMPIRE THEATRES
115 King St.
Stellarton, Nova Scotia B0K 150
902-755-7620
fax: 902-755-7640
screens: 101

38. B & B THEATRES
114 W. Second St.
P.O. Box 171
Salisbury, MO 65281
816-388-5219
screens: 100

39. MANN THEATRES OF
MINNESOTA
704 Hennepin Ave., Suite 225
Minneapolis, MN 55403
612-332-3303
fax: 612-332-3305
screens: 98

40. SOCAL CINEMAS
(Sanborn Theatres)
13 Corporate Plaza
Newport Beach, CA 92660
714-640-2370
fax: 714-640-7816
screens: 98

41. LANDMARK OF CANADA
522-11 Avenue S.W., 4th floor
Calgary, Alberta T2R OC8
403-262-4255
fax: 403-266-1529
screens: 95

42. SIGNATURE THEATRES LLC
1600 Broadway, Suite 300
Oakland, CA 94612
510-268-9498
fax: 510-268-9843
screens: 95

43. R/C THEATRES
231 W. Cherry Hill Ct.
P.O. Box 1056
Reisterstown, MD 21136
410-526-4774
fax: 410-526-6871
screens: 86

44. DOUGLAS THEATRES
1300 P St.
Lincoln, NE 68508
402-474-4909
fax: 402-474-4914
screens: 83

45. MUVICO THEATRES
3101 N. Federal Hwy,6th Floor
Fort Lauderdale, FL 33306-1042
954-564-6550
fax: 954-564-6518
muvico@muvico.safari
screens: 83

46. CENTRAL STATES THEATRES
Insurance Exchange Bldg.
505 Fifth Ave.Suite 414
Des Moines, IA 50309
515-243-5287
fax: 515-243-5892
screens: 80

47. CINEMASTAR LUXURY THE-
ATERS
431 College Blvd.
Oceanside, CA 92057
760-630-2011

428

fax: 760-630-8593
www.cinemastar.com
screens: 79

48. JACK LOEKS THEATRES
1400 28th St. S.W.
Grand Rapids, MI 49509
616-532-6302
fax: 616-532-3660
www.jack-loeks.com
screens: 77

49. R.L. FRIDLEY THEATRES
1321 Walnut St.
Des Moines, IA 50309
515-282-9287
fax: 515-282-8310
screens: 77

50. CROWN THEATRES
64 North Main St.
South Norwalk, CT 06854
203-846-8800
fax: 203-846-9828
www.crown-theatres.com
screens: 69

# LIMITED PARTNERSHIP AGREEMENT

**Limited Partnership Agreement (Sample)**

Here is a sample Limited Partnership Agreement. It is helpful to read and understand how business is conducted. This document, along with a Confidential Summary and a Subscription Agreement, given to your limited partners for signature. Space considerations prohibit us from including the Summary and Subscription Agreement.

> *Disclaimer:*
>
> *This document is for educational and informational uses only.*
>
> *The publisher accepts no responsibility nor is in any way liable for how the reader of this document chooses to use this information. The publisher has no legal background and cannot verify the accuracy nor legality of this document.*
>
> *Readers intending to produce their own motion pictures through Limited Partnerships should contact an experienced entertainment attorney. We make no claims whatsoever as to be able to provide any advice through this document.*

A recommended entertainment attorney
who can prepare your Limited Partnership Agreement.

Greg S. Bernstein, Rosenfeld, Meyer & Susman, 9601 Wilshire Blvd., 4th Floor, Beverly Hills, CA 90210 310-246-3222, fax 310-271-6430, gbernste@rmslaw.com

A Word 4.0 diskette of this document, plus the Confidential Summary along with an additional hard copy, is available for $95.00. Call 1-800-833-5738.

FORM OF PARTNERSHIP AGREEMENT

AGREEMENT OF LIMITED PARTNERSHIP

OF

_____PARTNERS, L.P.

A California Limited Partnership

THIS AGREEMENT OF LIMITED PARTNERSHIP ("Agreement") is hereby
entered into as of August, 1995, by and among_____, Inc., a
newly-formed California corporation (the "General Partner ") and all persons, who become limited partners of this limited partnership
("Limited Partners"), the identities of whom are attached hereto in
the Subscription Agreements.

The Partnership was formed as of_____ 1998, with the filing
of Form LP-1 with the Secretary of State of California the Partners
hereby agree to continue the Partnership as a limited partnership
pursuant to the provisions of the California Revised Limited
Partnership Act (the "Act") and upon the terms and conditions set
forth in this Agreement.

SECTION 1

DEFINITIONS

The following terms, when used in this Agreement, shall have the
meaning set forth in this section.

1.1 Adjusted Invested Capital. The Invested Capital of a Limited
Partner (including the amount in the Deemed Capital Account), less
all amounts distributed to that Partner as Cash Available for
Distribution and Cash From Sales or Refinancings, provided that
Adjusted Invested Capital shall not be reduced below zero.

1.2 Affiliate. An Affiliate means (i) any person directly or indirectly owning, controlling, or holding with power to vote, ten percent (10%) or more of the outstanding voting securities of such
other person; (ii) any person ten percent (10%) or more of whose
outstanding voting securities are directly or indirectly owned, controlled or held with power to vote, by such other person; (iii) any
person directly or indirectly controlling, controlled by or under
common control with, such other person; (iv) any officer, director
or General Partner of such other person; and (v) if such other person is an officer, director or General Partner, any company for
which such person acts in any such capacity.

1.3 Assignee. A person who has acquired a beneficial interest in
this Partnership from a Limited Partner but who is not a substituted
Limited Partner.

431

1.4 Bankruptcy. The institution of any proceedings under federal or state laws for relief of debtors, including filing of a voluntary or involuntary petition in bankruptcy or the adjudication as insolvent or bankrupt, or the assignment of the person's property for the benefit of creditors, or the appointment of a receiver, trustee or a conservator of any substantial portion of the person's assets or the seizure by a sheriff, receiver, trustee or conservator of any substantial portion of the person's assets, and the failure, in the case of any of these events, to obtain the dismissal of the proceeding or removal of the conservator, receiver or trustee within thirty (30) days of the event.

1.5 Capital Account. The "Capital Account" of a Partner shall mean |the capital account of that Partner determined from the inception of the Partnership strictly in accordance with the rules set forth in Section 1.704-I(b) (2) (iv) of the Treasury Regulations.

Subject to the previous paragraph, "Capital Account" shall mean:

a. The amount of money contributed by the Partner to the Partnership, increased by

b. The fair market value of the property contributed by the Partner to the Partnership (net of liabilities secured by the property or to which the property is subject), and

c. The amount of income allocated to the Partner, and decreased by:

d. The amount of money distributed to the Partner, and

e. The fair market value of property distributed to the Partner by the Partnership (net of liabilities secured by the property or to which the property is subject), and

f. The Partner's share of expenditures of the Partnership described in Section 705(a)(2)(B) of the Code (including, for this purpose, losses which are nondeductible under Section 267(a)(1) or Section 707(b) of the Code), and

g. The Partner's share of amounts paid or incurred by the Partnership to organize the Partnership (except to the extent properly amortizable for tax purposes), and

h. The amount of loss allocated to the Partner.

For this purpose, "income" refers to all items of income (including all items of gain and including income exempt from tax) as properly determined for "book" purposes, and "loss" refers to all items of loss (including deductions) as properly determined for "book" purposes. "Book" income and loss shall be determined based on the value of the Partnership's assets as set forth on the books of the Partnership in accordance with the principles of Section 1.704-1(b) (2) (iv) (g) of the Treasury Regulations. Otherwise, income and loss shall be determined strictly in accordance with federal income tax principles (including rules governing depreciation and amortiza-

432

tion), applied hypothetically based on values of Partnership assets as set forth on the Partnership's books.

An assumption of a Partner's unsecured liability by the Partnership shall be treated as a Distribution of money to the Partner. An assumption of the Partnership's unsecured liability by a Partner shall be treated as a cash contribution by the Partner to the Partnership. For this purpose, the assumption of a secured liability in excess of the fair market value of the security shall be treated as the assumption of an unsecured liability to the extent of that excess.

In the event that assets of the Partnership other than cash are distributed to a Partner in kind, Capital Accounts shall be adjusted for the hypothetical "book" gain or loss that would have been realized by the Partnership if the distributed assets had been sold for their fair market value in a cash sale (in order to reflect unrealized gain or loss).

In the event of the liquidation of a Partner's Interest or of the Partnership, Capital Accounts shall be adjusted for the hypothetical "book" gain or loss that would have been realized by the Partnership if all Partnership assets had been sold for their fair market values in a cash sale (in order to reflect unrealized gain or loss).

Capital Accounts also shall be adjusted upon the constructive termination of the Partnership as provided under Section 708 of the Code in accordance with the method set forth in the immediate preceding paragraph (as required by Section 1.704-1(b) (2) (iv) (e) of the Treasury Regulations). In the event that a Partner shall be both a General Partner and a Limited Partner of the Partnership, a single Capital Account shall be maintained for that Partner.

1.6 Capital Contributions. The aggregate cash contribution of a Partner made to the Partnership. The minimum Capital Contribution by a Limited Partner shall be $_____in cash, unless the General Partner waives the prohibition on the purchase of Fractional Units. The General Partner shall have the right to cause the Partnership to issue up to ____ Units (or a fractional amount thereof) in lieu of cash in exchange for services to be rendered in a like amount to the laboratory. The General Partner will contribute one percent (1%) of the aggregate Capital Contributions of the Limited Partners.

1.7 Capital Event. Capital Event means the sale or other disposition of the Partnership's assets of a capital type, the receipts of insurance and other proceeds derived from the involuntary conversion of the Partnership's property, or the borrowing or the refinanced borrowing upon the security of the Partnership's property, or from a similar event with respect to the Partnership's property.

1.8 Cash Available for Distribution. Total cash revenues generated by the Partnership including interest earned on the Partnership's reserves and excess funds in the reserve account, as may be determined by the General Partner in its sole discretion (other than Cash

From Sales or Refinancings), less cash expenditures, including fees for services of the General Partner or any Affiliate of the General Partner and operating expenses, and less amounts set aside for reserves. The General Partner may withhold funds from Cash Available for Distribution, if the General Partner, in its sole discretion, determines that reserves are necessary for the Partnership's future expenses, capital or growth. Notwithstanding the foregoing, to the extent not otherwise restricted by any loan agreement, covenant or other contractual restriction, Cash Available for Distribution will not be less than the aggregate amount which would be owing by the Limited Partners in any year determined by reference to the then applicable federal and California state individual tax rates.

1.9 Cash From Sales or Refinancings. The cash proceeds from a sale or refinancing of any Partnership assets remaining after retirement of debt secured by the Partnership's assets, payment of all expenses relating to the transaction (including payment of fees to the General Partner and Affiliates) and retention of reasonable reserves.

1.10 Code. "Code" means the Internal Revenue Code of 1986, as amended or modified by subsequent revenue laws

1.11 Deemed Capital Account. "Deemed Capital Account" shall be the amount of services rendered by the Laboratory in exchange for the Units received by it. The amount of the Deemed Capital Account shall be subject to all of the adjustments and provisions set forth herein, including those set forth in Section 1.5 above.

1.12 Direct Expenses. Fees and expenses incurred directly by or for the benefit of the Partnership including, but not limited to: legal, accounting, and audit fees; fees and expenses for preparing Partnership tax returns, Investor reports, and filings and reports required by federal and state securities authorities; fees and expenses for qualification of a Partnership in various jurisdictions; all associated printing, duplicating, and postage charges; fees and expenses relating to the development and operation of the Partnership; and all other costs incurred directly by or for the benefit of the Partnership and not otherwise reimbursed or paid under any other category of expense.

1.13 Distributions. Any cash or property distributed to Partners arising from their interests in the Partnership, other than payments to Partners for services or as repayment of loans

1.14 General Partner. _____ Inc., or any person or entity succeeding it as the General Partner.

1.15 Gross Proceeds. In general, the total amounts received from the operations of the Partnership.

1.16 Invested Capital. The Capital Contributions of Partners.

1.17 Laboratory. _____or any affiliate thereof, including _____ Laboratories who may render service to the Partnership in exchange for Units. The Laboratory may be replaced in the sole discretion of the General Partner.

1.18 Limited Partner. Any Limited Partner to this Agreement _____and any person who becomes a Limited Partner by substitution after receiving an assignment from one of the original Limited Partners and the consent of the General Partner

1.19 Majority. The Limited Partners collectively holding more than one-half of the Percentage Interests of all the Limited Partners

1.20 Management Fee. A fee payable to the General-Partner for its services in providing oversight management services for the Partnership. The Management Fee is equal to the greater of five percent (5%) of the Gross Proceeds of the Partnership, which shall be treated as a guaranteed payment.

1.21 Memorandum. The Partnership's Confidential Private Placement Memorandum, dated _____1998, which is made a part hereof and incorporated herein by this reference.

1.22 Net Income and Net Loss. The "Net Income" and "Net Loss" of the Partnership shall mean the net income and net loss, respectively, of the Partnership; however, the following items shall be excluded from the computation of Net Income and Net Loss:

a. Any gain, income, deductions or losses specifically allocated under Sections 6.1, 6.2, 6.3, 6.6, and 6.7.

b. Any Nonrecourse Deductions

c. Any Partner Nonrecourse Deductions. For purposes of computing Net Income and Net Loss, the "book" value of an asset shall be substituted for its adjusted tax basis if the two differ, but otherwise Net Income and Net Loss shall be determined in accordance with federal income tax principles.

1.23 Net Operating Cash Flow. The net amount of Gross Proceeds received by the Partnership for distribution to the Partners after deduction of all expenses, including reserves, incurred in connection with the operation and management of the Partnership.

1.24 Nonrecourse Deductions. "Nonrecourse Deductions" in any taxable year means the Partnership deductions that are characterized as "nonrecourse deductions" under Section 1.704-2(c) of the Treasury Regulations. Subject to the previous sentence, "Nonrecourse Deductions" for the Partnership's taxable year means the excess, if any, of:

a. The net increase in the amount of Partnership Minimum Gain during the year, over

b. The aggregate amount of any distributions during the taxable year of proceeds of a Nonrecourse Liability that are allocable to an increase in Partnership Minimum Gain.

If the amount of Nonrecourse Deductions during the Partnership taxable year exceeds the total amount of items of Partnership loss, deduction and Section 705(a)(2)(B) expenditure for the year, then that excess shall carry forward and shall be treated as an increase in Partnership Minimum Gain for the immediately succeeding Partnership taxable year for purposes of determining whether there is a net increase or decrease in Partnership Minimum Gain (and Nonrecourse Deductions) during that succeeding Partnership taxable year. For this purpose, the items of Partnership loss, deduction and Section 705(a)(2)(B) expenditure for the year are determined without regard to any item that is treated as a Partner Nonrecourse Deduction.

The Nonrecourse Deduction shall be comprised of the following partnership items (as determined for "book" purposes) as provided in Section 1.704-2(c) of the Treasury Regulations:

(i) First, depreciation or cost recovery deductions (as determined for "book" purposes) with respect to items of Partnership property subject to one or more Nonrecourse Liabilities to the extent of the increase in Partnership Minimum Gain attributable to the Nonrecourse Liabilities to which each item is subject. If the depreciation or cost recovery deductions exceed the amount of Nonrecourse Deductions for the year, then a proportionate share of each of these deductions shall constitute Nonrecourse Deductions.

(ii) Thereafter, a pro rata portion of the Partnership's other items (as determined for "book" purposes) of deduction, loss, and Section 705(a)(2)(B) expenditures for the year.

Any item of loss, deduction, and Section 705(a)(2)(B) expenditure for a taxable year that is treated as a Partner Nonrecourse Deduction shall be excluded in determining Nonrecourse Deductions.

1.25 Nonrecourse Liabilities. "Nonrecourse Liabilities" means nonrecourse liabilities of the Partnership as defined in Section 1.752-1(a)(2) of the Treasury Regulations. Subject to the foregoing sentence, "Nonrecourse Liabilities" means liabilities of the Partnership (or a portion thereof) for which no Partner bears the economic risk of loss.

1.26 Operating Costs. In respect to any period, all costs, risks and liabilities directly or indirectly paid or incurred by or on behalf of the Partnership in connection with the operation of the Partnership.

1.27 Partner. Any person who is a General Partner or a Limited Partner in this Partnership.

1.28 Partner Nonrecourse Debt. "Partner Nonrecourse Debt" means liabilities of the Partnership defined in section 1.704-2(b)(4) of the Treasury Regulations. Subject to the foregoing sentence, "Partner Nonrecourse Debt" means "nonrecourse debt" of the Partnership for which no Partner bears the economic risk of loss For this purpose, "nonrecourse debt" means any Partnership liability that is considered nonrecourse for purposes of Section 1.1001-2 of the Treasury Regulations and any Partnership liability for which the creditor's right to repayment is limited to one or more assets of the Partnership.

1.29 Partner Nonrecourse Deductions. "Partner Nonrecourse Deductions" in any Partnership taxable year means Partnership deductions defined in Section 1.704-2(0 (2) of the Treasury Regulations. Subject to the previous sentence, "Partner Nonrecourse Deductions" with respect to a Partner Nonrecourse Debt for a Partnership taxable year means the excess, if any, of:

a. The net increase in the minimum gain attributable to the Partner Nonrecourse Debt during such year, over

b. The aggregate amount of any distributions during the taxable year to the Partner that bears the economic risk of loss for the Partner Nonrecourse Debt of proceeds of the Partner Nonrecourse Debt that are allocable to an increase in the minimum gain attributable to the Partner Nonrecourse Debt.

The determination of which items of Partnership loss, deduction, and Section 705(a) (2) (B) expenditure constitute Partner Nonrecourse Deductions with respect to a Partner Nonrecourse Debt shall be made in a manner that is consistent with the principles of Section 1.704-2(j) of the Treasury Regulations.

The determination of which items of Partnership loss, deduction, and Section 705(a) (2) (B) expenditure constitute Partner Nonrecourse Deductions for a Partnership taxable year shall be made before the determination of which items constitute Nonrecourse Deductions. If the amount of Partner Nonrecourse Deductions with respect to a Partner Nonrecourse Debt during the Partnership taxable year exceeds the total amount of items of Partnership loss, deduction and Section 705(a) (2) (B) expenditure for the year that is treated as Partner Nonrecourse Deductions with respect to the Partner Nonrecourse Debt, then that excess shall carry forward and shall be treated as an increase in minimum gain attributable to the Partner Nonrecourse Debt for the immediate succeeding taxable year for purposes of determining the net increase or decrease in the minimum gain attributable to the Partner Nonrecourse Debt (and Partner Nonrecourse Deductions) during that succeeding, taxable year.

1.30 Partnership. The Partnership formed by this Agreement, _____Partners, L.P., A California Limited Partnership.

1.31 Partnership Minimum Gain. "Partnership Minimum Gain" with respect to any taxable year of the Partnership means the "partnership minimum gain" computed strictly in accordance with the principles of Section 1.704-2(d) of the Treasury Regulations. Subject to the previous sentence, "Partnership Minimum Gain" means the amount determined as follows: (i) first, compute, with respect to each Nonrecourse Liability of the Partnership, the amount of taxable income or gain that would be realized by the Partnership if the

Partnership disposed of (in a taxable transaction) the Partnership property subject to the Nonrecourse Liability in full satisfaction of that Nonrecourse Liability (and for no other consideration), and (ii) then, add together the amounts so computed for all Nonrecourse Liabilities of the Partnership. This sum is the "Partnership Minimum Gain."

For this purpose, where the asset is subject to multiple secured liabilities of unequal priority, the adjusted basis of the asset (or "book" value if" book" value differs from adjusted tax basis) shall be allocated among the liabilities in order of priority from most senior first to least senior last. Where two or more secured lia-bilities are of equal priority, basis (or "book" value if "book" value differs from adjusted tax basis) shall be allocated among the liabilities pro rata in accordance with the outstanding balances of the liabilities. For purposes of computing Partnership Minimum Gain, the "book" value of an asset shall be substituted for its adjusted tax basis if the two differ, but otherwise Partnership Minimum Gain shall be determined in accordance with federal income tax princi-ples.

For purposes of determining the net increase or decrease in Partnership Minimum Gain during any Partnership taxable year in which the Capital Accounts of Partners are increased pursuant to section 1.704-1(b) (2) (iv) f) or (r) of the Treasury Regulations to reflect a revaluation of Partnership property subject to one or more Nonrecourse Liabilities, any decrease in Partnership Minimum Gain attributable to this revaluation shall be added back to the net decrease or increase otherwise determined.

1.32 Percentage Interest(s). The Percentage interest of a Limited Partner in the Partnership based on the ratio of Adjusted Invested Capital from any one Limited Partner divided by the Adjusted Invested Capital of all the Limited Partners.

1.33 Person. The term "Person" means and includes a natural person, partnership, corporation, association or other legal entity.

1.34 Subscription Agreement. The Subscription Agreement for purchase of the Units offered pursuant to the Memorandum.

1.35 Subscription Price. $_____per Unit, paid in cash or, in the cost of the Laboratory, by rendering approved services.

1.36 Treasury Regulations. "Treasury Regulations" means the regula-tions of the United States Treasury Department pertaining to the income tax, as amended, and any successor provision.

1.37 Unit(s). An interest in the Partnership representing a Capital Contribution of $_____.

SECTION 2

FORMATION

2.1 Form and Certificate. The parties hereby enter into a limited partnership under the provisions of the California Revised Limited Partnership Act (the "Act"), and the rights and liabilities of the Partners shall be as provided in that Act except as herein provided. The Partnership shall acquire, hold, operate, manage, and sell the Partnership and enter contracts as a limited partnership.

A "Certificate of Limited Partnership" under California Corporations Code Section 15621 has been or will be prepared, signed by the General Partner, and filed in the Office of the California Secretary of State

2.2 Purpose. The purpose of the Partnership will be to develop, produce, market and distribute three movies.

2.3 Name. The name of the Partnership is _____L.P., A California Limited Partnership.

2.4 Place of Business. The Partnership's principal place of business shall be _____ such other address as the General Partner may _____.

SECTION 3

TERM

3.1 Commencement. The Partnership term begins as of _____, 1998; however, the effective date for doing business shall be the date of the initial closing of the offering of Units pursuant to the Memorandum.

3.2 Dissolution. The Partnership shall dissolve upon:

a. Approval by all the Partners; or

b. December _____20___, or

c. Sale of all or substantially all of the assets of the Partnership, and distribution of the proceeds to the Partners: provided, however, that the General Partner may elect to continue the existence of the Partnership after sale of all the Partnership's property, should such sale require the Partnership to finance any portion of the sale price. Any such continuation shall be for the purpose of collection of any payments due under such financing; or

d. The removal, bankruptcy, or dissolution of the General Partner.

3.3 Reconstitution. The occurrence of any of the events described in Section 3.2 shall cause a dissolution of the Partnership and of the agency relationship between the Limited Partners and the General Partner. The Limited Partners may, upon the occurrence of any of

439

these events, reconstitute the business of the Partnership in a new limited partnership on the same terms as this Agreement and with a new General Partner elected by a Majority, provided that if the General Partner ceases to be a General Partner other than by removal, and there is no remaining or surviving General Partner, admission of a new General Partner or a decision to continue the business of the Partnership must be approved by the affirmative vote of all of the Limited Partners. Expenses incurred in the reformation, or attempted reformation, of the Partnership shall be deemed expenses of the Partnership.

3.4 Proceeds from Liquidation. The proceeds from the liquidation of the assets of the Partnership and the collection of the receivables of the Partnership, together with the assets distributed in kind, to the extent sufficient therefor, shall be applied and distributed in the following order of priority:

a. To the payment and discharge of all of the Partnership's debts and liabilities, including fees payable to the General Partner (other than the claims of secured creditors whose obligations will be assumed or otherwise discharged upon the liquidation, of Partnership assets), the claims of secured creditors which are non-recourse liabilities, with respect to which the creditor may look only to its security for satisfaction of its claim, but including debts and liabilities owing to Partners to the extent permitted by law other than liabilities for Distributions to Partners under Sections 15661, 15664 and 15665 of the Act) and the expenses of liquidation;

b. To the creation of any reserves which the General Partner may deem necessary for any contingent or unforeseen liabilities or obligations of the Partnership and, at the expiration of such period as the General Partner may deem advisable, for distribution in the manner hereinafter provided;

c. To the payment and discharge of all of the Partnership's debts and liabilities owing to Partners remaining unpaid, but if the amount available for such payment and discharge shall be insufficient, then pro rata in accordance with the amounts of such debts and liabilities; and

d. Thereafter, the balance, if any, shall be distributed to the Partners in accordance with their respective positive Capital Account balances (including the Deemed Capital Account), as determined after taking into account all Capital Account (and Deemed Capital Account) adjustments for the Partnership taxable year during which the liquidation occurs, as provided in Section 1.7041(b)(2)(ii)(b)(2) of the Treasury Regulations

3.5 Deficit Capital Account. No Partner shall have any liability to the Partnership, to any other Partner or to the creditors of the Partnership on account of any deficit balance in any Partner's Capital Account (or Deemed Capital Account), either prior to or at the time of liquidation of the Partnership.

3.6 Recourse to Partnership Assets Only. Each Partner shall look solely to the Partnership assets for the return of his investment, and if the Partnership assets remaining after the payment or discharge of all debts and liabilities of the Partnership are insufficient to return the investment of any Limited Partner, such Limited Partner shall have no recourse against the General Partner or against any other Limited Partner.

SECTION 4

MANAGEMENT

4.1 Control in General Partner. Except as otherwise expressly stated in this Agreement, the General Partner and its Affiliates shall have exclusive control over the business of the Partnership, including the power to sign contracts and leases; and to assume management and direction of business operations, and shall have all rights, power and authority generally conferred by law or necessary, advisable or consistent with accomplishing the purpose of the Partnership. Without limiting the generality of the foregoing, the General Partner has the right:

a. To cause this Partnership to enter other partnerships as a general or limited partner and exercise the authority and perform the duties required of them or of this Partnership as a partner in any other partnership;

b. To purchase, sell, hold, exchange, dispose of or refinance any assets of the Partnership;

c. To borrow money on behalf of the Partnership and to encumber the Partnership assets or place title in the name of a nominee for the purpose of obtaining financing;

d. To prepay in whole or in part, refinance, increase, modify or extend any obligation;

e. To employ from time to time, directly or through the General Partner or Affiliates, at the expense of the Partnership, among others, bookkeepers, consultants, advisors, accountants, and attorneys;

f. To pay, on behalf of the Partnership, and out of Partnership funds all organization expenses incurred in the creation of the Partnership and expenses of the offering of Units;

g. To pay, on behalf of the Partnership, and to reimburse certain Affiliates of the Partnership, who have contributed to the development of the Partnership, the costs incurred by the Partnership or such Affiliates with respect to the development of the Partnership;

h. To assume the overall duties imposed on the General Partner by the California Revised Limited Partnership Act;

i. To alter the basis for tax-related items, such as the distribution of net profits and losses if, on the advice of the Partnership's tax counsel or accountants, it would be more equitable or required by current or future Code or Regulation provisions;

j. To acquire by purchase, lease, or otherwise any real or personal property that may be necessary, convenient, or incidental to the accomplishment of the purposes of the Partnership;

k. To execute any and all agreements, contracts, documents, certifications, and instruments necessary or convenient in connection with the management, maintenance, and operation of the Partnership, and contract on behalf of the Partnership for the employment and services of employees and/or independent contractors to operate and manage the Partnership, which employees or independent contractors may be Affiliates of the General Partner, and delegate to such persons the duty to manage or supervise any of the assets or operations of the Partnership;

l. To operate, maintain, finance, improve, construct, own, grant options with respect to, sell, convey, assign, mortgage, and lease any real estate and any personal property necessary, convenient, or incidental to the accomplishment of the purposes of the Partnership;

m. To participate in the development and operation of the Partnership; and

n. To provide oversight management services with respect to the Partnership.

4.2 Limitation on General Partner's Authority. The General Partner shall not have authority to:

a. Do any act in contravention of this Agreement;

b. Do any act that would make it impossible to carry on the ordinary business of the Partnership;

c. Admit a Person as an additional General Partner without the approval of a Majority;

d. Amend this Agreement without the approval of a Majority, other than as set forth in Section 4.1 (i).

4.3 Devotion of Time. The General Partner is not obligated to devote full time to the affairs of the Partnership. The General Partner may become involved in other businesses and occupations and other partnerships. The General Partner shall devote a reasonable amount of time as necessary in managing the Partnership business and performing the General Partner's duties.

4.4 Indemnification of General Partner. The Partnership, its receiver or its trustee, shall indemnify, hold harmless and pay all judgments and claims against the General Partner, its officers, directors, shareholders, employees, agents, subsidiaries, affiliates and assigns, from any liability, loss or damage incurred by them by reason of any act performed or omitted to be performed by them in connection with the Partnership's business and purpose, including costs and attorneys' fees and any amounts expended in the settlements of any claims of liability, loss or damage, other than for an act of gross negligence or fraud.

4.5 Investment Opportunities. Neither the General Partner nor any Affiliate of the General Partner shall be obligated to present any particular investment opportunity to the Partnership, even if the opportunity is of a character which, if presented to the Partnership, could be taken by the Partnership, and it shall have the right to take for its own account or to recommend to others any investment opportunity.

4.6 Business Relationships with Partnership. The General Partner, its Affiliates, officers, directors, shareholders, agents and employees, and any of their respective business enterprises may transact business with the Partnership without thereby accruing any liability to the Partnership or any Partner for self-dealing, conflict of interest or breach of any duty of loyalty to the Partnership or any Partner. Among other things, these permitted activities include the following:

a. The General Partner and/or its Affiliates may acquire Units in its own name and for its own account, then sell, at a profit, all or part of them to the Partnership; retain all or a portion of them for its own account; and/or allocate undivided interests therein among several business enterprises with which it is associated.

b. The General Partner and/or its Affiliates may perform legal, accounting, construction and/or other services, including providing }day-today management services for the Partnership, that, if performed by third parties would be properly chargeable to the Partnership, and may itself charge such services to the Partnership, in addition to the reimbursable charges for the general and administrative costs, Direct Expenses, and for the Management Fee.

c. The General Partner may lend money to the Partnership.

d. The General Partner may enter into agreements with other parties directly or indirectly owned, controlled or Affiliated with the General Partner. To the extent that the General Partner may control any such transactions, however, they shall be carried out on terms and conditions which the General Partner believes to be competitive The terms of any transaction shall be deemed competitive if they are not substantially more onerous to the Partnership than the terms of the same or similar transactions conducted at arm's length by other parties in the same general area at the same general time.

SECTION 5

CAPITAL CONTRIBUTIONS

5.1 Capital Contributions.

a. Other than the Laboratory, each Limited Partner shall contribute to the Partnership the amount set forth in his/her executed Subscription Agreement.

b. The General Partner shall contribute to the capital of the Partnership, one percent (1%) of the Capital Contributions of the Limited Partners and shall have the right, but not the obligation, to acquire Units in the Partnership and be admitted to the Partnership as a Limited Partner.

c. If the General Partner determines that the Partnership requires Capital Contributions in addition to the Capital Contributions provided herein above, then it may, without the consent of existing Limited Partners, admit additional persons as Limited Partners on such terms and conditions as it shall deem reasonable and in the best interests of the Partnership, notwithstanding any resulting dilution in the Percentage Interests of existing Limited Partners.

d. No Partner shall be obligated to lend money or other property to the Partnership, but any Partner may do, so upon reasonable arm's length commercial terms. All such loans shall be repaid prior to any Distributions to Partners.

5.2 Capital Account. Each Partner shall have a Capital Account (or in the case of the Laboratory, a Deemed Capital Account) as defined in Section 1.5 above.

SECTION 6

DISTRIBUTIONS AND ALLOCATIONS

6.1 Minimum Gain Chargeback. In the event that there is a net decrease in the Partnership Minimum Gain during a Partnership taxable year, each Partner shall be allocated items of income and gain in accordance with Section 1.704-2(f) of the Treasury Regulations and its requirements for a "minimum gain chargeback."

Subject to the immediately preceding sentence, each Partner shall be allocated items of Partnership income and gain for that year equal to that Partner's share of the net decrease in Partnership Minimum Gain (within the meaning of Section 1.7042(g)(2) of the Treasury Regulations).

The allocation required by this Section 6.1 shall be made prior to any other allocation for the year.

Allocations of income and gain shall be made as follows as required by Section 1.704-2(f)(6) of the Treasury Regulations:

a. First, from gains recognized from the disposition of Partnership property subject to Nonrecourse Liabilities, to the extent of the decrease in Partnership Minimum Gain attributable to the disposition of this property (or if these gains exceed the minimum gain chargeback for the taxable year, then a proportionate share of those gains).

b. Thereafter, the remainder, if any, from a pro rata portion of the Partnership's other items of income and gain for the year.

"Book" income and gain shall be determined by reference to values set forth on the books of the Partnership in accordance with the principles of Section 1.5.

6.2 Partner Minimum Gain Chargeback. In the event that there is a net decrease in the minimum gain attributable to a Partner Nonrecourse Debt of the Partnership during a Partnership taxable year, each Partner with a share of the minimum gain attributable to the Partner Nonrecourse Debt at the beginning of the taxable year shall be allocated income and gain for the year (and, if necessary, subsequent years) in accordance with Section 1.704-2(i)(4) of the Treasury Regulations.

The allocation required by this Section 6.2 shall be made after the allocation required by Section 6.1 but prior to any other allocation for the year.

"Book" income and gain shall be determined by reference to the values set forth on the books of the Partnership in accordance with the principles of Section 1.5.

6.3 Qualified Income Offset. Any Limited Partner who unexpectedly receives an adjustment, allocation, or distribution described in subparagraphs (4), (5) or (6) of Section 1.704-1(b)(2)(ii)(d) of the Treasury Regulations, which adjustment, allocation or distribution creates or increases a deficit balance in that Partner's Capital Account, shall be allocated items of "book" income and gain in an amount and manner sufficient to eliminate the deficit balance in that Partner's Capital Account so created or increased as quickly as possible in accordance with Section 1.704-1(b)(2)(ii)(d) of the Treasury Regulations and its requirements for a "qualified income offset."

Allocations under this Section 6.3 shall be comprised of a pro rata portion of each item of Partnership income (including gross income) and gain for the year; however, items of income and gain allocated under Sections 6.1 and 6.2 shall be excluded from the operation of this Section 6.3.

"Book" income and gain shall be determined by reference to values set forth on the books of the Partnership in accordance with the principles of Section 1.5.

6.4 Allocations of Net Income. Net Income shall be allocated as follows: (i) First, in an amount equal to the amount of Net Income previously allocated hereunder and not previously offset by an allocation of Net Loss under Section 6.5 below; (ii) Second, 1% to General Partner and 99% to the Limited Partners (except to the extent that any Net Loss was previously allocated to the General Partner, in which case Net Income allocated under this Paragraph Section 6.4 shall first be allocated to the General Partner until all prior Net Loss allocated to it hereunder has been recouped in accordance with the partnership percentage); and (iii) Third, any Net Income not allocated under the foregoing shall be allocated 50% among the Limited Partners in accordance with their partnership percentage and 50% to the General Partner.

6.5 Allocation of Net Losses.

a. Net Losses shall be allocated first in an amount equal to the amount of Net Income previously allocated under Section 6.4 above and not previously offset by an allocation of Net Loss under this Section 6.5, and all Net Loss shall be allocated 99% to the Limited Partners until the amount of Net Losses so allocated equals the Adjusted Invested Capital of the Limited Partners, and 1% to the General Partner. Thereafter, Net Losses shall be allocated 50% to the Limited Partners and 50% to the General Partners. In no event, however, such an allocation of Net Loss be made to a Limited Partner in an amount that would (1) cause such Limited Partner's deficit capital account to exceed his share of the Partnership's "minimum gain" (as defined in Treasury Regulation Section 1.704-1(b)(4)(iv)(f')) taking into account any adjustment pursuant to Treasury Regulation Section 1.704-1(b)(2)(ii)(d)(4)-(6) or (2) cause such Limited Partner's basis to be negative. Any excess Net Loss shall be allocated to the other Limited Partners, to the extent per-mitted above, and the balance to the General Partner.

b. After the allocations of Net Losses and Nonrecourse Deductions, Partner Nonrecourse Deductions shall be allocated between the Partners as required in Section 1.704-2(i)(1) of the Treasury Regulations, in accordance with the manner in which the Partner or Partners bear the economic risk of loss for the Partner Nonrecourse Debt corresponding to the Partner Nonrecourse Deductions, and if more than one Partner bears such economic risk of loss for a Partner Nonrecourse Debt, the corresponding Partner Nonrecourse Deduction must be allocated among such Partners in accordance with the ratios in which the Partners bear the economic risk of loss for the Partner Nonrecourse Debt.

c. Except as otherwise provided in this section, no allocation of Net Loss shall be made to a Partner to the extent that the alloc-ation would create or increase a negative balance in that Partner's Capital Account. In the event and to the extent that a Partner may not be allocated Net Losses as a result of the application of the preceding sentence, Net Losses shall be allocated to those Partners with positive Capital Account balances in proportion to the ratio of their positive Capital Account balances. In the event that no Partner has a positive Capital Account balance, Net Losses shall be allocated in accordance with Section 6.5(a) above.

6.6 Allocation of Net Gain From Capital Events.

a. In general, net "book" gain and income (in excess of deductions and loss) of the Partnership resulting from a Capital Event, shall be allocated to the Partners as follows: 99% to the Limited Partners in accordance with their Percentage Interests and 1% to the General Partner until the allocations provided for in Section 6.4 (i) and

(ii) have been made in full, and thereafter 50% to the Limited Partners and 50% to the General Partner.

b. In computing net "book" gain and income of the Partnership resulting from a Capital Event, the following items are excluded:

(i) Any losses that are characterized as Partner Nonrecourse Deductions or Nonrecourse Deductions; and

(ii) Any income or gain of the Partnership that is specially allocated under Sections 6.1, 6.2 or 6.3.

   "Book" income and gain shall be determined by reference to values set forth on the books of the Partnership in accordance with the principles of Section 1.5.

6.7 Allocation of Net Loss from Capital Events.

a. In general, net "book" loss and deductions (in excess of income and gain) of the Partnership resulting from a Capital Event, shall be allocated to the Partners as follows: 99% to the Limited Partners in accordance with their Percentage Interests and 1% to the General Partner until the allocations provided for in Section 6.4 (i) and (ii) have been made in full, and thereafter 50% to the Limited Partners and 50% to the General Partner, to the extent the aggregate Net Losses allocated to the Limited Partners equal their Adjusted Invested Capital.

b. Except as otherwise provided in this section, no allocation of Net Loss from Capital Events shall be made to a Partner to the extent that the allocation would create or increase a negative balance in that Partner's Capital Account. In the event and to the extent that a Partner may not be allocated Net Losses from Capital Events as a result of the application of the preceding sentence, Net Losses from Capital Events shall be allocated to those Partners with positive Capital Account balances in proportion to the ratio of their positive Capital Account balances. In the event that no Partner has a positive Capital Account balance, Net Losses from Capital Events shall be allocated in accordance with Section 6.7a.

"Book" loss and deductions shall be determined by reference to values set forth on the books of the Partnership in accordance with the principles of Section 1.5.

c. In computing net "book" losses and deductions of the Partnership resulting from a Capital Event, the following items are excluded:

i. Any losses that are characterized as Partner Nonrecourse Deductions or Nonrecourse Deductions

ii. Any income or gain of the Partnership that is specially allocated under Sections 6.1, 6.2 or 6.3.

6.8 Distributions. Subject to the provisions of Sections 6.9 and 3.4 of this Agreement, Distributions of Cash Available for Distribution

447

and Distributions of Cash from Sales or Refinancings shall be made first one percent 1% to the General Partner and ninety 99% to the Limited Partners until each Limited Partner has received an amount equal to such Limited Partner's Adjusted Invested Capital; and thereafter fifty percent (50%) to the Limited Partners and fifty percent (50%) to the General Partner.

6.9 Apportionment Among Partners. The Net Income, Net Loss and Distributions allocated to the Limited Partners shall be apportioned among them according to their respective Percentage Interests.

6.10 Miscellaneous Tax Allocation Matters.

a. Relationship to Book Values. To the extent permitted by Section 1.704-1(b) (4) (i) of the Treasury Regulations, all items 'of income, gain, loss, and deduction for Federal and state income tax purposes shall be allocated in accordance with the corresponding "book" items; however, all items of income, gain, loss, and deduction with respect to property with respect to which there is a difference between "book" value and adjusted tax basis shall be allocated in accordance with the principles of Section 704 (c) of the Code and Section 1. 704-1 (b) (4) (i) of the Treasury Regulations.

b. Recapture Income. In the event that the Partnership has taxable income that is characterized as ordinary income under the recapture provisions of the Code, each Partner's distributive share of taxable gain or loss from the sale of Partnership assets (to the extent possible) shall include a proportionate share of this recapture income equal to that Partner's share of prior cumulative depreciation deductions with respect to the assets which gave rise to the recapture income.

6.11 Application of Provisions. The provisions of this Section 6 shall be applied as if all distributions and allocations were made at the end of the Partnership's taxable year. Where any provision depends on the Capital Account of any Partner, that Capital Account shall be determined after operation of all preceding provisions for the year.

6.12 Allocations of Nonrecourse Liabilities. The nonrecourse liabilities of the Partnership shall be allocated to the Partners in accordance with their respective profits, subject to the provisions of Section 1.752-3 of the Treasury Regulations.

6.13 Authority of General Partner to Vary Allocations to Preserve and Protect Partners' Intent.

a. It is the intent of the Partners that each Partner's distributive share of income, gain, loss, deduction, or credit (or item thereof) shall be determined and allocated in accordance with this section 6 to the fullest extent permitted by Code Section 704(b). In order to preserve and protect the determinations and allocations provided for in this Section 6, the General Partner shall be, and it hereby is, authorized and directed to allocate income, gain, loss, deduction, or credit (or item thereof) arising in any year

448

differently than otherwise provided for in this Section 6, if, and
to the extent that the allocation provided for under such Section 6
would not be permitted by Code Section 704(b) and Treasury
Regulations promulgated thereunder. Any allocation made pursuant to
this Section 6 shall be deemed provided for in this Section 6, and
no amendment of this Agreement or approval of any Partner shall be
required.

b. In making any allocation (the "new allocation") under Section 6,
the General Partner is authorized to act only after having been
advised in writing, by the accountants to the Partnership that, in
its opinion, after examining Code Section 704(b) and the Treasury
Regulations thereunder, (i) the new allocation is necessary, and
(ii) the new allocation is the minimum modification necessary to
conform to Code Section 704(b) and the Treasury Regulations thereunder.

c. New allocations made by the General Partner in reliance upon the
written advice of the accountants described above shall be deemed
to be made pursuant to the fiduciary obligation of the General partner to the Partnership and the Limited Partners, and no such new
allocation shall give rise to any claim or cause of action against
the General Partner by any Limited Partner.

d. In the event that the General Partner is required by Section 6
to make any new allocation in a manner less favorable to the Limited
Partners than is otherwise provided for in this Section 6, the
General Partner shall be, and hereby is, authorized and directed,
insofar as it is permitted to do so by Code Section 704 (b), to
allocate income, gain, loss, deduction, or credit (or item thereof') arising in later years in a manner so as to bring the proportion of income, gain, loss, deduction, or credit (or item thereof)
allocated to the Limited Partners as close as possible to the proportion otherwise contemplated by this Section 6.

e. The General Partner shall have reasonable discretion, with
respect to each Partnership fiscal year, to (i) apply the provisions
of Paragraphs 11.4(b), I 1.4(c), and 11.4(d) hereof in whatever
order is likely to minimize the economic distortions that might otherwise result from the Regulatory Allocations, and (ii) divide all
allocations pursuant to Paragraphs I 1.4(b), 11.4(c), and 11.4(d)
hereof among the General Partner and Limited Partner s in a manner
that is likely to minimize such economic distortions.

f. Allocations Relating to Taxable Issuance of Partnership Interest.
Any income, gain, loss, or deduction realized as a direct or indi-
rect result of the issuance of a partnership interest by the partnership to a Partner (the "Issuance Items") shall be allocated among
the partners so that, to the extent possible, the net amount of such
Issuance Items, together with all other allocations under this
agreement to each partner, shall be equal to the net amount that
would have been allocated to each such Partner if the Issuance Items
had not been realized.

g. Other Allocations Rules.

(i) General Partner Fees. If any payments of fees to the General Partner are characterized as Partnership Distributions, the General Partner shall be allocated gross income equal to such payments. Any such allocations shall be deducted from the Partnership's Net Income and Net Loss.

(ii) Additional Partners. If additional Partners are admitted by the Partnership, in determining the character (but not the amount) of Net Income allocated under Paragraph 11.2 of this Agreement, any income attributable to inventory or unrealized receivables (as defined under Code Section 751) shall continue to be allocated (to the extent possible) to the Partners who had interests prior to the admission of the new Partners.

(iii) Tax Allocations: Code Section 704(c). In accordance with Code Section 704(c) and the Regulations thereunder, income, gain, loss, and deduction with respect to any property contributed to the capital of the Partnership shall, solely for tax purposes, be allocated among the General Partner and Limited Partners so as to take account of any variation between the adjusted basis of such property to the Partnership for federal income tax purposes and its initial Gross Asset Value.

In the event the Gross Asset Value of any Partnership asset is adjusted pursuant to Paragraph 22.21, subsequent allocations of income, gain, loss, and deduction with respect to such asset shall take account of any variation between the adjusted basis of such asset for federal income tax purposes and its Gross Asset Value in the same manner as under Code Section 704(c) and the Regulations thereunder. Any elections or other decisions relating to such allocations shall be made by the General Partner in any manner that reasonably reflects the purpose and intention of this Agreement. Allocations pursuant to this Paragraph 11.6 are solely for purposes of federal, state, and local taxes and shall not affect, or in any way be taken into account in computing, any Partner's Capital Account or share of Net Income, Net Loss, other items, or distributions pursuant to any provision of this Agreement.

(a) Restrictions on Distributions. The Partnership may be restricted from making Distributions under the terms of promissory notes, mortgages or other types of debt obligations which it may issue or assume in conjunction with borrowed funds, and Distributions also may be restricted or suspended in circumstances when the General Partner determines, in its sole subjective discretion, that such action is in the best interests of the Partnership. All Distributions are subject to the payment of Partnership expenses and to the maintenance of reasonable reserves for expenses.

(b) Partners' Consent to Distribution and Allocation Methods. The methods herein above set forth by which Distributions and allocations of Net Income and Net Loss are made and apportioned are hereby expressly consented to by each Partner as an express condition to becoming a Partner.

(c) Sale for Cash and Notes. Should the Partnership's assets be sold for a combination of cash and promissory notes, such promissory notes shall be valued at their principal amount less underlying encumbrances, if any, and pro rata individual portions thereof deemed divided and distributed among the Partners as if the Partnership were dissolved on the date of the sale for purposes of Distributions and allocations thereafter.

SECTION 7

COMPENSATION AND REIMBURSEMENT OF EXPENSES

TO THE GENERAL PARTNER AND AFFILIATES

7.1 Limits on Compensation. The General Partner or its Affiliates shall receive compensation only as specified in this Agreement.

7.2 Direct and Other Expenses. The General Partner and its Affiliates will receive reimbursement of Direct Expenses, and general and administrative costs of the General Partner as those costs relate to the General Partner's day-to-day management of the Partnership The General Partner and its Affiliates will also receive reimbursement of the fees, costs and expenses relating to the organization of the Partnership and the offering of Units therein, as well as any costs incurred by the General Partner which costs were incurred for the benefit of the Partnership.

7.3 Management Fee. In consideration for the management services to be performed by the General Partner, including without limitation, providing oversight management services with respect to the operation of the Partnership, monitoring all payments and costs of the Partnership; performing everyday bookkeeping and financial record keeping for the Partnership and making distributions and reports to the Partners, the General Partner will receive a management fee (the "Management Fee") equal to five percent (5%).

7.4 Production Services. _____the sole shareholder of the General Partner, is to receive _____ per individual film for directing and co-producing services. _____ is to be entitled to 50% of any of the contingency not used.

SECTION 8

BOOKS AND RECORDS

8.1 Records. The General Partner shall keep at _____ or at such other office of the General Partner as the General Partner may designate from time to time, the following Partnership documents:

a. A current list of the full name and last known business or residence address of each Partner, together with the contribution and share in profits and losses of each Partner.

b. A copy of the Certificate of Limited Partnership and all Certificates of Amendment, and executed copies of any power of

451

attorney pursuant to which any certificate has been executed.

c. Copies of the Partnership's federal, state and local income tax or information returns and reports, if any, for the six (6) most recent taxable years.

d. Copies of the original Agreement and all Amendments to the Agreement.

e. The Partnership's books and records for at least the current and past three (3) fiscal years.

8.2 Delivery to Limited Partner and Inspection.

a. Upon the request of a Limited Partner, the General Partner shall deliver to the requesting Limited Partner, at his or her expense, a copy of the information required to be maintained by subsection 8.1 a, b or d

b. Each Limited Partner has the right, upon reasonable notice, to each of the following:

(i) Inspect and copy at his own expense during normal business hours any of the Partnership records required to be maintained by Section 8.1.

(ii) Obtain from the General Partner, after becoming available, a copy of the Limited Partnership's federal, state and local income tax or information returns for each year.

c. The General Partner shall send to each Partner within a reasonable period following the end of each taxable year the information necessary for the Partner to complete its federal and state income tax or information returns. 8.3 Reports. The General Partner shall provide each partner with financial statements for each Partnership year, within 90 days after the end of each Partnership year, includ - ing a balance sheet, income statement and statement of changes in financial position for the year.

8.3 Tax Returns and Tax Matters. The Partnership's tax and fiscal year shall be the calendar year. The accountants shall be instruct- ed to prepare and file all required income tax returns for the Partnership. The General Partner shall be the Tax Matters Partner.

SECTION 9

ASSIGNMENT

9.1 Assignment of Units Prohibited. Except for transfers upon death, divorce or for estate planning purposes, no Partner may assign, transfer, sell, pledge, or hypothecate all or any part of his/her Units of the Partnership unless approval is given in advance by the General Partner and the procedures of Section 13 are followed.

9.2 Assignments. After receipt of the consent of the General

Partner, and compliance with Section 13, Limited Partner s may assign their rights to receive Distributions and Allocations of Net Income and Net Loss to any person of their choice. Upon receipt by the General Partner of a notice of assignment, signed by both the assignor and the assignee, in a form approved by the General Partner, and payment of a fee, not to exceed $500, to cover costs of the General Partner, the assignee shall become entitled to receive the assigning Limited Partner's share of Net Income, Net Loss and Distributions. In addition, at the request of the General Partner, the assignor may be requested to furnish at, his/her expense, either an opinion of counsel or other acceptable evidence, satisfactory in form and substance to the General Partner, to the effect that the transfer will not impair the Partnership's status as a Partnership under the federal income tax laws and that the transfer will not violate federal or state securities law An assignee is not a Limited Partner, and is not entitled to vote or entitled to the other rights of a Limited Partner, other than the right to receive allocations and distributions, unless the assignee is admitted as a Limited Partner as provided in Section 9.4 below.

9.3 Prohibited Assignments Void. Any assignment made in violation of this Section 9 shall be void.

9.4 Substitute Limited Partner. An assignee of a Limited Partner's interest may become a Limited Partner on satisfaction of the following conditions:

a. Filing with the Partnership a duly executed and acknowledged written instrument of assignment in a form approved by the General Partner specifying the interest being assigned and setting forth the intention of the assignor that the assignee succeed to the assignor's interest as a Limited Partner;

b. Execution and acknowledgment by the assignor and assignee of any other instruments required by the General Partner, including the acceptance and adoption by the assignee of the provisions of this Partnership Agreement and execution, acknowledgment and delivery to the General Partner of a special power of attorney, in substantially the form in Section 12;

c. Obtaining the written consent of the General Partner, the granting or denial of which shall be within the absolute discretion of the General Partner;

d. Complying with Section 13; and

e. Payment of a transfer fee, not to exceed $1,000 to the General Partner, sufficient to cover the reasonable expenses of the substitution. In addition, at the request of the General Partner, the assignor may be requested to furnish at his/her expense, either an opinion of counsel or other acceptable evidence, satisfactory in form and substance to the General Partner, to the effect that the transfer will not impair the Partnership's status as a Partnership under the federal income tax laws and that the transfer will not violate federal or state securities law.

9.5 Binding on Successors. The rights and obligations of the Partners shall inure to and be binding upon the heirs, successors, and assignees of the Partners.

9.6 Involuntary Assignment. A Limited Partner's heirs, successors, and estate shall not be subject to compliance with the requirements of Section 9.1.

9.7 Assignment by the General Partner. The General Partner's interest in the Partnership shall, subject to Section 3.3, be assignable (i) to an assignee approved by a Majority or (ii) to a successor corporation in connection with a merger, consolidation or corporate reorganization of the General Partner. Any entity to which the General Partner's interest in the Partnership is assigned in compliance with this Section 97 shall be substituted as the General Partner by the filing of appropriate amendments of the Partnership Agreement.

9.8 Assignee's Capital. An assignee shall have a Capital Account and shall have Adjusted Invested Capital in the same amount as attributed to the assigned interest when held by the assignor.

SECTION 10

POWERS AND APPROVAL

RIGHTS OF THE LIMITED PARTNERS

10.1 No Management and Control. Limited Partners shall take no part in the control, conduct or operation of the Partnership and shall have no right or authority to act for or bind the Partnership including during the winding up period following dissolution of the Partnership. If the General Partner has been removed and the Partnership has been dissolved, the Limited Partners may act for and bind the Partnership during the winding up period, as approved by a Majority.

10.2 Voting Rights. Except as expressly provided in this Agreement, Limited Partners shall have no voting rights.

10.3 Approval. Limited Partners shall have the right, by vote of a Majority, to approve or disapprove the following matters, and no others: election of a successor General Partner; and, with consent of the General Partner, the election of an additional General Partner.

10.4 Limitations. No Limited Partner shall have the right or power to: (i) withdraw or reduce his Invested Capital except as a result of the dissolution of the Partnership or as otherwise provided by law, (ii) bring an action for partition against the Partnership; (iii) cause the termination and dissolution of the Partnership, or (iv) demand or receive property other than cash in return for his Invested Capital. No Limited Partner shall have priority over any other Limited Partner either as to the return of Invested Capital

or as to Net Income, Net Loss or Distributions. Other than upon liquidation of the Partnership as provided by this Agreement, there has
been no time agreed upon when the Capital Contributions of each
Limited Partner may be returned.

10.5 Meetings of Partners.

a. Meetings of Partners may be held at the principal place of business of the Partnership as determined from time to time by the
General Partner.

b. Meetings shall be held only when called by either the General Partner
or by Limited Partner s representing a Majority

c. Meeting notices and procedures shall be in conformity with
California Corporations Code Section 15637.

SECTION 11

REMOVAL, BANKRUPTCY

OR DISSOLUTION OF THE GENERAL PARTNER

11.1 Removal. The General Partner may be removed from the
Partnership only by a vote of Limited Partner s holding a ninety
percent (90%) Percentage Interest and a showing of cause, or as otherwise provided herein.

11.2 Notice. Notice of removal shall be served on the General
Partner either by certified or by registered mail, return receipt
requested, or by personal service. The notice shall set forth the
effective date of the removal and the facts constituting cause. For
the purposes of this Section 11, "cause" shall mean the commission
by the General Partner of an act of fraud, breach of fiduciary duty,
misappropriation of funds and/or conviction of the General Partner
for a felony involving similar illegal actions.

11.3 Purchase of Interest and Payment of Fees.

a. On the removal of the General Partner the participation of the
General Partner in the Net Income, Net Loss and Distributions from
the Partnership shall be purchased by the Partnership for a purchase
price determined according to the provisions of Section 11.3.b.

b. The General Partner shall receive from the Partnership the following: (i) a return of all loans to the Partnership; (ii) reimbursement of all expenses incurred on behalf of the Partnership;
(iii) the fair market value of the General Partner's Units based
upon the Partnership's net worth. Payment to the General Partner
shall be made in cash at the time of the purchase of its Units by
the Partnership. The removal of the General Partner shall be effective only upon the payment herein provided.

SECTION 12

SPECIAL POWER OF ATTORNEY

12.1 Attorney-in-Fact. By his/her or its signature on the Subscription Agreement, each Limited Partner grants to the General Partner a special power of attorney irrevocably making, constituting and appointing the General Partner as the Limited Partners' attorney-in-fact, with power and authority to act in his name and on his behalf to execute, acknowledge and swear to in the execution, acknowledgment and filing of documents, which shall include, by way of illustration but not of limitation, the following:

a. The certificate of limited partnership, this Agreement, any amendment to either the certificate of limited partnership or this Agreement, any other document which, under the laws of the State of California or the laws of any other state, are required to be filed or which the General Partner elects to file;

b. Any other instrument or document required to be filed by the Partnership under the laws of any state or by any governmental agency, or which the General Partner elects to file, including, but not limited to, the Internal Revenue Service, the SEC and the California Corporations commission;

c. Any instrument or document that may be required to effect the continuation of the Partnership, the admission of an additional or substituted Limited Partner, or the dissolution and termination of the Partnership (provided that the continuation, admission or dissolution and termination are in accordance with the terms of this Agreement), or to reflect any reduction in amount of the Partner's Invested Capital or reduction in the Partner's Capital Accounts; and

d. Any instrument or document that may be required to effect the purchase, sale, financing or other operation of the Partnership.

12.2 Special Provisions. The special power of attorney being granted by each Limited Partner (i) is a special power of attorney coupled with an interest, (ii) is irrevocable, (iii) shall survive the death or incapacity of the granting Limited Partner, and (iv) is limited to the matters set forth in Section 12.1.

12.3 Signatures. The General Partner may exercise the special power of attorney on behalf of each Limited Partner by a facsimile signature of the General Partner or one of its officers, or by signature of the General Partner or one of its officers acting as an attorney-in-fact for all of the Limited Partners.

SECTION 13

RIGHT OF FIRST REFUSAL

13.1 Offer. Except for transfers upon death, divorce, disabilities or for estate planning purposes, before any Limited Partner assigns, transfers or sells his Units in this Partnership other than an involuntary assignment (as defined in Paragraph 9.6 herein above), that Partner (the "Selling Partner") shall first offer the Units to the General Partner by giving written notice of such desire to the General Partner, specifying the price, terms and conditions of such offer. The General Partner shall then have an option to purchase the Units at the price and on the terms and conditions set forth in the notice, which option shall be exercised in writing. If the General Partner does not exercise such option within thirty (30) days, then the Selling Partner shall give all of the other Limited Partners notice of the price and terms at which the Selling Partner is proposing to sell his Units. the Limited Partners shall have an option for fifteen (15) days after the expiration of the General Partner's option to purchase the Units at the price and on the terms and conditions set forth in the notice, which option shall be exercised in writing.

13.2 Acceptance. If more than one of the Limited Partners elects to purchase, those electing to purchase shall purchase a pro rata portion of the Selling Partner's Units according to the number of Limited Partners participating in the purchase. If no acceptance is given during the offer period by either the General Partner or the Limited Partners, the Selling Partner may sell his Units, subject to the provisions of Section 9 of this Agreement, for the price and on the terms described in the notice for a period of one hundred twenty (120) days following the end of the offer period to the Limited Partners. If the Selling Partner does not complete the sale of his Units in that one hundred twenty (120) day period, the provisions of this Section shall apply to any further sale or offer later proposed by the Selling Partner.

13.3 Rights of Buyer. A purchaser of the Selling Partner's Units, if not already a Limited Partner, shall be an assignee, and shall become a substitute Limited Partner only upon satisfaction of the requirements of Section 9.4. If the purchaser was already, before the purchase, a Limited Partner, the purchaser will continue as a Limited Partner.

SECTION 14

DEATH OR INCAPACITY OF A PARTNER

14.1 Death or Incapacity of a Partner. When a Limited Partner dies, the Partnership will not dissolve unless the remaining Partners elect by unanimous vote to dissolve the Partnership. The person or persons entitled to succeed to the deceased Partner's Partnership interest pursuant to the decedent's will or the laws of intestate succession shall become an assignee subject to the provisions of Section 9 herein above.

SECTION 15

MISCELLANEOUS

15.1 Readings. The titles and headings of the various paragraphs of this Agreement are intended solely for convenience of reference and are not intended to explain, modify or place any interpretation upon any of the provisions of this Agreement.

457

15.2 Time of Essence. All times and dates in this Agreement shall be of the essence.

15.3 Governing Law. This Agreement shall be governed by and construed in accordance with the laws of the State of California.

15.4 Attorneys' Fees. In any dispute between the Partners, whether or not resulting in litigation, the prevailing party shall be entitled to recover from the other party all reasonable costs, including, but not limited to, reasonable attorneys' fees.

15.5 Severability. If any part of this Agreement is determined to be illegal or unenforceable, all other parts shall be given effect separately and shall not be affected.

15.6 Notices. Notices given under this Agreement shall be in writing and shall either be served personally or delivered by first class (registered or certified, return receipt requested) U.S. mail, postage prepaid. Notices shall be deemed received at the earlier of actual receipt or five days following deposit in U.S. mail, postage prepaid Notices shall be directed to the addresses shown on the Subscription Agreement, provided that a Partner may change his/her address for notice by giving written notice to all other Partner in accordance with this notice section.

15.7 Gender and Number. As used in this Agreement, the masculine, feminine, or neuter gender, and the singular or plural number, shall each include the others whenever the context so indicates.

15.8 Counterpart Copies. This Agreement may be signed in counterpart or duplicate copies, and any signed counterpart or duplicate copy shall be equivalent to a signed original for all purposes.

15.9 Cross-References. All cross-references in this Agreement, unless specifically directed to another agreement or document, refer to provisions in this Agreement, and shall not be deemed to be references to the overall transaction or to any other agreements or documents.

15.10 Covenant to Sign Documents. Each Partner shall execute, with acknowledgment or affidavit, if required, all documents and writings reasonably necessary or expedient in the creation of this Partnership and the achievement of its purpose.

IN WITNESS WHEREOF, the Partner have signed this Agreement effective as of the date first set forth above.

GENERAL PARTNER
_____Partners, L.P.

_____INC.,as attorney-in-fact for the California
Corporation Limited Partners set forth in the attached
Subscription Agreements
By: _____

458

# BIBLIOGRAPHY

## Budgeting

*Film Budgeting: Or, How Much It Will Cost to Shoot Your Movie*, Ralph S. Singleton, Lone Eagle Press, Los Angeles, 1996.

*Film & Video Budgets - 2nd ed.*, Michael Wiese and Deke Simon, Michael Wiese Productions, Studio City, CA, 1995.

*The Hollywood Guide to Film Budgeting and Script Breakdown for Low Budget Features*, Danford Chamness, The Stanley J. Brooks Company, Los Angeles, 1988.

## Contracts

*Contracts in the Film and Television Industry*, Mark Litwak, Silman-James Press, Los Angeles, 1995.

*Deal Making in the Film and Television Industry*, Mark Litwak, Silman-James Press, Los Angeles, 1994.

*Limited Partnership Agreement on Word Diskette*, Michael Wiese Productions, Studio City, CA (800-833-5738).

*The Film Industries: Practical Business/Legal Problems in Production, Distribution, and Exhibition*, Michael Mayer, Hastings House.

*The Writer Got Screwed (But Didn't Have To): A Guide to the Legal and Business Practices of Writing for the Entertainment Industry*, Brooke A. Wharton, 1996.

## Directing

*Directing: Film Techniques and Aesthetics*, Michael P. Rabiger, 1996.

*Directing Actors: Creating Memorable Performances for Film and Television*, Judith Weston, Michael Wiese Productions, Studio City, CA, 1996.

*Directing Single Camera Drama*, Mike Crisp, 1998.

*Directing Television and Film* (Wadsworth Series in Television and Film), Alan A. Armer, 1991.

459

*Directing the Film: Film Directors on Their Art*, Eric Sherman, Little, Brown and Company, Boston, 1988.

*Directing Your Directing Career: A Support Book and Agent Guide for Directors*, K. Callan, 1994.

*Film Directing Cinematic Motion: A Workshop for Staging Scenes*, Steven D. Katz, Michael Wiese Productions, Studio City, CA, 1992.

*Film Directing: Killer Style & Cutting Edge Technique*, Renee Harmon, Lone Eagle Press, Los Angeles, 1997.

*Film Directing Shot by Shot: Visualizing from Concept to Screen*, Steven D. Katz, Michael Wiese Productions, Studio City, CA, 1991.

*Making Movies*, Sidney Lumet, Alfred A. Knopf, New York, 1995.

*The Director's Journey: The Creative Collaboration Between Directors, Writers and Actors*, Mark W. Travis, Michael Wiese Productions, Studio City, CA, 1997.

*The Film Director As Superstar*, Joseph Gelmis, Doubleday, New York, 1970.

*The Practical Director*, Mike Crisp, 1996.

### Documentaries

*The Search for Reality: The Art of Documentary Filmmaking*, Michael Tobias (Editor). Michael Wiese Productions, Studio City, CA, 1998.

### Editing

*In the Blink of an Eye*, Walter Murch, Silman-James Press, Los Angeles, 1996.

*When The Shooting Stops ... The Cutting Begins*, Ralph Rosenblum and Robert Karen, Penguin Books, New York, 1979.

### Financing

*Film Financing*, John Cones, Silman-James Press, Los Angeles, 1995.

*Film and Video Financing*, Michael Wiese, Michael Wiese Productions, Studio City, CA, 1991.

*Filmmakers and Financing: Business Plans for Independents*, Louise Levinson, Focal Press, 1994.

*Financing Your Film: A Guide for Independent Filmmakers and Producers*, Trisha Curran, Praeger Publishers, 1 Madison Avenue, New York, NY 10010.

*Movies and Money: Financing the American Film Industry*, Janet Wasko, 1982.

*Producing, Financing, and Distributing Film: A Comprehensive Legal and Business Guide*, Paul A. Baumgarten et al., 1992.

## Grants

*Catalog of Federal Domestic Assistance*, Superintendent of Documents, Washington, DC 20402.

*Corporate 500: The Directory of Corporate Philanthropy*, Public Management Institute, 358 Brannan, San Francisco, CA 94107.

*Dear Friend: Mastering the Art of Direct Mail Fund Raising*, Kay Partney Lautman and Henry Goldstein, The Taft Group, 12300 Twinbrook Pkwy, Suite 450, Rockville, MD 20852 (800-877-8238).

*Directory of International Corporate Giving in America*, Katherine E. Jankowski, ed., The Taft Group (800-877-TAFT).

*Encyclopedia of Associations*, Robert Thomas and Denise Allard, Detroit, MI, Gale Research, 1987, U.S. nonprofit organizations.

*Environmental Grantmaking Foundations 1992*, Environmental Data Research Institute, 797 Elmwood Ave., Rochester, NY 14620-2946.

*Financial Aid for Research, Study, Travel and Other Activities Abroad*, Schlacter and Weber, Reference Service Press, 1100 Industrial Road, Suite 9, San Carlos, CA 94070.

*Fiscal Sponsorship: 6 Ways to Do It Right*, Gregory Colvin, San Francisco Study Center, P.O. Box 425646, San Francisco, CA 94142-5646 (800-484-4173, ext. 1073).

Foundation Center, 79 Fifth Avenue, Dept. KM, New York, NY 10003, will do a computer search listing the foundations that regularly grant monies to fund film and video projects.

*Foundation Grants to Individuals* from The Foundation Center, New York.

*Fundraising for Social Change*, Kim Klein, Crain Books.

*Getting Funded: A Complete Guide to Proposal Writing*, PSU, P.O. Box 1491, Portland, OR 97207.

*Get the Money and Shoot: The DRI Guide to Funding Documentary Films*, Bruce Jackson and Diane Christian, Buffalo, NY, Documentary Research, revised edition 1986, DRI, 96 Rumsey Road, Buffalo, NY 14209 (716-885-9777).

*Grant Guides for the Arts*, The Foundation Center, New York.

*Grants and Grant Proposals That Have Succeeded*, Virginia White, Plenum, New York City (800-221-9369).

*Guide to California Foundations*, Northern California Grantmakers, 334 Kearny St., San Francisco, CA 94108. (Similar texts are available for many other states.)

*Maximum Gifts by Return Mail: An Expert Tells How to Write Highly Profitable Fund Raising Letters*, R. Kuniholm, The Taft Group (800-877-TAFT).

*Money for Film and Video Artists* and *Money for International Exchange in the Arts*, both from American Council for the Arts, One East 53rd St., New York, NY 10022. (800-321-4510).

*National Directory of Grants* and *Aid to Individuals in the Arts*, Washington International Newsletter, Washington, DC.

*Shaking The Money Tree: How to Get Grants and Donations for Film and Video*, Morrie Warshawski, Michael Wiese Productions, Studio City, CA, 1992.

*Sponsors: A Guide for Video and Film*, American Council for the Arts, New York, NY.

*Supporting Yourself as an Artist: A Practical Guide*, Deborah A. Hoover, American Council for the Arts/Oxford University Press, New York, NY.

*The Art of Winning Corporate Grants*, Howard Hillman, The Vanguard Press.

*The Foundation Center: Source Book Profile: Film, Media & Communications, Comsearch Printouts* (available by subject area on microfiche or in print), National Guide to Funding in Arts & Culture, Foundation Fundamentals, The Foundation Directory, Foundation Center's User Friendly Guide, The Foundation Grants Index Annual and Grants to Individuals. 79 5th Ave., New York, NY 10003. (800-424-9836).

*The Grantseekers Guide*, Shellow & Stella, National Network of Grantmakers, 919 No. Michigan Ave., Chicago, IL 60611.

*The Grass Roots Fundraising Book: How to Raise Money in Your Community*, and *Successful Fundraising*, both, Joan Flanagan, Contemporary Books, Chicago.

*Where the Money Is*, H. Bergen. Society for Non-Profit Organizations, 6314 Odana Rd., Suite 1, Madison, WI 53719.

*Where's the Money?*, a special report by Morrie Warshawski, Michael Wiese Productions, Studio City, CA, 1998 (800-833-5738).

## Myth

*Goddesses in Everywoman*, Jean Shinoda Bolen, M. D. Harper & Row, New York, 1985.

*Gods in Everyman*, Jean Shinoda Bolen, M. D. Harper & Row, New York, 1989.

*Myths of Greece and Rome*, Thomas Bulfinch, Penguin Books, New York, 1981.

*The Power of Myth*, Joseph Cambell with Bill Moyers, Doubleday, New York, 1988.

*The Hero With a Thousand Faces*, Joseph Campbell, Bollingen Series/Princeton University Press, 1973.

*The Greek Myths*, Robert Graves, Penguin Books, New York, 1979.

*The Odyssey*, Homer, transl., E. V. Rieu, Penguin Books, New York, 1960.

*He: Understanding Masculine Psychology*, Robert A. Johnson, Harper & Row Perennial Library, 1977.

*She: Understanding Feminine Psychology*, Robert A. Johnson, Harper & Row, New York, 1977.

*We: Understanding the Psychology of Romantic Love*, Robert A. Johnson. Harper & Row, New York, 1983.

*Awakening the Heroes Within*, Carol S. Pearson. Harper San Francisco, 1991.

## Marketing & Distribution

*16mm Distribution*, Judith Trojan & Nadien Convert; available from Educational Film Library Association, 43 W. 61st Street, New York, NY 10023.

*Alternative Visions: Distributing Independent Media in a Home Video World*, Debra Franco, AFI Press (Order from AIVF, 212-473-3400).

*Distribution* Guide, the Independent Film Journal, 1251 Avenue of the Americas, New York, NY.

*Doing It Yourself: A Handbook on Independent Film Distribution*, AIVF, Inc., Julia Reichert, 99 Prince Street, New York, NY 10012, 1977.

*Entertainment Industry Economics*, Harold L. Vogel, Cambridge University Press, New York, NY.

*Film Distribution Guide*, 1986-1992, Vol. 1, Gail McClellan, Rick Allen (Editor), 1994.

*Film & Video Marketing*, Michael Wiese, Michael Wiese Productions, Studio City, CA, 1988.

*Motion Picture Distribution (Business and/or Racket?)*, Walter E. Hurst and Wm Storm Hale. Seven Arts Press, Hollywood, 1977.

*Movie Marketing: Opening the Picture and Giving It Legs*, Tiiu Lukk, Silman-James, Los Angeles, 1997.

*Producing, Financing and Distributing Film*, Baumgarten, Farber & Fleischer. Limelight Editions, New York.

*Taking it to the Theaters: The Empowerment Project's Guide to Theatrical and Video Self-Distribution of Issue-Oriented Films and Videos*, Trent, Peale and Doroshow, 3403 Hwy. 54 W, Chapel Hill, NC 27516. (919-967-1963).

*The Beginning Filmmaker's Business Guide: Financial, Legal, Marketing, and Distribution Basics of Making Movies*, Renee Harmon, 1994.

*The Movie Business Book, 2nd ed.*, edited by Jason E. Squire, Fireside/Simon & Schuster, New York.

*The Next Step: Distributing Independent Films and Video*, edited by Morrie Warshawski, available from AIVF (212) 473-3400.

## PBS

*National Endowment for the Arts Guide to Programs, Media Arts Program Guidelines, and the Annual Report*, Information Office, NEA, Washington, DC 20506.

*National Endowment for the Humanities Program Announcement and Media Program Guidelines, and Media Log* (listing of 800 film, TV, and radio programs supported by NEH), NEH Public Information Office, Washington, DC 20506.

*PBS Program Producer's Handbook*, PBS, National Programming and Promotion Services, 1320 Braddock Place, Alexandria, VA 22314-1698; or call (703) 739-5450. Ask for a copy of the list of "Underwriters of PTV Programming."

*Producer's Guide to Public Television Funding* (free), CPB, 901 E St., NW, Washington, DC 20004-2006.

*Public Television's Programming Pipeline* (free), annual overview of series projects for public television currently in stages of development, PBS, National Programming and Promotion Services, 1320 Braddock Place, Alexandria, VA 22314-1698.

## Producing

*Breaking & Entering: Land Your First Job in Film Production*, April Fitzsimmons, 1997.

*Feature Filmmaking at Used Car Prices*, Rick Schmidt. Penguin Books, New York, 1988.

*Film Industries: Practical Business and Legal Problems in Production, Distribution and Exhibition, The*, Michael F. Mayer, available from Hastings House, New York, 1978.

*Film Producing: Low Budget Films That Sell*, Renee Harmon, 1989.

*Film Production*, Steven Bernstein, 1994.

*Film Production Management*, Bastian Cleve, 1994.

*Film Production: The Complete Uncensored Guide to Filmmaking*, Greg Merritt, 1998.

*Hollywood on $5,000, $10,000, or $25,000 a Day: A Survival Guide for Low-Budget Filmmakers*, Philip Gaines, David J. Rhodes, 1994.

*How I Made a Hundred Movies in Hollywood and Never Lost a Dime*, Roger Corman with Jim Jerome, Random House, New York, 1990.

*How to Make It in Hollywood*, Linda Buzzell, Harper Perennial.

*I Wake Up Screening!: Everything You Need to Know About Making Independent Films Including a Thousand Reasons Not To*, Frank D. Gilroy, 1993.

*Independent Feature Film Production*, Gregory Goodell, St. Martin's Press, New York, 1982.

*Killer Instinct: How Two Young Producers Took on Hollywood and Made the Most Controversial Film of the Decade*, Jane Hamsher, 1997.

*Making Films Your Business*, Mollie Gregory. Schocken Books, New York, 1979.

*Micro-Budget Hollywood: Budgeting (and Making Feature Films for $50,000 to $500, 000)*, Philip Gaines, David J. Rhodes, 1995.

*Movie Making: A Guide to Film Production*, Sumner Glimcher and Warren Johnson. Pocket Books/Simon & Schuster, New York, 1975.

*Off-Hollywood: The Making and Marketing of Independent Films*, Peter Hamilton and David Rosen. Grove Weidenfeld, New York, 1990.

*Persistence of Vision: An Impractical Guide to Producing a Feature Film for Under $30,000*, John Gaspard, Dale Newton, 1995.

*Producers on Producing: The Making of Film & Television*, Irv Broughton, MacFarland Publishing, 1986.

*Producer to Producer: Insider Tips for Entertainment Media*
Michael Wiese, Michael Wiese Productions, Studio City, CA, 1997.

*Production Management for Film and Video*, Richard Gates, 1995.

*Succeeding As an Independent Film Producer: Based on the UCLA Course*, Peter McAlevey, 1998.

*The Complete Film Production Handbook*, Eve Light Honthaner, Lone Eagle Press, Los Angeles, 1996.

*The Independent Producer: Film & Television*, Hourcourt, Howlett, Davies, Moskovic. Faber & Faber, London, 1986.

*The Grip Book*, Sabrina Uva, Michael G. Uva, 1997.

*The On Production Budget Book*, Robert J. Koster, 1997.

*The Seven Habits of Highly Effective People*, Stephen R. Covey. Simon & Schuster, New York.

## Resources and Directories

*AIVF Guide to Film and Video Distributors and AIVF Guide to International Film and Video Festivals*, Kathryn Bowser. AIVF (212-473-3400).

*American Demographics*, Dow Jones and Company Inc., Syracuse, NY.

*American Cinematographers Manual*, edited by Fred Detmers. The ASC Press, Hollywood, 1986.

*American Film and Video Association*, Computer searches for programs by titles or subject (800-358-1834); fax (708-823-1561).

*Art on Film Database*, Inventory of film/video productions on the visual arts,  980 Madison Ave., New York, NY, 10021. (212-988-4876).

*Baseline*, online services, an entertainment industry database, New York City (212-254-8235), or LA (310-659-3830).

*Bowker's Complete Video Directory*, edited by M.K. Reed. R.R. Bowker, New York City. (800-521-8110).

*Copyright Hotline*, Association for Information Media and Equipment (AIME); (800-444-4203). Free service answering questions about copyright. P.O. Box 865, Elkader, IA  52043. (319-245-1361).

*Dialog Information Services* (800-334-2564). On-line database accessible by individuals and institutions. Used by many libraries and universities. Contains The Foundation Center databases and NICEM's A-V Online.

*Eaglei.com*, a directory of directors, producers, cinematographers, composers, cross-referenced by title and production credits.

*Film Directories*: Film Directors, Film Producers, Studios and Agents Guide, Cinematographers, Production Designers, Costume Designers, Film Editors Guide from Lone Eagle Press, Los Angeles (see also www.eaglei/com).

*Index to AV Producers and Distributors*, Plexus, 143 Old Marlton Pl., Medford, NJ 08055.

*Motion Picture, TV and Theater Directory*, Motion Picture Enterprises, Tarrytown, NY 10591.

*New York Feature Film and Video Guide*, 90 Riverside Drive, New York, NY.

*Nicem EZ Custom Search* (800-468-3453). Will do customized computer search of its vast databases on films, videos, producers, distributors, filmstrips, etc.

*NICEM's Film and Video Finder*, Plexus, 143 Old Marlton Pl., Medford, NJ 08055.

*PBS VIDEOFINDERS*, computer search for film/video programs (by title, subject, filmmaker, etc.) for works on PBS or in R.R. Bowker's guide (900-860-9301).

*Producer's Master Guide*, New York Production Manual Inc., 611 Broadway, Suite 807, New York, NY 10012.

*Publisher's Marketing Association*, video marketing programs for video producers, Hermosa Beach, CA (310-372-2732).

*Sponsors: A Guide for Video and Filmmakers*, Goldman and Green. Center for Arts Information, New York City. Available from AIVF (212-473-3400).

*Television and Cable Contacts*, Larimi Communications Associates, Ltd., 5 W. 37th Street, New York, NY 10018 (212-819-9310).

## Screenwriting

*Adventures in the Screen Trade*, William Goldman. Warner Books, New York, 1983.

*Alternative Scriptwriting: Writing Beyond the Rules*, Ken Dancyger, 1995.

*American Screenwriters: The Insiders' Look at the Art, the Craft, and the Business of Writing Movies*, Karl Schanzer and Thomas Lee Wright. Avon Books, New York, 1993.

*Breaking Through, Selling Out, Dropping Dead and Other Notes on Filmmaking*, William Bayer. Limelight Editions, New York, 1971, 1989.

*Fade In: The Screenwriting Process*, 2nd ed., Robert A. Berman. Michael Wiese Productions, Studio City, CA, 1997.

*Film Scriptwriting: A Practical Manual*, Joye R. Swain, Dwight V. Swain, Focal Press, 1988.

*Film Writers Guide*, 6th ed., Susan Avallone (Compiler), 1996.

*Formatting Your Screenplay* (Paragon House Writer's Series). Rick Reichman, 1992.

*From Script to Screen, The Collaborative Art of Filmmaking,* Linda Seger, Edward Jay Whetmore, 1994.

*Getting Your Script Through the Hollywood Maze: An Insider's Guide,* Linda Stuart, 1993.

*Good Scripts, Bad Scripts: Learning the Craft of Screenwriting Through 35 of the Best and Worst Films in History,* Thomas Pope, 1998.

*How to Sell Your Screenplay: The Real Rules of Film and Television,* Carl Sautter. New Chapter Press, New York, 1992.

*How to Write a Selling Screenplay: A Step-By-Step Approach to Developing Your Story and Writing Your Screenplay by One of Today's Most Successful Screenwriters,* Christopher Keane, Lauren Marino (Editor), 1998.

*How to Write a Story...Any Story: The Art of Storytelling: A Directed Approach to Writing Great Fiction,* Michael B. Druxman, 1997.

*Lew Hunter's Screenwriting 434,* Lew Hunter, Perigee Books/Putnam Publishing Group, New York, 1993.

*Making A Good Script Great,* Linda Seger, Dodd, Mead & Company, New York, 1994.

*Opening the Doors to Hollywood: How to Sell Your Idea Story, Book, Screenplay, Manuscript,* Carlos De Abreu et al., 1997.

*Principles of Adaptation for Film and Television,* Ben Brady, 1994.

*Screen Adaption: A Scriptwriting Handbook,* Kenneth Portnoy, 1991.

*Screenplay: The Foundations of Screenwriting,* Syd Field. Dell Publishing Company, New York, 1979, 1982.

*Script Formatting With Microsoft Word on the Apple MacIntosh: The Complete Idiot's Guide to Make Script Writing Automatic,* Larry Hussar, 1991.

*Scriptwriters Market: How and Where to Sell What You Write for Film and TV,* Leslie Gates, 1991.

*Screen-Writing Tricks of the Trade,* William Froug, 1992.

*The Art of Adaptation: Turning Fact and Fiction into Film,* Linda Seger, 1992.

*The Art of Screenwriting: Story Script Markets,* William Packard, 1997.

*The Craft of the Screenwriter,* John Brady, Simon and Schuster, New York, 1981.

*The Elements of Screenwriting: A Guide for Film and Television Writers*, Irwin R. Blacker, 1996.

*The Insider's Guide to Writing for Screen and Television*, Ron Tobias, Ronald B. Tobias, 1997.

*The New Screenwriter Looks at the New Screenwriter*, William Froug. Silman–James Press, Los Angeles, 1992.

*The Screenwriter's Bible: A Complete Guide to Writing, Formatting, and Selling Your Script*, David Trottier, 1995.

*The Screenwriter's Guide: Almost Everything You Need to Know to Get Your Script Produced: With the Names and Addresses of over 220 Producers*, Joseph Gillis, Rod Granger, 1987.

*The Screenwriter's Problem Solver: How to Recognize, Identify, and Define Screenwriting Problems*, Syd Field, 1998.

*The Screenwriter's Workbook*, Syd Field. Dell Publishing Company, New York, 1984.

*The Understructure of Writing for Film and Television*, Ben Brady, Lance Lee, 1988.

*The Whole Picture: Strategies for Screenwriting Success in the New Hollywood*, Richard Walter, 1997.

*Screen Writing for Television and Film*, Ronald D. Dyas, 1993.

*Screenwriters on Screenwriting: The Best in the Business Discuss Their Craft*, Joel Engel, 1995.

*The Screenwriting Life: The Dream, the Job and the Reality*, Rich Whiteside, 1998.

*Script Is Finished, Now What Do I Do? The Scriptwriter's Resource Book & Agent Guide*, K. Callan, 1997.

*Script Planning: Positioning and Developing Scripts for TV and Film*, Tony Zaza, 1993.

*Story: Substance, Structure, Style, and the Principles of Screenwriting*, Robert McKee, 1997.

*Story Sense: Writing Story and Script for Feature Films and Television*, Paul Lucey, 1996.

*Television and Screen Writing: From Concept to Contract*, Richard A. Blum, 1995.

*The Tools of Screenwriting: A Writer's Guide to the Craft and Elements of a Screenplay*, David Howard et al., 1993.

*Top Secrets: Screenwriting*, Jurgen Wolff and Kerry Cox, Lone Eagle Press, Los Angeles, 1993.

*Vale's Technique of Screen and Television Writing*, Eugene Vale, 1998.

*Writer's Guide to Hollywood Producers, Directors, and Screenwriter's Agents*, Skip Press, 1997.

*The Writer's Journey: Mythic Structure for Writers*, 2nd ed., Christopher Vogler. Michael Wiese Productions, Studio City, CA, 1998.

*Writing Docudrama: Dramatizing Reality for Film and TV*, Alan Rosenthal, 1994.

*Writing for Video*, Gene Bjerke, 1997.

*Writing Great Characters: The Psychology of Character Development in Screenplays*, Michael Halperin, Ph.D., 1996.

*Writing Screenplays That Sell*, Michael Hauge, 1991.

*Writing Short Films: Structure and Content for Screenwriters*, Linda J. Cowgill, 1997.

*Writing Short Scripts*, William H. Phillips, 1991.

*Writing the Character-Centered Screenplay*, Andrew Horton, 1994.

*Writing the Screenplay: TV and Film*, Alan A. Armer, 1992.

*Writing the Short Film*, Pat Cooper, Ken Dancyger, 1994

*Writing Treatments That Sell: How to Create and Market Your Story Ideas to the Motion Picture and TV Industry*, Kenneth Atchity, Chi-Li Wong, 1997.

*Zen and the Art of Screenwriting: Insights and Interviews*, William Froug, 1996.

*1998 Film Writers Guide* (7th ed.), Susan Avallone (Editor), 1998.

## Sponsors

*Guide to the Sponsored Video*, Doug Duda et al., available from Knowledge Industry Publications, 701 Westchester Avenue, White Plains, NY 10604 (1987).

*Sponsorship, Principles and Practices*, Ron Bergin, Amusement Business, Box 24970, Nashville, TN 37302 (615-321-4254).

## Trade Publications

*Ad Age*, 200 E. 42nd Street, New York, NY 10017.

*Advertising Age*, Crain Communications, Inc., 740 N. Rush Street, Chicago, IL 60611.

*Adweek*, 49 E. 21st Street, New York, NY 10010.

*American Cinematographer*, 220 E. 42nd Street, Suite 930, New York, NY 10017.

*American Film*, The American Film Institute, Washington, DC.

*Backstage*, 5151 Wilshire Boulevard, Suite 302, Los Angeles, CA 90036.

*Billboard*, 9107 Wilshire Boulevard, #2265, Los Angeles, CA 90036. Also: 1515 Broadway, New York, NY 10036.

*Broadcasting*, 630 Third Street, 12th Floor, New York, NY 10017. Also: Broadcasting Publications Inc., Washington, DC.

*Chain Store Age*, Lebhar-Friedman, Inc., New York, NY.

*Channels*, 19 West 44th Street, #812, New York, NY 10036.

*Channels of Communications*, Media Commentary Council, Inc., New York, NY.

*Children's Video*, John L. Weber for Children's Video Magazine, Inc., Brooklyn, NY.

*Daily Variety*, 1400 N. Cahuenga Boulevard, Los Angeles, CA 90028.

*Direct Marketing*, Hoke Communications, Inc., Garden City, NY.

*DM* [Direct Marketing] News, c/o DMN Corp., 19 W. 21st Street, New York, NY 10010 (212-741-2095).

*Electronic Media*, 220 East 42nd Street, #1306, New York, NY 10017.

*Electronic* Retailing, Fairchild Publications, New York, NY.

*Film Comment*, 140 W. 65th Street, New York, NY 10023.

*Film Journal*, 244 W. 49th Street, #305, New York, NY 10019.

*Folio*, Folio Magazine Publishing Corp., New Canaan, CT.

*Hollywood Reporter*, 1501 Broadway, New York, NY 10036.

Also: 6715 Sunset Boulevard, Hollywood, CA 90028.

*Home Viewer*, 11 N. Second Street, Philadelphia, PA 19160 (215-629-1588).

*INTV Journal*, 80 Fifth Avenue, New York, NY 10011.

*Library Journal*, R.R. Bowker Co., New York, NY.

*Millimeter*, 826 Broadway, New York, NY 10003.

*Movieline*, 1141 S. Beverly Drive, Los Angeles, CA 90035-1139.

*Multi-Channel News*, 7 E. 12th Street, New York, NY 10003.

*News and Views*, 1560 Broadway, #714, New York, NY 10036.

*Paul Kagan and Associates*, 126 Clock Tower Place, Carmel, CA 93923.

*Premiere*, 755 Second Avenue, New York, NY 10017.

*Publishers Weekly*, R.R. Bowker Co., New York, NY.

*Rockamerica Magazine*, 27 E. 21st Street, New York, NY 10010.

*Screen International*, 8500 Wilshire Boulevard, Beverly Hills, CA 90211.

*Sight and Sound Marketing*, Dorbaugh Publications, New York, NY.

*Splice*, 10 Columbus Circle, #1300, New York, NY 10019.

*Television Digest*, Television Digest Inc., 475 Fifth Avenue, Suite 1021, New York, NY 10017.

*TV/Radio Age*, 1270 Avenue of the Americas, #502, New York, NY 10020.

*Variety* (daily and weekly editions), Variety, Inc., 154 W. 46th Street, New York, NY 10036.

*Video Business Weekly*, 345 Park South, New York, NY 10010.

*Video Insider*, 223 Conestoga Road, Wayne, PA 19087.

*Video Magazine*, 460 W. 34th Street, New York, NY 10001, (212) 947-6500.

*Videography*, PO Box 0513, Baldwin, NY 11510-0513.

*Video Software Dealer*, 5519 Centinela Avenue, Los Angeles, CA 90066.

*Video Store*, 545 Fifth Avenue, New York, NY 10017. Also: 1700 E. Dyer Road, Santa Ana, CA 92705.

*View: The Magazine of Cable TV Programming*, Subscription Services Department, P.O. Box 5011, FDR Station, New York, NY 10022.

## Trends

*Age Wave: How the Most Important Trend of Our Time Will Change Our Future*, Kenneth Dyctwald, Ph.D., et al., 1990.

*Cultural Democracy: Politics, Media, New Technology* (SUNY Series, Interruptions).

*Leisure and Society, Future Trend*, Jay Sanford Shivers, 1985.

*The Americanization of the World, or, The Trend of the Twentieth Century*, W. T. Stead.

*The Master Trend: How the Baby Boom Generation Is Remaking America*, Cheryl Russell, 1993.

*The Popcorn Report*, Faith Popcorn. Doubleday, New York, 1991.

*Timelines: Day by Day and Trend by Trend from the Dawn of the Atomic Age to the Gulf War*, Paul Dickson, 1991.

*Suburban Trend (Rise of Urban America)*, Harlan P. Douglass, 1974.

*Trend Tracking: The System to Profit from Today's Trends*, Gerald Celente, Tom Milton. Warner Books, New York, 1991.

*Video Purchasing Patterns in Schools: A Qed/Ait Survey* (Qed's School Trend Series), 1987.

## Video

*Alternative Visions: Distributing Independent Media in a Home Video World*, Debra Franco, AIVF, 625 Broadway, 9th Floor, New York, NY 10012.

*An Introduction to the 800# Revolution: Direct to Viewer Marketing of Home Video*, Peter Hamilton, in NVR Reports (1990), National Video Resources, 73 Spring Street, Suite 606, New York, NY 10012.

*Guide to Videotape Publishing*, ed., Ellen Lazer, available from Knowledge Industry Publications, 701 Westchester Avenue, White Plains, NY 10604, 1986.

*Home Video in Libraries: How Libraries Buy and Circulate Prerecorded Home Video*, Martha Dewing, Knowledge Industry Publications, White Plains, NY, 1988.

*Home Video: Producing for the Home Market*, Michael Wiese, Michael Wiese Productions, 1986.

*Home Video Publishing: The Distribution of Videocassettes 1986-90 by Presentation Consultants, Inc.*, Knowledge Industry Publications, Inc., White Plains, NY, 1986.

*The Age of Videography: Twenty Years That Changed the Way We See Ourselves*, edited by Brian McKernan, Miller Freeman, 460 Park Avenue South, New York, NY 10016, 1996.

473

*The Next Step*, Morrie Warshawski, AIVF, 625 Broadway, 9th Floor, New York, NY 10012.

*The Video Tape & Disc Guide to Home Entertainment,*

*Variety's Complete Home Video Directory,* R.R. Bowker, New York, NY.

*Video Product Marketplace,* Martin Porter, Martin Porter & Associates Publications, Port Washington, NY, 1987.

*National Video Clearinghouse, Inc.,* Syosset, NY (annual).

## Internet Databases

African-American Video Media Resource Center
www.lib.berkeley.edu/MRC/AfricanAmVid.html

Broadcasting Link
www.algonet.se/~nikos/broad.html

Chicago Filmmakers
www.tezcat.com/~chifilm

Cinema Connection
www.webcom.com/~3e-media/TMC/cineprax.html

Cinema Sites
www.webcom.com/~davidaug/Movie_Sites.html

CineMedia
www.afionline.org/CINEMEDIA/CineMedia.home.html

Clamen's Movie Information Collection
www.cs.cmu.edu/afs/cs.cmu.edu/user/clamen/misc/movies/

Moon
www.emoon.com/

Film.com
www.film.com/admin/linkrot.htm

GEWI Film Page
gewi.kfunigraz.ac.at/~puntigam/

Hollywood Online
www.hollywood.com

Internet Movie Database (IMDb)
us.imdb.com/

Michael Wiese Productions
www.mwp.com

Media-Link
www.dds.nl/~kidon/media.html

National Film Preservation Board
www.lcweb.loc.gov/film/

OMNIBUS-EYE
www.rtvf.nwu.edu/

Queer Media Resources
www.abacus.oxy.edu/qrd/media/

Movies & More
www.pages.ripco.com:8080/~bbb/movies.html

Rice Media
www.riceinfo.rice.edu/projects/depts/arts/Media/

RML's Movie Page
www. netspace.net.au/~haze/

SCREENSite
www.sa.ua.edu/TCF/welcome.htm

Take TWO
www.webcom.com/~taketwo/

Television Pointers
www.cs.cmu.edu/afs/cs.cmu.edu/user/clamen/misc/tv/README.html

TV Net
www.tvnet.com/

WebOvision
www.catalog.com/cgibin/var/media/index.html

Yahoo Entertainment
www.yahoo.com/Entertainment/

# CONSULTING SERVICES

Like you, I am interested in getting it done. That's why we publish these books. That's why we offer consulting services. Our philosophy is 'You want something done? Just do it.' Our goal is to make your films and videos as successful as possible.

We've consulted with film and videomakers on first features, documentaries, and special interest home videos. Depending on our availability, we are delighted to serve in whatever capacity that we can. Sometimes we meet with producers and review scripts, budgets, financial strategies, program development ideas, distribution contracts, or marketing plans. We can provide consulting on a per project basis or on a monthly retainer. When we consult, our entire knowledge base of experts and industry contacts are made available to you.

*Michael Wiese*

Our past clients have included: *National Geographic, The Smithsonian Institute, NOVA, Audubon, KCET, KQED, Hanna-Barbera Studios, Republic Pictures, PBS Home Video, The Apollo Theater, International Wildlife Coalition, Babies at Play, King World Television, The Buckminster Fuller Institute, Deepak Chopra, M. D.,* and dozens of first-time film and videomakers.

Learn more about how our consulting can assist you. Call Ken Lee (818) 379-8799 or e-mail kenlee@earthlink.net

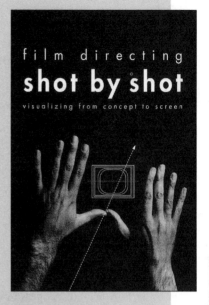

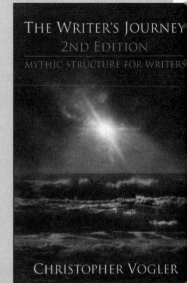

## SETTING UP YOUR SHOTS
### Great Camera Moves Every Filmmaker Should Know

**Jeremy Vineyard**

Written in straightforward, non-technical language and laid out in a nonlinear format with self-contained chapters for quick, on-the-set reference, *Setting Up Your Shots* is like a Swiss army knife for filmmakers! Using examples from over 140 popular films, this book provides detailed descriptions of more than 100 camera setups, angles, and techniques — in an easy-to-use horizontal "wide-screen" format.

*Setting Up Your Shots* is an excellent primer for beginning filmmakers and students of film theory, as well as a handy guide for working filmmakers. If you are a director, a storyboard artist, or an animator, use this book. It is the culmination of hundreds of hours of research.

Contains 150 references to the great shots from your favorite films, including *2001: A Space Odyssey*, *Blue Velvet*, *The Matrix*, *The Usual Suspects*, and *Vertigo*.

"Perfect for any film enthusiast looking for the secrets behind creating film. Because of its simplicity of design and straightforward storyboards, *Setting Up Your Shots* is destined to be mandatory reading at film schools throughout the world."
— Ross Otterman, *Directed By Magazine*

Jeremy Vineyard is a director and screenwriter who moved to Los Angeles in 1997 to pursue a feature filmmaking career. He has several spec scripts in development.

$19.95, 132 pages
Order # 8RLS
ISBN: 0-941188-73-6

## DIRECTING FEATURE FILMS
### The Creative Collaboration between Directors, Writers, and Actors

### Mark Travis

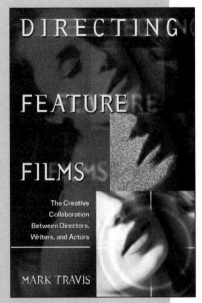

The director is the guide, the inspiration, the focus that can shepherd hundreds of artists through the most chaotic, complex collaboration imaginable. But how does one person draw all these individuals together to realize a single vision?

*Directing Feature Films* takes you through the entire creative process of filmmaking — from concept to completion. You will learn how to really read a script, find its core, determine your vision, and effectively communicate with writers, actors, designers, cinematographers, editors, composers, and all the members of your creative team to ensure that vision reaches the screen.

This edition of the best-selling *The Director's Journey* contains new material on all aspects of filmmaking, taking the reader even deeper into the process.

"A comprehensive and inspired examination of craft. A must read for any serious professional."
> — Mark Rydell, Director
> *On Golden Pond, The Rose, James Dean*

"With astonishing clarity Mark Travis articulates the techniques and skills of film directing."
> — John Badham, Director
> *Saturday Night Fever, War Games, Blue Thunder*

"Mark Travis is the only practical teacher of directing I've ever met — and simply the best. I learned more from him than I did in four years of film school."
> — Cyrus Nowrasteh, Writer/Director
> *The Day Reagan Was Shot*

Mark Travis has directed motion pictures, television programs, and stage shows. A graduate of the Yale School of Drama, Mark has shared his techniques on directing in courses around the world. He has served as a directing consultant on many feature films and top-rated television series.

$26.95, 402 pages
Order # 96RLS
ISBN: 0-94118-43-4

## CUT TO THE CHASE
### Forty-Five Years of Editing America's Favorite Movies

### Sam O'Steen as told to Bobbie O'Steen

Eclectic and unpredictable films such as *The Graduate*, *Cool Hand Luke*, *Chinatown*, and *Who's Afraid of Virginia Woolf?* ushered in what many historians and movie buffs call The Golden Age of Cinema. As diverse as these films are, they have one thing in common: They were all edited by one man, Sam O'Steen.

Sam O'Steen was a world-renowned editor whose talent, smarts, and desire to get the truth out of the film propelled him to an amazing level of success. He helped shape many of the most influential movies in motion-picture history.

This groundbreaking book takes the reader behind the closed doors of the editing room where Sam O'Steen controlled the fate of many celebrated films. Sam's absorbing stories — from on and off the set — are spiced with anecdotes about producers, directors, and such stars as Frank Sinatra, Elizabeth Taylor, Jack Nicholson, Meryl Streep, and Harrison Ford.

"Everything I know about film editing I learned from Sam O'Steen."
 — Roman Polanski, Director, *Rosemary's Baby, Chinatown, Frantic*

"Sam was listening to the currents that flow underneath human events."
 — Mike Nichols, Director, *Who's Afraid of Virginia Woolf?, The Graduate, Catch-22*

"Sam O'Steen was an American master and this book tells you where and how."
 — Robert Benton, Writer/Director, *Kramer vs. Kramer, Places in the Heart, Nadine*

Bobbie O'Steen is a writer with a background in story and film editing. As a film editor, she received an Emmy nomination for *Best Little Girl in the World*.

$24.95, 249 pages
Order # 19RLS | ISBN: 0-941188-37-X

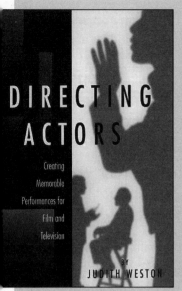

## DIRECTING ACTORS
### Creating Memorable Performances for Film & Television

*Judith Weston*

*Over 20,000 Sold!*

Directing film or television is a high-stakes occupation. It captures your full attention at every moment, calling on you to commit every resource and stretch yourself to the limit. It's the white-water rafting of entertainment jobs. But for many directors, the excitement they feel about a new project tightens into anxiety when it comes to working with actors.

This book provides a method for establishing creative, collaborative relationships with actors, getting the most out of rehearsals, troubleshooting poor performances, giving briefer directions, and much more. It addresses what actors want from a director, what directors do wrong, and constructively analyzes the director-actor relationship.

"Judith Weston is an extraordinarily gifted teacher."
— David Chase, Emmy Award-Winning Writer,
Director, and Producer
*The Sopranos, Northern Exposure, I'll Fly Away*

"I believe that working with Judith's ideas and principles has been the most useful time I've spent preparing for my work. I think that if Judith's book were mandatory reading for all directors, the quality of the director-actor process would be transformed, and better drama would result."
— John Patterson, Director
*The Practice, Law and Order, Profiler*

Judith Weston was a professional actor for twenty years and has taught Acting for Directors for over a decade.

$26.95, 314 pages
Order # 4RLS
ISBN: 0-941188-24-8

# DIRECTING & VISUALIZATION

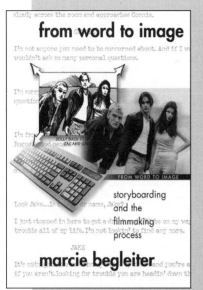

## FROM WORD TO IMAGE
### Storyboarding and the Filmmaking Process

### *Marcie Begleiter*

Whether you're a director, screenwriter, producer, editor, or storyboard artist, the ability to tell stories with images is essential to your craft. In this remarkable book, Marcie Begleiter offers the tools to help both word- and image-oriented artists learn how to develop and sharpen their visual storytelling skills via storyboarding.

Readers are taken on a step-by-step journey into the previsualization process, including breaking down the script, using overhead diagrams to block out shots, and creating usable drawings for film frames that collaborators can easily understand. Also includes discussions of compositional strategies, perspective, and figure notation as well as practical information on getting gigs, working on location, collaborating with other crew members, and much more.

"*From Word to Image* examines the how-to's of storyboard art, and is full of rich film history. It demystifies an aspect of filmmaking that benefits everyone involved — from directors, to cinematographers, to production designers."
— Joe Petricca, Vice Dean, American Film Institute

"Begleiter's process is a visual and organizational assist to any filmmaker trying to shift from story in words to story in moving image."
— Joan Tewkesbury, Screenwriter, *Nashville*
Director, *Felicity*

Marcie Begleiter is a filmmaker, an educator, and the owner of Filmboards, whose clients include Paramount, TriStar, New Line, HBO, ABC, and Lightspan Interactive.

$26.95, 224 pages
Order # 45RLS
ISBN: 0-941188-28-0

## FILM PRODUCTION MANAGEMENT 101
### The Ultimate Guide to Film and Television Production Management and Coordination

**Deborah S. Patz**

Two books in one, *Film Production Management 101* is a detailed insider's guide for managing a film or television production, covered from both the Production Manager's and the Production Coordinator's points of view.

In this greatly expanded second edition of *Surviving Production*, Deborah Patz taps into her eighteen years of independent production and studio experience to advise you from before the first day of preproduction through production and wrap, all the way into postproduction. Deborah shares detailed insights and tells it like it is. She delivers the nuts and bolts of the business in 35 in-depth chapters and 70 additional pages of essential forms (also downloadable from the Web).

Includes: how to get hired; budgeting and breakdowns; setting up the production office; how to hire crew; workspace organization; production scheduling; daily production reports; location management; production insurance and completion bonds; cast contracts; script format and revisions; customs & immigration; cost reporting; postproduction; audits; and much more.

This book is not only for production managers and production coordinators. It will also inform executive producers, producers, assistant directors, production assistants, film students, and anyone interested in knowing the true details of the business of filmmaking.

Deborah S. Patz is a filmmaker with experience in both film and television: from children's programming to science fiction extravaganzas, from video to IMAX 3D, from studio shoots to international co-productions. Deborah has arranged shoots around the world.

$39.95, 478 pages | Over 50 Production Forms, Lay Flat Binding for easy use
Order # 103RLS
ISBN: 0-941188-45-0 | **Available September 2002**

## THE PERFECT PITCH
### How to Sell Yourself and Your Movie Idea to Hollywood

**Ken Rotcop** *as told to James Shea*

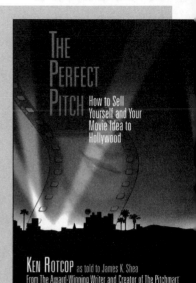

A good pitch can mean the difference between seeing your name on a lucrative studio contract or a form rejection letter. It's a well-known industry fact that film executives typically devote about two minutes of their attention to directors and screenwriters who bring them their ideas hoping for a deal. Can you capture their attention and pique their interest in the time it takes to order a latte at Starbucks? Your future as a successful screenwriter or director may depend on it.

Author Ken Rotcop writes from a unique perspective — he's made hundreds of pitches himself as a screenwriter and producer and heard many more as creative director of four studios. Using personal examples of successes and failures, Rotcop shows you how to walk the tightrope of a pitch meeting without falling off. Which attention-grabbing strategies can make a studio head put down his daily horoscope and listen to you? Once you've got his attention, how can you "reel him in" and get him excited about your idea? What if you forget what you were going to say? What if you make a faux pas? Does "no" always mean "no" in the language of movie deals?

Rotcop discusses these situations and others, as well as how to best present yourself and your idea, how and when to do "on-the-spot" pitching, and how to recognize and capitalize on future opportunities.

"Forget about snappy dialogue, characterization and plot. It's the pitch that gets a script read and a movie deal done. If it were not for Ken Rotcop, most new writers would be out of the loop."
                                    — John Lippman, *Wall St Journal*

Ken Rotcop produces Pitchmart™, Hollywood's biggest screenplay pitch event.

$16.95, 156 pages
Order # 14RLS | ISBN: 0-941188-31-0

# WRITING THE ACTION-ADVENTURE FILM
## The Moment of Truth

### Neill D. Hicks

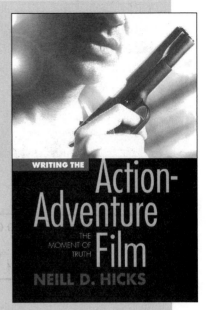

The Action-Adventure movie is consistently one of the most popular exports of the American film industry, drawing enormous audiences worldwide across many diverse societies, cultures, and languages.

But there are more than hot pursuits, hot lead, and hotheaded slugfests in a successful Action-Adventure script. With definitive examples from over 100 movies, *Writing the Action-Adventure Film* reveals the screenwriting principles that define the content and the style of this popular film genre. Neill Hicks furnishes a set of tools to build a compelling screenplay that fulfills the expectations of the motion picture audience.

You will discover how to create the Moment of Truth where the stakes are life and death, perfect a story structure that compels your characters to take immediate action, recognize the different forms of action and where to use them effectively, and develop the narrative context of adventure to surround the audience in the special world of the story.

"Dreaming about writing the next *The Matrix*, *Gladiator*, *The One*, or *Spy Game*? Neill clearly knows the Action-Adventure genre inside and out. I recommend the book highly!"
> — Eric Lilleør
> Publisher/Editor-in-Chief
> *Screentalk Magazine*

Neill D. Hicks, the author of the best-selling *Screenwriting 101: The Essential Craft of Feature Film Writing* (see page 21) and *Writing the Thriller Film: The Terror Within* (see page 8), is an L.A.-based professional screenwriter whose credits include two of the biggest Action-Adventure films of all time, *Rumble in the Bronx* and *First Strike*.

$14.95, 180 pages
Order # 99RLS
ISBN: 0-941188-39-6

# ORDER FORM

TO ORDER THESE PRODUCTS, PLEASE CALL 24 HOURS - 7 DAYS A WEEK
CREDIT CARD ORDERS 1-800-833-5738 OR FAX YOUR ORDER (818) 986-3408
OR MAIL THIS ORDER FORM TO:

**MICHAEL WIESE PRODUCTIONS**
11288 VENTURA BLVD., # 621
STUDIO CITY, CA 91604
E-MAIL: MWPSALES@MWP.COM
WEB SITE: WWW.MWP.COM

WRITE OR FAX FOR A FREE CATALOG

PLEASE SEND ME THE FOLLOWING BOOKS:

| TITLE | ORDER NUMBER (#RLS _____ ) | AMOUNT |
|-------|---------------------------|--------|
| | | |
| | | |
| | | |
| | | |
| | | |

|  | SHIPPING | |
|--|----------|-|
| | CALIFORNIA TAX (8.00%) | |
| | TOTAL ENCLOSED | |

SHIPPING:
ALL ORDERS MUST BE PREPAID, UPS GROUND SERVICE ONE ITEM - $3.95
EACH ADDITIONAL ITEM ADD $2.00
EXPRESS - 3 BUSINESS DAYS ADD $12.00 PER ORDER
OVERSEAS
SURFACE - $15.00 EACH ITEM    AIRMAIL - $30.00 EACH ITEM

PLEASE MAKE CHECK OR MONEY ORDER PAYABLE TO:

**MICHAEL WIESE PRODUCTIONS**

(CHECK ONE) ____ MASTERCARD ____VISA ____AMEX

CREDIT CARD NUMBER _____

EXPIRATION DATE _____

CARDHOLDER'S NAME _____

CARDHOLDER'S SIGNATURE _____

*SHIP TO:*

NAME _____

ADDRESS _____

CITY _____ STATE _____ ZIP _____

COUNTRY _____ TELEPHONE _____

ORDER ONLINE FOR THE LOWEST PRICES
24 HOURS    |    1.800.833.5738    |    www.mwp.com